NATURAL HISTORY OF THE
COLORADO PLATEAU AND GREAT BASIN

NATURAL HISTORY OF THE COLORADO PLATEAU AND GREAT BASIN

Kimball T. Harper, Larry L. St. Clair,
Kaye H. Thorne and Wilford M. Hess,
Editors

UNIVERSITY PRESS OF COLORADO

Published by the University Press of Colorado
P.O. Box 849, Niwot, Colorado 80544

The University Press of Colorado is a cooperative publishing enterprise
supported, in part, by Adams State College, Colorado State University, Fort
Lewis College, Mesa State College, Metropolitan State College of Denver,
University of Colorado, University of Northern Colorado, University of
Southern Colorado, and Western State College of Colorado.

Library of Congress Cataloging-in-Publication Data

Natural history of the Colorado Plateau and Great Basin/ [edited by]
    Kimball T. Harper . . . [et al.].
        p.   cm.
    Includes bibliographical references and index.
    ISBN 0-87081-335-8 (cloth)
    1. Natural history—Great Basin.   2. Natural history—Colorado
Plateau.   3. Glacial epoch—Great Basin.   4. Glacial epoch—Colorado
Plateau.   5. Great Basin.   6. Colorado Plateau.   I. Harper, K.T.
(Kimball T.), 1931–   .
QH104.5.G68N38   1994
508.79—dc20   94–11604
                                                                  CIP

The paper used in this publication meets the minimum requirements of the American
National Standard for Information Sciences—Permanence of Paper for Printed Library
Materials. ANSI Z39.48–1984.
    ∞

10 9 8 7 6 5 4 3 2 1

CONTENTS

CONTRIBUTORS

CHRISTOPHER J. BELL, Museum of Paleontology, Department of Integrated Biology, University of California, Berkeley, California 94720

DONALD K. GRAYSON, Department of Anthropology and Burke Memorial Museum, University of Washington, Seattle, Washington 98195

J. L. HAMRICK, Department of Botany, University of Georgia, Athens, Georgia 30602

KIMBALL T. HARPER, Department of Botany and Range Science, Brigham Young University, Provo, Utah 84602

W. M. HESS, Department of Botany and Range Science, Brigham Young University, Provo, Utah 84602

RICHARD H. JACKSON, Department of Geography, Brigham Young University, Provo, Utah 84602

JIM I. MEAD, Quaternary Studies Program and Department of Geology, Northern Arizona University, Flagstaff, Arizona 86011

THOMAS H. MORRIS, Department of Geology, Brigham Young University, Provo, Utah 84602

C. RILEY NELSON, Department of Zoology and Brackenridge Field Laboratory, University of Texas at Austin, Austin, Texas 78712

KENNETH LEE PETERSEN, Westinghouse Hanford Corporation, P.O. Box 1970, Mail Stop H4-14, Richland, Washington 99352

LARRY L. ST. CLAIR, Department of Botany and Range Science, Brigham Young University, Provo, Utah 84602

ANDREW F. SCHNABEL, Department of Botany, Iowa State University, Ames, Iowa 50011

JOHN W. SIGLER, Spectrum Sciences, 1780 North Research Park Way, Suite 106, Logan, Utah 84321

WILLIAM F. SIGLER, 309 East 2nd South, Logan, Utah 84321-5305

MELISSA A. STUBBEN, Department of Geology, Brigham Young University, Provo, Utah 84602

KAYE H. THORNE, Department of Botany and Range Science, Brigham Young University, Provo, Utah 84602

STEVEN D. WARREN, Department of the Army, Construction Engineering Research Lab, Corps of Engineers, Champaign, Illinois 61820-1305

P. V. WELLS, Departments of Botany, Systematics, and Ecology, University of Kansas, Lawrence, Kansas 66045

JAMES D. WILDE, Office of Public Archaeology, Brigham Young University, Provo, Utah 84602

JAMES A. YOUNG, United States Department of Agriculture/Agricultural Research Service, 920 Valley Road, Reno, Nevada 89512

NATURAL HISTORY OF THE
COLORADO PLATEAU AND GREAT BASIN

Sarcobatus vermiculatus (Hook.) Torr. (greasewood) is a common dominant of alkaline clays of broad alluvial drainage ways. This stiff, many-branched, spiny shrub is the escape cover of choice for small mammals being pursued by predators.

CHAPTER 1

Introduction

Kimball T. Harper, Larry L. St. Clair,
Kaye H. Thorne, and W. M. Hess

OVERVIEW

The Colorado Plateau and the Great Basin provide an exercise in topographic contrasts. The Plateau is world renowned for spectacular canyons deeply incised into a layer cake of brightly colored sedimentary strata. In contrast, the Great Basin is a huge depression without external drainage to the sea, where drab, fault-block mountains lie buried to their rugged shoulders in alluvium. Welsh (1979) has aptly described the Plateau as an excavational and the Basin as a depositional landscape.

The topographic differences that characterize these regions have left their marks on the associated biota. On the Plateau the constant removal of detritus from weathering processes necessitates that organisms (plants especially) adapt to one or another of a large array of highly distinctive parent materials. Edaphic endemism is rampant on the Plateau, but in the Basin the uniqueness of individual geologic strata is usually masked by a well-mixed alluvial veneer that discourages genetic novelties and results in a monotonous uniformity of flora (Welsh 1979). The deep canyons and rushing rivers of the Plateau have also left their marks on the fauna of the region. The Colorado River appears to have isolated populations of small mammals and sometimes produced distinct taxa across those barriers (Durrant 1952).

Lack of external drainage resulted in scores of lakes of variable size and permanence in the Great Basin during the Pleistocene (Smith 1978). The largest of those lakes (Bonneville and Lahontan) were huge and covered much of northwestern Utah and northwestern Nevada, respectively (Figure 1.1). As those lakes waxed and waned through the millennia, they alternately destroyed terrestrial life in their basins or exposed the basin floors for recolonization. Such drastic disturbances, with their potential for biological impoverishment, did not occur on the Plateau.

The environmental tapestry of both Basin and Plateau is enriched by mountains — islands of greenery in a sea of desert, their lushness caused by the combined effects of the greater precipitation and lower temperatures characteristic of increasing elevation

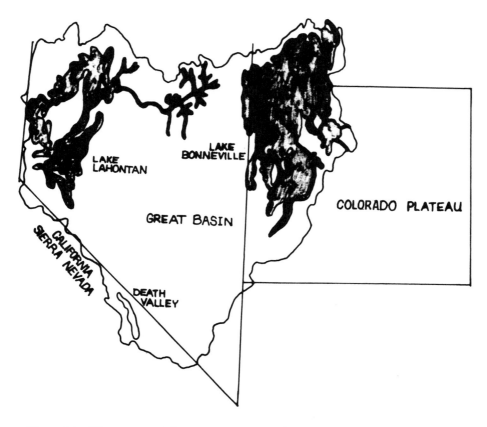

Figure 1.1   The maximum Pleistocene extent of Lakes Lahontan (western Nevada) and
Bonneville (western Utah).

*(Figure 1.2). The mountain vegetation is differentiated into more or less distinct types
along the elevational gradient. It is notable that the number and distinctness of vegetational zones on mountains decline steadily from the southeastern edge of the Colorado
Plateau to the northwestern corner of the Great Basin (Harper 1986; Billings 1990).*

*Marshes are common and often large in the Basin, but they are an uncommon feature of
the Plateau. The great primary productivity of marshes in a desert landscape of low productivity attracted burgeoning populations of numerous waterfowl and certain mammals. Those
animals and the large reserve of harvestable seeds attracted prehistoric humans, who invested
much of their foraging time in Great Basin wetlands (Janetski and Madsen 1990).*

*Despite these differences, the biological commonality of the Colorado Plateau and the
Great Basin is inescapable (Cronquist et al. 1972). That commonality is demonstrated
by the distribution of genera and species of Utah's 12 largest flowering plant families
between the Basin and Plateau (Table 1.1). Two clear conclusions emerge from analysis
of Table 1.1: (1) the Great Basin and Plateau regions of Utah have far more genera and
species in common than one would expect to occur by chance, and (2) the Colorado Plateau is more floristically diverse than the Basin, though the areas are of roughly equal size.*

Table 1.1 Distribution of Genera and Species of 12 Largest Flowering Plant Families

Family	Occurrence of Genera			Occurrence of Species		
	Great Basin Only	Both	Colorado Plateau Only	Great Basin Only	Both	Colorado Plateau Only
Asteraceae	5	65	16	46	221	122
Boraginaceae	0	9	1	8	41	24
Brassicaceae	2	20	3	21	60	20
Caryophyllaceae	0	7	1	3	29	2
Chenopodiaceae	1	11	2	2	23	10
Cyperaceae	0	5	1	9	62	30
Fabaceae	0	15	3	22	71	76
Poaceae	2	44	10	18	117	37
Polygonaceae	0	3	1	11	40	23
Ranunculaceae	0	10	2	2	38	11
Rosaceae	0	21	2	4	50	5
Scrophulariaceae	0	13	1	15	65	31
Totals	10	223	43	161	817	391

Source: Welsh et al. 1987 and Albee et al. 1988.

CULTURAL FEATURES

The Colorado Plateau and the Great Basin have sparse human populations. A few major population centers cluster along the bases of mountain ranges where perennial streams provide good water and broad expanses of fertile, essentially level land for agriculture and urban development. Laypeople often conclude that the remainder of the landscape is relatively natural and much as it was at the time of arrival of Europeans, but close scrutiny will usually provide evidence of human activity on all but the most remote landscapes.

The original European settlers in the region were ranchers or farmers. Today the regional economy is more often fueled by transportation enterprises, tourism, and businesses that support those activities. Visitors come to ski in the mountains or see the large number of spectacular national parks and monuments established to preserve the natural wonders of the region. Others come to gamble at Nevada's numerous casinos or to enjoy the water sports associated with the large reservoirs that control and harness the big rivers of the region. A few come because they are awed by the grand vistas that characterize portions of the Plateau and remote valleys of the Basin and Range Province of Nevada and western Utah. Those few find a renewed appreciation for the intrepid explorers who first encountered vast wildlands and charted routes across their often deadly expanses.

A final use of remote areas of the Basin involves military training. Millions of acres are closed to public entrance and used as weapons testing and target practice areas for both army and air force units.

THE INTENDED AUDIENCE AND OBJECTIVES

This volume was prepared with students and managers of the region's natural resources in mind. For the topics considered, scholars will find a ready reference to the best of recent studies that are relevant to the region. Resource managers will find much in all chapters that is relevant to their activities and useful for enrichment of resource interpretation programs for the general public. Interested laypeople will also discover much to enhance their understanding of and appreciation for the Colorado Plateau and the Great Basin.

This collection is designed to provide current, authoritative information on topics for which adequate information has been lacking or for which recent advances have significantly altered previous understanding. Where recent reviews are available, we call attention to their existence, but we do not cover their contents here. For instance, this volume does not attempt to duplicate monographic works on birds (Behle and Perry 1975; Hayward et al. 1976), mammals (Zoveloff 1988), or prehistoric humans on the Colorado Plateau (Jennings 1966). By the same token, there are no chapters on vegetation or plant adaptations because those topics have been recently reviewed more than once (e.g., MacMahon 1988 and West 1983, 1988, and 1989 for vegetation and Caldwell 1985 and Comstock and Ehleringer 1992 for plant adaptations).

We have provided a brief overview of each chapter to assist readers quickly to assess chapter contents and identify unique contributions. A final chapter summarizes

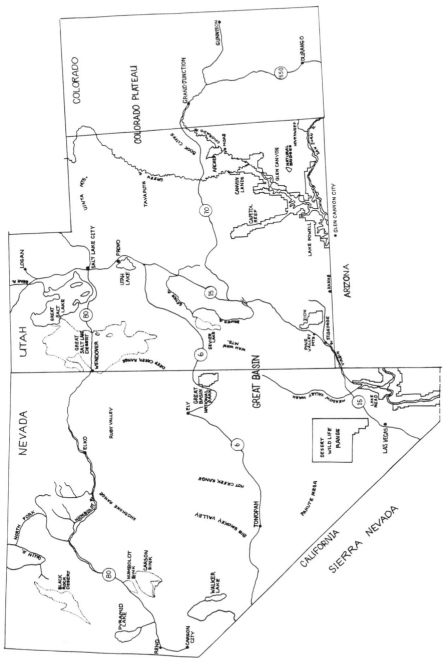

Figure 1.2 Major natural and cultural features in the Great Basin and on the Colorado Plateau.

the volume's contents and identifies problems worthy of future investigation in the region. For useful background information, readers may turn to earlier detailed analyses of the biology of the Great Basin and Colorado Plateau by Cronquist et al. (1972) and a symposium volume edited by Harper and Reveal (1978). Other valuable studies occur in the Great Basin volume (vol. 11) of *The Smithsonian Institution Handbook of North American Indians* (d'Azevedo 1986) and in Osmond et al. (1990). Late Pleistocene to modern changes in distribution of plants and animals in the region have been laboriously interpreted from packrat middens, which provide a surprisingly detailed record of the past 40,000 years (Betancourt et al. 1990).

We hope this collection will stimulate more research on the Colorado Plateau. Previous studies on the arid lands of the Intermountain West have concentrated on the Great Basin proper. That geographic bias for research, no doubt, has its origin in the remoteness of the Colorado Plateau from the region's major research institutions. Nevertheless, the Colorado Plateau is more bio-diverse and, perhaps, more fragile ecologically than the Great Basin. It also provides a climatic transition zone between the dry summer (Mediterranean) climatic region that dominates the Great Basin and the summer monsoon region of the American Southwest. That climatic gradient has had an effect (albeit poorly understood) on the modern biota of the Plateau and may noticeably alter organismal distributions in response to global warming patterns in the future.

LITERATURE CITED

Albee, B. J., L. M. Shultz, and S. Goodrich. 1988. Atlas of the vascular plants of Utah. Utah Museum of Natural History, Salt Lake City, Occasional Publication, No. 7. 670 p.

Behle, W. H., and M. L. Perry. 1975. Utah birds: checklist, seasonal and ecological occurrence charts, and guides to bird finding. Utah Museum of Natural History, Salt Lake City. 144 p.

Betancourt, J. L., T. R. Van Devender, and P. S. Martin, eds. 1990. Packrat middens: the last 40,000 years of biotic change. University of Arizona Press, Tucson. 467 p.

Billings, W. B. 1990. The mountain forests of North America and their environments. Pages 47–86 in C. B. Osmond, L. F. Pitelka, and G. M. Hidy, eds., Plant biology of the Basin and Range. Springer-Verlag, New York.

Caldwell, M. 1985. Cold deserts. Pages 198–212 in B. F. Chabot and H. A. Mooney, eds., Physiological ecology of North American plant communities. Chapman and Hall, New York.

Comstock, J. P., and J. R. Ehleringer. 1992. Plant adaptations in the Great Basin and Colorado Plateau. Great Basin Naturalist 52:195–215.

Cronquist, A., A. H. Holmgren, N. H. Holmgren, and J. L. Reveal. 1972. Plant geography of the Intermountain Region. Pages 77–161 in A. Cronquist, A. H. Holmgren, N. H. Holmgren, and J. L. Reveal, eds., Intermountain flora, Vol. 1. Hafner Publishing Co., New York. 270 p.

d'Azevedo, W. L., ed. 1986. Great Basin. Vol. 11, Handbook of North American Indians. Smithsonian Institution, Washington, D.C. 852 p.

Durrant, S. D. 1952. Mammals of Utah, taxonomy and distribution. University of Kansas Publications, Museum of Natural History, Vol. 6, Lawrence, Kansas. 549 p.

Harper, K. T. 1986. Historical environments. Pages 51–63 *in* W. L. d'Azevedo, ed., Great Basin, Vol. 11, Handbook of North American Indians. Smithsonian Institution, Washington, D.C.

Harper, K. T., and J. L. Reveal, eds. 1978. Intermountain biogeography: a symposium. Great Basin Naturalist Memoirs, No. 2, Provo. 268 p.

Hayward, C. L., C. Cottam, A. M. Woodbury, and H. H. Frost. 1976. Birds of Utah. Great Basin Naturalist Memoirs, No. 1. 229 p.

Janetski, J. C., and D. B. Madsen, eds. 1990. Wetland adaptations in the Great Basin. Brigham Young University, Museum of Peoples and Cultures, Provo, Occasional Papers, No. 1. 285 p.

Jennings, J. D. 1966. Glen Canyon: a summary. University of Utah Anthropological Papers, No. 81, Provo. 84 p.

MacMahon, J. A. 1988. Introduction: vegetation of Utah. Pages xiii–xx *in* B. J. Albee, L. M. Shultz, and S. Goodrich, Atlas of vascular plants of Utah. Utah Museum of Natural History, Salt Lake City, Occasional Publication, No. 7.

Osmond, C. B., L. F. Pitelka, and G. M. Hidy, eds. 1990. Plant biology of the Basin and Range. Springer-Verlag, New York. 375 p.

Smith, G. R. 1978. Biogeography of Intermountain fishes. Pages 17–42 *in* K. T. Harper and J. L. Reveal, eds., Intermountain biogeography: a symposium. Great Basin Naturalist Memoirs, No. 2, Provo.

Welsh, S. L. 1979. Endangered and threatened plants of Utah: a case study. Pages 69–80 *in* The endangered species: a symposium. Great Basin Naturalist Memoirs, No. 3, Provo.

Welsh, S. L., N. D. Atwood, S. Goodrich, and L. C. Higgins, eds. 1987. A Utah flora. Great Basin Naturalist Memoirs, No. 9, Provo. 894 p.

West, N. E., ed. 1983. Temperate deserts and semideserts. Vol. 5, Ecosystems of the world. Elsevier Scientific Publishing Co., Amsterdam. 522 p.

West, N. E. 1988. Intermountain deserts, shrub steppes, and woodlands. Pages 209–280 *in* M. G. Barbour and W. D. Billings, eds., North American terrestrial vegetation. Cambridge University Press, Cambridge.

West, N. E. 1989. Vegetation types of Utah. Pages 18–56 *in* K. L. Johnson, ed., Rangeland resources of Utah. Cooperative Extension Service, Utah State University, Logan.

Zevoloff, S. I. 1988. Mammals of the intermountain west. University of Utah Press, Salt Lake City. 352 p.

Cymopterus basalticus Jones (dolomite spring-parsley) is a Great Basin endemic of western Utah and eastern Nevada. The large orbicular leaflets without visible stalks are found nowhere else in the genus. The species name is a misnomer; the species usually grows on dolomite or calcareous alluvial fans.

CHAPTER 2

Geologic Contrasts of the Great Basin and Colorado Plateau

Thomas H. Morris and
Melissa A. Stubben

OVERVIEW

The geologic histories of the Great Basin and Colorado Plateau are significantly differ-
ent. The climate, physiography, and biology of these two Intermountain Provinces have
been influenced by their distinct geologic patterns. The Great Basin has no external or
surface outlet and consists of a series of mountain ranges alternating with valleys. The
Great Salt Lake currently occupies one of the internally drained basins and is a rem-
nant of the much larger Lake Bonneville. The Colorado Plateau, often called "the land
of color and canyons," is characterized by its high elevation, thick sedimentary strata,
monoclinal structures, igneous laccoliths, and arid to semi-arid climate. The Plateau is
bounded on the east by the southern Rocky Mountains, on the north by the central
Rocky Mountains, and on the south and west by the Basin and Range Province. In this
chapter the authors describe in detail the geologic structure and organization of the
Great Basin and Colorado Plateau.

THE GREAT BASIN AND COLORADO PLATEAU: DEFINING CHARACTERISTICS

A geologic basin is a topographic depression with no external or surface outlet. With few exceptions (e.g., the Klamath and Pitt Rivers of northern California drain to the Pacific Ocean), this definition holds true for the large physiographic province known as the Great Basin (Figure 2.1 Thornbury 1965). The Great Basin is composed of a series of uplifted mountain ranges (horsts) and their associated inter-vening valleys (grabens) (Figure 2.2). Perennial and ephemeral drainage systems, largely internal to the basins between the ranges, are widely developed throughout the province. These drainage systems can produce playa lakes, which by definition

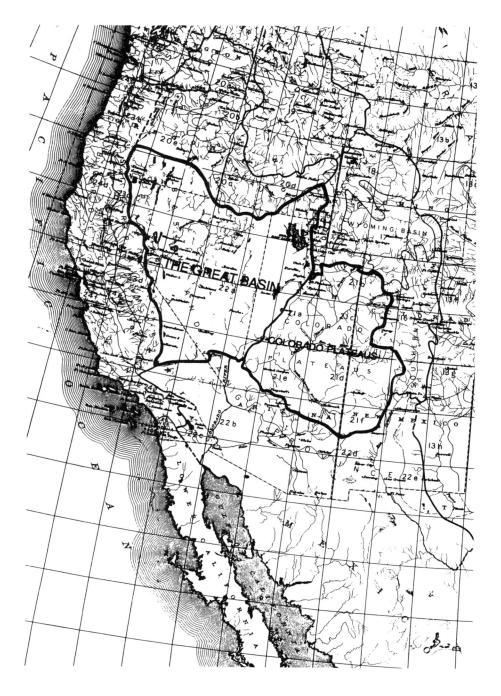

Figure 2.1   Index map showing the physical provinces of the western United States (after
Fenneman 1946).

Figure 2.2 Oblique aerial photograph of typical horst and graben topography of the Great Basin. There are approximately 100 internally drained basins between mountain ranges in the Great Basin (photo courtesy of W. K. Hamblin).

have no external drainage. Playa lakes can dry up, producing evaporite deposits and salt pans that are found extensively within the province. There are approximately 100 internally drained basins within the Great Basin province (Fenneman 1931). The center of one of the larger internally drained basins is the Great Salt Lake, presently a playa lake and a remnant of a larger ancient lake called Lake Bonneville. Lake Bonneville covered much of western Utah, parts of eastern Nevada, and southern Idaho during the last great Ice Age that ended 12 k.y.a. Lake Bonneville did have external drainage during its history, but as climatic conditions changed to the more arid environment of today, this large lake evaporated and drainage became internal.

The Great Basin embodies only a portion of a much larger geologic province called the Basin and Range. The Basin and Range Province is characterized by a series of horsts and grabens much like the Great Basin. The extent of this province is much larger, however, ranging from southern Idaho to central Mexico (Gerlach 1970). The Great Basin is bounded to the east by the Colorado Plateau and central Rocky Mountains, on the north by the Columbia Plateau, and on the west by the

Figure 2.3   Photo of the San Rafael Reef within the Colorado Plateau. The plateau is typified by high elevation, thick horizontal sedimentary strata, and monoclinal structures (photo courtesy of W. K. Hamblin). Monoclinal structures develop where sedimentary rocks fold over deeper-seated basement faults.

Cascade-Sierra Range (Figure 2.1). The limits of the Great Basin become more enigmatic as the Basin and Range Province continues to the south. The southern boundary is generally placed at the confluence of the Colorado River drainage and the Mojave Desert of southern California and southernmost Nevada.

A plateau is defined as an area of relatively flat terrain that has great extent and great elevation relative to surrounding terrains. The Colorado Plateau exhibits these features but locally has developed great relief by the erosive action of high-gradient, swift-flowing rivers that have downcut and incised the plateau (Figure 2.2). Approximately 90 percent of the Colorado Plateau is drained by the Colorado River and its tributaries (Thornbury 1965). For this reason and the existence of extensive red bed deposits, the Colorado Plateau has been called "the land of color and canyons" (Figure 2.3).

The Colorado Plateau can be characterized by its high elevation, thick horizontal sedimentary strata, monoclinal structures, igneous laccoliths, and arid to semi-arid climate. Elevations in the Plateau are generally above 5,000 feet and in some

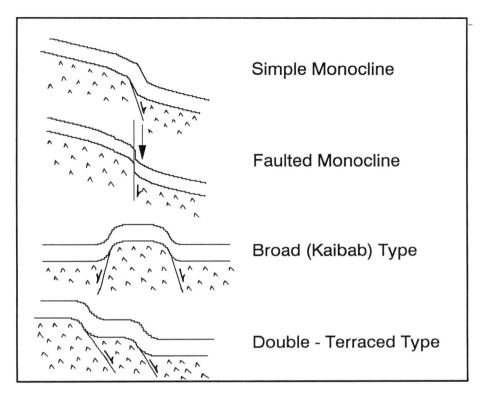

Figure 2.4 Variety of monoclinal structures found in the Colorado Plateau. Monoclines are the most characteristic structural feature of the Colorado Plateau.

areas are as high as 13,000 feet (Thornbury 1965). The Plateau can be thought of as an elevated, northward-tilted saucer (Rigby 1976). The northern section of the Colorado Plateau (Uinta Basin) has a thick sequence of relatively young (Tertiary) rocks yet has the lowest elevation within the Plateau. Monoclines are the single most characteristic structural feature of the Plateau (Kelley 1955). These structures are defined simply as a local steepening in otherwise uniform gently dipping strata (Figure 2.4). Laccoliths are flat-bottomed igneous intrusive bodies that dome up the overlying sedimentary rocks. They are typified in the Colorado Plateau by the Henry, La Sal, Navajo, Abajo, Ute, and Carrizo Mountains of southeastern Utah and northern Arizona (Pirkle and Yoho 1982; Hintze 1988).

The Colorado Plateau is bounded on the south and west by the Basin and Range, on the east by the southern Rocky Mountains, and on the north by the central Rocky Mountain geologic province (Gerlach 1970). The plateau itself can be sub-divided into six sections: the Uinta Basin in the north, the High Plateau to the west, the Grand Canyon section to the southwest, the Datil section to the south-east, the Navajo section in the south central area, and the Canyonlands section in the central plateau. Each of these sections is unique in physiography and geologic features (Hunt 1967; Rigby 1976).

CONTRASTS THROUGH TIME: LITHOLOGIC DIFFERENCES BETWEEN THE GREAT BASIN AND COLORADO PLATEAU

Just as human history is built on past events, so are present geologic relationships the cumulative product of the past.

— L. F. Hintze, *Geologic History of Utah*

It must be remembered that the topography and landscapes that are present on the earth's surface today were developed from relatively recent geologic events. In contrast, the rocks that compose these landscapes are generally much older. For example, the Great Basin's horst and graben (range and basin) topography developed only during the past 17 m.y., yet some of the rocks that compose the horsts were deposited more than 500 m.y.a. The Colorado Plateau may have had its beginning as a highly elevated physiographic province less than 30 m.y.a., yet includes Cambrian (<570 m.y.a.) bedrock that details events of sedimentation that occurred at and below sea level.

The various lithologies that were generated over geologic time have different rock properties such as porosity, permeability, and chemistry. These properties can dramatically impact the landforms and biologic communities that can develop in any given physiographic province.

The Phanerozoic (570 m.y.a. to the Holocene or present) geologic histories of the Great Basin and the Colorado Plateau have been outlined by a number of authors (see Hintze 1988; Dott and Batten 1988; Stokes 1986; Fiero 1986; Rigby 1976; Hunt 1967; and Thornbury 1965). A summary of broad depositional settings and associated lithologies from each of the geologic eras follows; this summary is based upon the above references and the maps listed at the end of the chapter. Particularly good reviews of the geologic histories of the major aspects of the two provinces can be found in both Hintze (1988) and Stokes (1986). These books detail the geologic history of Utah and are valuable because Utah is divided in half by the Great Basin to the west and the Colorado Plateau to the east (Table 2.1).

Also at the end of this chapter is a list of state geological surveys that can provide the reader with geological maps and additional information. Index maps available to the public outline the areas of the state covered by geologic maps. Topographic maps and a variety of other information (trails, road conditions, park boundaries, etc.) can also be accessed through these state agencies.

Paleozoic Era (570–245 m.y.a.)

The overriding lithologic theme of the Paleozoic Era was the deposition of clastic (conglomerates, sandstones, and shales) and volcanoclastic rocks in the western Great Basin, carbonate (dolomites and limestones) deposits in the eastern Great Basin, and clastic and local evaporite deposits in the area of the Colorado Plateau. Western Nevada, the sight of deep marine shales during the early Paleozoic, became a center of silicious and volcanoclastic deposition in middle Paleozoic time. This change was due to a supposed collision of an island arc (similiar to the Japanese island chain) and the western edge of the North American continent that resulted

Table 2.1   The Geologic History of Utah. Utah is divided in half by the Great Basin to the west and the Colorado Plateau to the east (table courtesy of L.F. Hintze).

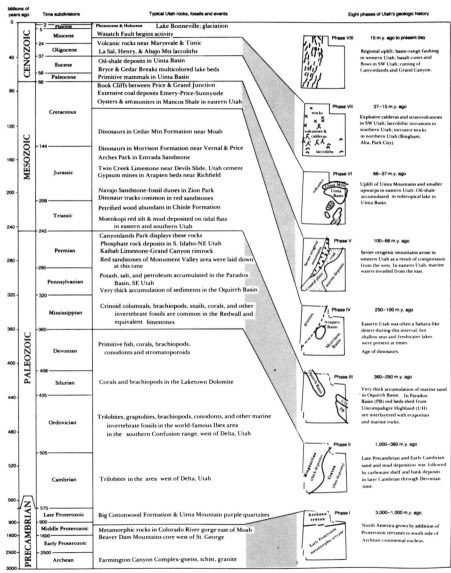

Source: Hintze 1988.

in a mountain-building event (orogeny) known as the Antler Orogeny (Fiero 1986). The eastern area of the Great Basin for most of the Paleozoic was inundated by shallow marine waters that were conducive to the deposition of thick sequences of carbonate rocks. Rapidly subsiding basins locally preserved continuous sequences of these carbonates. One such basin, called the Oquirrh Basin, accumulated more than 25,000 feet of carbonate rock before the end of the Paleozoic. In the area of the Colorado Plateau, a continental highland known as the Transcontinental Arch ran from Arizona to Wisconsin. This highland shed continental clastics locally but deposited few carbonate rocks. Locally in subsiding areas, the shallow seaway to the west would transgress (i.e., sea level would rise and move over the land) and deposit thin carbonate sequences and evaporite deposits, such as in the Paradox Basin of eastern Utah and western Colorado.

Mesozoic Era (245–66 m.y.a.)

As mentioned previously, the western Great Basin in the region of Nevada was located at the western edge of the North American continent during the Paleozoic Era. This changed during the Mesozoic. In the western Great Basin, the early Triassic Period (245–208 m.y.a.) evidences yet another orogenic event termed the Sonoman Orogeny. It is believed that this orogeny represents the collision of island arc chains and other suspect terrains (microcontinents) into the western edge of the North American continent from Nevada to Alaska. Thrust faults, which place older rocks on top of younger rocks, characterized the uplifted Sonoman Mountains. Volcanic ashes and clastic sediments from this orogeny were deposited eastward into the area of the Great Basin. On the eastern flank of the Great Basin and in the area of the Colorado Plateau, extensive low-gradient shoreline systems developed mudflats, lagoons, and evaporite sequences, as evidenced by the red beds of the Moenkopi and Chinle Formations. By the end of the Triassic Period, shallow continental seas were absent from most of the Colorado Plateau and the North American craton. Indeed, the Triassic marked the age of red bed deposits (typically, subaerially exposed sedimentary deposits) worldwide. Great quantities of eolian dune field sand and fluvial (river) sediments covered much of the Colorado Plateau and deposited the Wingate and Kayenta Sandstones.

The early Jurassic Period (208–144 m.y.a.) was typified by a vast eolian sand sea, or erg, that covered all of Utah, including major portions of the Colorado Plateau. This vast erg deposited the well-known Navajo Sandstone that provides spectacular vistas throughout areas of Utah, Colorado, and Arizona. Paleo-wind directions derived from the preserved dunes indicate that the winds blew toward the southwest. In the southwestern part of the Great Basin, the Navajo erg grades into erg margin (Aztec Sandstone) and alluvial plain deposits formed on the east flank of the volcanically active orogenic terrain located in western Nevada. A marine transgression inundated the eolian erg and deposited limestones and evaporite sequences locally. This marine transgression is preserved in the geologic record of Utah as the Carmel Formation and Twin Creek Limestone. Eventually this sea withdrew from the area and left evaporite and mudflat deposits of the upper Carmel, Entrada, and Summerville Formations. In eastern Utah the Entrada Sandstone was formed by eolian sand deposition and creates the arches of Arches National Park. In late Jurassic time, alluvial plains migrated eastward from the western orogenic belt and deposited the dinosaur- and uranium-rich Morrison Formation.

The great Western Interior Seaway developed through much of the Colorado Plateau during Cretaceous time (144–66 m.y.a.). This seaway connected the Arctic Ocean with the Gulf of Mexico and the Gulf of California. The seaway was flanked on the west by the Sevier orogenic belt, which was located in western Utah, and extended both to the north and south. The Sevier Orogeny was characterized by thin thrust sheets that were transported many miles from the west. Classic deltaic sequences were developed on the western edge of the Cretaceous seaway off of the Sevier Orogeny. These deltaic and shoreline sequences deposited the large coal reserves of the western Colorado Plateau. To the east, the seaway extended as far as Minnesota. Thick, dark, and sometimes organic-rich shales were deposited in deeper waters. In Utah and Colorado these thick shale sequences constitute the geographically widespread Mancos Shale. The Mancos Shale and its equivalents are thought to be the source rock for much of the hydrocarbon production within the Colorado Plateau.

Cenozoic Era (66 m.y.a.–Present)

The Great Basin and Colorado Plateau began to feel the effects of igneous plutonic activity and block faulting associated with Laramide orogenic events in latest Cretaceous and early Tertiary time. The Colorado Plateau was experiencing local uplifts, including the San Rafael Uplift, Douglas Creek Arch, Monument Uplift, and Circle Cliffs Uplift. These Laramide events helped develop the broad monoclines that typify the Colorado Plateau. Several of these uplifts were drained to the north and then dammed by the Uinta Uplift and the Sevier Orogeny to the west. This natural drainage pattern allowed several large lakes to develop in adjacent basinal areas. The Flagstaff Limestone, Green River, and Claron Formations were deposited in the Uinta and Flagstaff Basins of Utah and Colorado. Lacustrine and alluvial sediment accumulation in the Uinta Basin was more than 9,000 feet thick. Lithologies include kerogen-rich oil shale, fluvial sandstones, siltstones, mudstones, and lacustrine limestones.

About 30 m.y.a., during the Oligocene Epoch, the Great Basin and the Colorado Plateau became more structurally differentiated than they had been in the past. The Great Basin was experiencing uplift and associated block faulting. From middle Tertiary time to the Holocene, horst and graben topography of the Great Basin continued to develop. The thinning of the lithosphere and weakness of the crust along relatively deep-seated faults allowed magma chambers to reach near to the earth's surface and expel lavas, ash flow tuffs, and ashes over the area. Major volcanic eruptions occurred within the Great Basin and around the margins of the Colorado Plateau. Whereas volcanic fields and igneous plutons were evident in the Great Basin, laccoliths developed locally within the Colorado Plateau. The Colorado Plateau experienced relatively continuous uplift and associated erosion by major river systems and their tributaries during this time and up to the present.

The Pleistocene Epoch, or Ice Age (1.6–0.01 m.y.a.), dramatically affected the topography of all of the earth's surface by changing the climate patterns and therefore the amount of precipitation, runoff, and erosion. Climatic changes produced cooler and more humid conditions in the area of the Great Basin and Colorado

Plateau. The additional precipitation allowed large, internally drained lakes to develop in the Great Basin. The amalgamation of a number of these lakes developed the largest pluvial lake (a lake formed by exceptional rainfall and excessive river runoff) on the North American continent, Lake Bonneville. Lake Bonneville silts (and to a minor extent sand and gravel) were deposited over most of the grabens in western Utah and parts of eastern Nevada and southern Idaho. In the Colorado Plateau the elevation was high enough that snowfields and alpine glaciers developed. The accumulation of snow and ice added impetus to the ability of the river systems to downcut canyons and further erode the Plateau. Approximately 12 to 14 k.y.b.p., the climate system began to change to the arid and semi-arid conditions found in both provinces today.

STRUCTURAL MAKEUP

Great Basin

Topographically the Great Basin is divided evenly between mountain ranges (horsts) and adjacent basins (grabens). The relatively small mountain ranges are long and linear, averaging 50–75 miles in length and 6–15 miles in width (Fenneman 1931). Centers of the intervening grabens are spaced 15–20 miles apart (Stewart 1971). Horsts are composed of bedrock, whereas the adjacent grabens are composed largely of sediment and debris that was derived from the horst. The debris-filled grabens may be more than 15,000 feet deep (Baer, personal communication).

The onset of the Basin and Range Province began approximately 17 m.y.a., during the early Miocene Epoch of the Cenozoic Era in the southern part of the Basin and Range. In the southern Basin and Range, the distance between ranges is slightly greater. Also, the elevation of the ranges above the basin floor is less than in northern areas. It is thought that these two features of the southern Basin and Range evidence more mature weathering and therefore an older age.

Geologists are generally in agreement that horst and graben topography can develop only by tensile forces' acting on the earth's crust (i.e., the earth's crust has been pulled apart). These tensile forces have developed the extensional tectonic style of the Great Basin, which includes crustal topographic features of horsts and grabens, tilted fault blocks, and listric faults (Stewart 1980). The crust is the rigid outer layer of the lithosphere. Many of the topographic features of the Great Basin do not penetrate the lower lithosphere. Several theories suggest that the crust of the Great Basin has been uplifted and thinned by a large heat source beneath. The generation of heat in the Great Basin is evidenced not only in the recent past by the abundant volcanic and igneous activity in the area but also presently by the large number of geothermal hot springs of the province. There are more hot springs from Salt Lake City, Utah, to Reno, Nevada, than in any other place in the country (Hintze, personal communication). Hypotheses as to the source of this heat are numerous, but two ideas have gained the most acceptance among structural geologists. Both hypotheses rely on the theory of plate tectonics to explain the anomalous heat.

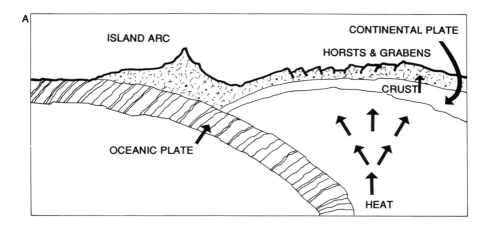

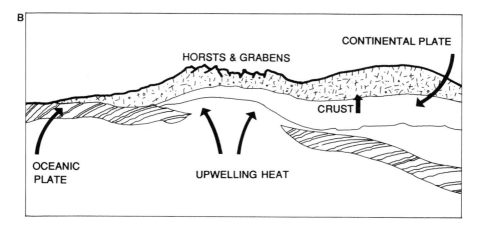

Figure 2.5   (a) The back-arc spreading hypothesis for development of the Great Basin topography. (b) The slab-window hypothesis.

   The back-arc spreading hypothesis proposes that as the North American continental plate overrode the more dense East Pacific oceanic plate, heat was generated both from friction and partial melting of the subducted plate as it dropped nearer to the upper mantle (Figure 2.5A). Hot magma chambers rose and bowed up the upper lithosphere (crust) in the vicinity of the Basin and Range. The relatively rigid crustal rocks could strain only to their breaking point, after which they faulted into a series of horsts and grabens (Stewart 1971).

A second hypothesis is similar to the back-arc spreading concept but proposes that as the North American continental plate completely overrode the divergent spreading center of the East Pacific plate, spreading stopped (Figure 2.5B). The east portion of this plate, known as the Farallon plate, continued to sink into the lower lithosphere and became detached from the former spreading center. The detachment produced a window between the Farallon plate and the spreading center. This window has allowed heat generated at the subducting plate and beneath it to rise and bow up that area of crust above it (Dickinson 1979). This hypothesis is appropriately called the slab-window concept.

Colorado Plateau

In contrast to the Great Basin, the Colorado Plateau has numerous structural features that developed a variety of landscapes. Kelley (1955) outlined seven structural features found in the province, including basins, uplifts and upwarps, monoclines, fault blocks, salt structures, igneous domal uplifts, and intermediate structures. The structural feature most characteristic of the plateau is the monocline (Figure 2.4). Monoclines may have gentle to steep dips (10° to 85°), multiple folds, faults, terraced surfaces, or a combination of these features. Monoclines in the Colorado Plateau commonly have five to ten times the relief of adjacent upwarps and basins. They are 10 to 200 miles long and have structural relief ranging from 200 to several thousand feet (Thornbury 1965).

The nearly circular Colorado Plateau has acted as a coherent block through the Cenozoic Era (i.e., the past 66 m.y.). During this time it has been uplifted more than 2 km (Beghoul and Barazangi 1989). Structural warping has occurred within the Plateau because of Laramide orogenic events and associated igneous plutonic emplacement. These features (uplift, warping, and igneous plutonic emplacement) must be considered when developing hypotheses as to the deeper earth mechanism that may have produced the Colorado Plateau. Two current hypotheses that are widely discussed include the thermal thinning model and the delamination model (Figure 2.6).

The thermal thinning model suggests that uplift occurred because of the thinning of the lithosphere by a deep-seated hot mantle plume. Lithospheric thinning is accompanied with crustal thickening, which results when molten asthenospheric material rises to a position just beneath the crust and injects magmatic fluids into the crust (Morgan and Swanberg 1985).

The second model used to explain the Colorado Plateau, the delamination theory, relies heavily on the plate tectonic theory. It involves the delamination (or horizontal detachment) of the subducted Farallon oceanic plate from the North American continental plate beneath the Colorado Plateau (Bird 1984). The hypothesis suggests that during early Cenozoic time, shearing between the two plates caused some of the Farallon plate to fuse to the North American plate. During mid-Cenozoic time, the remaining Farallon plate delaminated from the bottom of the North American plate. The Farallon plate sank into the lower lithosphere because it was composed of basaltic material, which is heavier than lower crustal continental rocks. The material that replaced the void made by the delamination was hot asthenospheric material that thermally expanded as it rose to the bottom of

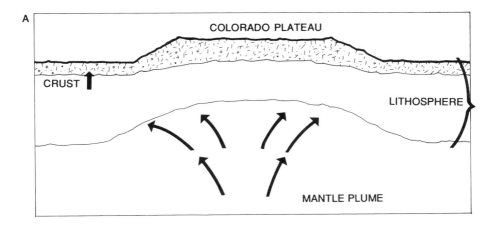

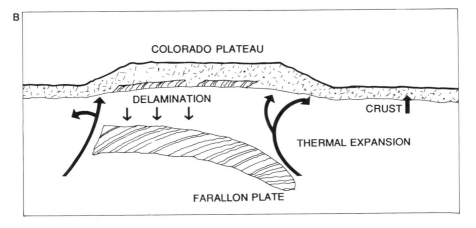

Figure 2.6 (a) The thermal thinning model used to explain the approximate 2 km of uplift of the Colorado Plateau. (b) The delamination model.

the crust. The thermal expansion and heating of the bottom of the North American plate, combined with the earlier crustal addition of Farallon material, could provide the estimated 2 km of crustal uplift seen in the Colorado Plateau. Recent velocity modeling of the lithosphere supports the delamination model over the thermal thinning model (Beghoul and Barazangi 1989).

SUMMARY

The sedimentologic and structural histories of the Great Basin and Colorado Plateau have been distinct through much of geologic time. The distinct geologic histories have contributed to the development of two discrete provinces not only geologically but also physiographically, climatically, and biologically. Through much of the Paleozoic Era, the Great Basin accumulated thick carbonate sequences as it was positioned at the western edge of the North American continent in a shallow marine depositional setting. Clastic rocks were deposited in the western edge of the Great Basin in response to the development of island arcs and amalgamation of suspect terrains (microcontinental blocks) during orogenesis. In contrast, throughout much of the northern Colorado Plateau, little or no carbonate sediments were deposited during this same time. The Transcontinental Arch caused much of the Plateau to be elevated above sea level, allowing only local and regional clastic sedimentation. These distinct depositional histories are reflected in the lithologies that are exposed today in the two provinces. The Great Basin of western Utah is dominated by Paleozoic carbonates (mostly dolomite), whereas the Colorado Plateau has a thinner Paleozoic section with a much greater percentage of sandstones and shales. Structural differentiation has been most prominent over the past 30 m.y. The thin, rigid crustal rocks of the Great Basin have been bowed upward by deeper-seated heat sources. The rocks responded to the tensile stress by straining to their breaking points and then faulting and collapsing into a series of horsts and grabens. The driving mechanism for the heat source is thought to come from the interaction of the subducted Farallon oceanic plate and the North American continental plate. The Farallon plate may have been key in the uplift of the Colorado Plateau as well. This plate may have temporarily laminated itself to the continental plate in the region of the Colorado Plateau. Upon delamination, the oceanic material sank and was replaced by thermally expanding asthenospheric material. The asthenospheric material was injected into the lower crust, increasing the thickness of the crust. The thickening of the crust and the thermally expanding material beneath it could have provided the 2 km of uplift within the Plateau.

Overprinting the depositional and structural histories of the two provinces is the more recent erosional surface history. Climate, precipitation, and surface runoff in the form of ephemeral (intermittent) streams, rivers, and alpine glaciation have modified the earth's suface. Moving water has downcut into the bedrock of the Colorado Plateau. In the Great Basin stream and river runoff processes have deposited sediments that have filled large areas between uplifted horsts. This has greatly modified the topographic expression of the Great Basin.

ADDRESSES OF STATE AGENCIES FOR GEOLOGIC INFORMATION

Arizona

Arizona Bureau of Geology and Mineral Technology
845 North Park Avenue
Tucson, AZ 85719

California

Division of Mines and Geology
California Department of Conservation
1516 Ninth Street, Fourth Floor
Sacramento, CA 95814

Colorado

Colorado Geological Survey
1313 Sherman Street, Room 715
Denver, CO 80203

Nevada

Nevada Bureau of Mines and Geology
University of Nevada–Reno
Reno, NV 89557-0088
(702) 784-6691

New Mexico

New Mexico Bureau of Mines and Mineral Resources
Campus Station
Socorro, NM 87801

Utah

Utah Geological and Mineral Survey
2363 South Foothill Drive
Salt Lake City, UT 84109-1491

GEOLOGIC MAPS USED

Arizona

Wilson, E. D., R. T. Moore, and J. R. Cooper, 1969, Geologic map of Arizona: Arizona Bureau of Mines and the United States Geological Society, Washington, D.C., 1:500,000.

Colorado

Tweto, O., 1979, Geologic map of Colorado: Geological Survey of Colorado and the United States Geological Society, Reston, Virginia, 1:500,000.

Nevada

Stewart, J. H., and J. E. Carlson, 1978, Geologic map of Nevada: United States Geological Survey in cooperation with the Nevada Bureau of Mines and Geology, Reston, Virginia, 1:500,000.

New Mexico

Dane, C. H., and G. O. Bachman, 1965, Geologic map of New Mexico: United States Geological Society in cooperation with the New Mexico Institute of Mining and Technology, State Bureau of Mines and Mineral Resources Division, and the University of New Mexico, Department of Geology, Washington, D.C., 1:500,000.

United States

Fenneman, N. M., 1946, Physical divisions of the United States: United States Geological Survey Separate Map, Denver, Colorado, 1:7,000,000.

Utah

Hintze, L. F., 1975, Geological highway map of Utah: Brigham Young University Geology Studies Special Publication 3, Provo, Utah, 1:1,000,000.

Hintze, L. F., 1980, Geologic map of Utah: Utah Geological and Mineral Survey, Salt Lake City, Utah, 1:500,000.

REFERENCES

Beghoul, N., and M. Barazangi, 1989, Mapping high Pn velocity beneath the Colorado Plateau constrains uplift models: Journal of Geophysical Research, vol. 94, pp. 7083–7104.

Bird, P., 1984, Laramide crustal thickening event in the Rocky Mountain foreland and Great Plains: Tectonics, vol. 3, pp. 741–758.

Dickinson, W. R., 1979, Cenozoic plate tectonic setting of the cordilleran region in the United States: in Armentrout, J. M.; M. R. Cole; and H. Terbest, (eds.), Cenozoic paleogeography of the western United States, Pacific Coast Paleogeography Symposium 3, Society of Economic Paleontologists and Mineralogists, Pacific Section, pp. 1–13.

Dott, R. H., Jr., and B. L. Batten, 1988, Evolution of the earth: McGraw-Hill, New York, 643 p.

Fenneman, N. M., 1931, Physiography of western United States: McGraw-Hill, New York, 534 p.

Fiero, B., 1986, Geology of the Great Basin: University of Nevada Press, Reno, 198 p.

Gerlach, A. C., 1970, The national atlas of the United States of America: United States Department of the Interior — Geology Survey, Washington, D.C., pp. 59–62.

Hintze, L. F., 1988, Geologic history of Utah: Brigham Young University Geology Studies Special Publication 7, 202 p.

Hunt, C. B., 1967, Natural regions of the United States and Canada: W. H. Freeman and Company, San Francisco, 725 p.

Kelley, V. C., 1955, Monoclines of the Colorado Plateau: Geological Society of America Bulletin, vol. 66, pp. 789–804.

Morgan, P., and C. A. Swanberg, 1985, On the Cenozoic uplift and tectonic stability of the Colorado Plateau: Journal of Geodynamics, vol. 3, pp. 39–63.

Pirkle, E. C., and W. H. Yoho, 1982, Natural landscapes of the United States, 3rd edition: Kendall/Hunt, Dubuque, Iowa, 399 p.

Rigby, J. K., 1976, Northern Colorado Plateau: field guide: Kendall/Hunt, Dubuque, Iowa, 207 p.

Stewart, J. H., 1971, Basin and Range structure: a system of horsts and grabens produced by deep seated extension: Geological Society of America Bulletin, vol. 82, no. 4, pp. 1019–1050.

Stewart, J. H., 1980, Regional tilt patterns of late Cenozoic basin-range fault blocks, western United States, part 1: Geological Society of America Bulletin, vol. 91, pp. 460–464.

Stokes, W. L., 1986, Geology of Utah: Utah Museum of Natural History, University of Utah, and Utah Geological and Mineral Survey, Salt Lake City, 280 p.

Thornbury, W. D., 1965, Regional geomorphology of the United States: John Wiley & Sons, New York, 609 p.

Pseudotsuga menziesii (Mirbel) Franco (Douglas fir) is a graceful tree with durable, artful cones. Douglas fir and other distinctive woody plant remnants in woodrat middens have helped paleobiogeographers recreate the vegetative scenes of the past 40,000 years in the Great Basin and on the Colorado Plateau.

CHAPTER 3

Modern and Pleistocene Climatic Patterns in the West

Kenneth Lee Petersen

OVERVIEW

Climate in the western United States is complex, and general patterns are linked to much larger global weather systems and to a deep geologic history. A perspective on the past should help us face our current concerns about human-induced global change, as such a view will better enable us to prepare for the future. A brief look at full glacial climates suggests that vast changes have been connected to the increase and decrease of global ice that occurs as the earth wobbles a bit in its slightly off-center orbit around the sun. Thus, in some ways the climate of the western United States is connected to the earth's cosmic journey.

Studies of the atmosphere, oceans, continents, ice cover, and biosphere over the past 30 years have revealed that the components of the global weather system are far more dynamic and complex than could have been imagined a few generations ago (Earth System Sciences Committee 1988). The launch of the first experimental satellite in 1960 showed images of the earth never before seen and provided a global perspective that was unheard of only a few years earlier. The launch of the first polar orbiting weather satellites in 1966 initiated a new era in weather forecasting that we now take for granted. Numerical simulation of atmospheric processes began to become practical in the 1960s with the advent of high-speed computers, although the beginning of numerical modeling had begun as early as 1948. All these advances have helped us better understand our global weather, which must be treated to some degree in this chapter to provide a basic backdrop for a more detailed discussion of the weather and climate in the western United States.

Weather is defined as a state or condition of the atmosphere at any particular time or place. A broad, integrated weather picture is known as a weather system. Meteorologists use satellites, balloons, ships, and computers to observe and forecast the day-to-day weather. Climate, in contrast, is really a statistical construct; a change in climate can be inferred only from a change in statistics, which by definition are gathered over long periods of time (Landsberg 1987). Climate can be viewed as the composite of all weather systems and events, and it fluctuates on all time scales: monthly, yearly, decadally, centennially, millennially, and longer.

To characterize past climate or even to project the future course of our climate, climatologists must take into consideration the wide complex of natural influences that affect climate: variations in the earth's orbit and tilt, breakup and clustering of continental plates and land masses, sporadic concentrations of volcanic dust in the atmosphere, great variations in area of snow and glaciers, changes in the concentration and composition of gases in the atmosphere, and the impact of humans. To assess these influences, climatologists turn to long-term instrumental records, old manuscripts, tree rings, fossil pollen, plant and animal remains, isotopes, ice from Greenland and the Antarctic, mud from the bottom of lakes and the ocean, and the world's fastest computers using extremely complex programs to simulate atmospheric and oceanic circulation.

GENERAL ATMOSPHERIC CIRCULATION

One cannot describe the climate in the Great Basin and the Colorado Plateau without first examining general concepts of atmospheric circulation. Most simply, the energy imbalance between lower and higher latitudes of the earth drives the general circulation system like a giant engine attempting to keep the earth in an energy equilibrium (for example, Oliver and Fairbridge 1987). Surplus energy in several forms is transported from the equatorial regions poleward to the higher latitudes, where outgoing radiation exceeds incoming solar radiation. This energy transport creates the general patterns of wind for the globe. A rotating earth produces a slight but persistent right-hand turn on air parcels moving poleward. This coriolis deflection, as it is known, results in a band of strong, westerly wind currents in the upper atmosphere of the middle latitudes that surrounds the pole. This band lies at the boundary of the cooler, polar air masses on its poleward side and the warmer, tropical air masses on its equatorward side. If the temperature gradient is relatively small between the lower and higher latitudes, these wind currents travel around the globe in a generally latitudinal fashion, referred to as zonal flow. However, if this temperature gradient steepens, the circulation flow forms a sinuous pattern moving around the hemisphere with a stronger north-south component, still at the boundary of the polar and tropical air masses. This second configuration that tends to move air in either a north or south direction is referred to as meridional flow. Whatever the configuration, the wind band, called the circumpolar vortex, significantly affects the weather and climate of the earth's surface, particularly in the middle latitudes, where the boundary between the polar and tropical air masses is normally located. The circumpolar vortex tends to persist (say with four descending wave troughs), but a change in the annual energy balance of the earth, for whatever reason, can force a stepwise change in the configuration of the circumpolar vortex (such as a contraction in size and a reconfiguration to three descending wave troughs), creating a climatic fluctuation.

At high altitude within the circumpolar vortex is a narrow band or stream of fast-moving air called the jet stream (Balling et al. 1987). Variation in wind velocities during the year is one of the interesting aspects of the jet stream — and of all the upper-air flow. According to the concept of thermal wind, the greater the contrast in thermal energy across a region, the greater the resulting wind velocity. Therefore, the jet stream, as well as most upper-air flow, reaches its maximum velocities during the fall and early winter and early spring, when the latitudinal thermal gradient is at a maximum. Conversely, during the summer season of either hemisphere, the velocity of the upper-air flow decreases as the latitudinal thermal gradient diminishes to a minimum. The undulations observed in the upper-air flow also reach the highest amplitude (crossing the largest amount of latitude) during the winter. During the summer the high-amplitude wave pattern becomes greatly reduced as a result of a reduced latitudinal thermal gradient.

The type of climatic condition found at the surface is associated with the position of the circumpolar vortex (Oliver and Fairbridge 1987). In the vicinity of a wave trough (counterclockwise circulation of the westerlies), where air flows from higher to lower latitudes, temperatures cool as polar air masses, transported southward by prevailing northwesterly flow, spread over the region. Beneath the wave ridge (clockwise circulation of the westerlies), in contrast, warmer air is advected northward and temperatures warm. Higher than normal pressures are found in the region dominated by an upper-level ridge, and lower pressures are found at the surface in the vicinity of the upper-level trough.

The mean position of these wave features also affects vertical motions in the atmosphere critical to precipitation (Oliver and Fairbridge 1987). Just ahead (downstream) of the upper-level ridge, air flows in a converging pattern, favoring subsidence of air parcels toward the surface that inhibits precipitation and fosters dry conditions. The subsidence pattern also favors slower than normal wind speeds. Ahead of the upper-level trough, divergence occurs in the upper atmosphere. This condition favors surface convergence and convection, with stronger wind speeds at the surface, increasing the potential for precipitation and prevailing wet conditions. Increases in the amplitude (north-south dimensions) of the long waves accentuate these vertical motions in the atmosphere and reinforce the wet-dry contrast. The surface weather data will reflect these patterns only if these long waves remain relatively stationary long enough so that they might be evident on daily or weekly weather maps.

During the Northern Hemisphere winter, all the circulation regimes migrate southward from their normal summertime positions. Conversely, these circulation features migrate northward with the advancement of summer into the Northern Hemisphere (Balling et al. 1987). One of the significant deviations from the generalized pattern of seasonal migration of circumpolar vortex is the development of regions of lower pressure over land during summer within the subtropical high-pressure belt. These low-pressure cells, called thermal lows, are predominantly surface manifestations, while aloft the controlling circulation pattern is still one of descending dry air with no precipitation.

Fronts (contrasting atmospheric conditions that mark the contact between two differing air masses) are one of the primary mechanisms for generation of precipitation and are often classified as being either cold, warm, or occluded, based on their individual characteristics and developmental history. Of all the regions of the world, the midlatitudes of each hemisphere are by far the most active in terms of moving atmospheric systems (Balling et al. 1987). The primary features that produce variations in surface winds are polar fronts, the low-pressure systems traveling along polar fronts, and the high-pressure systems that originate in either polar or subtropical regions.

IMPACT OF CONTINENTAL GEOGRAPHY ON CLIMATE

Land, which makes up about 30 percent of the global surface, can store relatively little heat compared to the oceans, so the continents have more dramatic climatological variation over the diurnal and seasonal cycles than do oceans (Barry and Chorley 1970). The climate of continents is strongly influenced by their latitudinal expanse, their physical configuration, and especially the arrangement and height of their mountain ranges. The African continent has one of the simplest patterns. It reaches across 70° of latitude, centered on the equator. Because of its low latitudes, the mean temperatures of Africa are perennially high so that the dominating pattern of the climatic belts is latitudinal, reflecting primarily the moisture regimes as controlled by the general circulation of the atmosphere. The African mountains, such as they are, do not significantly disrupt this pattern.

North America, although spanning slightly less latitude than Africa (60° vs. 70°), is located in the middle high latitudes and has a slightly more complex pattern than Africa. In North America there are latitudinal climatic belts that are conspicuous in the north, where the polar air mass exerts its frigid influence, but southward the latitudinal pattern is greatly disrupted by the effects of the high country of the western United States (Barry and Chorley 1970). This region of high mountains and plateaus acts to block out the Pacific moisture that would ordinarily dominate the continent, such as the Atlantic moisture that dominates Europe. Thus, in the United States the pattern of climatic belts is dominantly north and south, paralleling the global meridians. Because of its longitudinal structure, the western cordillera and plateaus themselves create a meridional series of cool, moist mountain climates alternating with warm, dry lowland climates. East of the western cordilleran highland is the dry area of the Great Plains grasslands. East of that the temperate forests reflect the dominance of the moist air masses out of the Gulf of Mexico and the west Atlantic, with the Appalachian Mountains serving to reinforce the meridional pattern.

Much of the United States is dominated by northerly flow during the winter season, driven in large part by the steeper temperature gradients from north to south. However, as the circulation belts migrate northward with the direct rays of the sun, the polar circulation gives way to a less vigorous summertime pattern. With the north and south migration of the circulation belts, the Great Basin is by far one of the most active in terms of moving atmospheric systems. It has the most frequent cyclogenesis (the spawning of low-pressure systems) in June and the most frequent occurrences of highs in December of any region in the Northern Hemisphere for any month (Barry and Chorley 1970).

EFFECTS OF MOUNTAINS AND PLATEAUS ON GENERAL CIRCULATION

Recent computer modeling experiments of general global circulation (Kerr 1989; Kutzbach et al. 1989; Ruddiman and Kutzbach 1989; Ruddiman and Kutzbach 1991; Ruddiman et al. 1989) suggest that one of the most significant influences on climate in recent earth history has been the thrusting of great mountain chains and plateaus (such as the Tibetan Plateau and the high country of the western United States) into the lower atmosphere. These uplifts resulted in a globe that can be pictured as having two major bulges on opposite sides of the Northern Hemisphere. The bulge over the western United States is roughly 2.5 million km^2 from the Sierra Nevada of California to the southern Rockies, which now stand 1.5 to 2 km high. These have risen more than 1 km during the past 20 million years, the uplift seeming to have accelerated during the past 15 million years (Kerr 1989). The bulge over the Tibetan Plateau is even larger.

These two high plateau regions, or global bulges, provoke a more complex circulation across much of the Northern Hemisphere through two mechanisms and through interactions between those mechanisms (Kerr 1989; Reiter and Tang 1984; Reyes and Cadet 1988; Shafer 1989; Tang and Reiter 1984). Computer models suggest that the first mechanism is the simple presence of an obstacle in the path of the prevailing westerly winds. Like a boulder in a stream, these plateaus divert the winds around them, including the jet stream, provoking undulations or wiggles in an otherwise smooth flow. The second mechanism is the generation of great columns of swirling air that in summer rise from the sun-baked plateau and in the winter descend while being dragged downward by the chill of the snow-covered heights. Throughout the troposphere (the lowermost, weather-generating layer of the atmosphere) the model plateau redirects winds to the north and south that would otherwise blow smoothly from west to east. These diversions induced by the high plateaus continue to set up a pattern of waves in the jet stream that are carried around the world. Some of these undulations or wiggles guide storms down across the United States and direct frigid air farther south and warm air farther north than would happen otherwise. The persistent routing of global winds around the high plateaus often results in a weather pattern characterized as a standing wave consisting of a ridge and adjacent trough.

Other computer experiments (Manabe and Broccoli 1990) suggest that there are further complex relationships fostered by the presence of the high plateaus and mountains acting as obstacles in the global wind system. The highlands actually led to extensive arid climates in their lee in middle latitudes of the Northern Hemisphere that were not simply a result of rainshadow effect (where a parcel of descending air in the lee of a mountain is warmed through compression to a temperature above that which would allow for moisture condensation). The experiments suggest that in the absence of mountains, stationary waves have relatively small amplitudes and a circumpolar jet axis is present between 45° and 50° north. In contrast, stationary waves have larger amplitudes traveling both farther north and south, and they establish a trough to the east of the Rocky Mountains. The jet streams in the mountain experiment are discontinuous and tend to be strongest downstream of the axes of the stationary troughs. The storm tracks show a similar discontinuity and are closely aligned with the jet axes. Precipitation tends to be heaviest in the areas downstream of the stationary trough (eastern United States). In the areas upstream of the troughs (western United States), general subsidence prevails, cyclonic activity is relatively weak, and precipitation is light. In summer the pattern of stationary waves in the mountain experiment is quite different from those in the other seasons. Wavelengths are shorter and the amplitudes are much smaller. But the upstream drought and downstream wet continues as it does in the other seasons.

In addition to the obstruction provided by the plateau itself, prevailing winds must also bypass wind systems induced by the plateau (Kerr 1989). In summer this system is the fountain-like, rising swirl of air known as the summer monsoon. In the simplest example of a monsoonlike circulation, the faster warming of the land than sea on a summer day induces a sea breeze at the beach because warm air rises over the land and draws in moist air from the sea. But the western highlands of the United States place the summer heating well up in the atmosphere. Because the atmosphere is less massive and thinner at those altitudes, winds can be driven faster by the same amount of heat energy. Given the breadth of the Colorado Plateau, the rising warm air forms an intense updraft that draws in air around its base. Under the influence of the earth's rotation, this air blows counterclockwise around the updraft, forming a huge, permanent low-pressure system. Winds such as the jet stream must swing to the north to get around the low. This makes for the start of another global undulation or wiggle. The air swirling into the plateau during the summer carries moisture off the Gulf of Mexico and Gulf of California to create the so-called Arizona monsoon (Kerr 1989; Tang and Reiter 1984). Airflow from the Gulf of California can be further enhanced with the development of a low trough in the Salton Sea region of southern California (Reyes and Cadet 1988).

To the north the dryness from loss of moisture to monsoon rains encourages the dry desert conditions of the northern Great Basin and the Columbia Plateau (Kerr 1989). The eastward traveling air that moves up and over the Columbia Plateau must come down eventually. The warming and drying of the air as it descends contribute to the arid nature of the Great Plains grassland (Borchert 1950).

During the winter the circulation about the plateaus reverses (Kerr 1989). Cooling now has the advantage, and there is less atmosphere above the ground to block heat loss to space. Dense, cold air sinks and swirls off a wintertime plateau, forming a permanent high-pressure system that the prevailing winds must also negotiate. This diversion of the westerlies results in a route that first goes north and then turns south around the high pressure, bringing cold air to the northern Great Plains from the north rather than milder air from the west.

RAPID REORGANIZATION OF THE ATMOSPHERE WITH CHANGING SEASONS

As discussed, the contrast of continental land temperatures during the winter and summer, as compared to the surrounding ocean surface temperature, leads to two distinctly different low-altitude circulation patterns over the elevated region of the western United States: clockwise around a high during the winter and counter-clockwise around a low during the summer (Kerr 1989). Like trying to change the direction of spin on a bicycle wheel, there can be no smooth transition between the two patterns.

In the spring a change begins as part of hemispheric readjustment of the circulation at about the beginning of April, when the Aleutian low-pressure cell, which from September to March is located at about 55° north and 165° west, splits into two cells, with one centered in the Gulf of Alaska and the other over northern Manchuria (Barry and Chorley 1970). Figure 3.1a illustrates that the arrival of spring is marked by a sharp decrease in precipitation from March to April in California. This reduction is due to the northward extension of the Pacific high, which establishes a high-pressure ridge off the West Coast of the United States. There is usually no rain during the remainder of the summer because of the blocking action of the high, and precipitation returns only with the cool season and the southward migration of the circulation belts following the direct rays of the sun (Pyke 1972).

In late March precipitation intensity increases east of the Rocky Mountains, with influences from both the north and south. In Figure 3.1a, more cyclogenesis can be seen between Colorado and Alberta, and at the same time, beginning in Texas, there is evidence of the northward extension of maritime tropical air over the Midwest from the Gulf of Mexico.

In late June there is a rapid northward displacement of the subtropical high-pressure cells in the Northern Hemisphere (Barry and Chorley 1970). In North America this pushes the depression tracks northward, resulting in June-to-July precipitation decreases over the northern Great Plains, parts of Idaho, and eastern Oregon (Figure 3.1b). Conversely, the southwestern anticyclone flow that affects Arizona in June is replaced by air from the Gulf of Mexico and the Gulf of California flowing around the western side of the Bermuda high, and this allows for the onset of the summer monsoon rains west of the Continental Divide. Bryson and Lahey (1958) have suggested that these circulation changes at the end of June may be connected with the disappearance of snow cover from the arctic tundra. This would lead to a sudden decrease of albedo (the reflection of incoming radiation) from about 75 to 15 percent, with a consequent rapid warming of the land surface and overlying atmosphere. Such warming would decrease the thermal gradient poleward and reduce the vigor of the thermal wind and related atmospheric circulation.

CLIMATIC PATTERNS IN THE WEST

The Pacific Ocean, the greatest ocean on earth, has little direct effect on the climate of much of the North American continent because of the high mountains and plateaus of the western United States (Hare 1966). One of the reasons is that much of the maritime character of the moist Pacific air is soon lost as it travels inland. As a parcel of air gains or loses altitude, it will change temperature in response to the changing pressure gradient. As the air parcel gains altitude — for example, when it goes over a mountain — its volume increases and its temperature cools. If the temperature of a parcel of air drops below its dew point, condensation occurs and water vapor changes to liquid water that can fall as precipitation. If, after crossing the

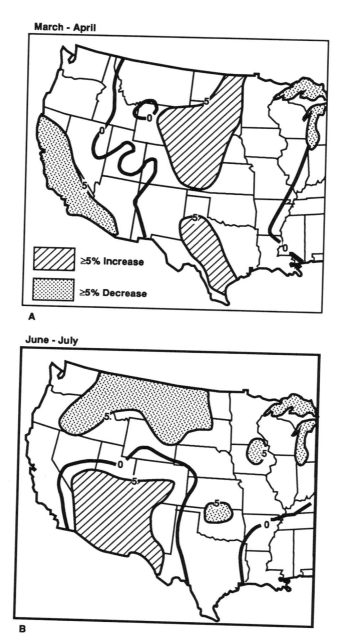

Figure 3.1   Precipitation changes in the western United States. Changes from March
through April (a) and June through July (b) are shown as a percentage of the
mean annual total (redrawn from Barry and Chorley 1970, fig. 5.9; after Bryson
and Lahey 1958).

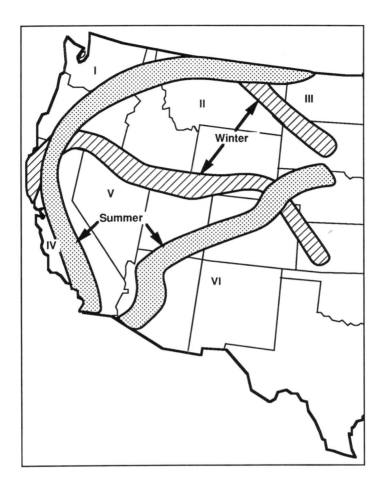

Figure 3.2 Western U.S. climatic regions. These regions are delineated by major summer and winter equivalent potential temperature boundaries (redrawn from Mitchell 1976, fig. 3).

mountain, the air parcel descends, its volume decreases and its temperature warms. As soon as its air temperature rises above its dew point, the liquid water within the parcel changes back to the vapor phase. It is quite difficult to trace Pacific moisture-bearing air masses that have to negotiate mountains and valleys as they travel across the western United States because of the changes in temperature, water phase, and moisture content connected to differences in elevation.

In this section I use a broad-brush approach to describe the modern climatic patterns in the western United States. For the interested reader, a selection of references containing more details can be found at the end of the chapter. Mitchell (1969, 1976) provides a useful classification of climatic regions of the western United States, as seen in Figure 3.2. His broad lines show the winter and summer boundaries that help to distinguish climatic regions with specific winter and sum-mer precipitation characteristics. Region I receives winter and much of the summer precipitation through frequent air mass intrusion from the Pacific. This region is largely shielded from outbreaks of winter arctic and polar air because of its proxim-ity to the ocean and mountains located to the north. Located in the zone of wester-lies, winters are very cloudy, which tends to modify temperature extremes. There is a definite winter maximum in precipitation. Region II receives winter precipitation through frequent air mass intrusion from the Pacific that provides considerable cloudiness, but the region receives little summer rainfall because it is mostly under the influence of what could be called interior air (mostly modified air coming from the southwest). Region III falls outside the major pathways of both summer and winter moisture-bearing air masses, and its winter is characterized by frequent out-breaks of polar and arctic air. Summer is warm with a precipitation maximum. Region IV is limited to southern California and receives winter moisture from infre-quent intrusion of Pacific air; winters are mild, but summers in the interior are hot and very dry (Figure 3.1b). Region V encompasses most of the Great Basin and falls largely outside the major pathways of both summer and winter moisture-bearing air masses. It receives winter moisture infrequently from Pacific air masses, and winter days are largely cloudless and mild, whereas summers are generally hot, with some cloud formation in late afternoon. This region is under the influence of interior air during the summer, with mostly southwest winds bringing dry air into the region. Region VI encompasses most of the Colorado Plateau and has a biseasonal regime with distinct winter and summer precipitation maxima. Winter is characterized by infrequent intrusions of Pacific air, but the summer has a rainy season brought about by the influx of monsoon air (Figure 3.1b).

The description of climate regions in Figure 3.2 shows that distinctions can be made between Great Basin and Colorado Plateau climates. As discussed, the winter rains are brought into the area by migrating low-pressure systems and troughs of low pressure associated with the westerly jet stream. This particular pattern is dominant from November to March (Figure 3.3a). These westerlies and accompanying storms normally follow a route to the north of the high-altitude ridge of high pressure off the coast of the western United States and enter the continent through Washing-ton and northern Oregon. They then follow a path that usually takes them south-ward along the eastern side of the Rockies, eastward through the Central Plains region, and then northeastward around a trough of low pressure centered over Hud-son Bay. Under these conditions, winter storms usually produce only partly cloudy skies and strong southwest winds throughout the western United States south of the Region II/V boundary (Figure 3.2).

The anomalous conditions that bring abundant winter precipitation south of the Region II/V boundary in the Great Basin and Colorado Plateau result from a westward displacement of the ridge of high pressure that normally resides over the western United States to a position well off the coast in the eastern Pacific Ocean and the formation of a low-pressure trough in its place (Figure 3.3b). Under these circumstances, storms follow the prevailing flow southward along the West Coast of the United States (often as far south as central California) before entering the

A
Mean 700-MB Contours
Outlook for February 1971

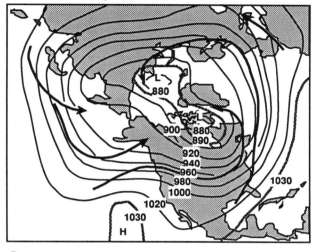

B
Mean 700-MB Contours Outlook
for Mid-February to Mid-March 1974

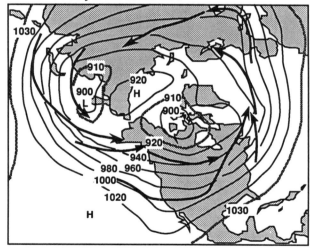

Figure 3.3 Winter circulation patterns. These examples show the patterns of prevailing airflow at an altitude of about 3,050 m. The arrows are principal cyclone tracks at sea level. (a)is more typical; however, conditions similar to (b) occur when the low over the Hudson Bay and the high off the coast of California are both shifted to the west (adapted from U.S. Department of Commerce, National Weather Service 1971, 1974; redrawn from Petersen 1988, fig. 7).

continent. Such storms pass through the Great Basin and Colorado Plateau region from the west and continue to the northeast. Once established, this pattern tends to persist or recur, thereby producing several storms in succession.

During May and June, Arizona and adjacent areas west of the Continental Divide are overlain by a warm, relatively dry air mass governed by a high-elevation anticyclone centered over the Mexican Highland. Not until this anticyclone shifts northward, usually around July 1 (Figure 3.1b), can the warm, moist air mass from the Gulf of Mexico and Gulf of California bring the convective storms of summer into Region VI west of the Continental Divide (Bryson and Lowry 1955; Hales 1974). Precipitation occurs mainly from convective cells initiated by surface heating, convergence, or, less commonly, orographic lifting. These summer convective storms form in clusters many tens of kilometers across, with individual storm cells covering altogether less than 3 percent of the surface area on regional weather maps at any one time and persisting for less than an hour on average (Barry and Chorley 1970). Figure 3.4 shows the monthly precipitation for three weather stations in the San Juan Mountain region located in the southwest corner of Colorado. Cool season and warm season precipitation are separated by lows in June and November. At this location summer monsoon precipitation is highest during the month of August.

Mountain Climates

In addition to the climatic effects already mentioned, mountain masses of the western United States produce other major effects upon regional and local climates (Rumney 1987). At the regional scale the highest ranges (for example, the Sierra Nevada and Cascade Ranges) funnel atmospheric flow (Bryson and Hare 1974) and create the large-scale rainshadows that contribute to the aridity of the western interior. At smaller scales most western mountains create local rainshadows that produce arid microclimates (climates on a very local scale) on their lee sides.

In many temperate areas precipitation in mountainous terrain increases rapidly with altitude up to a certain elevation, reaching a maximum that varies with latitude. In the western United States, the elevation for the maximum precipitation usually ranges between 1,200 and 2,400 m (Barry and Chorley 1970; Rumney 1987). The mountainous terrain also creates elevational gradients in microclimates. Temperature generally decreases with increasing elevation, but this trend can be reversed in areas where cold air collects in valley bottoms during clear nights and actually produces colder temperatures than those at higher elevations on the mountain above the cold air pool (Billings 1954). Less arid and more complex climates characterize mountain terrain where maximum climatic diversity can be encountered within short distances. The manifestation of the elevational trends are modified at any given locale by slope and aspect, with steep south-facing slopes being warmer and drier than most gentle or north-facing slopes. Plant and animal distributions in the mountains of a region are strongly influenced by changes in the gradient of temperature and precipitation. Often the higher mountains stand as humid islands above parched lowlands, and relatively dense vegetation develops in

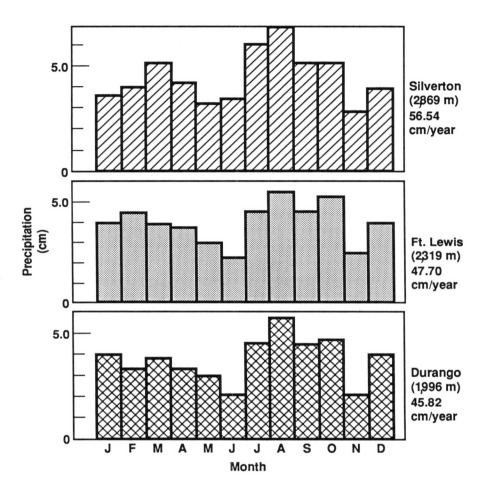

Figure 3.4 Monthly precipitation in southwestern Colorado. The bimodal distribution of precipitation is separated by lows in June and November, with the highest monthly averages occurring from July through October (redrawn from Petersen 1988, fig. 6; data from U.S. Department of Commerce, Weather Bureau 1964).

response to the increased moisture supply. Many of the mountain ranges accumulate sufficient moisture to support lakes, ponds, and feed streams.

Differences in altitude alone impose pronounced changes in atmospheric properties (Rumney 1987). With increasing altitude, both moisture and dust content, as well as atmospheric density and barometric pressure, diminish. The atmosphere's heat capacity also decreases, resulting in lower air temperatures. As density decreases, there is an increase in the intensity of solar radiation, particularly in the ultraviolet range of the spectrum. As a result, plant leaf temperatures may be higher than the surrounding air temperature, which may aid in plant survival at the highest elevations (Arno and Hammerly 1984:28). Wind speed increases with altitude. Turbulence can sometimes occur even in clear air over mountains and is most noteworthy over middle and upper slopes.

Airflow deflected upward over a mountain is cooled through lifting and encounters increasingly cooler atmospheric conditions in the process. The visible result of this movement is the development of clouds along windward mountain slopes that offer one of the striking features of the skies above mountains (Rumney 1987). Precipitation is commonly produced by such deflection and is known as orographic rain or snow. Convective motions that generate the cumulus clouds of mountain regions are often intensified sufficiently to form spectacular cumulonimbus clouds that can yield extremely heavy warm season showers. These cloudbursts, added to runoff from higher snowfields, often send sudden, destructive floods through lower stream courses, with disastrous consequences to life and property.

The proportion of precipitation that falls as snow becomes greater with rising altitude. Snowfields are seen at ever lower elevations as latitude increases (Rumney 1987). Annual release of meltwater to mountain streams in spring and summer is the chief source of water supply for many streams in the arid regions of the western United States.

Desert Climates

The term *desert* has traditionally been applied to regions afflicted by permanent drought (Rumney 1987). The capacity of a desert atmosphere to take up moisture is overwhelmingly greater than its capacity to release it, and the evaporation rate far exceeds precipitation. Thus, a desert area preserves an aspect of severe aridity despite the occurrence of random rain, snow, or even regular rain in small amounts. However, it is more difficult to provide a precise definition when a desert is compared to a near-desert or when arid climatic conditions are compared to semi-arid ones.

Most of the western U.S. deserts are in the elevated uplands between the Cascades–Sierra Nevada and Rocky Mountains (Rumney 1987). The largest desert region is the Great Basin, at an elevation of generally more than 1,500 m. It begins in southeastern Oregon and southwestern Idaho and extends into southern Nevada and eastward to the Salt Lake Desert in Utah. The arid region of the Colorado Plateau spreads over western Colorado, southern Utah, and northern Arizona and New Mexico at elevations similar to that of the Great Basin (above 1,500 m). The detailed distribution of actual desert climates is greatly complicated by the intermingling of mountains and plateaus that have foothill regions that are transitional between the arid desert lowlands and relatively moist highlands. The climatic boundaries surrounding persistently arid land change repeatedly because of the highly variable occurrence of precipitation.

Clear, cloudless skies from dawn until dusk are the overriding atmospheric condition of the desert climates around the globe. Most of the western deserts in the United States receive more than 80 percent of all possible sunshine from day to day in the summer (Rumney 1987). During the winter, clear skies are less frequent, although even then southern deserts receive more than 70 percent of the possible sunshine. In the deserts north of the Great Basin and the Region II/V boundary, frequent winter storms from the Pacific reduce the value to less than 50 percent in general and less than 40 percent in the Columbia Basin. Under clear skies the sun's rays, beginning at dawn, rapidly heat the bare ground, which in turn begins at once to warm the overlying air. Maximum air temperatures are reached in midafternoon, falling more slowly with the approach of evening. Low humidity and high temperatures are strongly characteristic of desert climates after midday.

In the western United States, mean yearly precipitation is generally less than 25 cm over most of the desert regions (Rumney 1987). However, the degree of variability, kinds of precipitation, and seasons of their occurrence are of far greater importance than the precipitation normals. Most precipitation in the desert areas of Region V falls mainly in winter, with 30 percent falling as snow in the central and northern sections. In the deserts of the southernmost section of Region V and in Region IV, snow falls infrequently and in trifling amounts, and the bulk of winter precipitation falls as light, steady rain. In Region VI 50 percent or more of the precipitation usually falls during the warm season. As discussed, the main moisture sources of warm season precipitation are the Gulf of Mexico and the Gulf of California, and thermal convective showers are the chief rain-generating mechanism. In the areas of summer maximum, departures from normal are over 20 percent, whereas in winter precipitation regions, variability averages between 25 percent and 35 percent. The random scattering of precipitation clouds is a common cause of the variability. In desert regions there is a notable phenomenon known as virga, when showers falling from a cloud base fail to reach the earth's surface.

PLEISTOCENE CLIMATE

Research has shown that some 18,000 years ago the climate on our planet was very different from the that of the present and may be related to changes in the earth's relationship to the sun. The 18,000-year date marks a point near the end of the geologic division of time called the Pleistocene, which spans about 1.6 million years and came to a conclusion 12,000 or so years ago. The subsequent geologic division of time is called the Holocene, and it represents climatic patterns that are much more like the present than those of the preceding late Pleistocene. In what follows, I give a global description to provide the reader a sense of the magnitude of contrast that exists between the present climate and that of 18,000 years ago; I then present specific evidence from the Great Basin and Colorado Plateau. By 10,000 years ago, global climate was more like it is today than in the late Pleistocene that preceded it. Although numerous researchers have found evidence for climatic change during the Holocene, these changes are usually not as dramatic as the relatively rapid and drastic changes that occurred when the earth shifted from a predominately glacial climate to that which is much more like the present.

Global Evidence

During the height of the Ice Age (24,000 to 14,000 years ago), continental glaciers in some regions rose nearly 3 km, and sea level was some 100 m lower than present;

tropical lake levels were lower, and monsoon circulation was weakened (Earth Systems Sciences Committee 1988). The world as a whole was substantially cooler, drier, and dustier than it is now. This reconstruction is based upon many different lines of evidence. The maximum extent of the ice sheets and mountain glaciers is well documented by terminal moraines and radiocarbon dating. Elsewhere, permafrost left characteristic signatures of subfreezing annual average temperatures on land. Past sea levels can be inferred from wavecut terraces, the downcutting of riverbeds, and ocean reef structure. The past temperature of the surface layers of the ocean can be inferred within 1° and 2°C by comparing the assemblages of species of planktonic microfossils in deep-sea sediments with those now being deposited. Sand dunes and eolian deposits reveal the direction and strength of prevailing winds. Ancient lake shorelines and sediments mark changes in lake levels, providing indicators of past regimes of precipitation and evaporation.

Satellite imagery has allowed the mapping of parts of the world that are now savannas but that were covered by sand dunes at the time of the last glacial maximum; using satellite images of the Sahara, scientists have identified the river channels from wetter, more recent interludes that are now buried beneath desert sand. The study of plant remains preserved in fossil packrat middens and pollen trapped in lake sediments reveals the past patterns of vegetation in the surrounding region that can be dated by radiocarbon techniques. In mountainous regions this type of information is translated into vertical displacement of vegetation zones and thus into changes of temperature that seem to be one of the primary limiting factors for plant growth. In more level terrain vegetation has also provided an indication of past temperature and rainfall, but substantial lags in time may be introduced in migration that is dependent on the long-distance dispersal of seeds. In tropical regions marine sediments and lake and vegetational records show that the monsoon circulation waned during glacial and waxed during nonglacial or interglacial periods in response to changes in the seasonal distribution of solar radiation associated with orbital and solar geometry.

The study of deep-sea sediments in recent years has also yielded persuasive evidence that the recurring ice ages characteristic of the past million years are indeed closely associated with the so-called Milankovitch cycles (Earth Systems Sciences Committee 1988). These cycles (related to slow changes in the earth's distance from and polar orientation to the sun) cause subtle but apparently critical changes in the seasonal variation of the incoming solar radiation, particularly in high latitudes. And these cycles may be reliably calculated from celestial mechanics. The waxing and waning of the ice ages themselves are recorded in the ratio of oxygen isotopes in deep-sea sediments because the reduced fraction of heavy isotopes in freshwater evaporated at the ocean surface is reflected in an enhanced ratio in the precipitated carbonate skeletons of microorganisms living in the seawater remaining. Although there are still some issues of interpretation and dating, variation in the stable oxygen isotope ratios of $^{16}O/^{18}O$ with depth in an ocean sediment core are widely interpreted as measuring total ice volume on land as a function of the passage of time. As more informative cores have been examined and dating procedures have become more refined, it has become more apparent that the changes in insolation and subsequent changes in ice volume are highly interrelated. However, a correspondence between the two records requires an allowance for the relatively slow buildup of ice sheets as contrasted with their relatively rapid decay.

Evidence in the Western United States

In the western United States about 18,000 years ago, immense lakes were evident in many closed basins, and glaciers advanced down high mountain valleys. Herds of mammoths, llamas, camels, and native horses as well as individuals of other exotic animals now extinct roamed over the region; and pikas, now restricted to a few of the highest mountain ranges, lived in talus near the valley bottoms. During the late Wisconsin, subalpine woodlands and mountain forests dominated vast areas now occupied by pygmy conifer woodlands. Studies of lake and wind deposits, faunal remains, pollen, and the relatively new study of fossilized waste piles of packrats have made tremendous strides in the efforts to shed light on the vast changes that took place in the western United States in the Pleistocene. The specific evidence used to deduce these climatic changes is not described here because it has been reviewed elsewhere (Betancourt et al. 1990; Bryant and Holloway 1985; Jacobs et al. 1985; Mehringer 1977, 1986; Ruddiman and Wright 1987; Thompson 1988; Van Devender et al. 1985; Wells 1983; Wright 1983; Wright and Frey 1965).

Pleistocene Climatic Patterns in the Western United States

At approximately 18,000 B.P., a summer radiation minimum corresponded with the maximum expansion of continental glaciers (Imbrie and Imbrie 1980) that I refer to as the full glacial in the following discussion. Field data suggest that, as compared to today, the principal features of full glacial climate were the strong summer cooling and the expansion of winter precipitation from Pacific frontal storms and greatly diminished monsoonal flow. Computer simulation experiments of full glacial climates by the Cooperative Holocene Mapping Project (COHMAP) (COHMAP Members 1988) and Manabe and Broccoli (1985) suggest that the very presence of the Laurentide ice sheet thrust up into the lower atmosphere acted as a physical barrier and split the jet stream into two branches. The COHMAP simulations suggest that the mean position of the southerly branch was 20° south of the modern position of the jet stream and the summer monsoon was essentially nonexistent in the western United States. The existence of a vast, very cold, and elevated ice sheet created a perpetual high-pressure system with cold, dense, sinking air swirling clockwise that most likely would have placed the Pacific Northwest under easterly flow off the ice sheet (a complete reversal from the dominant westerly air flow of today), and summer temperatures may have been as much as 5° to 10°C below the modern mean (Barnosky et al. 1987).

Concurrently during the full glacial, the modern southwestern deserts received abundant precipitation from storms following the southern branch of the jet stream. Both the COHMAP model runs and the paleoenvironmental data (Van Devender and Spaulding 1979; Van Devender 1990) indicate that temperatures were only moderately depressed below modern temperatures. Milder winters seem to be suggested by the upward expansion of desert scrub.

Between the cold Pacific Northwest and the relatively warm southwestern deserts lies the region of the Colorado Plateau and the Great Basin. Thompson (1990) notes that the depiction of physiography and the spacial resolution in the COHMAP models are too coarse to determine whether this middle region would have been under desiccating winds from the midcontinent or under western-bearing flow off the Pacific during the full glacial. In the Colorado Plateau Betancourt (1990) and Cole (1990) indicate that, depending on the site location, inferences can be made for either a decrease or increase in soil moisture during the full glacial. In general the climate seems to have been quite continental, with cooler and drier summers than present, which is consistent with the decreased monsoon circulation at that time.

Thompson (1990) believes the predominance of cold-tolerant species and the downward expansion of subalpine trees, like bristlecone pine, along with the apparent absence of thermophiles in plant assemblages from packrat middens dated to the full glacial in the Great Basin, possibly indicate that summers were cooler and winters still colder. This may have been because the westerly flow was not as dependable in the Great Basin as areas in much of the Southwest, where winter temperatures apparently were moderated. Siegal's (1983) and Flynn and Buchanan's (1990) isotopic hydrogen (H/D) ratios from packrat midden cellulose and aged groundwater, respectively, seem to indicate that major temperature depressions did occur in the Great Basin during the full glacial.

Thus, there is evidence of a steepening of the temperature gradient from north to south in the western United States. In addition, there was possibly also a steepening of the temperature gradient elevationally as compared to that of today. In the mountains of North America there is a correspondence to the elevation of the average 10°C July isotherm (a line connecting points of equal temperature) and the elevation of alpine timberline (the upper elevational limit of trees). Under modern climatic conditions there is a regular depression of the elevation of the 10°C July isotherm and the elevation of alpine timberline as one moves from the Continental Divide in Montana to the Olympic Mountains near the Pacific Ocean (a distance of about 720 km) (Arno and Hammerly 1984). The elevational difference between the two extreme points on the transect is about 1,000 m and is the result of decreasing continental climate westward with increased cloudiness, snowfall, and cooler summer temperatures at any given elevation. Thus, the climatic gradient is steeper (changes more rapidly with elevation) under coastal climatic conditions than it is under continental conditions. A southern displacement of the jet stream 20° to the south during the full glacial would have resulted in more Pacific air masses crossing the Great Basin and Colorado Plateau, bringing with them increased precipitation, cloudiness, and generally cooler conditions. The increased cool season storminess in the central portion of the region probably helped maintain the high pluvial levels of lakes (Benson and Thompson 1987) and supported lower-elevation glaciation and other related phenomena in the mountains (Brakenridge 1978; Dohrenwend 1984; Phillips et al. 1990; Zielinski and McCoy 1987).

Kukla (1975) and Young and Bradley (1984) suggest that 5,000 to 10,000 years prior to the maximum extent of global ice (18,000 years ago) there could have been climatic conditions very favorable for the rapid growth of ice sheets in the northern latitudes. These climatic conditions might also have favored the initial filling of pluvial lakes and the expansion of mountain glaciers in the western United States prior to the southern displacement of the jet stream. As already indicated in the discussion above on thermal winds, a strong solar insolation gradient in the winter results in the displacement of the subtropical highs toward the equator, an expansion of the circumpolar vortex, a more intense circumpolar westerly flow, and increased moisture flux to high latitudes due to the increased amplitude of the circumpolar vortex. However, celestial mechanics suggest that at certain times during the past several hundred thousand years or so, all seasons have varied in their solar insolation gradients (Berger 1978; Kukla 1975). Young and Bradley (1984) use modeling experiments to suggest that with a steepening of the autumn insolation gradient in the Northern Hemisphere, there would have been an increase in the vigor of the global wind system during that season. Autumn would be characterized by a more expanded winterlike circumpolar vortex and greater transport of moisture poleward (contributing to ice sheet growth) earlier in the cool season. Such conditions would suggest a longer and (because of the added length) wetter cool season with a corresponding shorter and cooler warm season. Such conditions would have been further amplified when the continental ice sheets reached the critical size or shape necessary to divert the jet stream south (Lao and Benson 1988). Many radiometric dates on moderately deep pluvial lakes (Lao and Benson 1988) and maxima of mountain glaciers (Phillips et al. 1990) show that these are largely synchronous with maxima in global ice volume.

Soon after 18,000 years ago, global temperatures began to warm. Even so, the sher size and volume of the continental ice sheets meant that it would take thousands of years for the ice mass to waste away (Ruddiman and Wright 1987). With warming global conditions, the capacity for Pacific air masses to hold more moisture increased, but their route was still maintained far to the south in the western United States as they negotiated the barrier of continental ice. This would have allowed for continued cool season storminess in the Great Basin and Colorado Plateau. Thompson (1990) indicates that in the Great Basin the deepest lake phases were reached and maintained for a few thousand years after the coldest period of the full glacial but rapidly desiccated thereafter. With the shrinking of the continental ice mass below the critical threshold, the jet stream was allowed to establish a pattern more like that of the present (COHMAP Members 1988).

SUMMARY

Climate in the western United States is complex, and the patterns have links to a much larger global weather system and an even longer geologic history. As we can see from studying full glacial climates, vast changes in the past have been linked to the amount of global ice that builds up and melts as the earth orbits the sun off-center. In some respects, then, the climate of the Great Basin and Colorado Plateau depends on the earth's movement through space. The western United States is a strangely provocative and hauntingly beautiful place that, once studied, can never be viewed in the same way again.

ACKNOWLEDGMENTS

This chapter benefited from the constructive reviews of Peter J. Mehringer, Jr., Robert S. Thompson, and David S. Shafer. It was prepared while the author was employed by Westinghouse Hanford Company in Richland, Washington (Hanford Operations and Engineering Contractor for the U.S. Department of Energy under Contract DE-AC06-87RL10930), and is Westinghouse Document No. WHC-EP-0523. The views and opinions of authors expressed herein do not necessarily state or reflect those of the U.S. government or any agency thereof.

LITERATURE CITED

Arno, S. F., and R. P. Hammerly. 1984. Timberline: mountain and arctic forest frontiers. The Mountaineers, Seattle, WA.

Balling, R. C., Jr., R. S. Cerveny, and K. E. Dewey. 1987. Wind and wind systems, pp. 933–41. In: J. E. Oliver and R. W. Fairbridge (eds.), The encyclopedia of climatology. Encyclopedia of earth sciences, volume 11. Van Norstrand Reinhold, New York.

Barnosky, C. W., P. M. Anderson, and P. J. Bartlein. 1987. The northwestern U.S. during deglaciation; vegetation history and paleoclimatic implications, pp. 289–321. In: W. F. Ruddiman and H. E. Wright, Jr. (eds.), North America and adjacent oceans during the last deglaciation. The geology of North America, volume K-3. Geological Society of America, Boulder, CO.

Barry, R. G., and R. J. Chorley. 1970. Atmosphere, weather, and climate. Holt, Rinehart and Winston, New York.

Benson, L. V., and R. S. Thompson. 1987. The physical record of lakes in the Great Basin, pp. 241–60. In: W. F. Ruddiman and H. E. Wright, Jr. (eds.), North America and adjacent oceans during the last deglaciation. The geology of North America, volume K-3. Geological Society of America, Boulder, CO.

Berger, A. L. 1978. Long-term variation as daily insolation and Quaternary climatic changes. Journal of Atmospheric Sciences 35:2362–67.

Betancourt, J. L. 1990. Late Quaternary biogeography of the Colorado Plateau, pp. 259–92. In: J. L. Betancourt, T. R. Van Devender, and P. S. Martin (eds.), Packrat middens: the last 40,000 years of biotic change. University of Arizona Press, Tucson.

Betancourt, J. L., T. R. Van Devender, and P. S. Martin (eds.). 1990. Packrat middens: the last 40,000 years of biotic change. University of Arizona Press, Tucson.

Billings, W. D. 1954. Temperature inversion in the pinyon-juniper zone of a Nevada mountain range. Butler University Botanical Studies 11:112–18.

Borchert, J. R. 1950. The climate of the central North American grassland. Association of American Geographers Annals 40:1–39.

Brakenridge, G. R. 1978. Evidence for a cold, dry full-glacial climate in the American Southwest. Quaternary Research 9:22–40.

Bryant, V. M., Jr., and R. G. Holloway. 1985. Pollen records of Late-Quaternary North American sediment. American Association of Stratigraphic Palynologists Foundation, Dallas, TX.

Bryson, R. A., and F. K. Hare. 1974. Climates of North America, pp. 1–47. *In:* R. A. Bryson and F. K. Hare (eds.), Climates of North America. World survey of climatology, volume 11. Elsevier, Amsterdam.

Bryson, R. A., and J. F. Lahey. 1958. The march of the seasons. University of Wisconsin Meteorology Department, Madison. (Cited in Barry and Chorley 1970.)

Bryson, R. A., and W. P. Lowry. 1955. Synoptic climatology of the Arizona summer precipitation singularity. Bulletin of the American Meteorological Society 36:329–39.

COHMAP Members. 1988. Climatic changes of the last 18,000 years: observations and model simulations. Science 241:1043–52.

Cole, K. L. 1990. Late Quaternary vegetation gradients through the Grand Canyon, pp. 240–58. *In:* J. L. Betancourt, T. R. Van Devender, and P. S. Martin (eds.), Packrat middens: the last 40,000 years of biotic change. University of Arizona Press, Tucson.

Dohrenwend, J. C. 1984. Nivation landforms in the western Great Basin and their paleoclimatic significance. Quaternary Research 22:275–88.

Earth System Sciences Committee, NASA Advisory Council. 1988. Earth system science: a closer view. National Aeronautics and Space Administration, Washington, DC.

Flynn, T., and P. K. Buchanan. 1990. Geothermal fluid genesis in the Great Basin. Division of Earth Sciences, Report 90R1. Environmental Research Center, University of Nevada, Las Vegas.

Hales, J. E., Jr. 1974. Southwestern United States summer monsoon source—Gulf of Mexico or Pacific Ocean? Journal of Applied Meteorology 13:331–42.

Hare, F. K. 1966. The restless atmosphere, 4th edition. Harper and Row, New York.

Imbrie, J., and J. Z. Imbrie. 1980. Modeling the climatic response to orbital variations. Science 207:943–53.

Jacobs, B. F., P. L. Fall, and O. K. Davis (eds.). 1985. Late Quaternary vegetation and climates of the American Southwest. AASP Contribution Series no. 16. American Association of Stratigraphic Palynologists Foundation, Dallas, TX.

Kerr, R. A. 1989. Research news: did the roof of the world start an ice age? Science 244:1441–42.

Kukla, G. J. 1975. Missing link between Milankovitch and climate. Nature 253:600–603.

Kutzbach, J. E., P. J. Guetter, W. F. Ruddiman, and W. L. Prell. 1989. Sensitivity of climate to Late Cenozoic uplift in southern Asia and the American West: numerical experiments. Journal of Geophysical Research 94:18, 393–407.

Landsberg, H. E. 1987. Climatology, pp. 327–88. *In:* J. E. Oliver and R. W. Fairbridge (eds.), The encyclopedia of climatology. Encyclopedia of earth sciences, volume 11. Van Norstrand Reinhold, New York.

Lao, Y., and L. Benson. 1988. Uranium-series age estimates and paleoclimatic significance of Pleistocene tufas from the Lahontan Basin, California and Nevada. Quaternary Research 30:165–76.

Manabe, S., and A. J. Broccoli. 1985. The influence of continental ice sheets on the climate of an ice age. Journal of Geophysical Research 90:2167–90.

Manabe, S., and A. J. Broccoli. 1990. Mountains and arid climates of middle latitudes. Science 247:192–95.

Mehringer, P. J., Jr. 1977. Great Basin Late Quaternary environments and chronology, pp. 113–67. In: D. D. Fowler (ed.), Models and Great Basin prehistory: a symposium. Publications in the Social Sciences no. 12. Desert Research Institute, University of Nevada System, Reno.

Mehringer, P. J., Jr. 1986. Prehistoric environments, pp. 31–50. In: W. L. d'Azevedo (ed.), Great Basin. Handbook of North American Indians, volume 11. Smithsonian Institution, Washington, DC.

Mitchell, V. L. 1969. The regionalization of climate in montane areas. Ph.D. dissertation, University of Wisconsin, Madison.

Mitchell, V. L. 1976. The regionalization of climate in the western United States. Journal of Applied Meteorology 15:920–27.

Oliver, J. E., and R. W. Fairbridge (eds.). 1987. The encyclopedia of climatology. Encyclopedia of earth sciences, volume 11. Van Norstrand Reinhold, New York.

Petersen, K. L. 1988. Climate and the Dolores River Anasazi. University of Utah Anthropological Papers no. 113. University of Utah Press, Salt Lake City.

Phillips, F. M., M. G. Zreda, S. S. Smith, D. Elmore, P. W. Kubik, and P. Sharma. 1990. Cosmic chlorine-36 chronology for glacial deposits at Bloody Canyon, eastern Sierra Nevada. Science 248:1529–32.

Pyke, C. B. 1972. Some meteorological aspects of the seasonal distribution of precipitation in the western United States and Baja California. Water Resources Center Contribution no. 139. University of California, Los Angeles.

Reiter, E. R., and Tang, M. 1984. Plateau effects on diurnal circulation patterns. Monthly Weather Review 112:638–51.

Reyes, S., and D. L. Cadet. 1988. The southwest branch of the North American monsoon during summer 1979. Monthly Weather Review 116:1175–87.

Ruddiman, W. F., and J. E. Kutzbach. 1989. Forcing of Late Cenozoic Northern Hemisphere climate by plateau uplift in southern Asia and the American West. Journal of Geophysical Research 94:18, 409–27.

Ruddiman, W. F., and J. E. Kutzbach. 1991. Plateau uplift and climatic change. Scientific American 264(3):66–75.

Ruddiman, W. F., W. L. Prell, and M. E. Raymo. 1989. Late Cenozoic uplift in southern Asia and the American West: rationale for general circulation modeling experiments. Journal of Geophysical Research 94:18, 379–91.

Ruddiman, W. F., and H. E. Wright, Jr. (eds.). 1987. North American and adjacent oceans during the last deglaciation. The geology of North America, volume K-3. Geological Society of America, Boulder, CO.

Rumney, G. R. 1987. Climate of North America, pp. 613–23. In: J. E. Oliver and R. W. Fairbridge (eds.), The encyclopedia of climatology. Encyclopedia of earth sciences, volume 11. Van Norstrand Reinhold, New York.

Shafer, D. S. 1989. The timing of late Quaternary monsoon precipitation maxima in the southwest United States. Ph.D. dissertation, University of Arizona, Tucson.

Siegal, R. D. 1983. Paleoclimatic significance of D/H and $^{13}C/^{12}C$ ratios in Pleistocene and Holocene wood. Master's thesis, University of Arizona, Tucson. (Cited in Thompson 1990.)

Tang, M., and E. R. Reiter. 1984. Plateau monsoons of the Northern Hemisphere: a comparison between North America and Tibet. Monthly Weather Review 112:617–37.

Thompson, R. S. 1988. Western North America: vegetation dynamics in the western United States; modes of response to climatic fluctuation, pp. 415–58. *In*: B. Huntley and T. Webb III (eds.), Vegetation history. Kluwer Academic Publishers, Dordrecht, the Netherlands.

Thompson, R. S. 1990. Late Quaternary vegetation and climate in the Great Basin, pp. 200–39. *In*: J. L. Betancourt, T. R. Van Devender, and P. S. Martin (eds), Packrat middens: the last 40,000 years of biotic change. University of Arizona Press, Tucson.

U.S. Department of Commerce, National Weather Service. 1971. For February 1971. Average Monthly Weather Outlook 25(3).

U.S. Department of Commerce, National Weather Service. 1974. For mid-February to mid-March 1974. Average Monthly Weather Outlook 28(4).

U.S. Department of Commerce, Weather Bureau. 1964. Decennial census of United States. Climatic summary of the United States, Supplement for 1951 through 1960: Colorado. Climatography of the United States 86–5.

Van Devender, T. R. 1990. Late Quaternary vegetation of the Sonoran Desert, United States and Mexico, pp. 134–63. *In*: J. L. Betancourt, T. R. Van Devender, and P. S. Martin (eds.), Packrat middens: the last 40,000 years of biotic change. University of Arizona Press, Tucson.

Van Devender, T. R., P. S. Martin, R. S. Thompson, K. L. Cole, A.J.T. Jull, A. Long, L. J. Toolin, and D. J. Donahue. 1985. Fossil packrat middens and the tandem accelerator mass spectrometer. Nature 317:610–13.

Van Devender, T. R., and W. G. Spaulding. 1979. Development of vegetation and climate in the southwestern United States. Science 204:701–10.

Wells, P. V. 1983. Paleobiogeography of montane islands in the Great Basin since the last Glaciopluvial. Ecological Monographs 53(4):341–82.

Wright, H. E., Jr. (ed.). 1983. Late Quaternary environments of the United States, volumes 1 and 2. University of Minnesota Press, Minneapolis.

Wright, H. E., Jr., and D. G. Frey (eds.). 1965. The Quaternary of the United States. Princeton University Press, Princeton, NJ.

Young, M. A., and R. S. Bradley. 1984. Insolation gradients and the paleoclimatic record, 707–13. *In*: A. L. Berger, J. Imbrie, J. Hays, G. Kukla, and B. Saltzman (eds.), Milankovitch and climate: understanding the response to astronomical forcing. D. Reidel, Dordrecht, the Netherlands.

Zielinski, G. A., and W. D. McCoy. 1987. Paleoclimatic implications of the relationship between modern snowpack and late Pleistocene equilibrium-line altitudes in the mountains of the Great Basin, western U.S.A. Arctic and Alpine Research 19:127–34.

SELECTED REFERENCES ON CLIMATE IN THE WESTERN UNITED STATES

Antevs, E. 1962. Late Quaternary climates of Arizona. American Antiquity 20:193–8.

Baker, F. S. 1944. Mountain climates of the western United States. Ecological Monographs 14:129–33.

Baldwin, J. L. 1973. Climates of the United States. U.S. Department of Commerce, National Ocean and Atmospheric Administrations, Silver Springs, MD.

Balling, R. C., Jr. 1979. Regional winter climatic variations associated with atmospheric circulation changes in the coterminous United States: 1939–1965. Ph.D. dissertation, University of Oklahoma, Norman.

Barry, R. G., and R. S. Bradley. 1976. Historical climatology, pp. 43–67. *In*: H. W. Steinhoff and J. D. Ives (eds.), Ecological impacts of snowpack augmentation in the San Juan Mountains, Colorado. U.S. Department of Interior, Bureau of Reclamation, Denver, CO (Accession no. PB 255 012, U.S. Department of Commerce, National Technical Information Service, Springfield, VA).

Bartlein, P. J. 1982. Streamflow anomaly patterns in the U.S.A. and southern Canada, 1951–1970. Journal of Hydrology 57:49–63.

Batchelor, L. D., and F. L. West. 1915. Variation in minimum temperature due to topography of a mountain valley and its relation to fruit growing. Utah Agricultural College Experiment Station Bulletin 141, Logan.

Betancourt, J. L. 1984. Late Quaternary plant zonation and climate in southeastern Utah. Great Basin Naturalist 44:1–35.

Bradley, R. S. 1976. Precipitation history of the Rocky Mountain states. Westview Press, Boulder, CO.

Bradley, R. S. 1976. Seasonal precipitation fluctuations in the western United States during the late nineteenth century. Monthly Weather Review 104:501–12.

Bradley, R. S. 1976. Secular changes of precipitation in the Rocky Mountain states. Monthly Weather Review 104:513–23.

Bradley, R. S. 1980. Secular fluctuations of temperature in the Rocky Mountain states and a comparison with precipitation fluctuation. Monthly Weather Review 108:873–85.

Bradley, R. S., and R. G. Barry. 1973. Secular climatic fluctuations in southwestern Colorado. Monthly Weather Review 101:264–70.

Brenner, I. S. 1974. A surge of maritime tropical air—Gulf of California to the southwestern United States. Monthly Weather Review 102:375–89.

Bryson, R. A. 1980. Ancient climes of the Great Plains. Natural History 89:65–73.

Byrne, R. J., O. Granger, and J. Monteverdi. 1982. Recent rainfall trends on the margins of the subtropical deserts: a comparison of selected northern regions. Quaternary Research 17:14–25.

Caine, N. 1976. Summer rainstorms in an alpine environment and their influence on soil erosion, San Juan Mountains, Colorado. Arctic and Alpine Research 8:183–96.

Dorroh, J. H., Jr. 1946. Certain hydrologic and climatic characteristics of the Southwest. Publications in Engineering no. 1. University of New Mexico, Albuquerque.

Douglas, A. V. 1976. Past air-sea interactions over the eastern north Pacific as revealed by tree-ring data. Ph.D. dissertation, University of Arizona, Tucson.

Douglas, A. V., and H. C. Fritts. 1972. Tropical cyclones of the eastern northern Pacific and their effects on the climate of the western United States: a study of circulation features that may be recorded by tree-rings. Final Report: NOAA Contract 1-35241. University of Arizona Laboratory of Tree-Ring Research. U.S. Department of Commerce, Environmental Data Service, Washington, DC. (Accession no. COM-73-11230, U.S. Department of Commerce, National Technical Information Service, Springfield, VA).

Erdman, J. A., C. L. Douglas, and J. W. Marr. 1969. Environments of Mesa Verde, Colorado. Publications in Archaeology 7B. U.S. Department of Interior, National Park Service, Washington, DC.

Farmer, E. E., and J. E. Fletcher. 1971. Precipitation characteristics of summer storms at high-elevation stations in Utah. Research Paper INT-110. U.S. Department of Agriculture, Forest Service, Ogden, UT.

Gregory, H. E., and M. R. Thorpe. 1938. The San Juan country: a geographic and geologic reconnaissance of southeastern Utah. Professional Paper 188. U.S.Geological Survey. U.S. Government Printing Office, Washington, DC.

Hack, J. T. 1942. The changing physical environment of the Hopi Indians of Arizona. Papers of the Peabody Museum of American Archaeology and Ethnology 35, no. 1. Cambridge, MA.

Hansen, E. M. 1975. Moisture source for three extreme local rainfalls in the southern Intermountain Region. Technical Memorandum, Hydrometeorological Report no. 26. National Weather Service, National Oceanic and Atmospheric Administration, Silver Springs, MD.

Hansen, E. M., and F. K. Schwartz. 1981. Meteorology of important rainstorms in the Colorado River and Great Basin drainages. Technical Memorandum, Hydrometeorological Report no. 50. National Weather Service, National Oceanic and Atmospheric Administration, Silver Springs, MD.

Harper, K. T. 1986. Historical environments, pp. 51–63. *In*: W. L. d'Azevedo (ed.), Great Basin. Handbook of North American Indians, volume 11. Smithsonian Institution, Washington, DC.

Hastings, J. R., and R. M. Turner. 1965. The changing mile. University of Arizona Press, Tucson.

Horn, L. H., and R. A. Bryson. 1960. Harmonic analysis of the annual march of precipitation over the United States. Association of American Geographers Annals 50:157–71.

Houghton, J. G. 1969. Characteristics of rainfall in the Great Basin. Desert Research Institute, University of Nevada System, Reno, NV.

Houghton, J. G. 1979. Model for orographic precipitation in the north-central Great Basin. Monthly Weather Review 107:1462–75.

Houghton, J. G., C. M. Sakamoto, and R. O. Gifford. 1975. Nevada's weather and climate. Nevada Bureau of Mines and Geology Special Publication 2. Mackay School of Mines, University of Nevada, Reno.

Huntington, E. 1914. The climatic factor as illustrated in arid America. Publication 192. Carnegie Institution of Washington, Washington, DC.

Irons, W. V., C. H. Hembree, and G. L. Oakland. 1965. Water resources of the Upper Colorado River Basin—technical report. Professional Paper 441. U.S. Department of the Interior, Geological Survey, Washington, DC.

Jameson, D. A. 1969. Rainfall patterns on vegetation zones in northern Arizona. Plateau 41:105–11.

Jurwitz, L. R. 1953. Arizona's two-season rainfall pattern. Weatherwise 6:96–99.

Kay, P. A. 1982. A perspective on Great Basin paleoclimates, pp. 76–81. *In*: D. B. Madsen and J. F. O'Connell (eds.), Man and environment in the Great Basin. SAA Papers no. 2. Society for American Archaeology, Washington, DC.

Kittle, T.G.F. 1986. The distribution of vegetation in North America with repect to tropospheric circulation parameters. Ph.D. dissertation, University of California, Davis.

Kuo, M., and S. K. Cox. 1975. Analysis of Colorado precipitation. Completion Report Series 63. Environmental Resource Center, Colorado State University, Fort Collins.

Leighley, J. 1956. Weather and climate, pp. 25–37. *In*: C. M. Zierer (ed.), California and the Southwest. John Wiley and Sons, New York.

Martin, P. S. 1963. The last 10,000 years: a fossil pollen record of the American Southwest. University of Arizona Press, Tucson.

Martin, R. J. (ed.). 1933. Section 22—western Colorado. *In*: Climatic summary of the United States: climatic data herein from the establishment of the stations to 1930, inclusive. U.S. Department of Agriculture, Weather Bureau, Washington, DC.

Martin, R. J., and E. Corbin (eds.). 1933. Section 21—eastern Utah. *In*: Climatic summary of the United States: climatic data herein from the establishment of the stations to 1930, inclusive. U.S. Department of Agriculture, Weather Bureau, Washington, DC.

Meko, D. M., and C. W. Stockton. 1984. Secular variations in streamflow in the western United States. Journal of Climate and Applied Meteorology 23:889–97.

Murphy, D. R. 1978. One hundred years of Utah climate. Utah Historical Quarterly 46:369–75.

Neilson, R. P. 1986. High-resolution climatic analysis and Southwest biogeography. Science 232:27–34.

Neilson, R. P. 1987. Biotic regionalization and climatic controls in western North America. Vegetation 70:135–47.

Neilson, R. P., and L. H. Wullstein. 1983. Biogeography of two southwest oaks in relation to atmospheric dynamics. Journal of Biogeography 10:275–97.

Pearson, G. A. 1913. A meteorological study of parks and timbered areas in the western yellow-pine forests of Arizona and New Mexico. Monthly Weather Review 41:1614–29.

Peterson, D. H. (ed.). 1989. Aspects of climate variability in the Pacific and western Americas. Geophysical Monograph 55. American Geophysical Union, Washington, DC.

Price, R., and R. B. Evans. 1937. Climate and the west front of the Wasatch Plateau in central Utah. Monthly Weather Review 65:291–301.

Sellers, W. D. 1960. Precipitation trends in Arizona and western New Mexico, pp. 81–94. *In*: Proceedings of the 28th annual meeting, Western Snow Conference, Santa Fe, New Mexico, April 1960. Colorado State University, Fort Collins.

Sellers, W. D. 1968. Climatology of monthly precipitation patterns in the western United States, 1931–1966. Monthly Weather Review 96:585–95.

Sellers, W. D., and R. H. Hill (eds.). 1974. Arizona Climate, 1931–1972, 2nd revised edition. University of Arizona Press, Tucson.

Siemer, E. G. 1977. Colorado climate. Colorado Experiment Station, Colorado State University, Fort Collins.

Steinhoff, H. W., and J. D. Ives (eds.). 1976. Ecological impacts of snowpack augmentation in the San Juan Mountains, Colorado. U.S. Department of Interior, Bureau of Reclamation, Denver, CO (Accession no. PB 255 012, U.S. Department of Commerce, National Technical Information Service, Springfield, VA).

Taun, Y., C. E. Everard, J. G. Widdison, I. Bennett, and J. Bateman. 1973. The climate of New Mexico, revised edition. New Mexico State Planning Office, Santa Fe.

Thomas, H. E. 1959. Reservoirs to match our climatic fluctuations. Bulletin of the American Meteorological Society 40:240–49.

U. S. Department of Agriculture. 1941. Climate and man. Year book of Agriculture. U.S. Department of Agriculture, Washington, DC.

Wallen, C. C. 1955. Some characteristics of precipitation in Mexico. Geografiska Annaler 37:51–85.

Weare, B. C., and M. A. Hoeschele. 1983. Specification of monthly precipitation in the western United States from monthly mean circulation. Journal of Climate and Applied Meteorology 22:1000–1007.

Wendland, W. M., and R. A. Bryson. 1981. Northern Hemisphere airstream regions. Monthly Weather Review 109:255–70.

Wexler, H., and J. Namias. 1938. Mean monthly isentropic charts and their relation to departures of summer rainfall, pp. 164–70. *In:* Transactions of the American Geophysical Union, 19th annual meeting. Papers, Joint Meeting, Meteorology and Oceanography. Geophysical Union, Washington, DC.

Whiteman, C. D. 1980. Breakup of temperature inversions in Colorado mountain valleys. Atmospheric Science Paper 328. Department of Atmospheric Science, Colorado State University, Fort Collins.

Williams, P. W., Jr., and E. L. Peck. 1962. Terrain influences on precipitation in the Intermountain West as related to synoptic situations. Journal of Applied Meteorology 1:343–47.

Atriplex confertifolia (Torr. and Frem.) Wats. (shadscale) is probably the most common shrub of the more arid regions of both the Great Basin and the Colorado Plateau. Since mammals of the boreal zones of high mountains of the Intermountain West are unable to survive in shadscale deserts — which now often form wide belts around many isolated mountains — biogeographers believe more mesic vegetation once dominated areas that now support shadscale.

The Extinct Late Pleistocene
Mammals of the Great Basin

Donald K. Grayson

OVERVIEW

Although information about the Pleistocene mammalian faunas of the Great Basin is limited, a great deal is known about the last 10,000 years of mammalian history in the Basin. Most of the data comes from studies conducted on archaeological and paleontological deposits. This information has been important in the development of effective management protocol for modern mammalian habitats. The record shows that during the Holocene there were significant changes in the distribution patterns of small mammals in the Great Basin, with few mammalian extinctions. However, at the end of the Pleistocene, there was a massive extinction of large animals in the Great Basin as elsewhere in North America. In this chapter the author proposes that more research is needed to effectively characterize the mammalian fauna and related environments of the late Pleistocene. These data will be useful in accurately predicting the effects of future environmental change on the biological diversity of the Great Basin.

The Great Basin has a remarkably dynamic record of mammalian colonization, extirpation, and extinction, much of which is solidly embedded in contemporary biogeographic theory. Our understanding of Great Basin mammalian history, however, is best developed for the Holocene, or the past 10,000 years. Indeed, Holocene mammalian history is probably better understood for the Great Basin than it is for anyplace else in North America (e.g., Brown 1971, 1978; Grayson 1982, 1987, 1993; Heaton 1990).

Once we cross the Holocene boundary into the Pleistocene, however, our understanding of Great Basin mammalian history becomes extremely weak. The late Pleistocene mammalian faunas of the Great Basin are poorly known, both in the sense that very few of them have been excavated and in the sense that there is little convincing chronological control available for those that have been excavated.

The reasons for this stark break between our understanding of late Pleistocene and Holocene mammalian history in the Great Basin are fairly straightforward. Our direct knowledge of prehistoric faunas in the Great Basin is derived from sites excavated for either paleontological or archaeological purposes. Archaeological sites are chosen for excavation because of the potential they seem to have for providing significant new information on the prehistoric human occupation of the region. Because many archaeologists are interested in the Basin, large numbers of archaeological sites from this region have been investigated. Many of these sites are rich in well-preserved mammalian specimens (e.g., Grayson 1983; Dansie 1987; Livingston 1988; Schmitt and Sharp 1990) and thus provide direct empirical access to understanding the distribution and abundance of Great Basin mammals through time. However, the Great Basin archaeological record is primarily Holocene in age: very few sites can be shown to predate 10,000 years ago, and none is demonstrably much older than 11,000 years. Our well-developed understanding of Great Basin Holocene mammalian history follows directly from efforts that have been made to understand the deeper human history of this area.

Paleontological sites, in contrast, are routinely selected for excavation or collection because of their great age, usually as inferred either from the presence of extinct mammals in the contained fauna or from geological context. Far fewer paleontological than archaeological sites have been scientifically excavated in the Great Basin. While there are many reasons for this, the basic reason is that there are simply far fewer paleontologists than archaeologists interested in this area. Our knowledge of late Pleistocene vertebrates in the Basin is thus limited because so few sites of this age have been excavated.

In addition, many paleontological sites that have provided late Pleistocene faunas have not provided them in a context that could be readily dated with techniques then (or even now) at hand. Gypsum Cave, southern Nevada (Harrington 1933), for instance, was excavated not only prior to the development of radiocarbon dating but also prior to the development of stratigraphic excavation techniques appropriate for the unraveling of complex depositional sequences. More recently, a number of paleontological sites have been excavated by people who had little or no training for the task, as if one could successfully practice amateur brain surgery.

But even modern scientific work cannot always successfully extract sequences and dates from some of the contexts in which Great Basin paleontological faunas are found. To take but one example, the rich mammalian fauna from Crystal Ball Cave in western Utah that has been reported in splendid detail by Heaton (1985) was retrieved from thin, unstratified deposits and clearly contains intermingled material of both late Pleistocene and Holocene age. Short of attempting to extract accelerator mass spectrometry (AMS) radiocarbon dates for every specimen in this rich fauna, there is little that can be done to derive a depositional chronology for this assemblage or for many others like it.

This is not to say that there are no late Pleistocene faunas from the Great Basin that were carefully excavated in settings that could be chronologically controlled. Such faunas do exist (e.g., Tule Springs: Mawby 1967). But they are few, and most late Pleistocene paleontological sites are known to be of this age simply because they contain species and genera of mammals that we know became extinct toward the end of the Pleistocene.

Here I provide a brief, primarily descriptive review of our current knowledge of the late Pleistocene (Wisconsinan) mammals of the Great Basin. I base my review on the published literature and focus on those species that became extinct as the Pleistocene came to an end. In order to provide breadth to my survey, I include sites from the Mojave Desert as well as from the floristic Great Basin.

NORTH AMERICAN PLEISTOCENE EXTINCTIONS

North America lost some 35 genera of mammals toward the end of the Pleistocene (see Table 4.1), either in the sense that they became extinct here while living on elsewhere (six genera) or in the sense that they were lost from the earth entirely (29 genera). Although many scientists have assumed that these extinctions occurred between 12,000 and 10,000 years ago, in fact our control over the chronology of the losses is extremely weak. Of the 35 genera that were lost, only nine can now be convincingly shown to have survived beyond 12,000 years ago (Grayson 1989, 1991; Gillette and Madsen 1992). Whether the remaining 26 genera were lost during the last 2,000 years of the Pleistocene is simply unknown, and it is at least equally likely that the extinctions began several thousand years before this time.

Table 4.1   Extinct Late Pleistocene North American Genera

Order	Family	Genus	Common Name
Edentata	Dasypodidae	*Pampatherium*	Southern Pampathere
		Holmesina	Northern Pampathere
	Glyptodontidae	*Glyptotherium*	Simpson's Glyptodont
	Megalonychidae	*Megalonyx*	Jefferson's Ground Sloth
	Megatheriidae	*Eremotherium*	Rusconi's Ground Sloth
		Nothrotheriops	Shasta Ground Sloth
	Mylodontidae	*Glossotherium*	Harlan's Ground Sloth
Carnivora	Mustelidae	Brachyprotoma	Short-faced Skunk
	Canidae	*Cuon**	Dhole
	Ursidae	*Tremarctos**	Florida Cave Bear
		Arctodus	Giant Short-faced Bear
	Felidae	*Smilodon*	Sabertooth
		Homotherium	Scimitar Cat
		Miracinonyx	American Cheetah
Rodentia	Castoridae	*Castoroides*	Giant Beaver
	Hydrochoeridae	*Hydrochoerus**	Holmes's Capybara
		Neochoerus	Pinckney's Capybara
Lagomorpha	Leporidae	*Aztlanolagus*	Aztlan Rabbit
Perissodactyla	Equidae	*Equus**	Horses
	Tapiridae	*Tapirus**	Tapirs
Artiodactyla	Tayassuidae	*Mylohyus*	Long-nosed Peccary
		Platygonus	Flat-headed Peccary

continues

Table 4.1   Extinct Late Pleistocene North American Genera   *(continued)*

Order	Family	Genus	Common Name
	Camelidae	*Camelops*	Yesterday's Camel
		Hemiauchenia	Large-headed Llama
		Palaeolama	Stout-legged Llama
	Cervidae	*Navahoceros*	Mountain Deer
		Cervalces	Elk-Moose
	Antilocapridae	*Capromeryx*	Diminutive Pronghorn
		Tetrameryx	Shuler's Pronghorn
		Stockoceros	Pronghorns
	Bovidae	*Saiga**	Saiga
		Euceratherium	Shrub Ox
		Bootherium	Harlan's Muskox
Proboscidea	Mammutidae	*Mammut*	American Mastodont
	Elephantidae	*Mammuthus*	Mammoths

Note: Common names are generally derived from particular species within genera.
*Genus survives elsewhere.

That the extinctions were complete by 10,000 years ago, however, is clear. Of the thousands of Holocene archaeological sites that have been excavated in North America, not one has provided the remains of any of the extinct mammals in a context suggesting that these animals still existed after the Pleistocene had come to an end. While it is certainly possible that straggling populations of a few genera lasted into the Holocene, the extinctions were functionally over by 10,000 years ago.

On the generic level, the breadth of the extinctions is astonishing (Table 4.1). The losses involve seven genera of Xenarthra, including four genera of huge, ground-dwelling sloths; seven genera of carnivores, ranging from the small short-faced skunk, *Brachyprotoma*, to the huge short-faced bear, *Arctodus*; three genera of rodents, including the giant beaver, *Castoroides*, and two genera of capybaras; a single genus of leporid; two genera of perissodactyls (horse and tapir); 13 genera of artiodactyls, ranging from peccaries to pronghorns and muskoxen; and two genera of proboscideans, mammoth and mastodon (for general reviews of the extinctions, see Grayson 1991 and Stuart 1991).

Two explanations of these extinctions have been debated intensely during the past 25 years. One group of scholars contends that human predation was the cause of these losses, an account generally referred to as the overkill model (e.g., Martin 1984, 1990; Spaulding 1983). A second group of scientists contends that climatic change was the driving cause (i.e, Grayson 1977; Guthrie 1984b; Graham and Lundelius 1984). The overkill account has fallen out of favor during recent years for a number of reasons (Grayson 1984a), the most important of which is that this approach appears to fail certain critical tests. Most significant, perhaps, is that only two of the extinct genera — mastodon (*Mammut*) and mammoth (*Mammuthus*) — have ever been found in association with artifacts in such a way as to provide compelling evidence that people hunted them. Indeed, of these two, only *Mammuthus* is fairly routinely found in such associations. This is the case even though horses and camels were at least equally abundant on the landscape (Grayson 1991).

At the same time as it has been impossible to find kill associations for all but two of the extinct mammals, archaeologists have begun to realize that older ideas as to the nature of the people who occupied North America between about 11,500 and 11,000 years ago — routinely referred to as Paleoindians — are likely to be incorrect. During the 1960s and 1970s, it was often assumed that these people were essentially big-game hunters, and the overkill hypothesis was in part built on this assumption. Indeed, some scholars even treated Paleoindians as if they had been obligate predators on large mammals. During the 1980s, however, it became increasingly clear that such a notion could not apply to North America as a whole (e.g., Grayson 1988; Meltzer 1988; Dillehay 1989) and that Paleoindians were far more eclectic in their diets than had once been thought. Finally, the fact that only nine of the 35 extinct genera can actually be shown to have overlapped in time with the earliest known human hunters in North America also diminishes the power of the overkill explanation. For all these reasons, overkill has fallen seriously out of favor.

At the same time that human predation has come to be seen as an unlikely explanation of the extinctions, accounts that focus on climatic change as the cause have become increasingly precise. These I return to below, after discussing what we know of the now extinct mammals that lived in the Great Basin during the Pleistocene.

THE EXTINCT PLEISTOCENE MAMMALS OF THE GREAT BASIN

Even though the late Pleistocene paleontology of the Great Basin cannot be said to be well known, the sites that are available document the presence of 16 of the 35 genera of extinct North American mammals within this region (Table 4.2: references to sites are provided in Table 4.3 and are not repeated in the text; site locations are provided in Figure 4.1; see Grayson 1991 for additional information on all extinct taxa).

Table 4.2 Extinct Late Pleistocene Mammals Known from the Great Basin

Genus	Common Name[*]
Megalonyx (Mg) Sites: 19	Jefferson's Ground Sloth
Nothrotheriops shastensis (No) Sites: 7, 10, 19, 31, 32	Shasta Ground
Glossotherium (Gl) Sites: 1, 14, 24	Harlan's Ground Sloth

continues

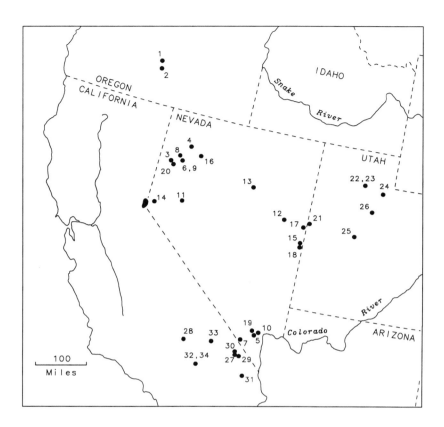

Figure 4.1   The location of Great Basin paleontological sites that have provided the remains of extinct Pleistocene mammals (key to sites is provided in Table 4.3).

Table 4.2   Extinct Late Pleistocene Mammals Known from the Great Basin   *(continued)*

Genus	Common Name[*]
Brachyprotoma brevimala (Br) Sites: 21	Short-faced Skunk
Arctodus simus (Ar) Sites: 1, 12, 23	Giant Short-faced Bear
Smilodon fatalis (Sm) Sites: 4, 21, 24, 28	Sabertooth
Panthera leo Sites: 3, 19	American Lion
Miracinonyx trumani (Mi) Sites: 6	American Cheetah

continues

Table 4.2   Extinct Late Pleistocene Mammals Known from the Great Basin   *(continued)*

Genus	Common Name*
Equus species (Eq) Sites: 1, 2, 3, 5, 8, 9, 10, 11, 13, 15, 16, 17, 18, 19, 20, 21, 22, 24, 27, 28, 29, 30, 31, 34	Horses
Platygonus (Pl) Sites: 1	Flat-headed Peccary
Camelops hesternus (Cm) Sites: 1, 4, 5, 9, 10, 11, 15, 16, 17, 18, 19, 20, 21, 22, 24, 25, 27, 28, 29, 31	Yesterday's Camel
Hemiauchenia macrocephala (Hm) Sites: 1, 10, 13, 21, 27, 28, 29	Large-headed Llama
Capromeryx (Cp) Sites: 34	Diminutive Pronghorn
Oreamnos harringtoni Sites: 17	Harrington's Mountain Goat
Euceratherium (Eu) Sites: 8, 13	Shrub Ox
Bootherium bombifrons (Bo) Sites: 22	Harlan's Muskox
Mammut americanum (Ms) Sites: 26	American Mastodon
Mammuthus columbi (Mm) Sites: 1, 4, 5, 16, 19, 20, 22, 24, 28, 33	Columbia Mammoth

Note: Sites are listed by number in Table 4.3. Abbreviations of extinct genera are used in Figure 4.2.
*Species names have been provided if a secure or reasonably secure species identification is available; these may not be correct in all cases.

Xenarthra

Three genera of extinct, ground-dwelling sloths are now known from the Great Basin. The bison-sized *Megalonyx* is known from Alaska to Florida. Within the Great Basin, however, it has been identified only at Tule Springs, southern Nevada, from sediments that were deposited more than 32,000 years ago. These deposits also provided the remains of the bear-sized Shasta ground sloth, *Nothrotheriops shastensis*. This sloth is best known from the American Southwest but is also known from Mexico, much of the western United States, and Alberta. Unlike *Megalonyx*, however, the Shasta ground sloth has been reported from a variety of Great Basin sites, all of which are in the southern reaches of this region. At Gypsum Cave, trustworthy radiocarbon dates establish that this animal was in southern Nevada until nearly the end of the Pleistocene. In fact, the Shasta ground sloth is one of the nine late Pleistocene mammals that can be shown to

Table 4.3 Great Basin Faunas with Extinct Late Pleistocene Mammals

Site	Location	Setting	Extinct Mammals	References
Oregon				
1. Fossil Lake	Fort Rock Basin	Lake	Harlan's ground sloth, Giant short-faced bear, Horse,.Flat-headed peccary, Camel, Large-headed llama, Mammoth	Allison 1966; Howe and Martin 1977
2. Paisley Five-Mile-Point Cave	Summer Lake Basin	Cave	Horse	Cressman 1942
Nevada				
3. Astor Pass	Pyramid Lake Basin	Lake gravels	American lion, Horse	Merriam 1915
4. Black Rock Desert (East arm)	Black Rock Desert	Alluvial deposits	Sabertooth, Camel, Mammoth	Dansie, Davis, and Stafford 1988; Livingston 1992
5. Centennial Parkway	Las Vegas Valley	Pond/marsh deposits	Horse, Camel, Mammoth	Reynolds, Mead, and Reynolds 1991
6. Crypt Cave	Winnemucca Lake Basin	Cave		Orr 1952, 1956, 1969, 1974; Thompson, Hattori, and Tuohy 1987; Van Valkenburgh, Grady, and Kurtén 1990
7. Devil Peak	Spring Mountains	Fissure	American cheetah Shasta ground sloth	Reynolds, Reynolds, and Bell 1991
8. Falcon Hill Caves	Winnemucca Lake Basin	Caves	Horse, Shrub ox	Hattori 1982; Thompson, Hattori, and Tuohy 1987
9. Fishbone Cave	Winnemucca Lake Basin	Cave	Horse, Camel	Orr 1956, 1974; Thompson, Hattori, and Tuohy 1987

continues

Table 4.3 Great Basin Faunas with Extinct Late Pleistocene Mammals *(continued)*

Site	Location	Setting	Extinct Mammals	References
Nevada				
10. Gypsum Cave	Frenchman Mountains	Cave	Shasta ground sloth, Horse, Camel, Large-headed llama	Stock 1931; Harrington 1933
11. Hidden Cave	Carson Desert	Cave	Horse, Camel	Grayson 1985
12. Labor-of-Love Cave	Schell Creek Range	Cave	Giant short-faced bear	Emslie and Czaplewski 1985
13. Mineral Hill Cave	Sulphur Spring Range	Cave	Horse, Large-headed llama, Shrub ox	McGuire 1980
14. Nevada State Prison	Carson City	Lake deposits	Harlan's ground sloth	Stock 1920, 1925
15. Owl Cave Two	Snake Range	Cave	Horse, Camel	Birnie 1986; Turnmire 1987
16. Rye Patch Dam	Humboldt River	Spring deposit	Horse, Camel, Mammoth	Firby, Mawby, and Davis 1987
17. Smith Creek Cave	Snake Range	Cave	Horse, Camel, Harrington's mountain goat	Stock 1936; Miller 1979; Mead, Thompson, and Van Devender 1982
18. Snake Creek Burial Cave	Snake Range	Cave	Horse, Camel	J. I. Mead and E. M. Mead 1985; Heaton 1987; E. M. Mead and J. I. Mead 1989
19. Tule Springs	Las Vegas Wash	Alluvial deposits	Jefferson's ground sloth, Shasta ground sloth, American lion, Horse, Camel, Mammoth	Mawby 1967
20. Wizards Beach	Pyramid Lake Basin	Lake deposits	Horse, Camel, Mammoth	Dansie, Davis, and Stafford 1988

continues

Table 4.3 Great Basin Faunas with Extinct Late Pleistocene Mammals (continued)

Site	Location	Setting	Extinct Mammals	References
Utah				
21. Crystal Ball Cave	Snake Valley	Cave	Short-faced skunk, Sabertooth, Horse, Camel, Large-headed llama	Miller 1982; Heaton 1985
22. Eastern Lake Bonneville	Bonneville Basin	Lake deposits	Horse, Camel, Harlan's muskox, Mammoth (multiple localities)	Madsen, Currey, and Madsen 1976; Nelson and Madsen 1978, 1980, 1983
23. Monroc	Bonneville Basin	Lake deposits	Giant short-faced bear	Nelson and Madsen 1983
24. Silver Creek Local Fauna	Wasatch Range	Alluvial/marsh deposits	Harlan's ground sloth, Sabertooth, Horse, Camel, Mammoth	Miller 1976
25. Tabernacle Crater	Sevier Desert	Cave	Camel	Nelson and Madsen 1979; Romer 1928, 1929
26. Utah Sinkhole	Wasatch Plateau	Sinkhole	Mastodon	Miller 1987
California				
27. Antelope Cave	Mescal Range	Cave	Horse, Camel, Large-headed llama	Reynolds et al. 1991a
28. China Lake	China Lake Basin	Alluvial/lake deposits	Sabertooth, Horse, Camel, Large-headed llama, Mammoth	Fortsch 1978
29. Kokoweef Cave	Kokoweef Peak	Cave	Horse, Camel, Large-headed llama	Goodwin and Reynolds 1989; Reynolds et al. 1991b
30. Mescal Cave	Mescal Range	Cave	Horse	Brattstrom 1958; Jefferson 1991
31. Mitchell Caverns	Providence Mountains	Cave	Shasta ground sloth, Horse, Camel	Jefferson 1991
32. Newberry Cave	Newberry Mountains	Cave	Shasta ground sloth	Davis and Smith 1981
33. Salt Springs	Southern Death Valley	Lake deposits	Mammoth	Jefferson 1990
34. Schuiling Cave	Newberry Mountains	Cave	Horse, Diminutive pronghorn	Downs et al. 1959

have survived beyond 12,000 years ago: superb analyses have documented that this animal became extinct in the Southwest at around 11,000 years ago (Long and Martin 1974; Thompson et al. 1980; Martin 1987).

Harlan's ground sloth, *Glossotherium harlani*, is characterized in part by the presence of pebblelike bones in its skin (dermal ossicles) and is the most abundant sloth in the deposits of Rancho La Brea, California. The Great Basin specimens of *Glossotherium*, known from Fossil Lake (south central Oregon), the nineteenth-century site of the Nevada State Prison (Carson City, western Nevada), and from the Silver Creek Local Fauna (Wasatch Range, central Utah), have been identified securely only to the genus level but probably represent G. *harlani*. The age of these specimens is not well controlled.

Carnivora

The short-faced skunk, *Brachyprotoma*, is known from a series of sites in the eastern United States, from the Yukon, and from Crystal Ball Cave on the Utah-Nevada border just east of the Snake Range. While the eastern specimens have been assigned to *B. obtusata*, Heaton (1985) has shown that the *Brachyprotoma* skeletal material provided by Crystal Ball Cave is distinctly different from *B. obtusata*; he assigns these specimens to a new species, *B. brevimala*. Unfortunately, there is no secure chronology available for the Crystal Ball Cave fauna. Although the short-faced skunk specimens from this site are most likely to date to the late Wisconsin, little more can be said of their age.

The noble marten, *Martes nobilis*, is known from a series of sites in the Yukon and western North America. In the Great Basin this large marten has now been reported from Hidden Cave (Carson Sink, western Nevada), Bronco Charlie Cave (Ruby Mountains, eastern Nevada), Smith Creek Cave (Snake Range, eastern Nevada), and Snake Creek Burial Cave (Snake Valley, eastern Nevada). Until recently, M. *nobilis* was thought to have become extinct by 10,000 years ago. However, a series of sites suggests that this animal survived until at least about 3,000 years ago (Grayson 1984b, 1985, 1987; Mead and Mead 1989). Both Hidden Cave and Bronco Charlie Cave provided M. *nobilis* specimens that appear to date to between 3,000 and 3,500 years ago. Dry Creek Cave, in southern Idaho, provided a specimen of M. *nobilis* stratigraphically above deposits dated to about 3,500 years ago; those deposits lie directly on bedrock (Webster 1978).

Hidden Cave contains late Pleistocene as well as Holocene sediments, and noble marten material was also present in those late Pleistocene deposits (Grayson 1985). Given the complex nature of cave deposits, it is possible that the Hidden Cave M. *nobilis* specimen that appeared to be late Holocene in age was in fact brought up from deeper levels. In an effort to determine whether this had been the case, the specimen was submitted to the University of Washington Quaternary Isotope Laboratory for an AMS radiocarbon date on bone protein. Unfortunately, during laboratory processing the combustion tube holding the CO_2 from the sample cracked, and the sample was lost (P. Grootes, personal communication, 1990; the specimen of *Sylvilagus idahoensis* discussed in Grayson 1985 met with the same fate). A conventional date was obtained on the carbonate fraction of this specimen

(6,070 ± 110 years ago, QLA-097), but carbonates are easily contaminated, and this date is essentially meaningless. Of the known Great Basin M. *nobilis* specimens of apparent late Holocene age, only the Bronco Charlie material still exists.

The giant short-faced bear, *Arctodus simus*, has been reported from Fossil Lake, Labor-of-Love Cave (east slope, Schell Creek Range, eastern Nevada), and the Monroc quarry on the eastern edge of the Lake Bonneville Basin. *A. simus* was huge, some 30 percent larger than the North American grizzly (*Ursus arctos*), and was until recently thought to have been almost totally carnivorous (Kurtén 1967). Emslie and Czaplewski (1985), however, have presented a detailed morphological analysis of the relatively complete *Arctodus* skeletal material from Labor-of-Love Cave. Their analysis strongly suggests that this bear was not the huge carnivore as was once thought but was instead largely omnivorous or herbivorous. Several radiocarbon dates have been reported for the Monroc *Arctodus* (Nelson and Madsen 1980, 1983). These dates range between 11,690 and 12,650 years ago, but all are conventional radiocarbon dates on material prone to contamination and so cannot be trusted (Meltzer and Mead 1985). Gillette and Madsen (1992) report convincing dates of 11,420 and 11,200 years ago on material associated with *Arctodus* at the Huntington Mammoth Site, in the Wasatch Mountains of central Utah just east of the eastern edge of the Great Basin. These dates provide the first secure sub-12,000-year ages for this genus in North America.

The lion-sized sabertooth cat, *Smilodon fatalis*, is known from Alberta in the northwest to Florida in the southeast. In the Great Basin *Smilodon* specimens have been reported from China Lake (southeastern California), Crystal Ball Cave, the Silver Creek Local Fauna, and the east arm of the Black Rock Desert in northern Nevada. *Smilodon* is one of the nine late Pleistocene genera that we know to have survived beyond 12,000 years ago. Unfortunately, none of the Great Basin material is well dated. The Silver Creek Local Fauna appears to be greater than 40,000 years old; the remaining Great Basin specimens are late Wisconsin in age.

Detailed morphological analyses of *Smilodon* teeth have shown that little contact was made between those teeth and the bones of *Smilodon* prey. This, in turn, suggests that a good deal of meat was left on the carcasses of sabertooth victims, providing opportunities for various scavengers (Akersten 1985; Van Valkenburgh and Ruff 1987; Van Valkenburgh, Teaford, and Walker 1990). Those scavengers may have included the extinct dire wolf (*Canis dirus*), and the distributions of dire wolves and sabertooth cats in North America south of glacial ice are extremely similar (compare Kurtén and Anderson 1980, fig. 11.17, and Nowak 1979, fig. 54). Nonetheless, while *Smilodon* has been reported from central Utah and from northern Nevada to southeastern California, the Great Basin has not, to my knowledge, provided a single securely identified specimen of dire wolf. Dire wolves were surely in the Great Basin during the late Pleistocene; the lack of records for them probably reflects the weakness of our understanding of the Great Basin paleontological record.

The American cheetah, *Miracinonyx trumani*, is known only from Colorado, Wyoming, and Nevada. This New World cheetah differs from its Old World counterpart in many ways, including larger size and the possession of fully retractile claws (Adams 1979; Van Valkenburgh, Grady, and Kurtén 1990). The Nevada material, from Crypt Cave in the Winnemucca Lake Basin of northwestern Nevada, is undated but is rather clearly late Wisconsin in age.

Lions (*Panthera leo*) were widespread in North America during the late Pleistocene, found from California to Florida and from Alaska into Mexico and beyond. The two secure records for lions in the Great Basin were both initially assigned to *Panthera atrox*, subsequently synonymized with *P. leo*. The first of these is from Tule Springs, where it is greater than 32,000 years old, while the second is from Astor Pass, northwest of Pyramid Lake. The Astor Pass fauna lacks trustworthy radiocarbon dates (the dates reported in Broecker and Kulp 1957 are on materials that often provide invalid results) but is late Wisconsin in age.

Perissodactyla

Horses have been reported from numerous late Pleistocene sites in the Great Basin. Indeed, given that few sizable faunas of this age lack horses, these animals must have been common throughout at least the lower elevations of the Great Basin toward the end of the Pleistocene. The taxonomy of late Pleistocene North American horses remains confused, but several species are clearly represented in Great Basin paleontological sites. Horses are known to have survived to beyond 12,000 years ago in North America; the Tule Springs site contains horses that are between 13,100 and 11,500 years old.

Artiodactyla

The flat-headed peccary, *Platygonus compressus*, has been reported from coast to coast and from the edge of glacial ice in the north into Mexico in the south. Often found in groups of multiple skeletons, this peccary appears to have been gregarious. Floral and faunal remains found in sites that have provided the remains of *P. compressus* also suggest that this animal occupied fairly open environments, unlike the European wild boar, *Sus scrofa*. There is but a single record for *Platygonus* in the Great Basin, from Fossil Lake, where it has been identified only to the genus level.

During the late Pleistocene, North America supported two genera of llamas and one genus of llamalike camel. Of these, the camel, *Camelops hesternus*, and the llama, *Hemiauchenia macrocephala*, are known from the Great Basin. *Camelops*, in fact, is found in most sizable late Pleistocene Great Basin faunas, suggesting that camels, like horses, were abundant on the late Pleistocene Great Basin landscape. In life, *C. hesternus* would have looked much like a large version of the dromedary (*Camelus dromedarius*), although its legs were longer, its head narrower and longer, and its single hump placed somewhat further forward (Webb 1965). The Wizards Beach camel, from the northwest end of Pyramid Lake in northwestern Nevada, is well dated to about 25,000 years ago (Dansie, Davis, and Stafford 1988), while a *Neotoma* midden from near Garrison, Utah, has provided secure dates for *Camelops* of about 13,500 years (Mead, Thompson, and Van Devender 1982). A number of sites outside the Great Basin have established that *C. hesternus* survived beyond 12,000 years ago. Within the Great Basin, the Tule Springs fauna contains *Camelops* remains that are between 13,100 and 11,500 years old. The Tabernacle Crater *Camelops* skull, discovered near Filmore in west central Utah and which had dried soft tissue adhering to it when first found, has been dated to 11,100 years ago. This, however, appears to have been a whole bone date and thus may not give a valid indication of the antiquity of the specimen (Romer 1928, 1929; Nelson and Madsen 1979).

The large-headed llama, *Hemiauchenia macrocephala*, was widespread in the more southerly United States, known from southern California to Florida. *Hemiauchenia* sp. and *H*. cf. *macrocephala* have been reported from a number of sites of late Wisconsin age in the Great Basin, from Oregon to southeastern California, none of which is well dated. Given that *H. macrocephala* is the only known latest Pleistocene member of the genus, it is likely that all reported Great Basin specimens represent this species (see Heaton 1985).

Capromeryx minor, a tiny pronghorn some 0.5 m tall at the shoulder, was known from California to Texas. There is only one Great Basin record, assigned to *Capromeryx* sp., from Schuiling Cave in California's Mojave Desert and of unknown age, though it appears to date to the latest Pleistocene.

The shrub ox, *Euceratherium collinum*, has been reported from late Pleistocene deposits ranging from California to Iowa and as far south as central Mexico. Apparently related to muskoxen, these animals seem to have been grazers that occupied hilly but not mountainous terrain. There are two Great Basin records for *Euceratherium*: from Mineral Hill Cave in north central Nevada and from Falcon Hill in the Winnemucca Lake Basin. Both are late Wisconsin in age; neither is well dated. An attempt to date the *Euceratherium* mandibles from Falcon Hill failed because of the preservative that had been applied to them (Thompson, Hattori, and Tuohy 1987).

Harlan's muskox, *Bootherium bombifrons*, is known from nearly all of unglaciated North America, with the exception of the far southeast and southwest, and seems to have occupied fairly open terrain. In the Great Basin *Bootherium* has been reported from a number of localities along the eastern margin of the Bonneville Basin (Nelson and Madsen 1980). Many of these specimens have been attributed to *Symbos cavifrons*, but it has now been established that *S. cavifrons* and *B. bombifrons* were males and females, respectively, of the same species (McDonald and Ray 1989). While there are radiocarbon dates available for several of these specimens, they are conventional bone or bone collagen dates and may not be valid. Most specimens, however, are rather clearly late Wisconsin in age (Nelson and Madsen 1978, 1980).

The mountain goat, *Oreamnos americanus*, is doing well in the mountains of northwestern North America. The smaller Harrington's mountain goat, *O. harringtoni*, however, failed to survive the late Pleistocene. It was best known from the Colorado Plateau to the immediate south of the Great Basin, but remains of Harrington's mountain goat were first described from Smith Creek Cave in the Snake Range of eastern Nevada (Stock 1936), still the only known Great Basin locality for this animal. Exquisite work has shown that *O. harringtoni* became extinct at almost precisely 11,000 years ago in the Southwest (Mead 1983; Mead, O'Rourke, and Foppe 1986; Mead et al. 1986; Mead et al. 1987).

Proboscidea

The American mastodon was widespread in unglaciated North America from coast to coast and from Alaska to Mexico, but it appears to have been most abundant in the woodlands and forests of the east. These massive, stocky animals were browsers, apparently thriving in open spruce woodlands. There is a single secure record for mastodon in the Great Basin, from a sinkhole at an elevation of approximately 3,000 m (9,850 feet) in the Wasatch Plateau just west of the Continental Divide (and thus just barely within the Great Basin; see Miller 1987). Two radiocarbon dates on bone provided ages of between 7,000 and 7,600 years ago for this individual, but these dates more likely indicate the problems involved in dating whole bone than they indicate the late survival of mastodon. Gillette and Madsen (1992) note that a date of 10,800 years is now available for this site, but that date is on bone collagen and may not be valid. Mastodon are known to have survived beyond 12,000 years ago, but there are no secure dates indicating that they lasted into the Holocene.

Spurr (1903:157) noted "mastodon teeth and bones" of apparent late Pleistocene age in the Tule Springs area of southern Nevada. Since Spurr did not see these specimens himself but was simply reporting what he had been told, his report cannot be evaluated. Certainly, recent work in this area has not replicated this discovery (Mawby 1967; Reynolds, Mead, and Reynolds 1991).

Closely related to living elephants, the two species of late Pleistocene North American mammoths (the Columbian mammoth, *Mammuthus columbi*, and the woolly mammoth, *M. primigenius*) are known from Alaska and the Yukon in the north, south into Mexico. As yet, there are no secure records for woolly mammoths in the Great Basin (W. Miller, personal communication, 1991; see also Agenbroad 1984). *M. columbi*, in contrast, appears to have been fairly common in the Great Basin toward the end of the Pleistocene. Most Great Basin mammoths, however, have been identified only to the genus level. The sites listed in Table 4.3 indicate but a small fraction of the localities that have provided mammoth remains in this region (see, for instance the tabulation of proboscidean sites provided in Tuohy 1986; the genus of proboscidean is not identified in Tuohy's review, nor is the age of the site, but it is likely that most are late Pleistocene mammoths). Mammoths are also known to have survived beyond 12,000 years ago in North America. In the Great Basin Tule Springs has provided mammoth remains that are between 13,100 and 11,500 years old.

IS THE LIST COMPLETE?

Although only 16 of the 35 genera of extinct late Pleistocene North American mammals have been reported from the Great Basin, and although only a small number of Great Basin paleontological sites of this age have been studied, there is good reason to suspect that many of the 19 genera that are unknown from the Great Basin simply did not occur here during the late Pleistocene. Many of the missing taxa do not seem to have occupied the western United States. To take but a few examples, the capybaras, *Neochoerus* and *Hydrochoerus,* are known only from the southeast; the massive sloth, *Eremotherium*, is known only from the southeast and Texas; the peccary, *Mylohyus*, is known only east of about 100° longitude; the elk-moose, *Cervalces*, is known primarily from the central and eastern United States and Canada on the one hand and from the Yukon and Alaska on the other; the saiga is unknown in the New World outside of the eastern terminus of the Bering Land Bridge. In short, unless distributional inferences drawn from the much better known paleontological records of areas outside the Great Basin are extremely misleading, many of the taxa listed on Table 4.1 are not to be expected in the late Pleistocene Great Basin.

Yet some of them most certainly are to be expected. The Asiatic dhole, *Cuon alpinus*, for instance, is known only from eastern Beringia and northern Mexico. Assuming that the northern Mexican material has been correctly identified, the dhole most certainly occurred in intervening areas, and it would not be surprising if it occupied the Great Basin during the late Pleistocene. The mountain deer, *Nava-hoceros*, is known from localities in or near the Rocky Mountains and may have entered at least the eastern edge of the Great Basin during the late Pleistocene. There are records for the tapir in the southwestern United States, and these animals may have occupied the southern edge of the Great Basin.

An almost certain indication that we have yet to record all of the larger extinct late Pleistocene mammals of the Great Basin is provided by the dire wolf. As I have noted, this large carnivore was widespread, may have scavenged with great frequency, and is often found associated with the sabertooth cat, *Smilodon*. Given that records for *Smilodon* are not rare in the Great Basin, the dire wolf was almost certainly here as well, even though it has yet to be securely identified. While there are reasons to think that we have identified most of the extinct mammals that occupied the Great Basin toward the end of the Pleistocene, there are equally good reasons to think that our list remains incomplete.

Even if the list were complete, our knowledge of Great Basin late Pleistocene mammals would still be remarkably weak. Because there are so few well-excavated, stratified sites, we know little about the distribution and abundance of these animals, either through time or at any one point in time.

It is, however, possible to get a feel for the relative abundances of the Great Basin's extinct Pleistocene mammals by counting the number of sites listed on Table 4.3 in which each extinct mammal occurs. The results of doing that are provided in Figure 4.2. I note that the eastern Lake Bonneville entry in Table 4.3 includes a number of separate sites; these have not been listed on Table 4.3 but are included in Figure 4.2.

Because Figure 4.2 is not based on a complete inventory of finds of extinct late Pleistocene mammals in the Great Basin (no such inventory exists), and because some of the localities involved include more than a single discovery (several mammoths have been reported from the east arm of the Black Rock Desert, for instance), Figure 4.2 cannot be taken as more than suggestive.

What it clearly suggests, however, is that horses, camels, and mammoth were relatively common on the Great Basin landscape during the late Pleistocene. While Figure 4.2 makes it appear that Harlan's muskox was also common here, it is important

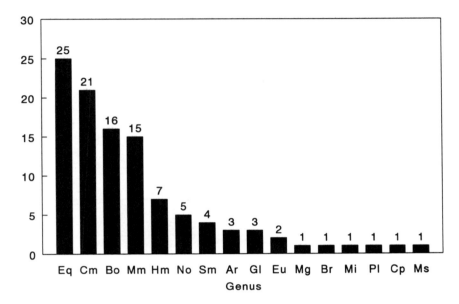

Figure 4.2   The number of localities at which extinct genera of Pleistocene mammals have been reported in the Great Basin (key to genera is provided in Table 4.2).

to realize that all of the Great Basin records for this animal are from the eastern edge of Lake Bonneville. It has yet to be reported from other Great Basin localities.

My point is simple: the existing list of extinct late Pleistocene Great Basin mammals is probably reasonably complete, but there can be little doubt that the list will expand as more paleontological work is done in this area. Camels, horses, and mammoths were fairly abundant in the Great Basin during the late Pleistocene, but we know very little about the distribution and abundance as a whole of the Great Basin's late Pleistocene extinct mammals.

CHRONOLOGICAL CONTROL

It is also true that our control over the ages of the Great Basin's late Pleistocene paleontological sites is extremely weak, even though a substantial array of radiocarbon dates does exist for those sites. The dates, exclusive of those from sites that provide clear evidence of stratigraphic mixture (for instance, Hidden Cave, which contains fossilized camel and horse specimens in late Holocene deposits), are presented in Table 4.4; standard deviations for these dates may be found in the primary references (the Huntington Mammoth Site is not within the Great Basin and thus is not included in this table).

While the list is substantial, however, the list of dates that can be accepted at face value is much shorter. Many kinds of material that were once believed to provide reliable radiocarbon dates are now known to give results that are often highly misleading. As Table 4.4 shows, the vast majority of dates available for the extinct late Pleistocene mammals of the Great Basin are on precisely that kind of untrustworthy material. Others were run during the earliest days of radiocarbon dating, using methods that are now seen as unreliable. Our current understanding of the difficulties involved in dating bone directly suggests that the only secure way to obtain such dates is by extracting individual amino acids from the organic fraction of bone and dating those acids with the AMS method (e.g., Stafford et al. 1991). To date, however, there is only a single AMS date for an extinct late Pleistocene mammal from the Great Basin.

Table 4.4   Radiocarbon Dates Associated with Extinct Pleistocene Mammals in the Great Basin

Site	Date	References
Astor Pass	16,800[*]	Broecker and Kulp 1957
China Lake	18,600[*]	Fortsch 1978; Davis 1978a, 1978b
Crystal Ball Cave	12,980[*]	Heaton 1985
	18,600[*]	
	18,820[*]	
	>23,200[*]	
East Arm, Black Rock Desert	11,080[*]	Stout 1986
East Bonneville Localities		
City Creek Mammoth	14,150[*]	Madsen et al. 1976
Logan City *Bootherium*	7,080[*]	Nelson and Madsen 1980
Monroc Gravel Pit		
Bootherium	11,690[*]	Nelson and Madsen 1980, 1983
Arctodus	12,650[*]	
Sandy Mammoth	5,985[*]	Madsen et al. 1976
	7,200[*]	
	8,815[*]	
	14,150[*]	Nelson and Madsen 1980
Fishbone Cave	10,900[*]	Orr 1956
	11,555[*]	
	12,280[*]	Thompson et al. 1987
Fossil Lake	29,000[*]	Allison 1966a
Garrison	13,480	Mead et al. 1982
Gypsum Cave *Nothrotheriops*	8,527[*]	Arnold and Libby 1951

continues

Table 4.4   Radiocarbon Dates Associated with Extinct Pleistocene Mammals in the Great Basin   *(continued)*

Site	Date	References
	10,455[*]	
	11,360	Long and Martin 1974
	11,690	
	21,470	Thompson et al. 1980
	23,700	Long and Muller 1981
	33,910	Thompson et al. 1980
Equus	13,310	Long and Muller 1981
	25,000	
Labor-of-Love Cave	5,320[*]	Emslie and Czaplewski 1985
Newberry Cave *Nothrotheriops*	11,600[*]	Davis and Smith 1981
Owl Cave Two	8,520[*]	Turnmire 1987
Silver Creek Local Fauna	>40,000[*]	Miller 1976
Smith Creek Cave	12,600	Bryan 1979; Mead et al. 1982
	28,650[*]	
Tabernacle Crater	11,075[*]	Nelson and Madsen 1979
Tule Springs Unit E_1	11,500	Haynes 1967
	11,900	
	12,270	
	12,300	
	12,400	
	12,400	
	12,450	
	12,650	
	12,920	
	13,000	
	13,100	
	13,900[*]	
	15,920[*]	
	17,600[*]	
	16,900[*]	
	>28,000[*]	

continues

Table 4.4   Radiocarbon Dates Associated with Extinct Pleistocene Mammals in the Great
                 Basin   (*continued*)

Site	Date	References
Tule Springs Unit D	22,600[*]	
	31,300[*]	
	>23,000[*]	
	>31,000[*]	
	>35,000	
Tule Springs Unit B$_2$	26,000[*]	
	>30,000[*]	
	>32,000	
	>32,000	
	>35,000	
	>37,000	
	>40,000	
Utah Sinkhole	7,080[*]	Miller 1987
	7,590[*]	
	7,650[*]	
Wizards Beach	25,470	Dansie et al. 1988

[*]Date was obtained from material or using techniques now considered to give untrustworthy results, or date is not well associated with the extinct mammals.

If the untrustworthy dates that are listed in Table 4.4 are eliminated, the status
of the available chronology for extinct Pleistocene mammals in the Great Basin
becomes clear. The trustworthy radiocarbon dates associated with extinct mammals
in the Great Basin come from only five sites (see Table 4.5). At Smith Creek Cave,
a single date suggests that the horse and camel remains here are older than 12,600
years. The Garrison packrat midden (Snake Valley, Utah) documents the presence
of camels in this area about 13,500 years ago. The Wizards Beach camel (Pyramid
Lake, Nevada), which provides the only AMS age determination for an extinct
Great Basin mammal, is about 25,500 years old. At Tule Springs, Vance Haynes's
exquisite results, along with John Mawby's paleontology, document the presence of
horses, camels, and mammoths between 13,100 and 11,500 years ago (Haynes 1967;
Mawby 1967). And radiocarbon dates of ground sloth dung from Gypsum Cave
document that Shasta ground sloths survived here until almost 11,000 years ago.

Five sites are not much to go on if we wish to understand the changing distributions and abundances of now extinct mammals in the Great Basin during the late

Table 4.5 Trustworthy Radiocarbon Dates Associated with Extinct Mammals in the Great Basin

Site	Mammals	Date
Garrison	*Camelops*	13,480
Smith Creek Cave	*Equus*	>12,600
	Camelops	
	Oreamnos harringtoni	
Gypsum Cave	*Nothrotheriops*	11,360
		11,690
		21,470
		23,700
		33,910
	Equus	13,310
		25,000
Tule Springs Unit E_1	*Equus*	11,500–13,100
	Camelops	(11 dates)
	Mammuthus	
Tule Springs Unit D	*Camelops*	>35,000
	Mammuthus	
Tule Springs Unit B_2	*Nothrotheriops*	>32,000–>40,000
	Megalonyx	(5 dates)
	Panthera leo	
	Equus	
	Camelops	
	Mammuthus	
Wizards Beach	*Camelops*	25,470

Pleistocene. It is worth noting that the four extinct genera that Tule Springs and Gypsum Cave show to have survived in the Great Basin until the tail end of the Pleistocene are among the small number of genera we know to have survived this late elsewhere in North America. As I have noted, *Nothrotheriops, Equus, Camelops,* and *Mammuthus* all have excellent dates from outside the Great Basin documenting that they became extinct after 12,000 years ago.

EXPLAINING THE EXTINCTIONS

I have mentioned that two distinctly different kinds of explanations have been forwarded to account for the extinctions of late Pleistocene mammals in North America as a whole: those that depend on human predation to provide the primary cause and those that depend on climatic change to provide that cause. I have also noted that one of the major weaknesses of the overkill account is that only mammoths and mastodon have been found in what archaeologists reasonably interpret as kill sites (Grayson 1991), even though the overkill hypothesis maintains that all the extinct large herbivores were lost as a result of human predation (Martin 1984, 1990). This pattern is not likely to reflect sampling bias, since camels and horses are at least equally abundant in known paleontological sites (Grayson 1991).

The Great Basin archaeological record extends back 11,200 years and perhaps further (see, for instance, Aikens and Madsen 1986). As a result, there is no reason to doubt that people coexisted with extinct late Pleistocene mammals in this region. Nonetheless, there is not a single Great Basin site that has provided an association between an extinct late Pleistocene mammal and human artifacts in a convincing kill context (for an excellent discussion of how associations between artifacts and extinct mammals can come about accidentally, see Dansie, Davis, and Stafford 1988).

Since human occupation of the Great Basin began before the extinctions were complete, there is an excellent chance that sooner or later such an association will be found. As I have discussed, only mammoths and, to a far lesser extent, mastodons have been found in kill sites in other parts of North America. Given the extreme rarity of mastodons in the Great Basin, if a kill site is discovered in this region, it will almost undoubtedly involve mammoths. Unfortunately, most known Great Basin archaeological sites of late Pleistocene age are surface sites (e.g., Davis 1979; Willig 1988, 1989). Convincing evidence of an association between extinct Pleistocene mammals and people in the Great Basin will most likely require the discovery of buried open sites.

I noted that overkill explanations of North American late Pleistocene extinctions have lost popularity because some of the key requirements of those explanations have not been met, including the requirement that there be kill sites for at least the abundant herbivores involved. At the same time as this has occurred, climatic accounts have become increasingly precise. Climatic explanations focus on a small number of key environmental factors as the driving force in causing the extinctions. Those key factors include decreased length of the growing season, increased seasonal swings in temperature, and vegetational simplification. The importance given to each of these factors differs from region to region within North America, but some combination of them is argued to have occurred at the time of the extinctions and to have caused those extinctions (Guthrie 1984a, 1984b, 1990a, 1990b; Graham and Lundelius 1984; Graham 1985a, 1985b, 1986, 1990; Graham and Mead 1987; Lundelius 1988, 1989).

Arguments depending on a decrease in the length of the growing season as the extinctions occurred are primarily based on the diminution in the size of the large mammals that survived the extinctions in eastern Beringia (e.g., Guthrie 1984a, 1990a, 1990b). Paleontological samples in the Great Basin are simply too small to allow this issue to be addressed here.

Our record for the latest Pleistocene and earliest Holocene vegetation of the Great Basin is also inadequate to address in detail whether or not massive vegetational simplification occurred in the Great Basin as the Pleistocene drew to a close. None-theless, it is certainly true that, as in eastern North America, the plant zonation typical of the modern Great Basin (Billings 1951) is entirely a Holocene phenome-non (e.g., Thompson 1990) and that plant associations that are unknown in the modern Great Basin are not uncommon in late Pleistocene plant assemblages. Such associations include shadscale (*Atriplex confertifolia*) with limber pine (*Pinus flexilis*) and desert almond (*Prunus fasciculata*) with bristlecone pine (*Pinus longaeva*) in the Sheep Range of southern Nevada (Spaulding, Leopold, and Van Devender 1983; Spaulding 1990; see also Spaulding 1985); many other examples exist. Whether, as in other parts of North America, such "anomalous" associations were broken apart at the same time as the extinctions were occurring is unknown. While the plant associations are well dated in the Great Basin, the extinctions are not.

It is also unclear whether the extinctions in the Great Basin were occurring as seasonal swings in temperature were increasing, as is called for by what is perhaps the most popular climatic account of the extinctions (Graham and Lundelius 1984; Graham 1990; Lundelius 1989). This is true not only because of our poor control over the chronology of extinction in the Great Basin but also because there is little agreement as to the nature of changes in seasonal temperature differences between late Pleistocene and early Holocene times here. Spaulding and Graumlich (1986), for instance, see no convincing evidence for dampened seasonal swings in tempera-ture during the late Pleistocene in the southern Great Basin (see also Spaulding 1990). Many paleobotanists, however, argue that late Wisconsin climates in the Great Basin were more equable than those that followed during the Holocene, and some of those arguments seem compelling (see Thompson 1990; Van Devender, Thompson, and Betancourt 1987; Woodcock 1986; for the Sonoran Desert, see Van Devender 1990).

Even if these paleoclimatological issues are resolved, however, the Great Basin will continue to remain on the edge of debates concerning the cause or causes of the extinctions. This is true simply because we know so very little about the distri-bution and abundance of the animals involved and because we know so little about the chronology of it all.

CONCLUSIONS

The contrast between our knowledge of the Pleistocene and of the Holocene mam-malian faunas of the Great Basin is stark. While our understanding of the history of Great Basin mammals during the past 10,000 years is arguably better than that for any other part of North America, our knowledge of the Pleistocene mammals of this region is quite weak.

This fact is of more than academic import. Our deep understanding of the Holocene history of Great Basin mammals has direct implications for the manage-ment of mammalian habitats in this region today (e.g., Grayson 1987, 1993; McDonald and Brown 1992). This understanding would not have been reached had we not been able to couple modern biogeographic theory and field observations with precise information on mammalian history drawn from archaeological and paleontological deposits spanning the past 10,000 years.

Although major changes in the ranges of Great Basin small mammals have occurred during the Holocene, mammalian extinction during this time has been minor. The end of the Pleistocene here, however, was marked by massive mammalian extinction, just as occurred elsewhere in North America. Graham (1985a, 1985b, 1988; Graham and Grimm 1990) has shown that without an understanding of the pattern of late Pleistocene North American extinctions, we are far less likely to be able to cope with significant climatic change in the future, including that which may be caused by our own behavior. Indeed, Graham's work has significant implications for the construction of wildlife reserves, implications drawn explicitly from our understanding of late Pleistocene mammalian extinctions and extirpations.

Our lack of knowledge of late Pleistocene mammalian extinctions in the Great Basin, and to an almost equal extent of changes in mammalian distributions here as the Pleistocene came to an end, greatly limits our ability to predict and to deal with the impacts of future environmental change on the mammalian fauna of this region. For those of us interested in the preservation of biological diversity, this is no small issue.

The Great Basin is rich in sources of information on late Pleistocene environments and environmental change (e.g., Thompson 1990). There is no doubt that this region is equally rich in late Pleistocene vertebrate faunas. If we are to understand the relationship between environmental change and mammalian history in the Great Basin, and if we are to use that information to safeguard the tremendous biological diversity that marks this region, then we must begin to focus serious efforts on developing a detailed understanding of the history of Great Basin mammals during the late Pleistocene.

ACKNOWLEDGMENTS

My sincere thanks to W. M. Hess, Stephanie D. Livingston, Jim I. Mead, and Wade E. Miller for help provided during preparation of this chapter.

REFERENCES

Adams, D. B. 1979. The cheetah: native American. Science 205:1155–1158.

Agenbroad, L. D. 1984. New World mammoth distribution, pp. 90–108. In, P. S. Martin and R. G. Klein (eds.), Quaternary Extinctions: A Prehistoric Revolution. University of Arizona Press, Tucson.

Aikens, C. M., and D. B. Madsen. 1986. Prehistory of the eastern area, pp. 149–160. In, W. L. d'Azevedo (ed.), Great Basin. Handbook of North American Indians, Vol. 11. Smithsonian Institution, Washington, D.C.

Akersten, W. A. 1985. Canine function in Smilodon (Mammalia; Felidae; Machairodontinae). Natural History Museum of Los Angeles County, Contributions in Science 356:1–22.

Allison, I. S. 1966. Fossil Lake, Oregon: Its geology and fossil faunas. Oregon State University Studies in Geology 9.

Arnold, J. R., and W. F. Libby. 1951. Radiocarbon dates. Science 113:111–120.

Billings, W. D. 1951. Vegetational zonation in the Great Basin of western North America. In, Les Bases écologiques de la régénération de la végétation des zones arides. International Union of Biological Sciences, Series B, No. 9:101–122.

Birnie, R. I. 1986. Late Quaternary environments and archaeology of the Snake Range, east central Nevada. M.S. thesis, University of Maine, Orono.

Brattstrom, B. H. 1958. New records of Cenozoic amphibians and reptiles from California. Bulletin of the Southern California Academy of Sciences 57:5–12.

Broecker, W. S., and J. L. Kulp. 1957. Lamont natural radiocarbon measurements IV. Science 126:154–165.

Brown, J. H. 1971. Mammals on mountaintops: Nonequilibrium insular biogeography. Journal of Mammalogy 105:467–478.

Brown, J. H. 1978. The theory of insular biogeography and the distribution of boreal mammals and birds. *In*, K. T. Harper and J. L Reveal (eds.), Intermountain Biogeography: A Symposium. Great Basin Naturalist Memoirs 2:209–228.

Bryan, A. L. 1979. Smith Creek Cave. *In*, D. R. Tuohy and D. L. Rendall (eds.), The Archaeology of Smith Creek Canyon, Eastern Nevada. Nevada State Museum Anthropological Papers 17:162–251.

Cressman, L. S. 1942. Archaeological Researches in the Northern Great Basin. Carnegie Institute of Washington Publication 538.

Dansie, A. J. 1987. The Rye Patch archaeofaunas: Change through time. *In*, M. K. Rusco and J. O. Davis (eds.), Studies in Archaeology, Geology, and Paleontology at Rye Patch Reservoir, Pershing County, Nevada. Nevada State Museum Anthropological Papers 20:156–182.

Dansie, A. J., J. O. Davis, and T. W. Stafford, Jr. 1988. The Wizards Beach Recession: Farmdalian (25,500 yr B.P.) vertebrate fossils co-occur with early Holocene artifacts. *In*, J. A. Willig, C. M. Aikens, and J. L. Fagan (eds.), Early Human Occupation in Far Western North America: The Clovis-Archaic Interface. Nevada State Museum Anthropological Papers 21:153–200.

Davis, C. A., and G. A. Smith. 1981. Newberry Cave. San Bernardino County Museum Association, Redlands, California.

Davis, E. L., ed. 1979. The ancient Californians: Rancholabrean hunters of the Mojave lakes country. Natural History Museum of Los Angeles County Science Series 29:173–176.

Dillehay, T. D. 1989. Monte Verde: A Late Pleistocene Settlement in Chile. Vol. 1: Palaeoenvironment and Site Context. Smithsonian Institution Press, Washington, D.C.

Downs, T., H. Howard, T. Clements, and G. A. Smith. 1959. Quaternary Animals from Schuiling Cave in the Mojave Desert, California. Los Angeles City Museum Contributions in Science 29.

Emslie, S. D., and N. J. Czaplewski. 1985. A New Record of Giant Short-Faced Bear, *Arctodus simus*, from Western North America with a Re-evaluation of Its Paleobiology. Los Angeles County Museum Contributions in Science 731:1–12.

Firby, J. R., J. E. Mawby, and J. O. Davis. 1987. Vertebrate paleontology and geology of the Rye Patch paleontological locality. *In*, M. K. Rusco and J. O. Davis (eds.), Studies in Archaeology, Geology, and Paleontology at Rye Patch Reservoir, Pershing County, Nevada. Nevada State Museum Anthropological Papers 20:23–40.

Fortsch, D. E. 1978. The Lake China Rancholabrean Faunule. *In*, E. L. Davis (ed.), The Ancient Californians: Rancholabrean Hunters of the Mojave Lakes Country. Natural History Museum of Los Angeles County Science Series 29:173–176.

Gillette, D. D., and D. B. Madsen 1992. The short-faced bear *Arctodus simus* from the late Quaternary in the Wasatch Mountains of central Utah. Journal of Vertebrate Paleontology 12:107–112.

Goodwin, H. T., and R. E. Reynolds. 1989. Late Quaternary Sciuridae from Kokoweef Cave, San Bernardino County, California. Bulletin of the Southern California Academy of Sciences 88:21–32.

Graham, R. W. 1985a. Diversity and community structure of the Late Pleistocene mammal fauna of North America. Acta Zoologica Fennica 170:181–192.

Graham, R. W. 1985b. Response of mammalian communities to environmental changes during the late Quaternary, pp. 300–313. In, J. Diamond and T. J. Case (eds.), Community Ecology. Harper and Row, New York.

Graham, R. W. 1986. Plant-animal interactions and Pleistocene extinctions, pp. 131–154. In, D. K. Elliot (ed.), Dynamics of Extinctions. Wiley, Chicago.

Graham, R. W. 1988. The role of climatic change in the design of biological reserves: The paleoecological perspective for conservation biology. Conservation Biology 2:391–394.

Graham, R. W. 1990. Evolution of new ecosystems at the end of the Pleistocene. In, L. D. Agenbroad, J. I. Mead, and L. W. Nelson (eds.), Megafauna and Man: Discovery of America's Heartland. Mammoth Site of Hot Springs Scientific Papers 1:54–60.

Graham, R. W., and E. C. Grimm. 1990. Effects of global climatic change on the patterns of terrestrial biological communities. Trends in Ecology and Evolution 5:289–292.

Graham, R. W., and E. L. Lundelius, Jr. 1984. Coevolutionary disequilibrium and Pleistocene extinctions, pp. 223–249. In, P. S. Martin and R. G. Klein (eds.), Quaternary Extinctions: A Prehistoric Revolution. University of Arizona Press, Tucson.

Graham, R. W., and J. I. Mead. 1987. Environmental fluctuations and evolution of mammalian faunas during the last deglaciation. In, W. F. Ruddiman and H. E. Wright, Jr. (eds.), North America and Adjacent Oceans During the Last Glaciation, pp. 371–402. The Geology of North America, Vol. K3. Geological Society of America, Boulder.

Grayson, D. K. 1977. Pleistocene avifaunas and the overkill hypothesis. Science 195:691–693.

Grayson, D. K. 1982. Toward a history of Great Basin mammals during the past 15,000 years. In, D. B. Madsen and J. F. O'Connell (eds.), Man and Environment in the Great Basin. Society for American Archaeology Papers 2:82–101.

Grayson, D. K. 1983. The paleontology of Gatecliff Shelter: Small mammals. In, D. H. Thomas, The archaeology of Monitor Valley, Vol. 2: Gatecliff Shelter. American Museum of Natural History Anthropological Papers 59(1):98-126.

Grayson, D. K. 1984a. Explaining Pleistocene extinctions: Thoughts on the structure of a debate, pp. 807–823. In, P. S. Martin and R. G. Klein (eds.), Quaternary Extinctions: A Prehistoric Revolution. University of Arizona Press, Tucson.

Grayson, D. K. 1984b. The time of extinction and nature of adaptation of the noble marten, Martes nobilis. In, H. H. Genoways and M. R. Dawson (eds.), Contributions in Quaternary Vertebrate Paleontology: A Volume in Memorial to John E. Guilday. Carnegie Museum of Natural History Special Publication 8:233–240.

Grayson, D. K. 1985. The paleontology of Hidden Cave: Birds and mammals. In, D. H. Thomas (ed.), The Archaeology of Hidden Cave, Nevada. American Museum of Natural History Anthropological Papers 61(1):125–161.

Grayson, D. K. 1987. The biogeographic history of small mammals in the Great Basin: Observations on the last 20,000 years. Journal of Mammalogy 68:359–375.

Grayson, D. K. 1988. Americans before Columbus: Perspectives on the archaeology of the first Americans. In, R. C. Carlisle (ed.), Americans Before Columbus: Ice-Age Origins. Ethnology Monographs 12:107–123.

Grayson, D. K. 1989. The chronology of North American late Pleistocene extinctions. Journal of Archaeological Science 16:153–165.

Grayson, D. K. 1991. Late Pleistocene mammalian extinctions in North America: Taxonomy, chronology, and explanations. Journal of World Prehistory 5:193–231.

Grayson, D. K. 1993. The Desert's Past: A Natural Prehistory of the Great Basin. Smithsonian Institution Press, Washington, D.C.

Guthrie, R. D. 1984a. Alaskan megabucks, megabulls, and megarams: The issue of Pleistocene gigantism. *In*, H. H. Genoways and M. R. Dawson (eds.), Contributions in Quaternary Vertebrate Paleontology: A Volume in Memorial to John E. Guilday. Carnegie Museum of Natural History Special Publication 8:482–510.

Guthrie, R. D. 1984b. Mosaics, allelochemics, and nutrients: An ecological theory of late Pleistocene megafaunal extinctions, pp. 259–298. *In*, P. S. Martin and R. G. Klein (eds.), Quaternary Extinctions: A Prehistoric Revolution. University of Arizona Press, Tucson.

Guthrie, R. D. 1990a. Frozen Fauna of the Mammoth Steppe. University of Chicago Press, Chicago.

Guthrie, R. D. 1990b. Late Pleistocene faunal revolution: A new perspective on the extinction debate. *In*, L. D. Agenbroad, J. I. Mead, and L. W. Nelson (eds.), Megafauna and Man: Discovery of America's Heartland. Mammoth Site of Hot Springs Scientific Papers 1:42–53.

Harrington, M. R. 1933. Gypsum Cave, Nevada. Southwest Museum Papers 8.

Hattori, E. M. 1982. The Archaeology of Falcon Hill Cave, Winnemucca Lake, Washoe County, Nevada. Nevada State Museum Anthropological Papers 18.

Haynes, C. V., Jr. 1967. Quaternary geology of the Tule Springs area, Clark County, Nevada. *In*, H. M. Wormington and D. Ellis (eds.), Pleistocene Studies in Southern Nevada. Nevada State Museum Anthropological Papers 13:15–104.

Heaton, T. H. 1985. Quaternary paleontology and paleoecology of Crystal Ball Cave, Millard County, Utah: With emphasis on mammals and description of a new species of fossil skunk. Great Basin Naturalist 45:337–390.

Heaton, T. H. 1987. Initial investigation of vertebrate remains from Snake Creek Burial Cave, White Pine County, Nevada. Current Research in the Pleistocene 4:107–109.

Heaton, T. H. 1990. Quaternary mammals of the Great Basin: Extinct giants, Pleistocene relicts, and recent immigrants, pp. 422–465. *In*, R. M. Ross and W. D. Allmon (eds.), Causes of Evolution: A Paleontological Perspective. University of Chicago Press, Chicago.

Howe, K. M., and J. E. Martin. 1977. Investigation of the Paleontological Resources of Fossil Lake, Lake Co., Oregon, With Recommendations for Their Management. Bureau of Land Management, Lakeview, Oregon.

Jefferson, G. T. 1990. Rancholabrean age vertebrates from the eastern Mojave Desert, California, pp. 109–116. *In*, R. E. Reynolds, S. G. Wells, and R. H. Brady III (eds.), At the End of the Mohave: Quaternary Studies in the Eastern Mojave Desert. San Bernardino County Museum Association, Redlands, California.

Jefferson, G. T. 1991. Rancholabrean age vertebrates from the southeastern Mojave Desert, California, pp. 163–176. *In*, R. E. Reynolds (ed.), Crossing the Borders: Quaternary Studies in Eastern California and Southwestern Nevada. San Bernardino County Museum Association, Redlands, California.

Kurtén, B. 1967. Pleistocene bears of North America, part 2. Genus *Arctodus*, short-faced bears. Acta Zoologica Fennica 117.

Kurtén, B., and E. Anderson. 1980. Pleistocene Mammals of North America. Columbia University Press, New York.

Livingston, S. D. 1988. The avian and mammalian faunas from Lovelock Cave and the Humboldt Lakebed site. Ph.D. dissertation, Department of Anthropology, University of Washington, Seattle.

Livingston, S. D. 1992. The DeLong Mammoth Locality, Black Rock Desert, Nevada. Current Research in the Pleistocene 8:94–97.

Long, A., and P. S. Martin. 1974. Death of American ground sloths. Science 186:638–640.

Long, A., and A. B. Muller. 1981. Arizona radiocarbon dates X. Radiocarbon 23:191–217.

Lundelius, E. L., Jr. 1988. What happened to the mammoth? The climatic model. In, R. C. Carlisle (ed.), Americans Before Columbus: Ice-Age Origins. Ethnology Monographs 12:75–82.

Lundelius, E. L., Jr. 1989. The implications of disharmonious assemblages for Pleistocene extinctions. Journal of Archaeological Science 16:407–417.

Madsen, D. B., D. R. Currey, and J. H. Madsen. 1976. Man, Mammoth, and Lake Fluctuations in Utah. Utah Division of State History, Antiquities Section Selected Papers 5.

Martin, P. S. 1984. Prehistoric overkill: The global model, pp. 354–403. In, P. S. Martin and R. G. Klein (eds.), Quaternary Extinctions: A Prehistoric Revolution. University of Arizona Press, Tucson.

Martin, P. S. 1987. Late Quaternary extinctions: The promise of TAMS 14C Dating. Nuclear Instruments and Methods in Physics Research B29:179–186.

Martin, P. S. 1990. 40,000 years on the planet of doom. Palaeogeography, Palaeoclimatology, Palaeoecology 82:187–201.

Mawby, J. E. 1967. Fossil vertebrates of the Tule Springs Site, Nevada. In, H. M. Wormington and D. Ellis (eds.), Pleistocene Studies in Southern Nevada. Nevada State Museum Anthropological Papers 13:105–129.

McDonald, J. N., and C. E. Ray. 1989. The Autochthonous North American Musk Oxen Bootherium, Symbos, and Gidleya (Mammalia: Artiodactyla: Bovidae). Smithsonian Contributions to Paleobiology 66.

McDonald, K. A., and J. H. Brown. 1992. Using montane mammals to model extinctions due to global climatic change. Conservation Biology 6:409–415.

McGuire, K. R. 1980. Cave sites, faunal analysis, and big-game hunters of the Great Basin: A caution. Quaternary Research 14:263–268.

Mead, E. M., and J. I. Mead. 1989. Snake Creek Burial Cave and a review of the Quaternary mustelids of the Great Basin. Great Basin Naturalist 49:143–154.

Mead, J. I. 1983. Harrington's extinct mountain goat (Oreamnos harringtoni) and its environment in the Grand Canyon, Arizona. Ph.D. dissertation, University of Arizona, Tucson.

Mead, J. I., and E. M. Mead. 1985. A natural trap for Pleistocene animals in Snake Valley, eastern Nevada. Current Research in the Pleistocene 2:105–106.

Mead, J. I., L. D. Agenbroad, A. M. Phillips III, and L. T. Middleton. 1987. Extinct mountain goat (Oreamnos harringtoni) in southeastern Utah. Quaternary Research 27:232–331.

Mead, J. I., P. S. Martin, R. C. Euler, A. Long, A.J.T. Jull, L. J. Toolin, D. J. Donahue, and T. W. Linick. 1986. Extinction of Harrington's mountain goat. Proceedings of the National Academy of Science 83:836–839.

Mead, J. I., M. K. O'Rourke, and T. M. Foppe. 1986. Dung and diet of the extinct Harrington's mountain goat (Oreamnos harringtoni). Journal of Mammalogy 67:284–293.

Mead, J. I., R. S. Thompson, and T. R. Van Devender. 1982. Late Wisconsinan and Holocene fauna from Smith Creek Canyon, Snake Range, Nevada. Transactions of the San Diego Society of Natural History 20:1–26.

Meltzer, D. J. 1988. Late Pleistocene human adaptations in eastern North America. Journal of World Prehistory 2:1–52.

Meltzer, D. J., and J. I. Mead. 1985. Dating late Pleistocene extinctions: Theoretical issues, analytical bias, and substantive results, pp. 145–173. *In*, J. I. Mead and D. J. Meltzer (eds.), Environments and Extinctions: Man in Late Glacial North America. Center for the Study of Early Man, Orono, Maine.

Merriam, J. C. 1915. An occurrence of mammalian remains in Pleistocene lake deposits at Astor Pass, near Pyramid Lake, Nevada. University of California Publications, Department of Geology, Bulletin 8(21):377–384.

Miller, S. J. 1979. The Archaeological fauna of four sites in Smith Creek Canyon. *In*, D. R. Tuohy and D. L. Rendall (eds.), The Archaeology of Smith Creek Canyon, Eastern Nevada. Nevada State Museum Anthropological Papers 17:272–331.

Miller, W. E. 1976. Late Pleistocene vertebrates of the Silver Creek Local Fauna from north central Utah. Great Basin Naturalist 36:387–424.

Miller, W. E. 1982. Pleistocene vertebrates from deposits of Lake Bonneville, Utah. National Geographic Society Research Reports 14:473–478.

Miller, W. E. 1987. *Mammut americanum*, Utah's first record of the American mastodon. Journal of Paleontology 61:168–183.

Nelson, M. E., and J. H. Madsen, Jr. 1978. Late Pleistocene musk oxen from Utah. Kansas Academy of Science Transactions 81:277–295.

Nelson, M. E., and J. H. Madsen, Jr. 1979. The Hay-Romer camel debate: Fifty years later. University of Wyoming Contributions to Geology 18:47–50.

Nelson, M. E., and J. H. Madsen, Jr. 1980. A summary of Pleistocene fossil vertebrate localities in the northern Bonneville Basin of Utah. *In*, J. W. Gwynn (ed.), Great Salt Lake: A Scientific, Historical, and Economic Overview. Utah Geological and Mineral Survey Bulletin 116:97–114.

Nelson, M. E., and J. H. Madsen, Jr. 1983. A giant short-faced bear (*Arctodus simus*) from the Pleistocene of northern Utah. Transactions of the Kansas Academy of Science 86:1–9.

Nowak, R. M. 1979. North American Quaternary *Canis*. University of Kansas Museum of Natural History Monograph 6.

Orr, P. C. 1952. Preliminary excavations of Pershing County Caves. Nevada State Museum Department of Archaeology Bulletin 1.

Orr, P. C. 1956. Pleistocene Man in Fishbone Cave, Pershing County, Nevada. Nevada State Museum Department of Archaeology Bulletin 2.

Orr, P. C. 1969. *Felis trumani*, a new radiocarbon dated cat skull from Crypt Cave, Nevada. Bulletin of the Santa Barbara Museum of Natural History Department of Geology 2:1–8.

Orr, P. C. 1974. Notes on the archaeology of the Winnemucca caves, 1952–1958. Nevada State Museum Anthropological Papers 16:47–59.

Reynolds, R. E., J. I. Mead, and R. L. Reynolds. 1991. A Rancholabrean fauna from the Las Vegas Formation, North Las Vegas, Nevada, pp. 140–146. *In*, R. E. Reynolds (ed.), Crossing the Borders: Quaternary Studies in Eastern California and Southwestern Nevada. San Bernardino County Museum Association, Redlands, California.

Reynolds, R. E., R. L. Reynolds, and C. J. Bell. 1991. The Devil Peak Sloth, pp. 115–116. *In*, R. E. Reynolds (ed.), Crossing the Borders: Quaternary Studies in Eastern California and Southwestern Nevada. San Bernardino County Museum Association, Redlands, California.

Reynolds, R. E., R. L. Reynolds, C. J. Bell, and B. Pitzer. 1991a. Vertebrate remains from Antelope Cave, Mescal Range, San Bernardino County, California, pp. 107–109. *In*, R. E. Reynolds (ed.), Crossing the Borders: Quaternary Studies in Eastern California and Southwestern Nevada. San Bernardino County Museum Association, Redlands, California.

Reynolds, R. E., R. L. Reynolds, C. J. Bell, N. J. Czaplewski, H. T. Goodwin, J. I. Mead, and B. Roth. 1991b. The Kokoweef Cave faunal assemblage, pp. 97–103. *In*, R. E. Reynolds (ed.), Crossing the Borders: Quaternary Studies in Eastern California and Southwestern Nevada. San Bernardino County Museum Association, Redlands, California.

Romer, A. S. 1928. A "fossil" camel recently living in Utah. Science 68: 19–20.

Romer, A. S. 1929. A fresh skull of an extinct American camel. Journal of Geology 37:261–267.

Schmitt, D. N., and N. D. Sharp. 1990. Mammals in the marsh: Zooarchaeological analysis of six sites in the Stillwater Wildlife Refuge, Western Nevada. *In*, J. C. Janetski and D. B. Madsen (eds.), Wetland adaptations in the Great Basin. Brigham Young University Museum of Peoples and Cultures Occasional Papers 1:75–95.

Spaulding, W. G. 1983. The overkill hypothesis as a plausible explanation for the extinctions of late Wisconsin megafauna. Quaternary Research 20:110–112.

Spaulding, W. G. 1985. Vegetation and Climates of the Last 45,000 Years in the Vicinity of the Nevada Test Site, South-Central Nevada. U. S. Geological Survey Professional Paper 1329.

Spaulding, W. G. 1990. Vegetational and climatic development of the Mojave Desert: The last glacial maximum to the present, pp. 166-199. *In*, J. L. Betancourt, T. R. Van Devender, and P. S. Martin (eds.), Packrat Middens: The Last 40,000 Years of Biotic Change. University of Arizona Press, Tucson.

Spaulding, W. G., and L. J. Graumlich. 1986. The last pluvial climatic episodes in the deserts of southwestern North America. Nature 320:441–444.

Spaulding, W. G., E. B. Leopold, and T. R. Van Devender. 1983. Late Wisconsin paleoecology of the American Southwest, pp. 259–292. *In*, S. C. Porter (ed.), Late Quaternary Environments of the United States, Vol. 1: The Late Pleistocene. University of Minnesota Press, Minneapolis.

Spurr, J. E. 1903. Descriptive Geology of Nevada South of the Fortieth Parallel and Adjacent Portions of California. United States Geological Survey Bulletin 208.

Stafford, T. W., Jr., P. E. Hare, L. Currie, A.J.T. Jull, and D. Donahue. 1991. Accelerator radiocarbon dating at the molecular level. Journal of Archaeological Science 18:35–72.

Stock, C. S. 1931. Problems of antiquity presented in Gypsum Cave, Nevada. Scientific Monthly 32:22–32.

Stock, C. S. 1936. A new mountain goat from the Quaternary of Smith Creek Cave, Nevada. Bulletin of the Southern California Academy of Sciences 35:149–153.

Stout, B. 1986. Discovery and dating of the Black Rock Desert mammoth. Nevada Archaeologist 5(2):21–23.

Stuart, A. S. 1991. Mammalian extinctions in the late Pleistocene of northern Eurasia and North America. Biological Review 66:453–562.

Thompson, R. S. 1990. Late Quaternary vegetation and climate in the Great Basin, pp. 134–165. *In*, J. L. Betancourt, T. R. Van Devender, and P. S. Martin (eds.), Packrat Middens: The Last 40,000 Years of Biotic Change. University of Arizona Press, Tucson.

Thompson, R. S., E. M. Hattori, and D. R. Tuohy. 1987. Paleoenvironmental and archaeological implications of early Holocene–late Pleistocene cave deposits from Winnemucca Lake, Nevada. Nevada Archaeologist 6(1):34–38.

Thompson, R. S., T. R. Van Devender, P. S. Martin, T. Foppe, and A. Long. 1980. Shasta ground sloth (*Nothrotheriops shastense* Hoffstetter) at Shelter Cave, New Mexico: Environment, diet, and extinction. Quaternary Research 14:360–376.

Tuohy, D. R. 1986. Nevada's fossil elephants. Nevada Archaeologist 5(2):8–18.

Turnmire, K. L. 1987. An analysis of the mammalian fauna from Owl Cave One and Two, Snake Range, east-central Nevada. M.S. thesis, University of Maine, Orono.

Van Devender, T. R. 1990. Late Quaternary vegetation and climate of the Sonoran Desert, United States and Mexico, pp. 134–165. *In*, J. L. Betancourt, T. R. Van Devender, and P. S. Martin (eds.), Packrat Middens: The Last 40,000 Years of Biotic Change. University of Arizona Press, Tucson.

Van Devender, T. R., R. S. Thompson, and J. L. Betancourt. 1987. Vegetation history of the deserts of southwestern North America: The nature and timing of the late Wisconsin-Holocene transition, pp. 323–352. *In*, W. F. Ruddiman and H. E. Wright, Jr. (eds.), North America and Adjacent Oceans During the Last Glaciation. The Geology of North America, Vol. K3. Geological Society of America, Boulder.

Van Valkenburgh, B., F. Grady, and B. Kurtén. 1990. The Plio-Pleistocene cheetah-like cat *Miracinonyx inexpectatus* of North America. Journal of Vertebrate Paleontology 10:434–454.

Van Valkenburgh, B., and C. B. Ruff. 1987. Canine tooth strength and killing behaviour in large carnivores. Journal of Zoology 212:379–397.

Van Valkenburgh, B., M. F. Teaford, and A. Walker. 1990. Molar microwear and diet in large carnivores: Inferences concerning diet in the sabretooth cat, *Smilodon fatalis*. Journal of Zoology 222:319–340.

Webb, S. D. 1965. The Osteology of *Camelops*. Los Angeles County Museum Science Bulletin 1.

Webster, G. S. 1978. Dry Creek Rockshelter: Cultural chronology in the western Snake River region of Idaho ca. 4150 B.P.–1300 B.P. Tebiwa 15:1–35.

Willig, J. A. 1988. Paleo-Archaic adaptations and lakeside settlement patterns in the northern Alkali Basin, Oregon. *In*, J. A. Willig, C. M. Aikens, and J. L. Fagan (eds.), Early Human Occupation in Far Western North America: The Clovis-Archaic Interface. Nevada State Museum Anthropological Papers 21:417–482.

Willig, J. A. 1989. Paleo-Archaic broad spectrum adaptations at the Pleistocene-Holocene boundary in far western North America. Ph.D. dissertation, Department of Anthropology, University of Oregon, Eugene.

Woodcock, D. 1986. The late Pleistocene of Death Valley: A climatic reconstruction based on macrofossil data. Palaeogeography, Palaeoclimatology, Palaeoecology 57:272–283.

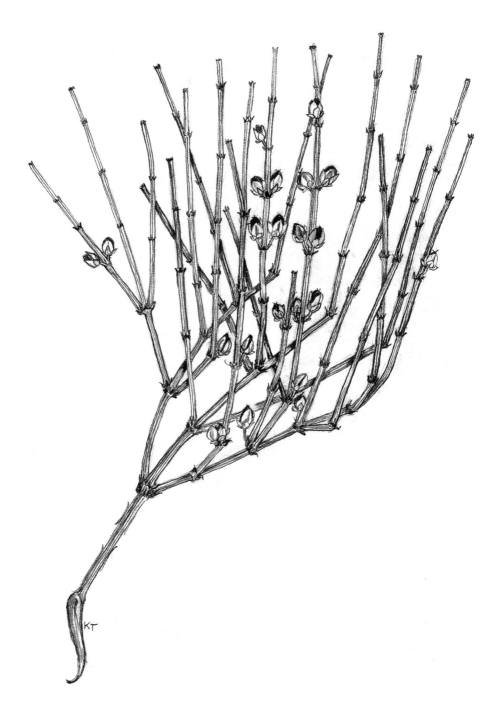

Ephedra viridis Coville (Mormon green tea) and its close congener, *E. nevadensis* S. Wats., were important ingredients of medicinal teas widely used by native peoplesof the Intermountain West.

CHAPTER 5

Western Great Basin Prehistory

James D. Wilde

OVERVIEW

To date, archaeological studies in the Great Basin have focused on basic questions about when the region was first occupied, the technological development of the early inhabitants, and their relationships with other cultures in the region. In this chapter the author summarizes available information on western Great Basin cultures and discusses several synthetic approaches to understanding regional cultural models. He points out that most of the regional models have centered on data from valleys with relatively abundant marsh, stream, and lakeside resources. Studies outside of this habitat type are limited but essential to a complete understanding of prehistoric human cultures of the region.

In this chapter I consider the western Great Basin (Figure 5.1) to be that portion of the Basin and Range Province between central Nevada on the east, the spine of the Sierra Nevada of California on the west, the internally draining portions of south central and southeastern Oregon on the north, and the southern extent of Owens and Panamint Valleys, California, on the south. It includes all of the area once covered by pluvial Lake Lahontan in northwestern Nevada, as well as other not quite so large Pleistocene lakes in the Fort Rock, Summer Lake, Abert, Goose Lake, Warner, Catlow, Malheur, and Alvord Basins of Oregon; Surprise Valley and Honey Lake Basin in northeastern California; and Owens, Long, Antelope, Panamint, and Mono and Walker Lake Basins of eastern California and western Nevada. Various overviews of the basic prehistory of this region have been presented in the last decade by Aikens (1982, 1983a, 1983b), Aikens and Witherspoon (1986), Cressman (1986), Elston (1982, 1986), and Thomas (1982b). My goal is not to rehash the work of these authors but to present a brief outline of our ideas of western Great Basin archaeology in terms of time and space, and then to discuss some synthetic approaches to understanding regional cultural/environmental models that attempt to describe patterns that have endured and evolved for many thousands of years.

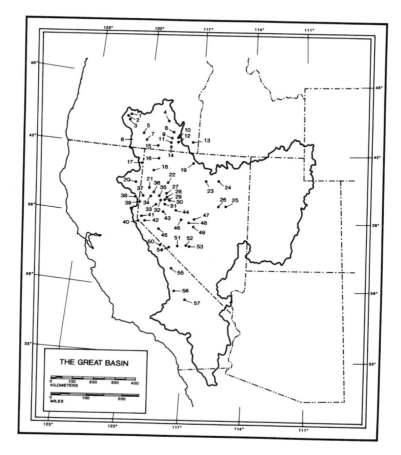

Figure 5.1 The Great Basin of North America, showing locations of archaeological sites
and geographical features discussed in the text. 1. Cougar Mountain Caves; 2.
Fort Rock Cave; 3. Connley Caves; 4. Malheur Lake; 5. Lake Abert; 6.
Chewaucan Marsh; 7. Warner Valley; 8. Steens Mountain; 9. Roaring Springs
Cave; 10. Coyote Flat; 11. Skull Creek Dune Locality 1; 12. Tule Springs
Hearth Site; 13. Dirty Shame Rock shelter; 14. Catlow Cave; 15. Alkali Lake;
16. Last Supper Cave; 17. Surprise Valley; 18. Silent Snake Springs; 19. Ezra's
Retreat; 20. Karlos; 21. Falcon Hill; 22. Rye Patch Reservoir; 23. James Creek
Shelter; 24. South Fork Shelter; 25. Sunshine Well Locality; 26. Newark Cave;
27. Old Humboldt; 28. Leonard Rock shelter; 29. Lovelock Cave; 30. Carson
Sink; 31. Stillwater Marsh; 32. Humboldt Cave; 33. Sadmat; 34. Winnemucca
Lake; 35. Cocanour; 36. Fishbone Cave; 37. Pyramid Lake; 38. Long Valley
Creek; 39. Bordertown; 40. Hobo Hot Springs; 41. Spooner Lake; 42. Dangberg
Hot Springs; 43. Hidden Cave; 44. Wagon Jack Shelter; 45. Walker Lake; 46.
Reese River Valley; 47. Gatecliff Shelter; 48. Triple T Shelter; 49. Alta
Toquima; 50. Long Valley Caldera; 51. Lake Tonapah; 52. Lowe Shelter; 53.
Mud Lake; 54. White Mountains; 55. Owens Valley; 56. Stahl; 57. China Lake.

TIME AND SPACE

For the past 100 years, archaeologists interested in the Great Basin have concerned themselves primarily with problems of time and space. Central questions have included, When did people first occupy the region? What kinds of tool kits did Great Basin people have? Will the technologies evident in these tool kits reveal where people came from and how they got here? How are the technologies of the early and later residents of the Basin related to each other and to other technologies in more culturally elaborate areas such as the Southwest? And, How and why did these technologies change over time? These kinds of questions are related to an understanding of "culture" as a set of shared ideas and standards that are represented in the archaeological record as common traits. Such items as projectile points, house types, ceramics, baskets, sandals, milling stones, and other artifacts contain these shared elements, allowing archaeologists to determine patterns of past similarities and differences across space and through time. Groups of artifacts with these shared traits that are confined to certain areas and times are considered archaeological cultures. A number have been defined to constitute the prehistoric ebb and flow of peoples for the past 12,000 years in the western Great Basin. These include supergroups such as Paleoindian and Archaic, both of which are divided into regional and temporal subunits.

Paleoindians: The First People in the Basin

Several general Paleoindian "cultures" existed over a large portion of North America between about 12,000 and 8000 B.P. (Jennings 1989). The identifying characteristics are suites of chipped stone tools that include large bifacial knives, stemmed and concave base projectile points with edge grinding, crescents, gravers, punches, choppers, and several types of scrapers. Some of the most distinctive projectile points, called Clovis and Folsom, are also "fluted," or thinned, with relatively long, parallel-sided flake scars on either side that originate at the base of the object and presumably assisted in hafting (Figure 5.2; k, l). These suites of artifacts are similar in most details to those found in terminal Pleistocene sites in the Great Plains. In contrast to that area, however, most Paleoindian sites in the Great Basin are surface scatters or isolated finds. In any case, the similarity of tool types and the scarcity of seed-processing tools in these sites have suggested to some that Basin Paleoindians were primarily hunters of now extinct megafauna, the commonly accepted adaptation during terminal Pleistocene times in the Great Plains. Basin cultures associated with this period include regional manifestations of Clovis-Llano, Folsom, Plano, Western Clovis, and Western Stemmed, all named for projectile point styles that predominate the record during portions of the overall Paleoindian period (Willig and Aikens 1988).

The most common manifestations of these "cultures" in the western Great Basin are Western Clovis and Western Stemmed. Sites with these traditions occur in a variety of environments, but most are associated in some way with the margins of ancient lakes. Such sites have been found on shores, gravel bars, caves, and near extinct or extant spring-fed marshes. A few sites and isolated artifacts have also been found in upland areas in the region. Western Clovis sites fall into two categories:

those with Clovis projectile points that may or may not have been independently dated and those without Clovis points that have been radiocarbon dated to the Western Clovis period, between about 11,500 and 10,500 B.P. (Willig and Aikens 1988). Cougar Mountain Cave 2 and Connley Cave No. 4B (both Bedwell and Cressman 1971) in Oregon and Fishbone Cave (Thompson et al. 1987) in western Nevada fall into the latter category. Surface and other finds from Alkali Lake, Oregon (Willig 1988); China Lake, California (Davis 1978); and Mud and Tonapah Lakes, Nevada (for example, Tuohy 1988); plus a number of individual finds throughout the western Great Basin fall into the former category. None of these sites shows any clear association of Western Clovis and extinct or extant large game animals.

Typology and radiocarbon dates indicate a Western Clovis–Western Stemmed cultural continuum in the western Basin (Willig and Aikens 1988). The Western Stemmed tradition includes a variety of somewhat similar regional stemmed or lanceolate point styles, including Windust, Haskett, Lake Mojave, Silver Lake, Parman, Cougar Mountain, Mount Moriah, Borax Lake Wide Stemmed, Great Basin Stemmed, and Black Rock Concave Base (Willig and Aikens 1988, with references) that were widespread in the region between 10,500 and 7500 B.P. The large stemmed projectile point varieties from the central and northern Basin (Figure 5.2; i, j) are often grouped into the Western Pluvial Lakes tradition (Bedwell 1973), a subgroup of the more widespread Western Stemmed tradition. A relatively large number of sites contain Western Stemmed assemblages. A few of the most important in Oregon include Fort Rock Cave (Bedwell and Cressman 1971), Connley Cave No. 5B (Bedwell 1970, 1973), Dirty Shame Rock Shelter (Hanes 1988), and several sites in Coyote Flat (Butler 1970) and the Alkali Lake Basin (Fagan 1988; Willig 1989). Sites in Nevada include Last Supper Cave (Layton 1970, 1979), Falcon Hill (Hattori 1982), Sadmat (Tuohy 1981), Old Humboldt (Rusco and Davis 1987), and a number of sites in ancient lake basins such as Lake Tonapah (Tuohy 1988) and the Sunshine Well Locality (Hutchinson 1988). Several important California sites are also known, although most are outside the western Great Basin.

The spatial correlation of many early sites to ancient lakeside features has triggered some lively debate on the nature of general Western Clovis and Western Stemmed adaptive strategies, particularly in regard to the use of lacustrine or other specific resources (for example, Baumhoff and Heizer 1965; Bedwell 1973; Heizer and Baumhoff 1970; Tuohy 1974; Willig 1989). Although the common perception, held by many members of the public and some North American archaeologists, is that present evidence suggests that Paleoindians hunted megafauna and other large game, there are no acceptable data to support such a claim for all of far western North America. This purported big-game hunting specialization is more of a myth suggested by analogy to the Great Plains than a reality (Dansie et al. 1988; Haynes 1988). The question of wetland- (lake and marsh) focused strategies is also intriguing, as a growing body of data suggests that such a settlement focus was not a particularly specialized adaptation to these shifting environments but was only "one regional manifestation of a larger, more encompassing, broad-spectrum adaptation which existed throughout the Far West in the early Holocene . . . and late Pleistocene" (Willig and Aikens 1988:28).

If such a broad-spectrum adaptation was indeed in place, what subsistence differences really existed between Paleoindian strategies and those of the subsequent Archaic peoples? One major difference is evidenced in the scarcity of seed-grinding and storage technologies in Paleoindian sites compared to their relative abundance in Archaic contexts. These are important differences, but in the absence of direct subsistence data from Paleoindian sites, a general consensus is developing around the idea that overall, large-scale subsistence strategies of both cultures were similar. The details of regional subsistence foci, however, particularly as related to plant processing and storage, remain distinct between the two cultures. Even so, broad-spectrum adaptations of Western Archaic groups are rooted in the more limited but still wide-ranging strategies of Clovis and later Paleoindian adaptations.

It should also be noted that one site in the western Basin contains artifacts that may be older than the accepted age of Paleoindians. This is Fort Rock Cave in south central Oregon, where a small assemblage of flakes and flake tools was found in association with Pleistocene beach gravels dated to 13,200 B.P. (Bedwell 1970, 1973; Bedwell and Cressman 1971). This evidence for "pre-Clovis" peoples in North America is not well accepted, and it is generally assumed that the materials were intruded into this early horizon from more recent deposits overlaying the gravels (for example, Haynes 1971).

Archaic Adaptations: Questions of Mobility

For many of the past several decades, a substantial subsistence shift has been presumed to characterize the difference between terminal Pleistocene Paleoindian and Holocene Archaic cultures. This has revolved around the extent to which the various Paleoindian groups outside the Great Plains have specialized in the hunting of now extinct mammoths, mastodons, bison, and other megafauna. A long-standing but untested assumption has been that these early strategies throughout North America have been similar to those centered to varying degrees around large-game hunting in the Plains. So when Clovis, Folsom, and other Paleoindian projectile points have been found in, for example, the western Great Basin, they are assumed to be diagnostic of terminal Pleistocene large-game hunters. As mentioned, no clear evidence exists in the region to support this assumption. Instead, the little subsistence-related information that has been obtained from sites in the western Basin suggests broader-based strategies, similar in many aspects to those of the Archaic.

The Archaic here is used to define both a period of time between around 8,000 and 200 years ago and a series of archaeological "cultures" based on generalized subsistence. The latter is evidenced by certain projectile points, seed-processing and storage technologies, and relatively wide-ranging settlement patterns. The primary dichotomy in traditional terms was between the Paleoindian hunting specialty and the Archaic seed, plant, and animal generality. Now that the earlier "cultures" seem to have been less specialized than thought, the differences between the two major strategies are diminished. Several authors have called for new terms, such as *pre-Archaic* (Elston 1982, 1986; Jennings 1986), *Initial Archaic* (Oetting 1990), and *paleo-Archaic* (Willig 1989) for at least the latter part of the earlier period, to conceptualize the perceived continuum between the two. Others have argued that both *Paleoindian* and *Archaic* should be dropped and replaced by more regional cultural definitions, such as Western Pluvial Lakes tradition (Simms 1988). The replacement of *Paleoindian* may be warranted, although the term *Archaic* remains useful as a widely understood designator of both the overall time period and a long-lasting generalized adaptive strategy (see, however, Willig 1989; Willig and Aikens 1988).

EARLY ARCHAIC (CA. 8000–4000 B.P.)   This time in the western Great Basin saw a warming and drying trend that characterized the early Holocene in the entire region. Lakes and mountain glaciers shrank or disappeared as the precipitation pattern shifted to summer predominance. Sites dated to this period are rare, perhaps because of small human populations at the time or because many sites are buried under later alluvium. Diagnostic artifacts for the earliest portion of this period are Lake Mojave, Great Basin Stemmed, Black Rock Concave Base, and other of the stemmed varieties of projectile points included in the Western Stemmed tradition described above. Around 7,000 years ago, large Pinto stemmed varieties and Humboldt lanceolate styles, as well as large Northern side-notched and Elko corner-notched points (Figure 5.2; e–h) began to appear in the record. These were accompanied at a few sites by seed-grinding implements, bifacial knives and drills, unifacial scrapers, and a variety of flake tools. Nonlithic items found in cave sites included woven sage bark sandals, atlatl darts, nets, baskets, and bone awls. Important sites for this period are Fort Rock and Cougar Mountain caves (Bedwell 1973), Dirty Shame Rock Shelter (Aikens et al. 1977), and the pre-Mazama component at Skull Creek Dune Locality 1 (Wilde 1985) in Oregon. Nevada sites include Sadmat, Leonard Rock Shelter (Heizer and Hester 1978), the Falcon Hill caves (Hattori 1982), Last Supper Cave (Layton 1979), Fishbone Cave (Adovasio 1970), and possibly Spooner Lake (Elston 1971). Important sites dated to the latter part of this period include Gatecliff and Triple T Shelters (Thomas 1983), Hidden Cave (Thomas 1985), Silent Snake Springs (Layton and Thomas 1979), and Lovelock Cave (Heizer and Napton 1970). Most interesting are several sites in Surprise Valley, California, with large, substantial, semi-subterranean houses dated between 6500 and 4500 B.P. (O'Connell 1975). Shallow circular structures dated to this general period are known from the Cocanour (Stanley et al. 1970) and Stahl (Harrington 1957) sites.

Settlement and subsistence almost everywhere except Surprise Valley during this period appear to have been focused on small mobile groups who traveled from resource to resource, with perhaps some more intensive settlement centered around lacustrine environments (Elston 1982, 1986; Layton 1970). Population density was low, especially near the end of the period, and little direct subsistence data has been found. The much greater degree of sedentism implied by the labor-intensive structures in Surprise Valley suggests the presence of early centrally based collecting economies in that area that presaged later settlement and subsistence systems in various locations throughout the western Great Basin.

MIDDLE ARCHAIC (CA. 4000–1500 B.P.)   This period saw the end of the general drying and warming trend that characterized the middle Holocene. Many of the basin lakes that had shrunk or dried during the early Holocene began to reappear after about 4200 B.P., during what has been called the neoglacial or neopluvial interval (Davis 1982; Mehringer 1986; Weide 1982). Lake Tahoe resupplied the Truckee River, Pyramid Lake rose, the first Fallon Lake appeared in the Carson Sink, and intermittent lakes appeared in the Black Rock Desert and in many other basins throughout the western region. Mountain glaciers expanded, and winter precipitation prevailed. These environmental changes coincided with marked increases in cultural complexity in the western Basin, evidenced by the wide variety of textiles, baskets, wooden items, snares, bone tools, mountain sheep horn tools, projectile points, stone sculpture, and other artifacts found in caves and other sites throughout the region. The most widespread characteristic projectile point styles (Figure 5.2; d–f, h) are Gypsum, Gatecliff Split-stem, and members of the Elko series (Holmer 1986; Wilde 1985). Bifaces made from quarried materials are common during this time (Singer and Ericson 1977). Other more geographically restricted diagnostics include multiple-warp sandals in Oregon, marine shell beads and Martis series projectile points in California, and Lovelock wickerware baskets in the Lahontan Basin.

Important middle Archaic sites include many of those mentioned above, such as Dirty Shame Rock Shelter, the Falcon Hill caves, Lovelock Cave, and Gatecliff Shelter. Others of importance in Oregon include Catlow and Roaring Springs caves (Wilde 1985) and sites in Warner Valley (Weide 1968; Cannon et al. 1990) and around Lake Abert and Chewaucan Marsh (Pettigrew 1985; Oetting 1990). Ezra's Retreat (Bard et al. 1979), South Fork Shelter (Heizer et al. 1968), Wagon Jack Shelter (Heizer and Baumhoff 1961), Newark Cave (Fowler 1968), Lowe Shelter (Self 1980), James Creek Shelter (Elston and Budy 1990), and Dangberg Hot Springs (Elsasser 1960; Elston 1970) are some of the important Nevada sites. California sites include the Martis Complex camps at Bordertown (Elston 1979), Karlos (Riddell 1960), and Hobo Hot Springs (Elsasser 1960; Elston 1970). The Martis Complex sites are considered winter campsites with shallow pit houses, earth ovens, and abundant artifactual remains, and they are similar in some of these regards to other middle Archaic sites around Pyramid Lake and in the Humboldt Sink. Many of these winter camps are associated with hunting, seed-gathering, and lithic procurement sites in valley margin and upland environments. The semi-subterranean houses in Surprise Valley were abandoned just prior to this period and were replaced with less labor-intensive, shallow, basin-shaped ephemeral structures. A shift also occurred in Owens Valley, as riverine environments were abandoned in favor of desert scrub ecozones and upland areas between 3500 and 1500 B.P. (Bettinger 1977). These settlement changes may have been related to a combination of increased human population pressure and the ameliorating climate that enhanced productivity in the desert scrub and pinyon communities.

As Elston noted (1982:197), the middle Archaic period is more of an intensification of early Archaic patterns than a shift of any remarkable degree:

> The transition . . . was gradual and cannot be defined precisely. There are no large technological breaks between the two, and the changes are those of emphasis and quality.

There is more of everything in the Mid[dle]-Archaic. In most places there seems to have been an increase in the diversity of the resources utilized, which involved a greater emphasis on seeds in addition to big game. The increase in resource diversity was accompanied in some areas by a decrease in the range of ecozones exploited because climatic improvement resulted in the increased variety and productivity of plant communities in particular ecozones, and fewer zones had to be exploited.

LATE ARCHAIC (CA. 1500–200 B.P.)   The transition between middle and late Archaic is more abrupt, marked by technological transitions and additions. One major transition was from atlatl and dart to bow and arrow. This occurred earlier in the northwestern Great Basin than in the area to the south but had been accomplished throughout the region by 1500 B.P. (Wilde 1985: fig. 14). The most visible diagnostic change was the replacement, beginning around 2,000 years ago, of larger Elko series dart points with smaller Rose Spring and Eastgate (Rosegate; Thomas 1981) arrow points (Figure 5.2; b, c). In addition, hullers and various mortar forms were added to the mano and metate for processing seeds and other kinds of hard-coated resources. Brownware pottery and Desert series projectile points (Figure 5.2; a) had spread throughout the region by about 1,000 years ago. Such suites of changes suggest that major social or ethnic changes were under way in the late Archaic, culminating in patterns observed in ethnographic times. These patterns further suggest that ancestors of Numic-speaking historic groups, such as Northern and Owens Valley Paiute and Western Shoshone, came into the region during the beginning of this period (for example, Bettinger and Baumhoff 1982; Lamb 1958). Others see the development of Numic languages as an in situ development in the western and central Great Basin (Aikens and Witherspoon 1986; Goss 1977). Those who interpret linguistic and archaeological data as supporting migrations of new people into the region from southern California often call the late Archaic the Numic or late prehistoric period. In any case, speculations about invading peoples do not provide testable models (Simms 1983), and no clear-cut material culture attributes have been shown to correlate to linguistic and ethnic boundaries in the Great Basin (Elston 1982; O'Connell et al. 1982; see also Adovasio 1986, for a dissenting view).

The late Archaic began about the same time as the late Holocene warming and drying trend in the western Basin. This was relatively mild compared to earlier climatic shifts and was accompanied by predominately summer precipitation patterns until around 800–600 B.P., when the region returned to more effective moisture and a predominately winter precipitation pattern (Davis 1982). This ameliorating climatic pattern seems to have begun somewhat later (ca. 400 B.P.) in the northwestern Basin (Mehringer and Wigand 1984).

Sites occupied during the late Archaic are more abundant than those of previous periods, partly because of increased populations and partly because of their more recent, hence more visible, nature. Oregon sites include the Headquarters and other sites around Malheur Lake (Aikens and Greenspan 1988), Tule Springs Hearth site (Wilde 1989), Lake Abert sites (Oetting 1990), Dirty Shame Rock Shelter (Aikens et al. 1977), and Warner Valley sites (Weide 1968). Gatecliff Shelter (Thomas 1983), South Fork Shelter (Heizer et al. 1968), James Creek Shelter

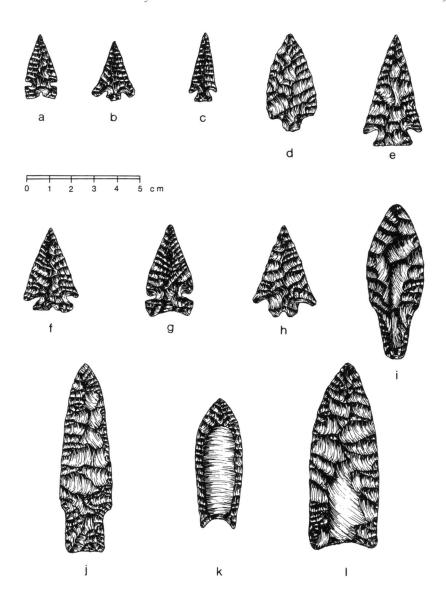

Figure 5.2 Projectile points used as chronological markers in the Great Basin. (a) Desert Side-notched. (b) Eastgate Expanding Stem (Rosegate). (c) Rose Spring Corner-notched (Rosegate). (d) Gypsum (Gatecliff Contracting Stem). (e) Elko Corner-notched. (f) Elko Eared. (g) Northern Side-notched; (h) Gatecliff Split Stem. (i) Great Basin Stemmed (Parman). (j) Great Basin Stemmed (Windust). (k) Folsom. (l) Clovis.

(Elston and Budy 1990), Lovelock Cave (Heizer and Napton 1970), Alta Toquima (Thomas 1982a), and abundant sites in and around Stillwater Marsh and the Carson Sink (Kelly 1985; Raven 1990; Raven and Elston 1988a, 1988b, 1989; Raymond and Parks 1990; Tuohy et al. 1987) are important west central Nevada sites. Humboldt Cave (Heizer and Krieger 1956), Winnemucca and Pyramid Lake sites (Tuohy 1974, 1990), and sites at Rye Patch Reservoir (Rusco and Davis 1987) are in the Lahontan Basin. Late sites in northern California are part of the Kings Beach Complex, thought to be the precursor of the ethnographic Washoe (Heizer and Elsasser 1953; James et al. 1982). Important sites are also known from Owens and Long Valleys in California (Bettinger 1982) and the Walker Lake region of western Nevada (Rhode 1990).

The general late Archaic pattern seems to have been focused on fish, seeds, and animal resources, with evidence from many areas suggesting increased emphasis on a variety of fauna (Elston 1986). Winter villages may be evident in the Malheur, Warner Valley, and Lake Abert regions of Oregon. The Kings Beach Complex in northern California saw a shift from larger pit houses to smaller and shallower houses after around 800 years ago. People in this area focused on seeds, fishing, jackrabbits, and other small game. Sites in the Stillwater Marsh–Carson Sink area suggest that general exploitation of marsh resources did not change much between around 3,200 and 1,500 B.P., when a slight intensification of residential usage of marsh resources occurred, evidenced primarily by increased numbers of Rosegate points (Kelly 1988; Raven 1990). Another slight shift occurred in the area around 550 B.P. that may be related to the influx of Numic speakers (Raymond and Parks 1990). Owens Valley is an apparent cultural anomaly, as its sites suggest intensive exploitation of pinyon nuts from midaltitude base camps, associated, at least after about 1,000 B.P., with high-altitude hunting camps in the White Mountains (Bettinger 1977, 1989, 1991). The high-altitude site of Alta Toquima, on Mount Jefferson, indicates a similar focus on hunting and seed processing in the central Basin during this time (Thomas 1982a).

The period of Euroamerican contact began around 200 B.P. in the western Great Basin. This is usually called the Ethnographic Period, and much of what we know about it is based on ethnohistoric data. The highly mobile Western Shoshone groups in the central Basin, described by Steward (1938), provided the basis for the majority of inferences regarding human adaptation in the Great Basin until only recently, when regional differences were illuminated. Much recent work has focused on questions of mobility and sedentism and around the environmental conditions that might allow one pattern or the other. Most past environments that are associated with degrees of sedentism in the western Great Basin are lakes and marshes. One current research focus is on defining the degree of "limno-mobility" and "limno-sedentism" that obtained throughout the past in various major drainage areas within the Great Basin (for example, Fowler and Fowler 1990; Kelly 1990, 1992; Madsen 1990; Rhode 1990; Thomas 1985, 1990). Many of these discussions grow out of and are related to regional models of settlement, subsistence, and environmental reconstruction, essentially past human ecology.

The next section goes beyond questions of time and space and presents some proposed models of human paleoecology in the western Great Basin. This change in emphasis reflects broad shifts over the past three decades in archaeological thought and research foci, from those primarily related to questions of time and space to those also dealing with human ecology and behavior. It is appropriate to include these brief discussions of models of human adaptations in an overview of general biogeography in western North America.

REGIONAL MODELS OF WESTERN GREAT BASIN PREHISTORY

The primary foci of cultural/environmental models in the region have been reconstructions of climatic patterns over the past 12,000 years. The most pervasive climatological theory was proposed by Antevs in 1948. It involves the concept of an increasingly warm and drying postglacial climate until an arid thermal maximum or "Altithermal" Period was reached in the middle Holocene. The climate ameliorated from that point to relatively mild modern conditions. Into this scheme were placed prehistoric human adaptations in the Great Basin and elsewhere, to suggest a proposed long cultural abandonment of various regions in response to an inhospitable environment during the Altithermal (for example, Antevs 1948; Baumhoff and Heizer 1965; Fagan 1974; Hurt 1966; Mulloy 1958; and Stephenson 1965). The controversy surrounding the utility of this climatic framework as an explanatory model for regional or local cultural change has sparked the current intense research emphasis on climates of the past 12,000 years. Essentially independent avenues of research, such as sedimentation, tree-ring studies, paleobiogeography, paleolimnology, tectonism, and archaeology, have been used concomitantly for interpreting specific microclimates and local or regional human adaptive systems.

The term *paleoecological model* is here taken to refer to a construct that attempts to explain past human behavior as an adaptation or series of adaptations to regional environmental factors. This group contains works that attempt systematically to relate the settlement patterns of a particular regional group to the resources of a circumscribed area. The relations thus described are termed "settlement-subsistence systems" (Winters 1963; Struever 1968, 1971) and are defined as "regional patterns of cultural ecology" or "ecological adaptive patterns" (Aikens 1970:202). Thus, a settlement-subsistence system is the set of rules that generate a particular settlement pattern. The system "cannot be empirically derived, but at least some of the rules can be deduced by simulation or the use of probabilistic models" (Flannery 1976:162). They cannot be empirically defined because climate and environment are multidimensional and can only be reconstructed through proxy data, or "nonclimatic variables that covary with climate" (Bryson 1985:285). These include pollen, geomorphological, botanical, archaeological, and soil data. Hence, paleoecological models can be deduced only from interpretations of such data and are not directly observable. The following are some western Great Basin paleoecological models.

Steward's Ethnographic Model

The earliest model considered here was one Steward proposed in 1938. Using his ethnographic studies of Shoshonean subsistence patterns and culture, Steward argued that the Great Basin had a socially fragmenting effect upon its prehistoric inhabitants. The harsh, unpredictable environment placed such constraints upon the social system that institutions more complex than the nuclear family were notably absent. Ecological relationships predetermined the population density; limited the size, mobility, and distribution of village groups; and restricted economic cooperation. The Shoshonean subsistence pattern was based on the exploitation of contiguous but dissimilar microenvironments. Pinyon nuts and seeds formed the staples of the system, while hunting was essentially a supplemental resource-obtaining activity.

The Shoshonean settlement and subsistence system was centered on a well-defined seasonal round that permitted the coordination of resource gathering into an overall network. Dispersed resources necessitated a small and fragmented social group system throughout the year. The availability and abundance of pinyon nuts, however, enabled social group coalescence into semi-permanent winter camps. These were often located in ecotonal environments between sagebrush-grassland flatlands and the pinyon-juniper foothill regions of the eastern Great Basin. Conditions necessary for this coalescence were "accessibility to stored seeds, especially pine nuts, water, sufficient wood for house building and fuel, and the absence of extremely low winter temperatures" (Steward 1938:232). During group coalescence enough people and energy were available for communal jackrabbit and less frequent antelope hunts. Family groups resumed nomadic rounds in the summer, exploiting plant resources as they became available. Most groups returned the following winter to reoccupy the winter village site or its general vicinity so that group winter village areas remained stable for long periods.

Steward proposed this model as a generalization of the basic hunter-gatherer settlement and subsistence system in the Great Basin; it is not directly applicable to any particular location. He also understood that more productive areas within the Basin may have supported essentially different systems. Since 1938, this proposal has been pervasive as the basic model of hunter-gatherer ecology.

The Desert Culture Model

Although not based on any regional systemic study, Jennings's (1957) concept of a Desert Culture adaptation has been applied to the whole of the Great Basin as well as other arid regions of North America and elsewhere. Originally set out to account for the record of Danger Cave in northwestern Utah, this model of hunter-gatherer ecology proposed a stable settlement and subsistence system that did not change significantly for the past 10,000 years. Beginning at the end of the Pleistocene and lasting into the historic period, regional subsistence patterns were broadly similar and were based on the intensive but unspecialized exploitation of all available food resources. Seen as a response to the relatively unproductive desert environment, this adaptation was thought to have been essentially unaffected by long-term climatic changes, especially the Altithermal (Antevs 1948). The major outlines of this argument were based on the model of Shoshonean ecological adaptation Steward proposed. Indeed,

Jennings (1957:8) claimed that the subsistence pattern of the Shoshone was a "vivid contemporary description of the Desert Culture lifeway." Although unsubstantiated by settlement pattern data, this view of human adaptation persisted for some time as the model of Archaic lifeways not only in the Great Basin but throughout North and South America.

With the shift in American archaeology toward more systemic explanations of culture change and continuity, the models Jennings and Steward proposed have come to be regarded as inadequate to describe the full range of human adaptations in the Great Basin. As regions and regional systems became the focus of paleoenvironmental studies, both the diversity and richness of Great Basin environments and cultures became apparent.

Lower Humboldt Valley Model

Heizer (1956), Heizer and Napton (1970), Napton (1969), and Rozaire (1963) proposed a regional settlement and subsistence system for the lower Humboldt Valley of west central Nevada. This system is characterized by permanent or semi-permanent settlements located along the margins of Humboldt Lake and the broad marshy sloughs of the lower Humboldt River. The earliest clearly definable regional adaptation dates from 4,600 to 1,500 years ago, although evidence exists for earlier occupations in the area 7,100 to 8,700 years ago. Strong evidence of a marsh and lakeside adaptation comes from several sites, most of which are not fully reported (Livingston 1986, 1988). Remains of several semi-subterranean houses were found in the Humboldt Lake Bed Site and at a site within the town of Lovelock, Nevada. Because pit house structures require a relatively high energy expenditure to build and maintain, they indicate a high degree of occupational sedentism based on the rich marsh and lakeside resources. These include cattail, bulrush, tule, waterfowl, and small mammals abundant in localized areas (Livingston 1988).

Heizer (1956) and Napton (1969) have interpreted the lower Humboldt River Valley lacustrine system as directly contradicting the Desert Culture model. They argued that diverse regional subsistence patterns vary according to local environmental conditions, sometimes involving specialized use of a few abundant resources to the exclusion of others potentially exploitable. They further argued that many of these regional subsistence patterns bear little resemblance to Steward's Shoshonean model.

Warner Valley Model

In 1968 Weide described the marsh and lakeside adaptations of the Warner Valley of south central Oregon. She tested the efficacy of the lacustrine model proposed for the Humboldt River region to explain the more Desert Culture–like adaptations in the Warner Valley. Instead of the heavy marsh and lake resource dependence described by Heizer and Napton, Weide was able to define a Warner Valley settlement and subsistence system, operating between 3,500 and 1,500 years ago, as primarily lake- and marsh-oriented but with substantial reliance on upland animal resources. Some winter occupation sites were utilized by large groups over many years, whereas summer habitation sites appeared to be smaller, specific-resource-oriented camps, occupied for short periods by family-sized units.

> This sequence of community poses reconstructed for the Warner [Valley] . . . is not different in kind from that of the Desert Culture. The composition of the winter community may have been more consistent from year to year, however. The settlement pattern with the concentration of both winter village sites and family summer camps on the valley floor is a particular reflection of the great use of lake and marsh resources and contrasts with Desert Culture settlement patterns. (Weide 1968:389)

More recent work in Warner Valley has corroborated and refined this interpretation (Cannon et al. 1990). As Weide, Heizer, Napton, and Rozaire discovered, localized resource-rich environments associated with marsh and lake settings represented areas where the general models proposed by Steward and Jennings were not applicable. The majority of Great Basin valleys, especially in the central Basin, contained little or no marshlands; in these areas the Shoshonean model was thought to be more representative.

Reese River Model

Thomas (1971, 1973) has defined a settlement and subsistence system that apparently operated in central Nevada for the past 4,500 years. This model is similar to that proposed by Steward and was in fact designed as an empirical test of Steward's model. The Reese River system comprised two seasonally occupied base camps: one, inhabited during the summer, located in the sagebrush grassland of the valley floors, and the other, a large winter camp, located in the juniper-pinyon woodland on the valley flanks and hillsides. Subsistence at the winter camps was based on large stores of pinyon nuts, as well as on jackrabbit and antelope obtained through communal collections and hunts during the fall. Summer camps were characterized by foraging for roots, seeds, and small game by dispersed, possibly family-sized groups. "This adaptation, an 'on the fence' compromise between wandering and sedentary life, seemed to provide the flexibility required for success in a situation such as the central Great Basin" (Thomas 1973:173).

This model relies heavily on the assumption that pinyon nuts could be obtained in necessary quantities every year in the same locality. Actually, pinyon groves seem to produce heavy crops every five to seven years, necessitating a yearly movement of winter base camps to new locations or different winter strategies between good crop years.

Surprise Valley Model

The Surprise Valley of northeastern California was the scene of a system composed of two variants, the later apparently less stable than the earlier. O'Connell (1971, 1975) proposed a settlement-subsistence system that began operating about 6,500 years ago in Surprise Valley and possibly other well-watered regions along the northwestern edge of the Great Basin. During the early variant, called the Menlo phase, around 6,500 to 4,500 years ago, settlements were fully or semi-permanent the year round. They consisted of large semi-subterranean earth lodges exhibiting nearly continuous occupation for periods of several years. Subsistence at these sites was based primarily on marsh and grassland resources, supplemented by large upland animals in the winter months, with rabbits and waterfowl during the summer.

The later variant appeared about 4,500 years ago and lasted into historic times. It was characterized by small groups, possibly nuclear family units, occupying temporary brush wickiups for relatively short periods. Settlements apparently remained semi-sedentary, but occupation of particular sites was much less permanent than before. Marsh resources remained primary, but a greater proportion of plant foods was obtained from arid environments, especially greasewood and saltbush communities along the valley flanks. Faunal resources were exploited in patterns similar to those of the previous period.

The Surprise Valley system is similar to that proposed for the lower Humboldt Valley. One site in particular from that region, NV-Ch-15, was described as containing "domestic structures and . . . [an] array of artifacts . . . similar in nearly all respects to those found at post–Menlo phase lowland occupation sites in Surprise Valley. . . . Preliminary work indicates that fish, waterfowl, and the seeds of marsh plants were the most important foods" (O'Connell 1975:49).

Additional evidence for the importance of lake margin resources has been drawn from Lovelock Cave, about 2 miles southeast of NV-Ch-15 (Heizer and Napton 1970). Given this evidence, we can suggest that the principal difference between human-environment relationships in Surprise Valley and those from the past 4,500 years in the lower Humboldt Valley involves the details of subsistence, with the inhabitants of the latter more dependent upon lacustrine or marsh resources than those of the former. Settlement patterns in both areas involve fixed, semi-permanent camps occupied in all seasons of the year. Individual settlements in the lower Humboldt may have been somewhat larger than those in Surprise Valley, but with the exception of the earlier Menlo phase houses in the latter area, there is no evidence of difference in family size and composition or in complexity of social and political organization between the two areas (O'Connell 1975:49).

Owens Valley Model

Bettinger (1975, 1977, 1978, 1982) has described the dynamic nature of Owens Valley, California, settlement and subsistence systems over time. His analysis of site categories and artifact classes demonstrated that although the basic system in Owens Valley remained relatively stable, major settlement and subsistence changes were discernible. He found that lowland occupation sites served as base camps during most seasons of the year throughout the prehistoric period. He also found that subsistence for most of the prehistoric past was primarily based on lowland root and seed resources, with secondary emphasis on upland and animal resources.

In contrast to these broadly stable early systems, site analyses indicated that three important changes had occurred during the later Holocene: (1) A shift in the primary resource system from riverine plant to desert scrub exploitation was reflected in a similar shift in lowland base camp settlement from riverine to scrub environments. This occurred between 3,500 and 1,400 years ago and may have been the result of a climatic change from arid to relatively moist conditions (Bettinger 1977:15). (2) There was an increasing emphasis on pinyon exploitation between 1,400 and 1,000 years ago, as indicated by the appearance of pinyon-juniper zone sites. This may have been the result of another climatic change reducing productivity of the desert scrub zone (Bettinger 1977:15). (3) A shift away from large-game hunting occurred after around 1,000 years ago, as indicated by a decrease in the number of upland sites during this period, triggered by the intensification of lowland resource exploitation. This resulted in the establishment of large-scale, wild plant crop irrigation systems in the valley.

Bettinger utilized this view of dynamic and environmentally reactive settlement and subsistence systems in Owens Valley to argue that the Desert Culture concept is not valid in the western Great Basin (1977:15). He suggests that the model proposed by Heizer and Napton for the lower Humboldt is more consistent with the dynamic nature of the Owens Valley system.

Steens Mountain Model

A major attempt was made to obtain a comprehensive environmental record of the past 12,000 years during the Steens Mountain Prehistory Project (Aikens et al. 1982). This was correlated with cultural events on and around Steens Mountain to build a model of past settlement. In general, human habitation in the area has been stable throughout the past 10,000 years, although significant patterns can be seen in the archaeological record.

Site utilization and formation rates changed in response to population and environmental shifts, increasing in periods of cooler and wetter climate and decreasing in drier, warmer times (Beck 1984). Site numbers gradually increased from early low levels between around 10,000 and 5,000 years ago, during a time of relatively warm and dry conditions. The few sites known suggest that average site area was relatively large but was declining throughout the period. A marked increase in the overall number of sites occurred between 5,000 and 2,500 years ago, during the period of increased effective moisture and generally cooler temperatures. Mean site area decreased during this time, suggesting a more dispersed settlement pattern. The number of sites declined, but their average size was increased between about 2500 and 1,500 B.P., during the end of the cooler and wetter episode and the beginning of a drier and warmer climatic interval. Site frequency went up again after 1,500 years ago, and site size continued to decline as the drier and warmer interval progressed. Another cooler and wetter period began around 400 years ago, but no apparent changes in site frequency or size were noted in the record.

The inverse relationship between site frequency and site size suggests that people were aggregating and creating larger but fewer sites during certain periods, particularly between 2,500 and 1,500 years ago. This is when it appears that high resource productivity allowed population nucleation in both upland and lowland sites that were located to optimally exploit those particular resources (Beck 1984). Other periods, when relatively abundant but small sites predominated, appear to have been times of decreased productivity throughout the general region. The only sites with evidence of more intensive and long-term occupations were found near relatively rare springs, desert marshes, and other more productive environments. The Tule Springs Hearth site in the Alvord Basin east of Steens Mountain is one such site occupied during the late Archaic (Wilde 1985, 1989).

DIRECTIONS FOR FUTURE RESEARCH

Most regional models in the western Great Basin are centered on valleys with relatively abundant marsh, riverine, and lakeside resources. Models effectively describing settlement and subsistence patterns in areas outside these rich environments are rare but are expected to be the focus of future research. The Shoshone model may in fact adequately describe some prehistoric adaptations in these areas, as Thomas (1973) has suggested from work in the Reese River Valley.

The primary questions regarding past activities and behavior in the western Great Basin are still not adequately addressed, even in the regional models discussed above. Fundamental issues of why people respond the way they do are not really explained by invoking even strong correlations with environmental variables. These models may form relatively accurate descriptions of past events but do not as yet explain past behavior. A way toward explanation is to pose questions in terms of testable hypotheses within the frameworks of some explanatory theory. One approach toward such explanatory research is couched in terms of evolutionary ecology and relies on models that propose that "variation in the behavior of individual organisms is shaped by natural selection . . . and that it identifies a single goal, the maximization of potential reproductive success, toward which all behavior is directed and in terms of which it can be predicted" (O'Connell et al. 1982:233).

A way of measuring this kind of fitness is through use of optimal foraging theory, where generally more efficient strategies, those that produce greater returns of energy, will be chosen more often than those that are less efficient. These approaches usually rely on ethnographic analogy, especially in terms of food rank, energy expended, and energy returned in native systems. Comparisons are then made between patterns in the analog and patterns seen in the past to build foraging models that may explain past subsistence and, by extension, settlement practices.

Foraging models have been built in the Malheur region of Oregon (Couture 1980; Couture et al. 1986), the Carson Sink and Stillwater Marsh areas of western Nevada (Kelly 1990; Raven 1990; Raven and Elston 1988a, 1988b, 1989), James Creek Shelter in central Nevada (Elston and Budy 1990), and in portions of the eastern Basin (for example, Simms 1987; Madsen and Jones 1989). This line of inquiry is expected to form the theoretical foundation of more and more future research throughout the Great Basin. More basic questions of mobility and permanence and the conditions surrounding the long-term adoption of either or both are still at the center of regional research. Interregional research will focus on trade and exchange systems and will probably follow patterns recently established by Hughes (1986) in discussing long-range obsidian procurement and exchange in northeastern California and south central Oregon.

ACKNOWLEDGMENTS

I thank several people who aided in the preparation of this chapter: W. M. Hess, who helped initiate the project; C. Melvin Aikens and Deborah E. Newman, who reviewed various drafts; and Joel C. Janetski, Robert G. Elston, and an anonymous reviewer, who provided critical comments, additional references, and important suggestions. Tuula Rose illustrated the projectile points and drafted the map of sites in the Great Basin.

LITERATURE CITED

Adovasio, J. M. 1970. The Origin, Development, and Distribution of Western Archaic Textiles. Tebiwa: Miscellaneous Papers of the Idaho State University Museum of Natural History 13: 1–40.

Adovasio, J. M. 1986. Artifacts and Ethnicity: Basketry as an Indicator of Territoriality and Population Movements in the Prehistoric Great Basin. *In:* C. J. Condie and D. D. Fowler (eds.), Anthropology of the Desert West: Essays in Honor of Jesse D. Jennings. University of Utah Press, Salt Lake City.

Aikens, C. M. 1970. Hogup Cave. University of Utah Anthropological Papers No. 93. Salt Lake City.

Aikens, C. M. 1982. Archaeology of the Northern Great Basin: An Overview. *In:* D. B. Madsen and J. F. O'Connell (eds.), Man and Environment in the Great Basin. Society for American Archaeology Papers 2.

Aikens, C. M. 1983a. Environmental Archaeology in the Western United States, pp. 239–251. *In:* H. E. Wright, Jr. (ed.), The Holocene, Volume 2: Late Quaternary Environments of the United States. University of Minnesota Press, Minneapolis.

Aikens, C. M. 1983b. The Far West. *In:* J. D. Jennings (ed.), Ancient North Americans. W. H. Freeman, San Francisco.

Aikens, C. M., D. L. Cole, and R. Stuckenrath. 1977. Excavations at Dirty Shame Rockshelter, Southeastern Oregon. Tebiwa: Miscellaneous Papers of the Idaho State University Museum of Natural History 4.

Aikens, C. M., D. K. Grayson, and P. J. Mehringer, Jr. 1982. Final Report to the National Science Foundation on the Steens Mountain Prehistory Project. MS on file, Department of Anthropology, University of Oregon, Eugene.

Aikens, C. M., and R. L. Greenspan. 1988. Ancient Lakeside Culture in the Northern Great Basin: Malheur Lake, Oregon. Journal of California and Great Basin Anthropology 10: 32–61.

Aikens, C. M., and Y. T. Witherspoon. 1986. Great Basin Numic Prehistory: Linguistics, Archeology, and Environment. *In:* C. J. Condie and D. D. Fowler (eds.), Anthropology of the Desert West: Essays in Honor of Jesse D. Jennings. University of Utah Press, Salt Lake City.

Antevs, E. 1948. Climatic Changes and Pre-White Man, pp. 168–191. *In:* The Great Basin with Emphasis on Glacial and Postglacial Times. Biological Series 10, University of Utah Bulletin 38. Salt Lake City.

Bard, J. C., C. I. Busby, and L. S. Kobori. 1979. Ezra's Retreat: A Rockshelter/Cave in the North Central Great Basin. Center for Archaeological Research at Davis Publication 6.

Baumhoff, M. A., and R. F. Heizer. 1965. Postglacial Climate and Archaeology in the Desert West, pp. 697–707. *In:* H. E. Wright, Jr., and D. G. Frey (eds.), The Quaternary of the United States. Princeton University Press, Princeton.

Beck, C. 1984. Steens Mountain Surface Archaeology: The Sites. Ph.D. Dissertation, University of Washington, Seattle.

Bedwell, S. F. 1970. Prehistory and Environment of the Pluvial Fort Rock Lake Area of Southcentral Oregon. Ph.D. Dissertation, University of Oregon, Eugene.

Bedwell, S. F. 1973. Fort Rock Basin Prehistory and Environment. University of Oregon Books, Eugene.

Bedwell, S. F., and L. S. Cressman. 1971. Fort Rock Report: Prehistory and Environment of the Pluvial Fort Rock Lake Area of South-Central Oregon. University of Oregon Anthropological Papers 1: 1–25. Eugene.

Bettinger, R. L. 1975. The Surface Archaeology of Owens Valley, Eastern California: Prehistoric Man-Land Relationships in the Great Basin. Ph.D. Dissertation, University of California, Riverside.

Bettinger, R. L. 1977. Aboriginal Human Ecology in Owens Valley, Eastern California: Prehistoric Culture Change in the Great Basin. American Antiquity 42: 3–17.

Bettinger, R. L. 1978. Alternative Adaptive Strategies in the Prehistoric Great Basin. Journal of Anthropological Research 34: 27–46.

Bettinger, R. L. 1982. Archaeology East of the Range of Light: Aboriginal Human Ecology of the Inyo-Mono Region, California. Monographs in California and Great Basin Prehistory. Foundation for the Publication of Monographs in California and Great Basin Anthropology, Davis.

Bettinger, R. L. 1989. The Archaeology of Pinyon House, Two Eagles, and Crater Middens: Three Residential Sites in Owens Valley, Eastern California. Anthropological Papers of the American Museum of Natural History 67.

Bettinger, R. L. 1991. Aboriginal Occupation at High Altitude: Alpine Villages in the White Mountains of Eastern California. American Anthropologist 93: 656–679.

Bettinger, R. L., and M. A. Baumhoff. 1982. The Numic Spread: Great Basin Cultures in Competition. American Antiquity 47: 485–503.

Bryson, R. A. 1985. On Climatic Analogs in Paleoclimatic Reconstruction. Quaternary Research 23: 275–286.

Butler, B. R. 1970. A Surface Collection from Coyote Flat, Southeastern Oregon. Tebiwa: Miscellaneous Papers of the Idaho State University Museum of Natural History 13: 34–57.

Cannon, W. J., C. C. Creger, D. D. Fowler, E. M. Hattori, and M. F. Ricks. 1990. A Wetlands and Uplands Settlement-Subsistence Model for Warner Valley, Oregon. In: J. C. Janetski and D. B. Madsen (eds.), Wetland Adaptations in the Great Basin. Brigham Young University Museum of Peoples and Cultures Occasional Papers 1.

Couture, M. 1980. Some Notes on Harney Valley Paiute Spring Foraging Practices. Paper presented at the 17th Great Basin Anthropological Conference, Salt Lake City.

Couture, M. D., M. F. Ricks, and L. Housley. 1986. Foraging Behavior of a Contemporary Northern Great Basin Population. Journal of California and Great Basin Anthropology 8: 150–160.

Cressman, L. S. 1986. Prehistory of the Northern Area. In: W. L. d'Azevedo (ed.), Great Basin, Volume 11: Handbook of North American Indians. Smithsonian Institution, Washington D.C.

Dansie, A. J., J. O. Davis, and T. W. Stafford, Jr. 1988. The Wizards Beach Recession: Farmdalian (25,500 Yr B.P.) Vertebrate Fossils Co-occur with Early Holocene Artifacts. In: J. A. Willig, C. M. Aikens, and J. L. Fagan (eds.), Early Human Occupation in Far Western North America: The Clovis-Archaic Interface. Nevada State Museum Anthropological Papers 21.

Davis, E. L. 1978. The Ancient Californias: Rancholabrean Hunters of the Mojave Lakes Country. Natural History Museum of Los Angeles County, Sciences Series 29. Los Angeles.

Davis, J. O. 1982. Bits and Pieces: The Last 35,000 Years in the Lahontan Area. *In:* D. B. Madsen and J. F. O'Connell (eds.), Man and Environment in the Great Basin. Society for American Archaeology Papers 2.

Elsasser, A. L. 1960. The Archaeology of the Sierra Nevada in California and Nevada. University of California Archaeological Survey Reports 51. Berkeley.

Elston, R. G. 1970. A Test Excavation at Dangberg Hot Springs. Nevada Archaeological Survey Reporter 4: 3–5.

Elston, R. G. 1971. A Contribution to Washoe Prehistory. Nevada Archaeological Survey Research Paper 2. Carson City.

Elston, R. G. 1979. The Archaeology of U.S. 395 Right of Way Between Stead, Nevada, and Hallelujah Junction, California. Report submitted to the California Department of Transportation and the Nevada Department of Highways. Nevada Archaeological Survey, University of Nevada, Reno.

Elston, R. G. 1982. Good Times, Hard Times: Prehistoric Culture Change in the Western Great Basin. *In:* D. B. Madsen and J. F. O'Connell (eds.), Man and Environment in the Great Basin. Society for American Archaeology Papers 2.

Elston, R. G. 1986. Prehistory of the Western Area. *In:* W. L. d'Azevedo (ed.), Great Basin, Volume 11: Handbook of North American Indians. Smithsonian, Washington D.C.

Elston, R. G., and E. E. Budy (eds.). 1990. The Archaeology of James Creek Shelter. University of Utah Anthropological Papers 115. Salt Lake City.

Fagan, J. L. 1974. Altithermal Occupation of Spring Sites in the Northern Great Basin. University of Oregon Anthropological Papers 6. Eugene.

Fagan, J. L. 1988. Clovis and Western Pluvial Lakes Tradition Lithic Technologies at the Dietz Site in South-Central Oregon, pp. 389–416. *In:* J. A. Willig, C. M. Aikens, and J. L. Fagan (eds.), Early Human Occupation in Far Western North America: The Clovis-Archaic Interface. Nevada State Museum Anthropological Papers 21.

Flannery, K. V. 1976. The Evolution of Complex Settlement Systems, pp. 162–172. *In:* K. V. Flannery (ed.), The Early Mesoamerican Village. Academic Press, New York.

Fowler, D. D. 1968. The Archaeology of Newark Cave, White Pine County, Nevada. University of Nevada, Desert Research Institute Social Sciences and Humanities Publications 3. Reno.

Fowler, D. D., and C. S. Fowler. 1990. A History of Wetlands Anthropology in the Great Basin. *In:* J. C. Janetski and D. B. Madsen (eds.), Wetland Adaptations in the Great Basin. Brigham Young University Museum of Peoples and Cultures Occasional Papers 1.

Goss, J. A. 1977. Linguistic Tools for the Great Basin Prehistorian. *In:* D. D. Fowler (ed.), Models and Great Basin Prehistory: A Symposium. Desert Research Institute Publications in the Social Sciences 12: 49–70.

Hanes, R. C. 1988. Early Cultural Traditions of the Owyhee Uplands as Seen from Dirty Shame Rockshelter, pp. 361–372. *In:* J. A. Willig, C. M. Aikens, and J. L. Fagan (eds.), Early Human Occupation in Far Western North America: The Clovis-Archaic Interface. Nevada State Museum Anthropological Papers 21.

Harrington, M. R. 1957. A Pinto Site at Little Lake, California. Southwest Museum Papers 17. Los Angeles.

Hattori, E. M. 1982. The Archaeology of Falcon Hill, Winnemucca Lake, Washoe County, Nevada. Nevada State Museum Anthropological Papers 18.

Haynes, C. V., Jr. 1971. Time, Environment, and Early Man. Arctic Anthropology 8: 3–14.

Haynes, G. 1988. Spiral Fractures, Cutmarks and Other Myths About Early Bone Assemblages, pp. 145–152. *In:* J. A. Willig, C. M. Aikens, and J. L. Fagan (eds.), Early Human Occupation in Far Western North America: The Clovis-Archaic Interface. Nevada State Museum Anthropological Papers 21.

Heizer, R. F. 1956. Recent Cave Explorations in the Lower Humboldt Valley, Nevada. University of California Archaeological Survey Reports 33: 50–57.

Heizer, R. F., and M. A. Baumhoff. 1961. The Archaeology of Wagon Jack Shelter. University of California Anthropological Records 20: 119–138. Berkeley.

Heizer, R. F., and M. A. Baumhoff. 1970. Big Game Hunters in the Great Basin: A Critical Review of the Evidence. Contributions of the University of California Archaeological Research Facility 7: 1–12. Berkeley.

Heizer, R. F., M. A. Baumhoff, and C. W. Clewlow, Jr. 1968. Archaeology of South Fork Shelter (NV-EL-11), Elko County, Nevada. University of California Archaeological Survey Reports 7: 1–58. Berkeley.

Heizer, R. F., and A. B. Elsasser. 1953. Some Archaeological Sites and Cultures of the Central Sierra Nevada. University of California Archaeological Survey Reports 21. Berkeley.

Heizer. R. F., and T. R. Hester. 1978. Great Basin, pp. 147–199. *In:* R. E. Taylor and C. W. Meighan (eds.), Chronologies in New World Archaeology. Academic Press, New York.

Heizer, R. F., and A. D. Krieger. 1956. The Archaeology of Humboldt Cave, Churchill County, Nevada. University of California Publications in American Archaeology and Ethnology 47: 1–190. Berkeley.

Heizer, R. F., and L. K. Napton. 1970. Archaeology and the Prehistoric Great Basin Lacustrine Subsistence Regime as Seen from Lovelock Cave, Nevada. University of California Archaeological Research Facility Contributions 10. Berkeley.

Holmer, R. N. 1986. Common Projectile Points of the Intermountain West. *In:* C. J. Condie and D. D. Fowler (eds.), Anthropology of the Desert West: Essays in Honor of Jesse D. Jennings. University of Utah Press, Salt Lake City.

Hughes, R. E. 1986. Diachronic Variability in Obsidian Procurement Patterns in Northeastern California and Southcentral Oregon. University of California Publications in Anthropology 17. Berkeley.

Hurt, W. R. 1966. The Altithermal and the Prehistory of the Northern Plains. Quaternaria 15: 115–124.

Hutchinson, P. W. 1988. The Prehistoric Dwellers at Lake Hubbs, pp. 303–318. *In:* J. A. Willig, C. M. Aikens, and J. L. Fagan (eds.), Early Human Occupation in Far Western North America: The Clovis-Archaic Interface. Nevada State Museum Anthropological Papers 21.

James, S. R., B. Brown, and R. G. Elston. 1982. Archaeological Investigations at the Vista Site (26WA3017), Washoe County, Nevada. Intermountain Research, Silver City.

Jennings, J. D. 1957. Danger Cave. University of Utah Anthropological Papers 27. Salt Lake City.

Jennings, J. D. 1986. Prehistory: Introduction, pp. 113–119. *In:* W. L. d'Azevedo (ed.), Great Basin, Volume 11: Handbook of North American Indians. Smithsonian Institution, Washington, D.C.

Jennings, J. D. 1989. Prehistory of North America, 3rd Edition. Mayfield, Mountain View, CA.

Kelly, R. L. 1985. Hunter-Gatherer Mobility and Sedentism: A Great Basin Study. Ph.D. Dissertation, University of Michigan, Ann Arbor.

Kelly, R. L. 1988. Archaeological Context. *In:* C. Raven and R. G. Elston (eds.), Preliminary Investigations in Stillwater Marsh, Volume 2: Human Prehistory and Geoarchaeology. U.S. Fish and Wildlife Service Cultural Resources Series 1. Portland.

Kelly, R. L. 1990. Marshes and Mobility in the Western Great Basin. *In:* J. C. Janetski and D. B. Madsen (eds.), Wetland Adaptations in the Great Basin. Brigham Young University Museum of Peoples and Cultures Occasional Papers 1.

Kelly, R. L. 1992. Mobility/Sedentism: Concepts, Archaeological Measures, and Effects. *In:* Annual Review of Anthropology 21: 43–66.

Lamb, S. M. 1958. Linguistic Prehistory in the Great Basin. International Journal of American Linguistics 24: 95–100.

Layton, T. N. 1970. High Rock Archaeology: An Interpretation of the Prehistory of the Northwestern Great Basin. Ph.D. Dissertation, Department of Anthropology, Harvard University, Cambridge.

Layton, T. N. 1979. Archaeology and Paleoecology of Pluvial Lake Parman, Northwestern Great Basin. Journal of New World Archaeology 3: 41–56.

Layton, T. N., and D. H. Thomas. 1979. The Archaeology of Silent Snake Springs, Humboldt County, Nevada. Anthropological Papers of the American Museum of Natural History 55: 249–270. New York.

Livingston, S. D. 1986. The Archaeology of the Humboldt Lakebed Site. Journal of California and Great Basin Anthropology 8: 99–115.

Livingston, S. D. 1988. The Avian and Mammalian Faunas from Lovelock Cave and the Humboldt Lakebed Site. Ph.D. Dissertation, University of Washington, Seattle.

Madsen, D. B. 1990. Reply to Thomas. *In:* J. C. Janetski and D. B. Madsen (eds.), Wetland Adaptations in the Great Basin. Brigham Young University Museum of Peoples and Cultures Occasional Papers 1.

Madsen, D. B., and K. T. Jones. 1989. The Silver Island Expedition: Anthropological Archaeology in the Bonneville Basin, Part 1: Concepts and Contexts. MS on file, Museum of Peoples and Cultures, Brigham Young University, Provo.

Mehringer, P. J., Jr. 1986. Prehistoric Environments, pp. 31–63. *In:* W. L. d'Azevedo (ed.), Great Basin, Volume 11: Handbook of North American Indians. Smithsonian Institution, Washington, D.C.

Mehringer, P. J., Jr., and P. E. Wigand. 1984. Prehistoric Distribution of Western Juniper. Proceedings of the Western Juniper Management Short Course, Bend, Oregon, October 15–16, 1984.

Mulloy, W. B. 1958. A Preliminary Historical Outline for the Northwestern Plains. University of Wyoming Publications in Anthropology 22. Laramie.

Napton, L. K. 1969. The Lacustrine Subsistence Patterns in the Desert West. Kroeber Anthropological Society Special Publication 2: 28–98.

O'Connell, J. F. 1971. The Archaeology and Cultural Ecology of Surprise Valley, Northeastern California. Ph.D. Dissertation, University of California, Berkeley.

O'Connell, J. F. 1975. The Prehistory of Surprise Valley. Ballena Press Anthropological Papers 4. Pomona.

O'Connell, J. F., K. T. Jones, and S. R. Simms. 1982. Some Thoughts on Prehistoric Archaeology in the Great Basin. *In*: D. B. Madsen and J. F. O'Connell (eds.), Man and Environment in the Great Basin. Society for American Archaeology Papers 2.

Oetting, A. C. 1990. Aboriginal Settlement in the Lake Abert–Chewaucan Marsh Basin. *In*: J. C. Janetski and D. B. Madsen (eds.), Wetland Adaptations in the Great Basin. Brigham Young University Museum of Peoples and Cultures Occasional Papers 1.

Pettigrew, R. M. 1985. Archaeological Investigations in the Lake Abert–Chewaucan Basin, Lake County, Oregon, Volume 1. University of Oregon Anthropological Papers 32. Eugene.

Raven, C. 1990. Prehistoric Human Geography in the Carson Desert, Part 2: Archaeological Field Tests of Model Predictions. U.S. Fish and Wildlife Service Cultural Resources Series 4. Portland.

Raven, C., and R. G. Elston (eds.). 1988a. Preliminary Investigations in Stillwater Marsh, Volume 1: Human Prehistory and Geoarchaeology. U.S. Fish and Wildlife Service Cultural Resources Series 1. Portland.

Raven, C., and R. G. Elston (eds.). 1988b. Preliminary Investigations in Stillwater Marsh, Volume 2: Human Prehistory and Geoarchaeology. U.S. Fish and Wildlife Service Cultural Resources Series 1. Portland.

Raven, C., and R. G. Elston. 1989. Prehistoric Human Geography in the Carson Desert, Part 1: A Predictive Model of Land Use in the Stillwater Wildlife Management Area. U.S. Fish and Wildlife Service Cultural Resources Series 3. Portland.

Raymond, A. W., and V. M. Parks. 1990. Archaeological Sites Exposed by Recent Flooding of Stillwater Marsh, Carson Desert, Churchill County, Nevada. *In*: J. C. Janetski and D. B. Madsen (eds.), Wetland Adaptations in the Great Basin. Brigham Young University Museum of Peoples and Cultures Occasional Papers 1.

Rhode, D. 1990. Settlement Patterning and Residential Stability at Walker Lake, Nevada: The View from Above. *In*: J. C. Janetski and D. B. Madsen (eds.), Wetland Adaptations in the Great Basin. Brigham Young University Museum of Peoples and Cultures Occasional Papers 1.

Riddell, F. A. 1960. The Archaeology of the Karlo Site (Las-7) of California. University of California Archaeological Survey Reports 53. Berkeley.

Rozaire, C. 1963. Lake-Side Cultural Specializations in the Great Basin. Nevada State Museum Anthropological Papers 9: 72–77.

Rusco, M. K., and J. O. Davis. 1987. Studies in Archaeology, Geology, and Paleontology at Rye Patch Reservoir, Pershing County, Nevada. Nevada State Museum Anthropological Papers 20. Carson City.

Self, W. 1980. The Archaeology of Lowe Shelter: A Contribution to the Prehistory of the Western Great Basin. M.A. Thesis in Anthropology, University of Nevada, Reno.

Simms, S. R. 1983. Comments on Bettinger and Baumhoff's Explanation of the "Numic Spread" in the Great Basin. American Antiquity 48: 825–830.

Simms, S. R. 1987. Behavioral Ecology and Hunter-Gatherer Foraging: An Example from the Great Basin. BAR International Series 381. Oxford.

Simms, S. R. 1988. Conceptualizing the Paleo-Indian and Archaic in the Great Basin, pp. 41–52. *In*: J. A. Willig, C. M. Aikens, and J. L. Fagan (eds.), Early Human Occupation in Far Western North America: The Clovis-Archaic Interface. Nevada State Museum Anthropological Papers 21.

Singer, C. A., and J. E. Ericson. 1977. Quarry Analysis at Bodie Hills, Mono County, California: A Case Study, pp. 171–188. *In:* T. K. Earle and J. E. Ericson (eds.), Exchange Systems in Prehistory. Academic Press, New York.

Stanley, D. A., G. M. Page, and R. Shutler, Jr. 1970. The Cocanour Site: A Western Nevada Pinto Phase Site With Two Excavated "House Rings," pp. 1–46. *In:* Five Papers on the Archaeology of the Desert West. Nevada State Museum Anthropological Papers 15. Carson City.

Stephenson, R. L. 1965. Quaternary Human Occupation of the Plains, pp. 708–726. *In:* H. E. Wright, Jr., and D. G. Frey (eds.), The Quaternary of the United States. Princeton University Press, Princeton.

Steward, J. H. 1938. Basin-Plateau Aboriginal Sociopolitical Groups. University of Utah Press, Salt Lake City.

Struever, S. 1968. Woodland Subsistence-Settlement Systems in the Lower Illinois Valley, pp. 285–312. *In:* S. R. Binford and L. R. Binford (eds.), New Perspectives in Archaeology. Aldine, Chicago.

Struever, S. 1971. Comments on Archaeological Data Requirements and Research Strategy. American Antiquity 36: 9–19.

Thomas, D. H. 1971. Prehistoric Subsistence-Settlement Patterns of the Reese River Valley, Central Nevada. Ph.D. Dissertation, University of California, Davis.

Thomas, D. H. 1973. An Empirical Test of Steward's Model of Great Basin Settlement Patterns. American Antiquity 38: 155–176.

Thomas, D. H. 1981. How to Classify the Projectile Points from Monitor Valley, Nevada. Journal of California and Great Basin Anthropology 3: 7–43.

Thomas, D. H. 1982a. The 1981 Alta Toquima Village Project: A Preliminary Report. University of Nevada, Desert Research Institute, Social Sciences Center Technical Report Series 27. Reno.

Thomas, D. H. 1982b. An Overview of Central Great Basin Prehistory. *In:* D. B. Madsen and J. F. O'Connell (eds.), Man and Environment in the Great Basin. Society for American Archaeology Papers 2.

Thomas, D. H. 1983. The Archaeology of Monitor Valley, 2: Gatecliff Shelter. Anthropological Papers of the American Museum of Natural History 59. New York.

Thomas, D. H. 1985. The Archaeology of Hidden Cave, Nevada. Anthropological Papers of the American Museum of Natural History 61. New York.

Thomas, D. H. 1990. On Some Research Strategies for Understanding the Wetlands. *In:* J. C. Janetski and D. B. Madsen (eds.), Wetland Adaptations in the Great Basin. Brigham Young University Museum of Peoples and Cultures Occasional Papers 1.

Thompson, R. S., E. M. Hattori, and D. R. Tuohy. 1987. Paleoenvironmental and Archaeological Implications of Early Holocene–Late Pleistocene Cave Deposits From Winnemucca Lake, Nevada. Nevada Archaeologist 6: 34–38.

Tuohy, D. R. 1974. A Comparative Study of Late Paleo-Indian Manifestations in the Western Great Basin, pp. 90–116. *In:* R. Elston (ed.), A Collection of Papers on Great Basin Archaeology. Nevada Archaeological Survey Research Papers 5. Reno.

Tuohy, D. R. 1981. Pebble Mounds, Boulder Cairns, and Other Rock Features at the Sadmat Site, Churchill County, Nevada. Nevada Archaeologist 3: 4–15.

Tuohy, D. R. 1988. Paleoindian and Early Archaic Cultural Complexes from Three Central Nevada Localities, pp. 217–230. *In:* J. A. Willig, C. M. Aikens, and J. L. Fagan (eds.),

Early Human Occupation in Far Western North America: The Clovis-Archaic Interface. Nevada State Museum Anthropological Papers 21.

Tuohy, D. R. 1990. Pyramid Lake Fishing: The Archaeological Record. *In:* J. C. Janetski and D. B. Madsen (eds.), Wetland Adaptations in the Great Basin. Brigham Young University Museum of Peoples and Cultures Occasional Papers 1.

Tuohy, D. R., A. J. Dansie, and M. B. Haldeman. 1987. Final Report on Excavations in the Stillwater Marsh Archaeological District, Nevada. Nevada State Museum Archaeological Service Report to the U.S Fish and Wildlife Service, Portland Regional Office.

Weide, D. L. 1982. Paleoecological Models in the Southern Great Basin: Methods and Measurements, pp. 8–26. *In:* D. B. Madsen and J. F. O'Connell (eds.), Man and Environment in the Great Basin. Society for American Archaeology Papers 2.

Weide, M. L. 1968. Cultural Ecology of Lakeside Adaptation in the Western Great Basin. Ph.D. Dissertation, University of California, Los Angeles.

Wilde, J. D. 1985. Prehistoric Settlements in the Northern Great Basin: Excavations and Collections Analysis in the Steens Mountain Area, Southeastern Oregon. Ph.D. Dissertation, University of Oregon, Eugene.

Wilde, J. D. 1989. Interpreting Late Prehistoric Use of a Desert Marsh: The Tule Springs Hearth Site, Alvord Basin, Southeastern Oregon. Journal of California and Great Basin Anthropology 11: 215–230.

Willig, J. A. 1988. Paleo-Archaic Adaptations and Lakeside Settlement Patterns in the Northern Alkali Basin, Oregon, pp. 417–482. *In:* J. A. Willig, C. M. Aikens, and J. L. Fagan (eds.), Early Human Occupation in Far Western North America: The Clovis-Archaic Interface. Nevada State Museum Anthropological Papers 21.

Willig, J. A. 1989. Paleo-Archaic Broad-Spectrum Adaptations at the Pleistocene-Holocene Boundary in Far Western North America. Ph.D. Dissertation, University of Oregon, Eugene.

Willig, J. A., and C. M. Aikens. 1988. The Clovis-Archaic Interface in Far Western North America, pp. 1–40. *In:* J. A. Willig, C. M. Aikens, and J. L. Fagan (eds.), Early Human Occupation in Far Western North America: The Clovis-Archaic Interface. Nevada State Museum Anthropological Papers 21.

Winters, H. D. 1963. An Archaeological Survey of the Wabash Valley in Illinois. Reports of Investigations 10, Illinois State Museum, Springfield.

Camassia quamash Greene (camas root) was an important food plant of Native Americans, especially to the north of the Great Basin. Its preferred habitat was fertile, moist meadows, environments early occupied and drastically altered by European settlers in the Great Basin.

CHAPTER 6

Changes in Plant Communities in the Great Basin Induced by Domestic Livestock Grazing

James A. Young

OVERVIEW

To establish a meaningful agriculture in the wildland habitats of the Great Basin, early European colonists from the eastern United States relied heavily on management techniques developed by the Spanish. This eventually resulted in maintenance of large herds of domestic animals on the shrublands of the Great Basin. The general absence of large native herbivores in the Great Basin initially suggested that this habitat might not be suitable for large herds of domestic animals, especially in light of the relative unavailability of potable water. The author of this chapter evaluates the various factors that have influenced the development of a domestic grazing management scheme for the Great Basin. He also considers significant changes in the structure and dynamics of native communities following introduction of domestic grazing animals. Generally, grazing by domestic herds has resulted in the decline and in some cases the elimination of many native species of bunchgrasses. This eventually led to an increase in the density of shrub species and a substantial change in ecosystem dynamics. The chapter closes with an evaluation of modern issues, concerns, and successes relative to domestic grazing in the Great Basin.

The initial settlements of Europeans in the Great Basin were by necessity self-sufficient, agrarian communities. European colonization of the New World had for centuries been proceeding along increasingly arid gradients from humid tropical or temperate environments toward more arid conditions. From the south, Spanish colonists advanced into the hot deserts of northwestern Mexico and what was to become the southwestern United States. Northern Europeans and their American descendants traveled a more temperate version of this environmental gradient across the continent to the Great Basin. Many of the early American emigrants viewed the Great Basin as a dreaded wasteland, outside the potential of established agrarian practices, that was a purgatory through which they had to pass before reaching the promised land of the Pacific.

If an agrarian lifestyle in a temperate desert environment was outside the experience of the early colonizers of the Great Basin, then the colonizing process must be viewed as a grand experiment of humans and their domestic animals venturing into the wilderness.

The western Lahontan and eastern Bonneville Basins within the Great Basin provide subunits within the grand experiment. In the western part settlements initially grew around mining or transportation centers rather than deliberate, self-sufficient colonies as in the eastern portion of the Basin. Finally the agriculturalists in both halves of the Great Basin turned to the extensive ranging of livestock herds on the desert landscapes as the means of exploiting the renewable resource of the environment. In applying this type of animal husbandry, the Great Basin colonists borrowed from the experiences of the Spanish in exploiting semi-arid environments with free-roaming animals. By the time Spanish animal husbandry reached the Great Basin, it had been modified by Americans who had slunk from the piney woods of the southeastern United States to the woodlands of east Texas and had learned from the Spanish the management of cattle from horseback. Through this process the American cowboy arrived on the sagebrush (Artemisia) steppe of the Great Basin.

INITIAL REACTION OF VEGETATION TO DOMESTIC LIVESTOCK

The initial question in the grand experiment was, Can the environment of the Great Basin support the grazing of domestic animals? This may sound ridiculous, but if your total experience as an agriculturalist had been in subhumid to humid environments, the shrub-dominated plant communities of the Great Basin, with their sparse stands of bunchgrasses, certainly did not appear productive. Initial contact would soon illustrate that domestic livestock did not prefer the herbage of most species of sagebrush, the plants that characterized huge expanses of landscape. Yet fairly large brigades of trappers traveled in the Great Basin during the contact period, bringing with them bands of up to 300 riding horses and packhorses (e.g., Peter Skene Ogden, Cline 1974). Ogden's experiences in the Lahontan Basin during the 1820s illustrate how humans and their animals interacted with the environment. It was relatively easy to find forage for the horses, relatively difficult to find potable water, and very difficult to find sufficient game to feed the party even though they were largely highly skilled professional hunters. If you were using Ogden's experiences to evaluate the potential of a new environment to support concentrations of domestic livestock, there would be a plus in the ease of finding forage and two minuses in the lack of water and the low density of native large herbivores.

There are a lot of conflicting reports on the nature of the pristine vegetation of the Great Basin (e.g., Vale 1975 vs. Stewart 1941). The large number of different plant communities, aspect differences attributable to phenology and season, and the location of transportation routes in the bottoms of basins in salt desert vegetation areas all contributed to these variable reports. Most accounts agree on the lack of native large herbivores in the central Great Basin. Apparently, the American bison (*Bison*) occurred only in the northeastern portion of the Great Basin at contact times (see Hornaday 1889 for discussion of bison distribution during the nineteenth century). The only large herbivore that Odgen's hunters could find in the central Great Basin was the pronghorn (*Antilocapra americana*). The pronghorn is the only large herbivore native to the Great Basin whose evolution also occurred in western North America. Pronghorns are currently the only large herbivores that use significant amounts of big sagebrush (A. *tridentata*) in their diet during all seasons. However, pronghorns exist, and did exist, in environments with little or no sagebrush.

Compared to the Great Plains, where at contact time the American bison was one of the most numerous large herbivores on earth, the low density of large herbivores in the Great Basin did not speak well for the environment as a potential home for herds of domestic livestock. The absence of feral horses (*Equus caballus*) or their comparative rarity in the central Great Basin compared to other portions of western North America (see Ogden's discussion of horses, Cline 1974; and McNight 1964) was another strike against the Great Basin as a grazing area. In the central Great Basin, away from the influence of the adjacent mountainous rims, the endemic Indian cultures largely seemed associated with the jackrabbit (*Lepus* spp.) (Steward 1938). Jackrabbit populations are cyclic in nature, but concentrations of the animals can have a significant impact on plant communities (McAdoo and Young 1980). Virtually the only seedlings of native plants that can be planted on a small scale in the Great Basin without needing protection from jackrabbits are those of big sagebrush. If we accept jackrabbits as the major herbivore of many pristine environments in the Great Basin, their ability to survive on water obtained metabolically from herbage consumed does not enhance the potential of the environment to support herds of domestic animals that must have sources of free water to drink on a daily basis.

Despite all the negative indications on the potential of the environment to support grazing domestic animals, the initial experiments gave positive results. The native perennial grasses may have occurred in relatively sparse stands, but after brief periods of active growth, their herbage cured well under semi-arid conditions without leaching of nutrients. Per unit of land area, herbage production was a fraction of what could be obtained from subhumid or humid grasslands, but the self-curing and lack of leaching of nutrients were definite pluses for grazing animals.

The extremes in Great Basin topography were a plus for livestock production. The base level in the basin bottoms is high, but many are so arid they have limited snow cover during the winter. The many mountain ranges provided islands of summer range. The environment dictated transhuman forms of livestock production rather than fixed base production.

The early settlers of the eastern Great Basin followed the practice of communal herding of livestock that had its origin in northern Europe and eastern North America. Animals were herded on common grazing ground during the day and returned to the village at night. The grazing land was not owned by any individual but was held in common by the community. The semi-arid to arid nature of the Great Basin environment and the resulting relatively low productivity per unit of land area reacted negatively with this system. The cow and sheep herders had to travel longer and longer distances from the villages to find forage (Christensen and

Johnson 1964). Stewart (1941) believed the main reason for the failure of early Mormon settlements was lack of sufficient rangeland in the vicinity to support the common livestock resources.

The Spanish approach to the utilization of semi-arid rangelands probably evolved in the New World from roots in the ranching systems of the Extremadura region of southwestern Spain (Young and McKell 1976). In the relative harsh environmental conditions of the Extremadura, the Spanish evolved a system of running cattle loose in relatively large stone-walled pastures. Perhaps of more importance, they evolved the concept that the number of animals was of more importance than the quality of the individual animal. Transported to the New World, this method of cattle production was expanded through the vast ranchos of Mexico to south Texas and the Mediterranean climate of southern California. The stone-walled paddocks were lost during three centuries of expansion, and cattle became essentially free-roaming animals, left to fend for themselves without care from humans. Branding and ear marking evolved to identify these free roaming animals. The Spanish system of livestock production, originated in a Mediterranean environment, was transplanted to subtropical, humid, and warm desert environments. In south Texas the Spanish ranchos stood poised on the southern margins of one of the world's greatest expanses of temperate, semi-arid grasslands.

EXPANSION OF THE LIVESTOCK INDUSTRY

The second hypothesis to test in the grand experiment was the possibility of sustained livestock production in the Great Basin. The early agriculturalists in the Great Basin could not have been encouraged by cattle and horses' lack of preference for the landscape-dominant species of sagebrush. Equally disturbing was the very short green feed period for the native herbaceous species. Buds typically burst in the early spring, but growth is limited for a long period by low temperatures; when temperatures allow rapid growth in late spring, soil moisture is rapidly exhausted. Essentially, temperatures and soil moisture for plant growth are nearly completely out of phase in the Great Basin. This is in sharp contrast to the subhumid eastern United States or even the semi-arid Great Plains or the warm deserts of the Southwest, where some precipitation that results in moisture for plant growth occurs during the growing season.

The very short growing season that was sandwiched between the cold spring and hot summer would eventually haunt the domestic livestock industry in the Great Basin. Perennial grasses in the temperate deserts have to initiate growth from basal buds in the early spring. The new growth quickly produces enough photosynthetic surfaces to provide adequate carbohydrates both to compensate for the growth and to replenish the storage reserve for another growth cycle. Flowering and seed production also occur during the spring–early summer growing period, putting additional stress on the physiological system of the plants. If concentrations of domestic livestock are wintered so they have free access to the range, the animals will attack the growing grass as soon as there is sufficient aerial growth for grazing. During the winter, the animals are dependent on dry, coarse forage, which is often deficient in digestible protein. Cattle instinctively move to green feed as soon as it is available in the spring.

Intensive early spring grazing initially inhibits flowering and seed production and eventually leads to the death of the perennial grasses. In contrast, the woody plants with persistent leaves, such as big sagebrush, do not have to renew their entire photosynthetic surfaces in the spring, although many species may produce special ephemeral leaves. The landscape-dominant species of shrubs flower in the fall.

There is a very subtle balance between herbaceous and woody species in big sagebrush communities. Sneva (1972) illustrated this with a study of the production of the exotic perennial grass crested wheatgrass (*Agropyron cristatum*) in relation to the density of big sagebrush plants. Between 10 and 20 percent of projected crown cover of big sagebrush, there was a 10 percent drop in the production of crested wheatgrass herbage with every 1 percent increase in the cover of big sagebrush. If the reverse experiment has been reported, I am not familiar with it, but apparently the shrubs greatly benefited from the reduction in the herbaceous vegetation. Remember that domestic livestock do not prefer the dominant species of woody sagebrush that characterizes the landscape. When domestic livestock are driven by starvation to consuming excessive amounts of big sagebrush browse, the animals die because of the toxic influence of the browse on their rumen microorganisms (e.g., Nagy et al. 1964). The herbage of specific ecotypes of big sagebrush may provide an important portion of the winter diet of native large herbivores (e.g., Welch et al. 1981).

Reduction and eventual near removal of herbaceous vegetation in big sagebrush areas apparently resulted in an increase in density of the dominant shrub species. Perhaps of more lasting significance, the reduction in herbaceous vegetation reduced or eliminated the occurrence and spread of wildfires. Wildfire was the apparent method of stand renewal in the pristine big sagebrush communities. Big sagebrush does not sprout after the aerial portion of the plant is consumed by burning.

Did the early livestock ranchers of the Great Basin realize the negative effects that grazing of domestic livestock were having on the environment? As early as 1880 newspaper editorials suggested that something must be done to restore the range (e.g., Young and Sparks 1985). By 1900 the need to seed ranges to restore their productivity was apparent to scientist P. B. Kennedy (1903). At the turn of the century, during an inspection trip from Winnemucca, Nevada, to Burns, Oregon, botanist David Griffiths (1903) commented on the numerous fires burning on the mountain ranges. The fires seem to have been set to improve grazing the following season. This indicates both that there was a conscientious effort to reduce woody plant dominance and that there was still sufficient herbaceous understory vegetation to support fires on higher mountain ranges.

Growth of the livestock industry in the Great Basin was controlled by the availability of markets. The distribution of livestock was a factor of the physical and biological environment. The Great Basin is rimmed by mountains and desert. It was not feasible to drive livestock to markets outside the Basin and hope to have the animals arrive in a marketable condition. In contrast, on the Great Plains, steers were allowed to improve in condition on the grasslands of Kansas after being driven from Texas. The only market available to subsistence agriculturalists in the eastern Great Basin was to provide livestock for additional colonies. As mining developed in the western Great Basin, local markets developed for agricultural products to support the miners. The completion of the transcontinental railroad in the late 1860s changed the economic situation and made large-scale raising of livestock feasible (Young and Sparks 1985).

The distribution of livestock on the ranges of the Great Basin was controlled by the distribution of stock water and the topography. Distribution of pioneer ranches depended on the availability of potable water and the occurrence of meadows where hay could be conserved, primarily for winter use by stock horses. Stock water was scarce and poorly distributed on winter ranges. I. C. Russell, in his monograph of pluvial Lake Lahontan, was able to map precisely (largely by himself) the known springs below the maximum level of the former lake, which had a surface area of over 8,000 square miles (Russell 1885). During severe winters that preceded the disastrous winter of 1889–1890, it was common for cattle to starve on winter ranges even when they could see ungrazed forage resources (Young and Sparks 1985). The forage had to be close enough for the cattle to be able to walk, graze, and return to water daily. Generally, the optimal distance for this round-trip is given as 4 miles. As cattle became familiar with the winter ranges of the Great Basin, they could graze 10 miles from established water points by taking advantage of mud puddles on miniplayas (unpublished research ARS-USDA, Reno, NV). Experience demonstrated that the worst possible situation was an extremely cold, dry winter. Cold air drained to the bottom of enclosed basins and was trapped there by thermal inversions. The intense cold, which often freezes the ears and tails of calves, increased the needs of the cattle for metabolic heat, which could only be gained from the action of microorganisms on a full rumen. Starving cattle died from the cold before body reserves were exhausted.

Russell (1885) mapped about 75 springs below the maximum level of Lake Lahontan. If a 2-mile radius from water is the effective distance that cattle can graze under desert conditions, large portions of the Lahontan Basin would not have been available for grazing. The springs are not random but are clumped in distribution, reducing the area with natural stock water.

In the western Great Basin, portions of mountain ranges such as the Dogskins and Granite Peak are largely granitic. The coarse-textured surface soils are highly permeable to precipitation to the point that surface flow virtually never occurs. Vast areas on these mountain ranges are devoid of surface water except for very brief periods during snowmelt. Natural springs are rare in these mountains. Obviously, domestic livestock production was only possible in such environments through water developments.

Water developments took many forms, the simplest of which were digging out springs to increase the surface flow and installing wooden troughs. The technology that dramatically enhanced stock water in the temperate deserts was the windmill. On many of the lake plains that occupied the basin floors, water could be found at shallow depths. Sometimes shallow bores resulted in artesian flows, and there was a flurry of excitement in the Far West that such flows would provide an answer to the water problems inherent with semi-arid environments. Pumping was usually required. It became commonplace for cowboys to ride a circuit of windmills on winter ranges to make certain the stock had water.

We should not underestimate how important water development was and is to grazing animals in the Great Basin. Water development had a continued influence on the livestock industry that is much in evidence in the riparian area controversy. No one has ever studied the influence of water development for livestock production or the abundance and distribution of native or feral animals that are dependent on free water as opposed to metabolically obtained water.

The regionally severe winter of 1889–1890 nearly destroyed the livestock industry in the northern Great Basin (see Young and Sparks 1985 for appropriate literature). The major lesson learned from this disaster was that forage conserved as hay was necessary at the rate of .75 to 1.5 tons per brood cow for the cattle industry to survive in the Great Basin. Hay production was possible only from native meadows or from artificially irrigated areas. In northern Nevada only 4 to 5 percent of the total landscape was irrigatable with the maximum application of technology because of the finite amount of surface water.

Mountain ranges with extensive areas near 10,000 feet in elevation are necessary to produce sufficient runoff to permit consistent irrigation. In the Lahontan Basin this effectively limited irrigated hay production to the riparian areas of the five major rivers that originally fed pluvial Lake Lahontan: the Susan, Truckee, Carson, Walker, and Humboldt Rivers.

After the winter of 1889–1890, the range sheep industry grew rapidly in the Great Basin. Sheep do not require the production of hay for winter forage, and they are better adapted to wintering on the range because they are better browsers than cattle. But most importantly, they can utilize skiffs of snow for sources of water (Jardine 1915). The discovery that sheep did not have to be watered daily opened vast areas of winter range that had not been available to cattle. The lower relative water requirement of sheep compared to cattle made it feasible to haul water to sheep when necessary. The capital cost for getting into the sheep business was much lower than for entering cattle or horse production, and the expenses for operations were also lower when the sheep were kept on the range year-round. There were several giant range sheep operations in the Great Basin (Sawyer 1976) that had substantial capital investments and belonged to large landowners (e.g., Utah Construction, with about 40,000 ewes; Bowman 1958). However, the range sheep operations in the Great Basin became identified as lowly enterprises, those that did not own base property becoming known as tramp sheep operations.

If sheep were properly managed (e.g., animals were bedded at a site only one night rather than several times at the same bedgrounds; Fleming 1922), they were not inherently more destructive to the range than cattle. Unfortunately, sheep became associated with the destruction of ranges because tramp sheep operations were superimposed on ranges that had already been abused by excessive, continuous cattle grazing. The browsing potential of sheep offered a means for woody plant reduction, and their trampling action could be used to cover natural or artificially distributed seeds as tools in range improvement.

A system of acquiring land from the public domain in sufficient quantities to make private ranges economically feasible in the temperate deserts never evolved. As a result, ranges continued to be held in common, often used by more than one livestock enterprise. But this policy seldom led to conservation of natural resources, as it fostered an attitude of "If I don't get there first, my neighbor will get my rightful share." This problem was addressed in proposals for land reforms by John Wesley Powell, but the environment of the Great Basin was so foreign to the established political structure, elected from the largely humid eastern United States, that the reforms were never enacted (Young and Sparks 1985).

The move to establish forest reserves and eventually a national forest in the Great Basin was partially motivated to solve the problem of overutilization of rangelands. Under the system adopted by the Forest Service to allocate grazing resources, the privilege to graze was based on the history of use and on the ownership of property that commensurately supported the livestock enterprise during the portion of the year the animals were not grazing on the rangelands. National forests on the rim of the Great Basin often support extensive woodland and forest vegetation. Portions of some of the national forests in the interior of the Great Basin are largely treeless, and the establishment of the forest was more transparently a social economic rather than a timber conservation undertaking (Wooten 1932). Away from the mountain rims, the bulk of the rangelands of the Great Basin remained in the limbo of commons grazing until the passage of the Taylor Grazing Act, which allocated limited grazing privileges to specific operators only.

INTRODUCTION OF ALIEN PLANTS

The biological near vacuum created by overutilization of the herbaceous species on sagebrush rangelands was not maintained. A host of alien herbaceous species were accidentally introduced, and several species proved highly adapted to the Great Basin (Young et al. 1972). Russian thistle (*Salsola australis*) was perhaps the first of these to become widespread in disturbed habitats (Young 1988). Numerous introductions followed Russian thistle, with cheatgrass (*Bromus tectorum*) becoming the seral dominant of vast landscapes (Young et al. 1987).

The paramount ecological issue concerning the success of alien annual species in the Great Basin is their dominance of plant succession on disturbed habitats. The alien species influence subsequent succession through seedling competition and changing wildfire frequency and timing. Starting with Russian thistle and eventually culminating in cheatgrass, the alien species have pre-empted secondary succession in many plant communities (Piemeisel 1938).

Cheatgrass dominance essentially closes plant communities to the establishment of seedlings of native or exotic perennial grass species (Robertson and Pierce 1945). The alien species form a seral continuum that assures occupancy of the site by the aliens. Suppress cheatgrass by excessive grazing and tumble mustard (*Sisymbrium altissmum*) will occupy the site. Further intense disturbance will lead to dominance by Russian thistle. Relax the disturbance and succession will proceed to dominance by cheatgrass. Minimal disturbance perpetuates cheatgrass dominance.

In the early 1940s C. E. Fleming recognized that cheatgrass had become the major component of the forage base for the domestic livestock industry in the Great Basin (Fleming et al. 1942). The short green feed period for cheatgrass leads to selective grazing of remnant perennial grasses once the annuals have dried. Coupled with competition between cheatgrass and perennial seedlings for available soil moisture that permits seedling establishment (Evans et al. 1970), selective grazing pressure assured continued cheatgrass dominance. During the past two decades, cheatgrass has greatly increased in abundance — possibly a result of the implementation of grazing management systems. Although remnant stands of perennial grasses may benefit from this type of grazing management, cheatgrass also increases. Over a prolonged period (which would vary with the characteristics of each site), perhaps the perennials would gain dominance, but the accumulations of herbaceous fuel from ungrazed cheatgrass stands often lead to a rise in the frequency and extent of wildfires.

Domestic livestock are not the only animals to prey upon cheatgrass and the other annuals. Many native granivores have adapted to the collection and scatter-hoard caching of seeds of the alien species. Such seed collection and caching may aid in the regeneration of the species (e.g., Latourrette et al. 1971). This has been a problem with studies of the influence of nongrazing on the speed of recovery of degraded Great Basin rangelands. The grazing enclosure may serve as a protected habitat for rodents whose disturbance enhances the persistence of cheatgrass.

Cheatgrass matures 1 month to 6 weeks before native perennial grass species. The herbage of cheatgrass provides a fine fuel that is readily ignited, and the dense, near continuous cover of cheatgrass provides an excellent substrate to carry fire from shrub to shrub. Under the right environment, virtually all temperate desert plant communities will burn in wildfires. Cheatgrass-invaded plant communities would burn whereas native plant communities growing on sites of the same environmental potential would be fireproof. Changing the timing of wildfires in relation to the phenology of native plant species can have very detrimental effects.

Cheatgrass fires create optimum conditions for growth of cheatgrass, which preconditions the sites to burn again. Within the past decade there has been a documented increase in the distribution and density of cheatgrass in environments bordering the sagebrush/bunchgrass vegetation zone. Higher environmental potential woodlands and lower potential salt desert zones alike have fostered cheatgrass growth. The spread of cheatgrass into shadscale (*Atriplex confertifolia*) areas has brought stand renewal by wildfires to a zone that was considered fireproof.

Annual-dominated plant communities are open to invasion by seedlings of other colonizing species. The spread of halogeton (*Halogeton glomeratus*) in communities formerly dominated by Russian thistle and in turn the partial displacement of halogeton by barbwire Russian thistle (*Salsola iberica*) are examples of this process. The replacement of cheatgrass by medusahead (*Taeniatherum asperum*) is an example of an alien annual grass that is a forage species being replaced by another alien annual grass that will not support grazing animals. There is real concern that noxious species of *Centaurea* or *Euphorbia* will come to dominate extensive areas in the Great Basin as they have in the Columbia Basin. Perhaps the noxious species adapted to the drier portions of the Great Basin have not yet been introduced from the storehouse of species that exist in such genera as *Salsola* in Central Asia. As a measure of how disruptive such a species could be to the livestock industry and the environment in general, consider how halogeton contributed to the virtual extinction of the range sheep industry in many areas of the Great Basin.

PERSPECTIVE ON THE GRAND EXPERIMENT

The sagebrush-dominated ranges of the Great Basin today are in the best condition they have been in during this century, and all indications are that the century will close with a decade of well-documentable environmental restoration. How can this be, with the numerous environmental disasters associated with livestock in the temperate deserts? Livestock numbers are much lower than earlier in the century. The range sheep industry has virtually disappeared because of problems with predation, plant poisoning, labor, and a perceived lack of glamour. More importantly, every piece of public-administered rangeland is subject to some form of grazing management based on principles of plant ecology.

In the period from 1945 through 1960, large areas of badly degraded rangeland were seeded to exotic wheatgrass (*Agropyron* spp.). These seeded areas support a disproportionate share of the forage base for the livestock industry. Post-wildfire range management has greatly improved, often featuring 2 years of complete rest from grazing followed by some form of rotational-deferred grazing.

The bad news is the distribution and dominance of alien species, often perceived as weeds, are dramatically increasing in spite of vastly improved grazing management or perhaps as a partial function of grazing management. There is a very strong case that this increase would at least initially accelerate with the complete removal of domestic livestock from Great Basin ranges.

REFERENCES

Bowman, N. L. 1958. Only the mountains remain. Privately printed, Caldwell, Idaho.

Christensen, E. M., and H. B. Johnson. 1964. Pre-settlement vegetation and vegetation change in three valleys in central Utah. Brigham Young Univ. Bull. Biol. Series 4(4):1–16.

Cline, G. G. 1974. Peter Skene Ogden and the Hudson Bay Company. Univ. Okla. Press, Norman.

Evans, R. A., H. R. Holbo, R. E. Eckert, Jr., and J. A. Young. 1970. Functional environment of downy brome communities in relation to weed control and revegetation. Weed Science 18:154–162.

Fleming, C. E. 1922. Overnight camps versus established bedgrounds on Nevada sheep ranges. Nev. Agr. Exp. Sta. Bull. 103.

Fleming, C. E., M. A. Shipley, and M. R. Miller. 1942. Bronco grass (*Bromus tectorum*) on Nevada ranges. Nev. Agr. Exp. Sta. Bull. 159.

Griffiths, D. 1903. Forage conditions and problems in eastern Washington, eastern Oregon, northeastern California, and northwestern Nevada. U.S. Bur. Plant Indus. Bull. 38.

Hornaday, W. T. 1889. The extermination of the American bison. U.S. Natl. History Mus. Report for 1887. Washington, D.C., pp. 363–548.

Jardine, J. T. 1915. Grazing sheep on range without water. Natl. Wood Grower 50:7–10.

Kennedy, P. B. 1903. Summer ranges of eastern Nevada sheep. Nev. Agr. Exp. Sta. Bull. 55.

Latourrette, J. E., J. A. Young, and R. A. Evans. 1971. Seed dispersal in relation to rodent activities in seral big sagebrush communities. J. Range Manage. 24:118–120.

McAdoo, J. K. and J. A. Young. 1980. Jackrabbits. Rangelands 2:135–138.

McNight, T. 1964. Feral livestock in Anglo-America. Univ. Calif. Publ. Geol. 16:1–28.

Nagy, J. G., H. W. Steinoff, and G. M. Ward. 1964. Effect of essential oils of sagebrush on deer rumen: microbial function. J. Wildlife Manage. 28:788–790.

Piemeisel, R. L. 1938. Changes in woody plant cover on cleared sagebrush land and their probable cause. U.S. Dept. Agr. Cir.

Robertson, J. H., and C. K. Pierce. 1945. Artificial reseeding and closed communities. Northwest Science 19:58–66.

Russell, I. C. 1885. Geological history of Lake Lahontan, a quaternary lake of northwestern Nevada. U.S. Geol. Survey Mono.

Sawyer, B. W. 1976. Nevada nomads. Harlan-Young Press, San Jose, Calif.

Sneva, F. A. 1972. Grazing return following sagebrush control in eastern Oregon. J. Range Manage. 25:174–178.

Steward, J. H. 1938. Basin-plateau aboriginal sociopolitical groups. Bur. Amer. Ethnol. Bull. 120.

Stewart, G. 1941. Historic records bearing on agricultural and stream ecology of Utah. J. Forestry 39:363–375.

Vale, T. R. 1975. Presettlement vegetation in sagebrush/grass area of the intermountain west. J. Range Manage. 28:32–36.

Welch, B. L., E. D. McArthur, and J. N. Davis. 1981. Differential performance of wintering muledeer for accessions of big sagebrush and for black sagebrush. J. Range Manage. 34:409–411.

Wooton, E. O. 1932. The public domain of Nevada and factors affecting its use. U.S. Dept. Agr. Tech. Bull. 301.

Young, J. A. 1988. The public response to the catastrophic spread of Russian thistle and halogeton. Agr. History 62:122–130.

Young, J. A., R. A. Evans, R. E. Eckert, Jr., and B. L. Kay. 1987. Cheatgrass. Rangelands 9:266–269.

Young, J. A., R. A. Evans, and J. Mager. 1972. Alien plants in the Great Basin. J. Range Manage. 25:199–201.

Young, J. A., and C. M. McKell. 1976. Livestock under the Spanish oak trees. Rangeman's J. 3:172–174.

Young, J. A., and B. A. Sparks. 1985. Cattle in the Cold Desert. Utah State Univ. Press, Logan.

Artemisa tridentata Nutt. (valley big sagebrush) was the most common indicator of land suitable for tillage agriculture known to European settlers of the Intermountain West.

CHAPTER 7

People and Place in a Harsh Land:
The Cultural Geography of the Great Basin

Richard H. Jackson

OVERVIEW

This chapter presents an analysis of factors influencing modern human development of resources in the Great Basin. Modern human communities in the area have largely been agricultural; their general occurrence has been directly dictated by the availability of water. Initially, grazing of large herds of domestic animals was the principal agricultural activity of the region; however, over the past several years there has been a general decline in grazing. Settlement of the more arid areas of the Great Basin has been driven by mineral extraction, testing of military equipment, training of military personnel, and storage of toxic waste. The most significant concentration of humans in the Great Basin is restricted to the eastern margin of the Basin, with minimal development in the interior portions of the region.

Stretching across parts of six states and nearly 200,000 square miles, the Great Basin has only limited opportunities for human use, yet nearly 3 million people resided within its boundaries in 1990 (Houghton 1976; Atwood 1940; Fenneman 1931). The natural environment is characterized by arid climates and limited potential for traditional agriculture, yet it is a focus of many human activities. The Great Basin's harsh environment is a constant reality for Utah and Nevada, since approximately half of Utah and essentially all of Nevada fall within its boundaries. For California, Oregon, Arizona, and Idaho, the Great Basin is of less significance because it composes a smaller portion of each state's area. However, in all six states the environment of the Basin affects the cultural geography that has emerged as humans have attempted to occupy and utilize the resources of this vast area.

The cultural geography of the Great Basin mirrors the presence of the most important resource — water. Settlements are clustered around the eastern margins along the Wasatch Front and the edge of the Colorado Plateau, along the western margins at the eastern edge of the Sierra Nevada, and in the southeastern edge where the Colorado River provides water for Las Vegas (Moehring 1989). Settlement in the arid interior expanses of the region was in response to environmentally exploitive activities such as mining, testing of nuclear weapons or other military equipment, disposing of wastes from other areas of the United States, or grazing the sparse vegetation. In all of these activities, however, the human occupants wrestled with the reality that the natural environment was (and remains) a fragile setting with limited capacity to support large populations.

The human activities in the Great Basin are now reliant on outside support to a greater or lesser extent. The small farming communities of the nineteenth century based on the scant supply of water quickly outgrew the Basin's resources, leading to government-subsidized diversion of water from other regions. The exploitive mining and military activities continue at the discretion of forces far beyond the Great Basin. The modern urban centers of the Basin depend on national and international connections for food, transport, and jobs. The pattern of human geography evident in the Basin, however, remains one of concentrated population along the more readily accessible margins, with only isolated point settlements based on exploitive activities scattered throughout the broad expanse of the Basin.

THE CULTURAL HISTORY OF THE GREAT BASIN: EARLY EXPLORATIONS

Europeans first entered the Basin in 1776, when the Spanish explorers Francisco Atanasio Domínguez and Silvestre Vélez de Escalante, trying to find an overland route to the missions of California, entered the eastern margin from Spanish Fork Canyon in Utah (Figure 7.1). Turning south, they skirted the margins of the Great Basin near the Sevier River but then abandoned their journey and returned to Santa Fe (Houghton 1976:215–216; Jackson and Stevens 1981:12–13).

European contact with the Great Basin did not occur again until 1811, when trappers reached the Bear River Valley of northern Utah. While there is dispute over who first explored the eastern margin of the Great Basin, many believe Etienne Provost reached the Great Salt Lake in 1824. The first recorded evidence seems to be of Jim Bridger, who explored the Bear River and the shores of the Great Salt Lake in early 1825 (Jackson 1988:135–136). Jedediah Smith was the first to cross the Great Basin, reaching the San Gabriel Mission in California on November 26, 1826, and then returning the following year (Figure 7.1) (Elliott 1973:37; Houghton 1976:174–175). Peter Skene Ogden traversed much of the Great Basin between 1826 and 1830 (Figure 7.1), discovering the Humboldt River, which became a critical part of the overland trail to California (Houghton 1976:115–116). The first widely published account of the Great Basin was of Joseph R. Walker's exploration from the Great Salt Lake to California in 1833, published in 1837 as part of Washington Irving's *Adventures of Captain Bonneville in the Rocky Mountains and Far West* (Goetzmann 1966). Numerous California-bound immigrants crossed the Great Basin, beginning in 1841 with the Bartleson-Bidwell party, which went west along the Humboldt River from north of the Great Salt Lake, and the Workman-Rowland party, which used the old Spanish trail (Houghton

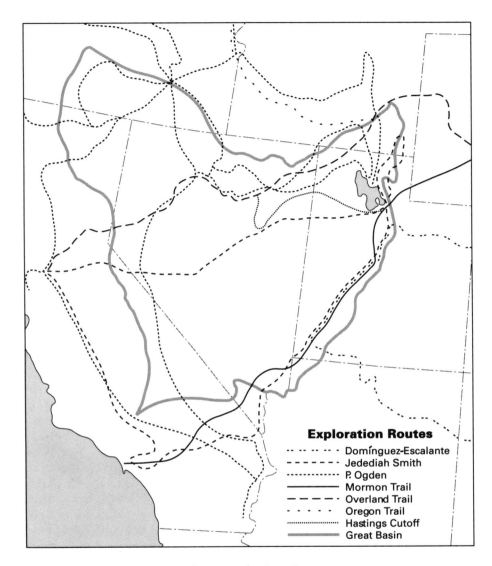

Exploration Routes

·· — ·· — ·· — Domínguez-Escalante
— — — — — — Jedediah Smith
············· P. Ogden
——————— Mormon Trail
— — — — Overland Trail
· · · · · Oregon Trail
······················ Hastings Cutoff
━━━━━━ Great Basin

Figure 6.1   Early exploration and routes in the Great Basin.

1976:218). These two trails became the major routes for subsequent immigrant groups and later modern transportation routes.

In the 1840s the U.S. government commissioned Lieutenant John Charles Fremont to travel across the Great Basin in search of routes to the coast. Reaching the Great Basin in September 1843, Fremont explored the Great Salt Lake (Jackson 1988:138–139). He visited Lake Tahoe, Pyramid Lake, and the Truckee and Carson Rivers in 1844, arriving at Utah Lake on May 24, 1844, after an eastward crossing of southern Nevada (Houghton 1976:63). Fremont explored the entire Great Basin, corroborating the reports of trappers that the region had no drainage to the sea. Widely disseminated, his information was particularly valuable to the first large group to settle the Great Basin, the Mormons (Jackson 1978:322–323).

ESTABLISHING THE GREAT BASIN'S CULTURAL GEOGRAPHY: MORMONS AND MINERS

The Mormon farmers were the first of five broad groups that have shaped the modern human geography of the Great Basin: Mormons, miners, ranchers, the military, and gamblers. While the imprint of these groups and their related activities are partially intermingled across the landscape of the region, in general terms Mormons occupied the eastern margin, the miners approached from the west, ranchers and the military utilized the vast open spaces of the central Great Basin for grazing, bases, and bomb testing, and gambling prompted the growth of Nevada's urban centers in the twentieth century. A variety of people created an intricate cultural mosaic in the Great Basin, but these five groups provided the impetus for permanent occupation of the region, shaping the towns, villages, ranches, military bases, and casinos that are evident upon its landscape today.

Under the leadership of Brigham Young, the Mormons reached the Great Salt Lake Valley in July 1847. Upon their arrival the pioneer party immediately laid out farms, diverted water from the creeks, established a fort and laid out homesites within it, and picked the location for the Salt Lake Temple (Arrington 1958:45–50). Once the first crops were planted, the Mormons began a systematic program of exploration, as Young stated that he intended to have "every hole and corner from the bay of San Francisco to the Hudson Bay known to us" (Arrington 1958:42). Using reports from these exploring parties, the Mormons began a process of colonization that would sketch the cultural geography of the eastern half of the Great Basin from Idaho to Arizona (Figure 7.2).

The most important element of this geography was provided by the adoption of irrigation, which allowed the Mormon settlers to continue to produce the same general types of crops and livestock they had had in the Midwest. Within days of their arrival, the Mormon pioneer group surveyed a city of 135 10-acre blocks, with a temple block in the center. Such division of the city and related land subdivisions provided a model that Mormons followed in general terms in most of their other settlements. Characterized by wide streets identified in typical Mormon efficiency (if somewhat prosaically) as First North, First West, and so forth, the resultant pattern is of large blocks made up of very large lots. Each block in Salt Lake City was divided into eight lots of 1.25 acres, creating a landscape of mini-farms based on irrigation. Observers of the Mormon settlement in the 1850s and 1860s commented that it resembled a large farm more than a town or city (Jackson 1988:146). The rigid orientation to cardinal direction, rectangular land division, irrigation, and small farms continue to make the Mormon communities of the Great Basin distinctive in the American landscape (Jackson and Layton 1976:140). Although the Provo–Salt Lake–Ogden region has now become a metropolitan area of over 1 million residents

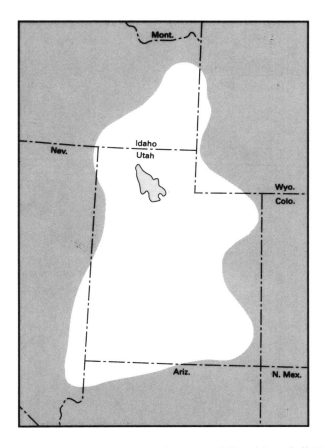

Figure 6.2   Mormon culture region (Meining 1965 and Campbell 1974).

reminiscent of other American cities, the imprint of the initial Mormon colonization effort is still highly visible.

Two events occurred in 1848 that significantly affected the cultural geography of
the Great Basin: the seizure of California from Mexico and the subsequent discovery of gold in the territory. In combination, the events sparked a level of overland
migration across the Great Basin unknown in the past. It is estimated that in 1849,
25,000 persons crossed the Great Basin on the California (or Overland) Trail
(Hulse 1978:60). The growth in numbers of overland travelers prompted establishment of supply posts beyond the Mormon settlements; the first permanent occupation of the western Great Basin took place in 1851 as John Reese established a
supply post in the Carson Valley (Earl 1986:50). The success of Reese and information about Carson Valley attracted other colonizers from Utah, leading to a small
settlement known as the Mormon station (Earl 1986:55). The growth of this settlement as a way station for migrants prompted Brigham Young to send Orson Hyde

and 36 colonizers to Carson Valley in 1855 (Hulse 1978:71). Under Hyde's direction the community of Franktown in Washoe Valley was established and a sawmill erected to provide timber for homes and farms. The Mormon settlers quickly founded the first church and school in the area and renamed the Mormon station settlement Genoa (Elliott 1973:110; Hulse 1978:71).

The Mormon settlement at Carson Valley was so successful that in 1856 the church sent additional colonizers. These settlers established communities in Carson, Eagle, and Washoe Valleys, complete with the Mormon system of irrigation and community organization (Elliott 1973:116). Mormon settlers also started a community in present-day Nye County, Nevada, but conflict with the federal government led to the so-called Utah war of 1857, and Young recalled the Mormon colonists to Utah to help defend it against the anticipated invasion of the U.S. Army (Earl 1986:54). The withdrawal of the Mormon settlers from the western Great Basin left only a few hundred miners scattered across this part of the region. These miners were generally concentrated in the Carson Valley, where they were engaged in placer mining (Earl 1986:54).

In 1858, after the threat of the Utah war dissipated, Young renewed his efforts to claim the Great Basin for a Mormon kingdom. Sending well-organized scouting parties into the interior of the Great Basin in search of new home sites, the Mormons gained the first exhaustive information of the great desert areas of the southern part of Nevada. The result of these explorations and their reports was the establishment of Panaca, southern Nevada's first permanent settlement (Paher 1981:321).

THE MINERS' FRONTIER: PEOPLING THE WESTERN GREAT BASIN

The Comstock lode was discovered in the western margin of the Great Basin in 1859, transforming the pattern of the cultural geography of the region. Where the incipient Mormon settlements had been replaced by scattered ranching and placer mining after 1857, there now emerged communities devoted to mining and mining-related activities. Discovery of the Comstock lode led to a boomtown atmosphere, as miners from California and elsewhere made the "rush to Washoe" and established Virginia City (Elliott 1973:65). The Comstock mines shaped the history of Nevada for the balance of the nineteenth century, creating a human landscape in the western region of the Great Basin as unique as the Mormon east. Between 1859 and 1880, the mines of the Comstock produced the majority of the mineral wealth of the entire state: $308,894,721 of Nevada's total income of $447,339,536 from mining between 1859 and 1880 (Elliott 1973:98). Mineral finds in other areas were prompted by expansion from the Comstock region, scattering towns such as Austin, Aurora, Belmont, Candelabra, Eureka, Hamilton, Pioche, and Unionville across the Great Basin of Nevada between 1860 and 1920 (Elliott 1973:99).

The cultural geography of the mining landscape centered on the mines themselves. There were massive timber frameworks supporting the cages that lowered workers into the shafts and brought up ore; vast stamp mills to process the ore; and the homes, bars, churches, and stores of the mining towns. The impact of the mining frontier in the western Great Basin extended far beyond the towns, as the demand for lumber for building stores, saloons, homes, churches, and mills and for providing the support timbers in the mines led to deforestation of much of the surrounding mountain slopes. The isolation of the region from food sources stimulated the economy of the Mormon towns in the eastern margins of the Great Basin, as supplies were freighted to the Nevada mining communities from the Mormon settlements. Demand from the booming mine towns encouraged expansion of agriculture in the western Great Basin, and ranching became a major economic activity across the region, while other crops were produced in the more favorable sites, such as the Carson Valley.

Unfortunately, in the rush to develop the gold and silver of the Great Basin, the inhabitants relied on crude exploitive techniques. The result was a cultural geography of exploitation and environmental destruction. In the words of John Muir:

> Many of [the mines] do not represent any good accomplishment and have no right to be. They are monuments of fraud and ignorance and sin against science. The drifts and tunnels in the rocks may be regarded as the prayers of the prospector offered for the wealth he so earnestly craves: like prayers of any kind not in harmony with nature, they are unanswered (Muir 1918:203).

Mining-related activities in the western Great Basin led to a fundamental division in the cultural geography of the region as the Nevada miners, centered in Virginia City, clamored for political recognition separate from that established by Brigham Young and the Mormons. The miners believed that their needs were not met by the Mormons in Salt Lake City, and Nevada was made a separate territory in 1861 and a state in 1864, formalizing the distinction between the Mormon east and the non-Mormon west of the Basin (Paher 1981:17).

MINING AND THE MORMONS: ERODING THE CULTURAL GAP

Brigham Young opposed mining, arguing that mining always cost more in effort than it returned. He stated that "the people have spent twenty dollars for every one they have obtained from the mines" (Arrington 1958:202). Young's opposition to mining effectively prevented the Mormon settlers from joining the exodus to California and Nevada's mines and limited prospecting in Utah Territory. Eventually, however, the military and the railroad brought mining activities to Utah. The military's role in the Great Basin began with troops dispatched to deal with rumors of Mormon treason. Movement of the American military to Utah in 1857 prompted establishment of the first military base in the Great Basin at Camp Floyd, some 40 miles southwest of Salt Lake City, in 1858. The base was abandoned after the Civil War began, and the Mormons were able to purchase wagons, buildings, and equipment for pennies on the dollar, foreshadowing the positive economic impact of the military on the Great Basin in the twentieth century. Equally important, the movement of the troops back to the East led to the stationing of the Third California Volunteers in Utah to protect the overland mail and telegraph during the Civil War.

Establishing Camp Douglas overlooking Salt Lake City, these volunteers began surveying the eastern Great Basin for minerals. Their explorations led to the growth of mining in the eastern Great Basin once the railroad arrived in 1869 and made hauling and processing of the lower-grade ores found in this area feasible (Arrington 1958: 192–193). Fourteen new mines in eight Utah counties began operations between 1869 and 1872, creating major mining districts in the areas of the eastern Great Basin. Important locations south of Great Salt Lake and west of Utah Lake included the Mercur and Tintic mining districts. In the eastern edge of the Great Basin, important and long-lived mines were located around the Park City area of the Rocky Mountains. But beyond these clusters the mining of gold and silver created smaller settlements that lasted for shorter periods of time, thirty years or so. South central Utah's Silver Reef and Frisco were examples of such boomtowns. The cultural impact of these communities is still seen in the names on the land, which recall miner optimism: Eureka, Mammoth, Silver City, Gold Hill. These are in stark contrast to Brigham City, Moroni, Pleasant Grove, and other Mormon towns named for leaders, religious heritage, or settlement potential. The mining communities quickly declined in importance once the higher-quality ores were exhausted. Twentieth-century mining activity in Utah is primarily associated with large corporate operations utilizing low-grade ores, such as at Bingham Canyon for copper; the extraction of magnesium and other minerals from Great Salt Lake; and the explorations for very low-grade gold, silver, and other ores of Utah's Great Basin.

DIVIDING THE LAND: POLITICAL BOUNDARIES IN THE GREAT BASIN

The diffusion of mining to Utah, however, did not end the split between Mormon east and non-Mormon west. The political geography of the Great Basin reflects this division, the boundaries of Utah and Nevada (which together total some 90 percent of the Great Basin) having little basis in the physical geography of the region.

The political boundaries of the Great Basin are rooted in the development of the area from the time of the first European contact. Shortly after the Mormons' arrival in the Great Basin, Brigham Young proposed a vast state of Deseret encompassing the Great Basin and its related drainage area extending from the Rockies to the Pacific. The actual boundaries of Utah Territory created by Congress were defined as part of the Compromise of 1850, in which California was admitted to the Union as a free state and the territories of Utah and New Mexico were created with the option of being free or slave based on popular vote. With the exception of small areas of the Great Basin located in today's California, Oregon, Idaho, and southern Nevada, Utah Territory included most of the Great Basin, even though half of Young's proposed state of Deseret was excluded (Wahlquist 1981:160–161).

Creation of Nevada Territory with Carson City as the seat of government in 1861 split the Great Basin, and over the next few years Nevada expanded east and south to its present borders. Political maneuvering in Washington ultimately led to determining today's boundaries of California, Nevada, Utah, Arizona, and Oregon. Thus, the Great Basin, a hydrological unit Brigham Young understood as a result of his exploration and analysis of government and explorers' documents, was fragmented among six political units to satisfy the penchant of Congress for geometric lines. They are simple to demarcate but fail to reflect the reality of the geography of the region. The importance of these political divisions lies in their impact on the subsequent development of the cultural geography of the area, including the numbers and natures of immigrants; the nature, focus, and development of economic activity; and the use and abuse of the environment by settlers and outside interests as well.

PEOPLE AND PLACE IN THE GREAT BASIN: THE EASTERN MARGINS

While the populating of the Great Basin by Mormons, miners, and military resulted in a cultural geography characterized by variety, people of western European ancestry dominate. The first great population boom occurred in the multiplying Mormon settlements at the eastern edge of the Basin as the Mormons first moved their people from the Midwest to Utah in the five years following initial colonization. Later they began bringing large numbers of foreign-born immigrants to the new Mormon kingdom. By the end of 1847, there were approximately 1,700 Mormon migrants in the Salt Lake Valley. More than 9,000 immigrants had flocked to the new settlements of Salt Lake City by 1850, and more than 17,000 Mormons had arrived in the Great Salt Lake Valley by 1852 (Wahlquist 1981:94). With natural population increase, by 1852 there were over 20,000 Mormon settlers in the valleys at the eastern margins of the Great Basin. By 1860 there were nearly 50,000 people in Utah Territory, while the total population of the Nevada portion of the Great Basin was estimated at 6,857 (Reed 1984) and the Oregon, California, and Idaho portions of the Great Basin were inhabited by only scattered trappers, miners, and traders involved with supplying overland immigrants. The great disparity in population numbers between the Mormon settlements of Utah and the western settlements has decreased since 1860, but as late as 1970 there were still three times as many people in the east as the west of the Great Basin.

The differences in total numbers of population between eastern and western margins of the Great Basin are also mirrored in the population characteristics. The Mormon settlements of the eastern Basin initially were composed of settlers who were nearly all American-born. After 1852 a large proportion of those immigrating to the Great Basin Mormon communities came from European countries. The majority of these European migrants were from the British Isles (mainly England but also significant numbers from Wales, Scotland, and even Ireland), with the second largest group from Scandinavia. One significant difference among the Mormon settlements as compared to the western portion of the Great Basin's population was the predominance of either married couples or young single males and females in sufficiently equal quantities to allow marriage and family formation among the majority. Their religious beliefs giving rise to a high birthrate, the large number of young adults produced an unusually high number of children, so that as early as 1870 the majority of Utah's population (62 percent) were native-born. The 1880 census (which first broke the population into age groups) indicated that only 30 percent of Utah's total population was foreign-born, but 57 percent of those over 20 years of age and 68 percent of those over 30 were foreign-born (Wahlquist 1981:94–95).

In 1870 all of the counties of Utah except three had a large majority of British stock among the foreign-born. The Mormon church was extremely successful in its proselyting efforts in Britain during 1840–1870, when the British Isles were experiencing displacements associated with the maturing industrial revolution; many people migrated to Utah. However, three counties, Sanpete, Sevier, and Box Elder, had a large proportion of Scandinavians in 1870. Danes dominated in Sanpete, where 73 percent of the foreign-born were of Scandinavian origin, while Box Elder had 32 percent. Other counties with a large proportion of Scandinavian immigrants included Cache, Millard, Morgan, and Rich Counties. The British Isles and Scandinavia accounted for 91 percent of Utah's foreign-born residents in 1870, while the rest of Europe contributed the balance, primarily Swiss and Germans (Wahlquist 1974).

Significant events that changed the composition of the population of the eastern Great Basin were the coming of the railroad, the expansion of mining after the railroad, and the influence of the military and industrialization in the twentieth century. The first non-European immigrants to the Mormon settlements of the eastern Great Basin were associated with the construction of the railroad, as Chinese workers came to Salt Lake and Box Elder Counties. In 1870, 20 percent of the foreign-born in Box Elder County and 4 percent in Summit County were Chinese. The numbers of Chinese in Utah decreased rapidly after the construction of the early railroads, until by 1900 there were only 417 in the entire state. Their annual numerical growth remained small, and not until the creation of relocation camps for Japanese American citizens from California, Oregon, and Washington between 1941 and 1945 were there many Asians among the Mormon communities. The population of the Topaz relocation camp for Japanese Americans near Delta, Utah, reached a total of some 12,700 at its peak, but most of those interned returned to their former homes after the war (Gurgel 1981:122). The Asian population in Utah grew primarily after World War II, reaching some 12,000 in 1980 and 32,497 in 1990. Asians tend to settle in urban locations, with over 62.7 percent in Salt Lake County and over 90 percent in the urban core of Salt Lake, Utah, Weber, and Davis Counties (U.S. Bureau of the Census 1991b).

Another minority group in Utah are Afro-Americans. The first Afro-Americans came with the Mormon pioneer company, which included several slaves and freed blacks. The population of Afro-Americans has always been low in Utah, with only 678 in the entire state in 1900, but this was still more than five times the 134 Afro-Americans in the state of Nevada at the same time. The Afro-Americans of the eastern Great Basin have resided primarily in the urban areas. With a total population of 11,418 in 1990, 95 percent were clustered in Salt Lake, Utah, Weber, and Davis Counties. The majority of Afro-Americans have been employed in jobs associated with the railroad, the military, and other federal activities (Figure 7.3)

There were seven times as many Hispanics (78,239) as Afro-Americans in Utah in 1990. The earliest permanent Hispanic residents in Utah were Spanish-speaking laborers of American origin from New Mexico. By 1900 only 40 Hispanic

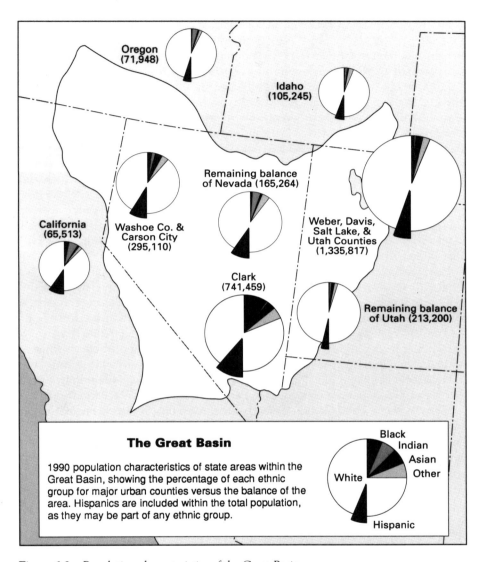

Figure 6.3 Population characteristics of the Great Basin.

individuals resided in Utah, and their numbers increased to only 4,012 by 1930. Hispanic population declined to only 1,069 in 1940 as a result of the Great Depression, but employment opportunities during and after World War II stimulated renewed immigration. The Hispanic population, too, is clustered in Salt Lake, Utah, Weber, and Davis Counties, which contain 90 percent of Utah's Hispanic residents. Outside of the urban centers of the eastern Great Basin, Hispanics have tended to remain concentrated in agricultural activities, while in the four urban counties, the Hispanic population has become involved in nearly all aspects of the economy.

Native Americans make up an important element of the cultural geography of the eastern Great Basin. The Native American population of the Basin decreased dramatically after colonization by the Mormons. It is estimated that there were approximately 6,000 Native Americans in the eastern Great Basin and the adjacent Rocky Mountains and Colorado Plateau when the Mormons arrived in 1847, but this number had declined to only 2,623 by the turn of the century (Gurgel 1981:122). Creation of reservations in eastern and southeastern Utah prevented the complete extinction of Native Americans in the eastern Great Basin, though today the majority (78 percent in 1990) are concentrated in the four urban counties of the state. Within the eastern margins of the Great Basin, Native Americans are also found in isolated reservations, including the Shivwits of southwestern Utah, the Deep Creek reservation near the Utah-Nevada border, Skull Valley (a Goshiute reservation southwest of the Great Salt Lake), Koosherum and Kanosh (Paiute reservations in central Utah), and Indian Peak in southwestern Utah. All have small populations, and the combined population of Native Americans on these reservations is less than 1,000 (Figure 7.3).

Others who have affected the cultural geography of the eastern Great Basin are the Pacific Islanders. The Mormons sent missionaries to the Pacific Islands in the 1850s and 1860s and converted many Hawaiians, Tongans, and Samoans. Iosepa, a colony of Hawaiians, was established in the desert west of the Great Salt Lake in the late 1800s. Hawaiians belonging to the Mormon faith immigrated to this area to be near Salt Lake City and the Mormon temple. Their attempts to create an agricultural community were unsuccessful, and today only a historic plaque and some graves remain at Iosepa. The descendants of these Hawaiians and other Polynesians have created an important element in the eastern Great Basin population.

Migrants from Italy, Greece, Poland, Czechoslovakia, and other eastern and southern European countries came to Utah in the early 1900s. Many of them found employment in coal mining in the Colorado Plateau province of Utah, but over time their descendants have moved to all areas of the state, bringing Greek Americans, Italian Americans, Polish Americans, and others to the eastern Great Basin. The greatest impact they have had on the cultural geography of the Great Basin has been the construction of churches, restaurants, and markets reflecting traditions of their homelands. As one example, there are Greek Orthodox churches in the towns of Ogden, Salt Lake, and Holladay, Utah. To these eastern and southern European migrants of the late nineteenth and early twentieth centuries have been added migrants from the Soviet Union in the post–World War II period. While few in number, they contribute to the ethnic and cultural diversity of the Great Basin's eastern region.

PEOPLE AND PLACE IN THE GREAT BASIN: THE WESTERN MARGINS

The population clustered at the edge of the Rocky Mountains in the Utah and Idaho Great Basin region makes up more than half of the total population of the Great Basin. The balance of the population is concentrated in the west in the Reno and Las Vegas metropolitan areas. Until the establishment of Las Vegas as a gambling center in the twentieth century, the mining of western Nevada had drawn the majority of the population of both the western region of the Basin and of the state of Nevada. The population in the western Great Basin boomed with the discovery of the Comstock mines in 1859, reaching 6,857 by 1860 and 42,491 by 1870 (Reed 1984).

The early population of the western region of the Great Basin was overwhelmingly male, composing 78 percent of the total population of Nevada in 1870. This predominance of males slowly decreased, but in the late nineteenth century there were two males to every female, and as late as 1920 the population was still 60 percent male (Reed 1984). The high proportion of men in the western Great Basin's mining towns also caused the population to be older than that found in the eastern Great Basin. The opportunity for family formation was smaller, and both the birthrate and family size were significantly lower than in the Mormon-occupied portion of the Basin. In consequence, natural increase of the population in the western Great Basin was slow, responding instead to the relative prosperity of the mines.

A second major distinction between the population of the western Basin and the eastern Mormon-occupied region reflected the importance of mining in the economy. The population of the Mormon-settled east continued to grow from decade to decade because of high birthrates and immigration, but in the western Great Basin the population fluctuated from census to census in response to economic conditions. After increasing to 62,266 in 1880, the population plunged to 45,761 by 1890 and to 42,355 in 1900. This trend continued in the twentieth century, with the population nearly doubling to 81,875 by 1910 but falling to only 77,407 by 1920. Since 1920 the total population of Nevada has increased each decade as the economy of the western Basin has diversified, particularly since the legalization of gambling in the area. Providing income even when prices for minerals are low, gambling has helped to stabilize the boom-bust cycle of the western Great Basin.

The boom-and-bust basis of early population growth in the western Great Basin of Nevada led to a highly diverse group of migrants to the region. When Nevada became a territory in 1861, nearly 33 percent of the population was foreign-born, and by 1870 the foreign-born population had increased to more than 44 percent. This figure is higher than that of the eastern Great Basin at the same time because the residents were primarily adults, and few children were being born to raise the proportion of native-born in the population. The American-born residents reflected primarily English, German, Irish, and other European ancestry.

As in the eastern settlements of the Great Basin, the western settlements also have several important non-European ethnic groups. The first large-scale non-European immigration into the western Great Basin was by Chinese. Then the Chinese were first brought to Nevada in 1850 by John Reese and other Mormons to help construct ditches for irrigation. The Chinese expanded and began operating their own businesses and became involved in mining. Conflict led to a regulation in 1859 prohibiting the Chinese from owning mining claims in the Gold Hill region (Hulse 1978:277). The numbers of Chinese in the Great Basin increased dramatically in 1863 when thousands of Chinese were hired to work on the Central Pacific Railroad, leading to even greater conflict. As a residual, by 1870 there

were 3,152 Chinese in the western Great Basin, many using intensive-labor practices to work old gold and silver mines that had been abandoned by Caucasian
miners as their yields declined (Hulse 1978:277). The peak of the Chinese placer
mining activities was between 1870 and 1880, and their population reached 5,419
in the 1880 census. After that time the Chinese population decreased, falling to
2,826 in 1890 and reaching a low of 689 in 1920 (Reed 1984).

A variety of other people came to Nevada in response to the various mining
booms. Italians and Swiss burned charcoal that was used in the smelters and
founded ranches and dairy farms in the valleys near Reno. Welsh and Irish immigrants worked in the mines of the Comstock and surrounding boomtowns, while
French Canadians worked to supply the lumber for the mine timbering from the
forests surrounding Lake Tahoe. Germans developed farms in the Carson Valley to
provide foodstuffs for the miners, and in the 1870s and 1880s, Slavs and Greeks
worked in the mines and smelters of Ruth and McGill in eastern Nevada. The cultural geography of other mining towns was shaped by the complex mixture of ethnic groups immigrating into the western Great Basin, as in the copper mining town
of McGill, which was divided into specific communities of Greeks, Slavs, Italians,
and Japanese. Basques as well as Scottish migrants herded sheep in the deserts and
mountains as sheep became an important part of the economy in the latter part of
the nineteenth century. The Basques were never a large group in the Great Basin,
but their impact on the cultural geography has remained. The Basque shepherds
sent home money to their families and founded small hotels or boardinghouses.
Bringing their future wives to the region, they created the tradition of the Basque
festivals that are still held annually in Elko, Ely, Winnemucca, and Reno.

The Afro-American population of Nevada was very small in the nineteenth cen-
tury and did not increase dramatically until the building of the Hoover Dam and
World War II. These events brought the first major influx of Afro-Americans to
southern Nevada, where they were concentrated in what was known as Westside
Las Vegas and in the western Great Basin tourism gambling communities such as
Reno (Shepperson 1989:39).

The present distribution of people and their unique cultural geography in Nevada
reflects the original boom growth of mining and related agricultural activities combined with twentieth-century economic changes. With the decline of the early gold
and silver rushes, the western Great Basin's cultural geography was dominated by
remnant mining towns, with their associated buildings and deteriorating cabins and
homes and the scattered towns, ranches, and farms that originally supplied the miners. Elko, Reno, Ely, Winnemucca, Fallon, and other towns of the Great Basin were
largely developed in response to the need for a market, financial services, and supplies for the mining and agricultural economy of Nevada's Great Basin.

Unique activities provided for the miners and cowhands in Nevada's towns were
gambling and prostitution. The two in combination have created some of the most
important characteristics of the cultural geography of the region. Gambling had
been a common form of entertainment among miners in both California and in the
Nevada mines in the 1860s, but when Nevada was incorporated as a territory in
1861, the legislature outlawed gambling. Widespread flaunting of this prohibition

caused the legislature to legalize gambling in 1869, but the decline of the mining industry in the late nineteenth century led to reversal of this law in 1909. This legislation was amended in 1915 to allow "friendly games." Friendly games included all types of gambling, especially during the Prohibition era, when private "clubs" provided alcohol, gambling, and prostitution. The Nevada legislature legalized all types of gambling in 1931, and this prompted an important change in the economy and cultural geography of the Great Basin beyond Utah's western border (Jackson and Hudman 1988:39). Although legalizing gambling did not prompt significant growth initially, in the 1930s a new phenomenon was added to the cultural geography of the Basin, gambling casinos. In both Reno and Las Vegas, these became the focus of tourist-related gambling in Nevada, and after World War II they emerged as the major element in the economy of Nevada and the western Great Basin. Reno and Elko were the most important of the gambling casino centers until after World War II. To the south on the margins of the Great Basin, Las Vegas remained a smaller community, pinning its hopes for growth on Hoover Dam and federal spending rather than gambling.

While gambling has shaped much of the more visible cultural geography the western Great Basin, population growth of there was triggered and sustained by federal spending. Beginning with the selection of a site for a dam on the Colorado in 1929 and the establishment of Boulder City in 1931, the federal government has played a significant role in the growth of population in the region (Moehring 1989:16). Las Vegas in Clark County, Nevada, had been simply a supply station on the overland route to California until 1902, when the San Pedro, Los Angeles, and Salt Lake City Railroad purchased the site. A town was established upon completion of the railroad, leading to creation of a Clark County railroad headquarters. The railroad was sold to the Union Pacific in 1921, but the population of Las Vegas was still only 5,000 in 1930. The establishment of Boulder City and construction of Hoover Dam swelled its population to 7,500 by 1931 (Moehring 1989:12–16). The great growth for the Basin came with Franklin Roosevelt's New Deal, which pumped more money per capita into the Great Basin region of Nevada than to any other state in the Union. Nevada was not only first in total per capita federal expenditures but also first in per capita amount of loans, in funds for the Civilian Conservation Corps and the Civil Works Administration, and in funds for public roads (Arrington 1958:311–317). The federal government also helped fund sewage systems, schools, a golf course, and an airport at Las Vegas. The Nevada congressional delegation also successfully lobbied for legislation that greatly benefited the mining interests of the region, particularly silver and copper, with copper becoming the most important mineral mined in the state (Elliott 1973:295–298).

The federal government affected the cultural geography of Nevada through defense spending after the beginning of World War II. The demand for metals led to establishment of communities such as Henderson near Las Vegas to develop magnesium from Nevada's magnesite ores using cheap power from Hoover Dam. The greatly inflated demand for copper and other ores from Nevada in turn stimulated a new mining boom in the state to replace the stagnant economy of the 1930s depression era (Elliott 1973:307–308; Moehring 1989:34–36).

The U.S. government established training centers in Nevada, including Stead Air Force Base north of Reno, a naval air station at Fallon, the army air base at Tonopah, the large training station for pilots at Wendover, and the Nellis Army Air Force Base near Las Vegas. By the end of the war, the Nellis base alone had been expanded to 13,000 residents with 3.3 million acres reserved for gunnery training (Moehring 1989:32–33; Elliott 1973:312–313). The soldiers based in Nevada's Great Basin became an important body of customers for the casinos that began to emerge in Elko and Winnemucca.

The wide-open atmosphere of Nevada during the war accompanied a population increase of more than 45 percent, from 110,247 in 1940 to 160,083 in 1950 (Elliott 1973:313). At the middle of the twentieth century, however, the biggest communities of Nevada's Great Basin remained Reno, with 32,492 people in 1950, and Las Vegas, with 24,624. Following World War II Nevada's cultural geography was further shaped by the growth in defense industries, nuclear testing, and the establishment of industries related to these activities in the 1960s through 1980s. The expansion of federal involvement in the western Great Basin since then has fostered the growth of Las Vegas and Clark County as a major focus of defense and space industries, while the climate and many recreation and tourist sites such as Hoover Dam and Lake Mead added to its appeal. Federal spending on defense, reclamation, and the interstate system made southern Nevada boom, both from defense industry employment and from tourists flocking to its gambling resorts. All federal investment in the state has not been so beneficial, as the government has also retained possession of most of the land in the state. Nevada has the highest percentage of federal ownership of land of any state, the government holding 86.1 percent of the state's area (Francis and Ganzel 1984:38).

The general pattern of human settlement in the western Great Basin is like that of the east, with a few large population clusters contrasting with scattered agricultural and mining communities struggling to maintain their population by hoping to capitalize on the largesse of the federal and state governments or seeking to become a focus of western migration by industry or retirees. The population of Las Vegas (741,459 in 1990) and Washoe County (254,667 in 1990) composes 83 percent of the state's population, rivaling the population and dominance of the metropolitan area of the Mormon settlements in Utah's Great Basin (86 percent of Utah's population and 1,335,817 people in 1990) (Figure 7.3).

The rapid growth of Las Vegas and Clark County to a position of dominance among the communities in or on the margins of the Great Basin reflects the tremendous change in the cultural geography of the Nevada portion of the Great Basin in the postwar era. As recreation associated with gambling and casinos replaced mining and agriculture as the basic elements in the economy of the Nevada Great Basin, Las Vegas occupied a better location for growth. The development of the interstate freeway system in the 1960s and 1970s tied Las Vegas to the Los Angeles Basin, with its burgeoning population, making the Nevada city a recreation magnet. The change in gambling in Nevada from small clubs to large casinos with floor shows, entertainment, food, recreation, and gambling gave Las Vegas an international image as a playground rivaling places such as the French Riviera and the casinos of Monaco. The resulting growth has created a city sprawling across the margins of the Great Basin but relying on areas beyond the Great Basin for its continued existence. The resultant cultural landscape of Las Vegas is unique in the Great Basin. Because of access to cheap hydroelectric power from Hoover Dam, Las Vegas is able to create an oasis of brilliance in the vast open spaces of the Great Basin, an image of bright lights and entertainment and excitement. While other Nevada towns and communities in the Great Basin also have gambling, none can compete with the resort atmosphere of Las Vegas.

Beyond the urban centers of Las Vegas and Reno, communities such as Elko, Ely, and Winnemucca play a dual role. Oriented toward their traditional function as service centers for mining and agriculture, they provide the stores, hospitals, schools, and other urban amenities for their own residents and the region that relies upon them. These communities also serve as rest stops for the restless American population that crosses the Great Basin each year. The volume of this traffic compared to the permanent residents of Nevada is overwhelming. In 1988 more than 7 million vehicles crossed the Nevada-California border on Interstate 15, while 4 million traveled the same road east and north from Las Vegas. On the western margin of the Great Basin, over 12 million vehicles crossed into or out of the state near Lake Tahoe, and 1.5 million vehicles traveled Interstate 80 at the Utah-Nevada border in the east (*Nevada Review* 1990:27). Although not all of these millions of travelers availed themselves of the unique services of Nevada communities, many did, including large numbers who come from the Mormon settlements of the eastern Great Basin to the gambling communities on Nevada's border at Jackpot, Wendover, and Mesquite (Jackson and Hudman 1988; Shepperson 1989:111–112). Thus, the cultural geography of even the smaller Nevada communities incorporates elements of the casino and gambling landscape, resulting in gambling-related activities being the single greatest element in the economy, employing more than half of all workers. The historic industries of mining (2.5 percent), manufacturing (5.2 percent), and agriculture (less than 1 percent) in combination provide but a fraction of the employment found in the gambling sector (*Nevada Review* 1990:24).

PEOPLE, PLACE, AND PROSPERITY: THE MODERN CULTURAL GEOGRAPHY OF THE GREAT BASIN

Growth in defense-industry-related manufacturing and military activity brought Las Vegas a greater share of minority groups than any other portion of the Great Basin, composing nearly 18 percent of the population in 1900. By comparison, in the Salt Lake metropolitan area, the next highest, only 7 percent of the population was part of minority groups. The Las Vegas and Reno metropolitan areas contain over 97 percent of Nevada's Afro-Americans, over 94 percent of the Asians, and more than 85 percent of the Hispanics. Only the Native American population of Nevada's Great Basin is relatively widespread across the state, yet 63.2 percent of them were concentrated in Clark and Washoe Counties (Carson City) in 1990 (Figure 7.3).

Beyond the twin metropolitan areas of the Salt Lake–Ogden–Provo area of the eastern margin and the Las Vegas–Clark County region of the southern, the people of the Great Basin are overwhelmingly Caucasian, with only 10.5 percent of the total population belonging to other groups. When the urban areas of the eastern Great Basin are removed from this equation and only the more rural counties are examined, this figure becomes even lower. The 1990 census reveals that Cassia County in the Idaho portion of the Great Basin had only 3 out of 19,532 people who were of Afro-American ancestry, while in Harney County of Oregon's Great Basin, only 2 of 7,060 people were Afro-American, and in Juab County of Utah's Great Basin only 2 of 5,817. The only minority group scattered across the rural counties of the Great Basin in significant numbers is Hispanics. Only in the urban areas are there a variety of peoples.

The cultural geography of the Great Basin thus reveals a series of dichotomies between east and west, north and south, urban and rural. In the eastern margins of the Basin, Mormon settlers created a cultural geography based on their experience in the frontier communities of the Midwest and their cultural origins in New England's Puritan villages. Utopian in nature, communitarian in practice initially, dedicated to enshrining agriculture as the ideal lifestyle, these Mormon communities emphasized subsistence through exploiting the natural resources of the locales in which they are found. Today the Mormon settlements of the east maintain their distinctiveness from the western Great Basin. Income from agriculture in Utah is nearly five times that in Nevada (U.S. Bureau of the Census 1991a:670), employment in manufacturing is more than four times as great in Utah (U.S. Bureau of the Census 1991a:740), and the violent crime rate in Nevada exceeds the national average and is more than three times as great as Utah's. In combination with the overwhelming cultural and political dominance of the Mormons, these differences create a cultural geography in the eastern Great Basin distinct from the western Basin and indeed from the rest of the United States.

Serendipity directed the settlement of the western Great Basin down paths different from the east. Based on mining and a boom-bust mentality, the broad division between the eastern and western Basin that resulted persists. The population fluctuation in the western margins in response to the quality of ore and external competition or demand is in stark contrast to the steady growth of the Mormon settlements to the east. The western and southern Great Basin emerges as a region whose cultural geography has been shaped by exploitive booms, the first based on providing for overland migrants. The subsequent mining boom and the expansion of ranching to the region continued the tradition of boom-bust cycles in the western Great Basin. In the twentieth century, military bases, bomb ranges, and the triad of gambling, quickie marriage, and just as quick divorce became the basis for an economic boom. The modern casino resorts of the 1970s and 1980s and the growing role of manufacturing and retiree population as part of the Sun Belt phenomenon in which the American population has moved south and west fuel the latest boom in Nevada. In spite of such diversification, Nevada's Great Basin settlements remain tied to the outside world, dependent on tourists, federal spending, and transfer payments such as retirement checks for their continued existence.

The contrast between the Mormon settlements of the eastern Great Basin based on prosaic farming and steady population growth, and the boom-or-bust excitement of the western Basin is obvious to even the casual observer. Less obvious is that like the west and south of the Basin, the Mormon settlements of the east are also reliant on outside support for their continued existence. This outside support, like Nevada's, comes in part from federal spending for reclamation, military spending, and federal payments to retirees and other transfer payments. A new element in the geography of this region is the tremendous growth of the Mormon church in the latter half of the twentieth century. Where historically the Mormon settlements were geared to self-sufficiency, the growth of the Mormon church into a worldwide organization has prompted the flow of money into Salt Lake City. The growth of support services for the membership of the Mormon church has provided a new element in the economy of the region, albeit another one based on external support.

The Great Basin has always been a land of limited resources, one that could not support large populations utilizing the traditional agricultural model or even local industry based on complementary resources. The rapid population growth of the region is a phenomenon of the postindustrial age in the United States. Ability to perform many economic activities by electronic means has prompted the growth of industries that do not rely on land or resources. In consequence, the Great Basin's population has surged in the last two decades as electronics, computers, and related industry moved into the area. This is especially true in the Mormon sector, where computing and processing of data play an ever important role in the economy. The cultural geography of the early history of the Great Basin has been overwhelmed by this modern transformation, creating two cultural geographies: one a relict geography of mining or agricultural communities and one composed of a few large urban centers, with their suburban sprawl replicating the experience of other urban areas of America. In this cultural geography the unique features are the gambling casinos, temples to recreation and hedonism on the western margins of the Basin; the Mormon temples and churches, symbols of the enduring belief of the descendants of the early Mormon settlers on the eastern margins; and the vast expanses of federally owned land used for bombing ranges, nuclear waste disposal, and other activities that other regions of the United States will not tolerate, scattered across the vast expanses of the center of the Basin.

This strange juxtaposition of religion and vice, destruction and recreation, is the enduring legacy of the human use of the natural environment of the Great Basin. The extreme differences in the human activities in the Great Basin are in stark contrast to the general unifying characteristics of the Basin's natural environment. The underlying geographic factor is that the Great Basin is an arid land, a fragile land, a dependent land, one whose people have always relied on the outside for support. Its austere beauty, open spaces, and climate will continue to attract migrants, but the region's present and future inhabitants can stay only as long as their lifelines to more richly endowed places remain in place.

REFERENCES

Arrington, Leonard J. *Great Basin Kingdom: An Economic History of the Latter-Day Saints, 1830–1900*. Cambridge: Harvard University Press, 1958.

Atwood, Wallace W. *The Physiographic Provinces of North America*. Boston: Ginn and Company, 1940.

Campbell, Lester D. "Perception and Land Use: The Case of the Mormon Culture Region." Master's thesis, Brigham Young University, Department of Geography, Provo, Utah, 1974.

Earl, Phillip. *This Was Nevada*. Reno: Nevada Historical Society, 1986.

Elliott, Russell. *History of Nevada*. Lincoln: University of Nebraska Press, 1973.

Fenneman, Nevin M. *Physiography of the Western United States*. New York: McGraw-Hill, 1931.

Francis, John G., and Richard Ganzel, editors. *Western Public Lands: The Management of Natural Resources in a Time of Declining Federalism*. Totawa, New Jersey: Roman and Allanfield, 1984.

Goetzman, William H. *Exploration and Empire*. New York: Alfred A. Knopf, 1966.

Gurgel, Klaus D. "Historic Population Growth in Utah," *Atlas of Utah*. Provo, Utah: Brigham Young University Press, 1981.

Houghton, Samuel G. *A Trace of Desert Waters*. Glendale, Calif.: Arthur H. Clark Company, 1976.

Hulse, James W. *The Nevada Adventure: A History*, 4th ed. Reno: University of Nevada Press, 1978.

Jackson, Richard H. "Great Salt Lake and Salt Lake City: American Curiosities," *Utah Historical Quarterly*, Vol. 56 (Spring 1988), 128–147.

Jackson, Richard H. "Mormon Perception and Settlement," *Annals of the Association of American Geographers*, Vol. 68 (September 1978), 317–334.

Jackson, Richard H., and Lloyd Hudman. "Border Towns, Gambling and the Mormon Culture Region," *Journal of Cultural Geography* (Summer 1988), 35–48.

Jackson, Richard H., and Robert Layton. "The Mormon Village: Analysis of a Settlement Type," *The Professional Geographer*, Vol. 28 (May 1976), 136–141.

Jackson, Richard H., and Dale J. Stevens. "Physical and Cultural Environment of Utah Lake and Adjacent Areas," Great Basin Naturalist Memoirs No. 5 (1981), 3–23.

Meining, Donald W. "The Mormon Culture Region: Strategies and Patterns in the Geography of the American West, 1847–1964," *Annals, Association of American Geographers*, Vol. 55 (1965), 191–220.

Moehring, Eugene P. *Resort City in the Sunbelt: Las Vegas, 1930–1970*. Reno: University of Nevada Press, 1989.

Muir, John. *Steep Trails*. Boston: Houghton Mifflin, 1918.

Nevada Review of Business Economics, 1990. Reno: University of Nevada Press, 1989.

Paher, Stanley, editor. *Nevada Towns and Tales*. Las Vegas: Nevada Publications, 1981.

Reed, Walter H. *Population of Nevada: Counties and Communities, 1860–1980*. Reno: Nevada Historical Society, 1984.

Shepperson, Wilbur S., editor. *East of Eden, West of Zion: Essays on Nevada*. Reno: University of Nevada Press, 1989.

U.S. Bureau of the Census. *Statistical Abstract of the United States, 1990*. Washington, D.C.: U.S. Department of Commerce, Bureau of the Census, 1991a.

U.S. Bureau of the Census. *United States Census of Population, 1990*. Washington, D.C.: U.S. Department of Commerce, Bureau of the Census, 1991b.

Wahlquist, Wayne L. "Migration to Utah," *Atlas of Utah*. Provo, Utah: Brigham Young University Press, 1981.

Wahlquist, Wayne L. "Settlement Processes in the Mormon Core Area, 1847–1890," Ph.D. dissertation, University of Nebraska, Lincoln, 1974.

Pinus longaeva D. K. Bailey (western bristlecone pine) individuals are the longest-lived organisms known on earth. Although this pine is now confined to the tops of widely separated, calcareous mountains, it occurs in many late Pleistocene woodrat middens in the bottoms of Great Basin valleys.

8

Distribution of Genetic Diversity Within and Among Populations of Great Basin Conifers

J. L. Hamrick, Andrew F. Schnabel,
and P. V. Wells

OVERVIEW

Using macrofossil data obtained from rat middens at various locations in the Great Basin, the authors of this chapter have been able to reconstruct accurately the evolutionary history of eight modern conifer species, documenting ancient fluctuations in conifer distribution both locally and regionally in the Great Basin. The authors have effectively correlated these changes with various paleoclimatic changes in the region. Specifically, they present the distribution of genetic diversity within and among populations of eight conifer species that now occupy the montane islands in the Basin. By examining the variation in several allozyme loci, the authors also test predictions based on the biogeographical history of these species.

The genetic composition of plant populations is dependent on past biogeographic and evolutionary events acting in concert with current evolutionary forces. The number and genetic composition of founding individuals, the duration and extent of fluctuations in population size, the duration and degree of isolation, and the direction and intensity of natural selection are among the historical factors influencing the genetic composition of contemporary populations. The reconstruction of past evolutionary events for most plant species is difficult, however, because the necessary historical information is not available. Usually the only recourse is to reconstruct those events from the current distribution of genetic diversity.

This generalization does not hold for populations of several conifer species inhabiting the Great Basin of western North America. Antecedents of populations of 10 conifer species are locally documented in ^{14}C-dated woodrat (Neotoma) middens from various sectors of the Great Basin (Wells 1976, 1979, 1983; Thompson and Meade 1982).

The availability of these detailed plant macrofossil records coupled with the varying degrees of isolation these populations have experienced for different numbers of millennia constitute large-scale microevolutionary experiments. Consequently, the known Quaternary history of these species suggests several straightforward genetic predictions that are amenable to testing by genetic analyses of existing populations.

Nine of the 10 conifer taxa that penetrate the central Great Basin have their main distributions in the Rocky Mountains; six wide-ranging species occur also in the Sierra Nevada of California (Table 8.1). Within the central Great Basin there is an east-

Table 8.1   Distribution of Montane Coniferous Taxa Among the Major Ranges of the Intermountain Region South of 43°N Latitude

Sierra Nevada	Great Basin Ranges	Rocky Mountains
A. concolor	Abies concolor (I, W)	A. concolor
var. lowiana	var. concolor	var. concolor
	Abies lasiocarpa (R, L)	A. lasiocarpa
J. communis	Juniperus communis (R, W)	J. communis
	Juniperus scopulorum (I, W)	J. scopulorum
	Picea engelmannii (R, L)	P. engelmannii
P. flexilis	Pinus flexilis (R, W)	P. flexilis
	Pinus longaeva (R, W)	P. longaeva
P. monophylla	Pinus monophylla (I, W)	P. edulis
P. ponderosa	Pinus ponderosa (I, L)	P. ponderosa
var. ponderosa	var. scopulorum	var. scopulorum
P. menziesii	Pseudotsuga menziesii (I, L)	P. menziesii
var. menziesii	var. glauca	var. glauca

Note: Letters in parentheses represent the biogeographical status and relative distribution of each species within the Great Basin: R = Pleistocene relict; I = Holocene immigrant; W = widespread distribution within the Great Basin; L = limited distribution within the Great Basin.
Source: Nomenclature after Little 1979.

west pattern of declining species richness of the 10 montane conifers that correlates with distance from the western Rocky Mountains. Detailed Neotoma macrofossil records (leaves, cones, seeds) imply that during the Wisconsin glacial (12,000–20,000 B.P.) several species of conifers currently found in the central Great Basin were absent from this region, though abundantly documented in the same time interval in the southern (Mojavean) sector. Other species have survived on the ranges they now occupy for the past 40,000 years or more but underwent major downward shifts in elevation during the Wisconsin glacial. A documented example is bristlecone pine, Pinus longaeva, which shifted its elevational range 600 m downward (Wells 1983).

The pleniglacial forests in the lowlands of the central Great Basin thus had only one to five species of conifers (Abies lasiocarpa, Pinus longaeva, Pinus flexilis, Picea engelmannii, Juniperus communis).

During the late-glacial/Holocene (12,000–8,000 B.P.) warming of climate, however, Pleistocene-relict species shifted upward in elevation and were augmented in the eastern Great Basin mountain ranges by as many as five additional species (Abies concolor, Pinus monophylla, Pinus ponderosa, Pseudotsuga menziesii, Juniperus scopulorum). These Holocene-immigrant species appear in the Neotoma macrofossil record from the central Great Basin only during the past 10,000 years; some date exclusively from the late Holocene (about 5,000 B.P.). Macrofossil evidence indicates that the later Holocene arrivals dispersed across desert barriers that by then isolated the shrunken montane islands. Timing of recolonization and actual distances traveled by the more recent immigrant species suggest that they were probably introduced by seed-eating birds (Wells 1983). Moderately long-range transport of seeds by birds is deduced as follows. A northward latitudinal shift of 500–640 km during the Holocene is documented for several conifer species, including the heavy-seeded, late-maturing pinyon pine, P. monophylla. A 640-km migration in 8,000 years (80 m/yr) is indicated for pinyon, but the most generous estimate of its dispersal rate via wind/gravity is 0.4 m/yr (3.2 km/8,000 yrs), two orders of magnitude too slow. Seed dispersal by nutcrackers (Nucifraga columbiana) and pinyon jays (Gymnorhinus cyanocephalus), however, is both the prevalent mode of dispersal in this and other conifer species (Balda and Bateman 1971; Van der Wall and Balda 1977; Ligon 1978; Tomback 1980; Lanner and Van der Wall 1980; Hutchins and Lanner 1982) and is amply swift to fit the known migrational history.

Population genetics theory predicts that founder events concomitant with long-distance dispersal should reduce genetic variation within populations and increase variation among populations, whereas long-established populations should retain their original genetic diversity. The present-day co-occurrence in the Great Basin of Pleistocene-relict and Holocene-immigrant species allows direct comparisons to be made between species with different evolutionary histories vis-à-vis the levels and distribution of genetic diversity.

In this chapter we examine the distribution of genetic diversity within and among populations of eight conifer species that presently occur on the montane islands of the Great Basin. We use variation patterns at several allozyme loci to test predictions based on the biogeographical history of these species.

PREDICTIONS

Given the recent paleoecology of the conifer species currently occupying the Great Basin mountain ranges, we can make several predictions concerning the distribution of genetic variation within and among their populations.

1.   Conifer populations of the western Rocky Mountains of Utah that served as sources for Holocene immigration ("mainland" populations) should have the same levels and patterns of variation as other continuously or nearly continuously distributed conifer species. Allozyme variation within populations

should be high, and less than 10 percent of the total variation should occur among populations.

2. Species with large, continuous populations in the Great Basin throughout the late Pleistocene that have subsequently contracted to Holocene refugia on isolated mountaintops (e.g., *P. longaeva*) should have genetic diversity distributed in a manner similar to mainland Rocky Mountain populations. These long-lived species have been isolated for only a few generations (<10,000 years). Where population sizes (though reduced) have generally remained substantial, intrapopulation variation should be large and interpopulation heterogeneity small, as on the mainland.

3. Holocene immigrants of low-elevation woodlands with larger population sizes and more nearly continuous distributions (e.g., *P. monophylla*) should experience more gene flow via pollen and seed. Thus, the more or less isolated (but recent) northern populations of pinyon may not differ greatly in genetic composition from mainland or source populations.

4. More restricted populations of Holocene immigrants of high-montane habitat (e.g., *Abies concolor*), colonized mainly by bird-mediated dispersal across semiarid lowland barriers, should have been initiated by very few individuals. As a consequence, levels of intrapopulational genetic variation in the Great Basin should be reduced relative to source populations of the Holocene-immigrant species (or relative to isolated populations of Pleistocene-relict species). Genetic variation among islandlike populations of these Holocene-immigrant species should be greater than that seen among conspecific mainland populations or among Great Basin populations of Pleistocene-relict species.

    The most noticeable genetic effect of long-distance dispersal should be the loss of relatively rare alleles (Nei et al. 1975) that are present in the Rocky Mountain source populations. As a result, the number of alleles per polymorphic locus should be lower in isolated Great Basin populations of the Holocene-immigrant species than in isolated populations of formerly continuous, Pleistocene-relict species. Since the most western and northern populations of recent immigrants (e.g., *A. concolor* in the Ruby and Pilot Ranges) were probably founded by individuals from populations to the east or south, the most western and northern populations should have lost the greatest number of alleles and should have lower levels of genetic diversity relative to possible intermediate sources (e.g., *A. concolor* in the Snake Range of east central Nevada).

Founder effects are assumed to be most marked if dispersal between mountains is an infrequent event, if few individuals from each founding event reach maturity, and if the time since founding has been insufficient for populations to recover genetic variation via mutation. Conversely, with many founders or multiple founder events, more alleles from the source population would be introduced and genetic diversity within new Great Basin island populations may show little, if any, reduction.

METHODS

The chief criterion for the selection of species was their paleobiogeography in the central Great Basin. While every species has its own history, the eight species selected for allozyme analysis readily fall into two groups of four: (1) Pleistocene relicts at high elevations that previously had much larger Pleistocene populations at lower elevations (600–800 m lower); and (2) Holocene immigrants — species that were absent or extremely local in the central Great Basin during the last glacial (Table 8.1).

A second criterion for selection was the existing distribution of each species, which also determined our sampling pattern. It is a fortunate circumstance that both the Pleistocene-relict group and the Holocene-immigrant group consist of species with wide and more localized distributions in the Great Basin region. Thus, a two-by-two factorial combination of the historical (Pleistocene relicts vs. Holocene immigrants) and modern distribution (wide-ranging vs. restricted) criteria constituted the sampling of the eight species for allozyme analysis. The four wide-ranging species include two relicts from the Pleistocene on subalpine mountaintops (*Pinus longaeva* and *P. flexilis*) and two Holocene immigrants to the central Great Basin, one a subalpine (*Abies concolor*) and one a xerophytic woodland species (*Pinus monophylla*). Similarly, there are four species with more restricted Great Basin distributions, again including two Pleistocene survivors, both strongly subalpine species (*Abies lasiocarpa* and *Picea engelmannii*), and two Holocene immigrants, the montane-subalpine *Pseudotsuga menziesii* and the more xerophytic montane *Pinus ponderosa*.

We sampled 78 populations of the eight species on 20 montane islands of the Great Basin. The number of populations per species ranged from three (*A. lasiocarpa*) to 18 (*P. monophylla*), depending on how common the species was in this region. An additional 47 mainland populations were sampled in the western Rocky Mountains of Utah (Uinta Mountains, Wasatch Mountains, High Plateaus, Uvada Prong), with the number of populations per species ranging from four to seven. The mainland populations of each species were generally chosen to span the latitudinal extent of the modern range in Utah. The locations and species sampled from each location are indicated in Figure 8.1.

A random sample of 72 individuals (all age classes) was obtained from each population. If population sizes were too small to achieve this number, a sample was taken from every available individual (minimum sample size = 32 individuals). Approximately 10 cm of branch and needle tissue were obtained from each individual. Each sample was labeled, placed in a plastic bag, and refrigerated the same day. Within four days of collection, the needles were shipped to the laboratory at the University of Kansas, where they were stored at 4°C.

Needles from each individual were placed in a mortar, covered with a layer of liquid nitrogen, and ground to a fine powder. An extraction buffer (Mitton et al. 1979) was then added, and the crude extract was passed through a synthetic filter and absorbed by filter-paper wicks. The wicks were placed in microliter plates and stored at −70°C until needed for electrophoresis.

Each species was analyzed for more than 21 isozyme loci. The number varied somewhat among species depending on expression and resolution (Tables 8.2 and 8.3). The

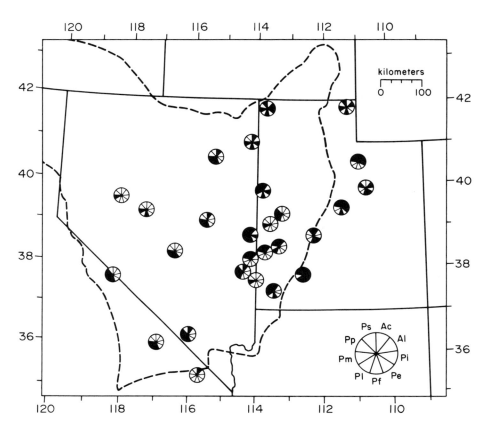

Figure 8.1   Locations of collection sites for nine conifer species. Species sampled in each
location are indicated by shading the appropriate sectors in the corresponding
circle. The dashed line indicates the boundaries of the Great Basin region.
Species are *Abies concolor* (Ac), *Abies lasiocarpa* (Al), *Picea engelmannii* (Pi),
Pinus edulis (Pe), *Pinus flexilis* (Pf), *Pinus longaeva* (Pl), *Pinus monophylla* (Pm),
Pinus ponderosa (Pp), and *Pseudotsuga menziesii* (Ps).

corresponding enzyme systems included aconitase, aldolase, diaphorase, esterase (colori-
metric and fluorescent), fructose-1,6-diphosphatase, glutamate oxalacetate transaminase,
isocitrate dehydrogenase, leucine aminopeptidase, malate dehydrogenase, malic enzyme,
peroxidase, phosphoglucoisomerase, phosphoglucomutase, 6-phosphogluconate dehydrogenase, shikimate dehydrogenase, and triosephosphate isomerase.

    Levels of genetic diversity within populations were estimated using three
parameters: percent of polymorphic loci per population (P); the number of alleles per polymorphic locus (A_p); and the Hardy-Weinberg expected percentage of
loci heterozygous per individual (H; where $H = 1 - \Sigma \, p_i^2$ and p_i is the frequency
of the ith allele). Mean values of these parameters were calculated for mainland
and island populations of the eight species. There are no truly mainland populations of *P. monophylla*. Genetic parameters of *P. monophylla* are compared to

Table 8.2   Allozyme Diversity Within and Among Populations of Four Pleistocene-Relict Conifer Species (Standard Deviations in Parentheses)

Species	Region	Pop.	Loci	P	A_p	H	G_{ST}
	Overall	9	22	70.0	2.36	0.211	0.102
				(3.3)	(0.09)	(0.016)	***
Abies	Mainland	6	22	69.8	2.38	0.213	0.065
lasiocarpa				(4.0)	(0.07)	(0.020)	***
	Island	3	22	70.3	2.34	0.208	0.072
				(5.8)	(0.12)	(0.027)	***
	Overall	10	25	56.5	2.49	0.181	0.109
				(3.1)	(0.17)	(0.014)	***
Picea	Mainland	5	25	52.2	2.58	0.171	0.050
engelmannii				(4.5)	(0.13)	(0.020)	***
	Island	5	25	60.8	2.39	0.192	0.089
				(4.3)	(0.17)	(0.019)	***
	Overall	19	26	63.5	2.53	0.182	0.101
				(2.2)	(0.13)	(0.010)	***
Pinus	Mainland	7	26	59.2	2.48	0.161	0.044
flexilis				(3.6)	(0.09)	(0.016)	***
	Island	12	26	66.0	2.55	0.195	0.101
				(2.7)	(0.15)	(0.012)	***
	Overall	16	27	65.1	2.41	0.223	0.149
				(2.4)	(0.10)	(0.011)	***
Pinus	Mainland	4	27	69.2	2.39	0.237	0.065
longaeva				(4.5)	(0.13)	(0.022)	***
	Island	12	27	63.8	2.42	0.218	0.169
				(2.8)	(0.09)	(0.013)	***
	Overall	—	—	63.8	2.45	0.199	0.115
				(1.4)	(0.06)	(0.006)	
Mean	Mainland	—	—	62.6	2.46	0.196	0.056
				(2.1)	(0.05)	(0.010)	
	Island	—	—	65.2	2.42	0.203	0.108
				(2.1)	(0.07)	(0.009)	

*** P < 0.001.

Table 8.3   Allozyme Diversity Within and Among Populations of Four Holocene-Immigrant Conifer Species (Standard Deviations in Parentheses)

Species	Region	Pop.	Loci	P	A_p	H	G_{ST}
	Overall	19	22	56.3	2.24	0.134	0.101
				(2.4)	(0.12)	(0.009)	***
Abies	Mainland	7	22	55.3	2.29	0.131	0.056
concolor				(4.0)	(0.14)	(0.015)	***
	Island	12	22	56.9	2.22	0.135	0.105
				(3.0)	(0.11)	(0.012)	***
Pinus	Mainland	4	26	72.8	3.00	0.159	0.018
edulis				(4.4)	(0.17)	(0.018)	*
Pinus	Island	18	26	67.9	2.80	0.150	0.033
monophylla				(2.2)	(0.13)	(0.009)	***
	Overall	17	26	67.5	2.36	0.172	0.091
				(2.2)	(0.17)	(0.010)	***
Pinus	Mainland	7	26	70.0	2.40	0.176	0.039
ponderosa				(3.6)	(0.12)	(0.016)	***
	Island	10	26	65.7	2.33	0.169	0.098
				(2.9)	(0.20)	(0.012)	***
	Overall	13	22	52.5	2.31	0.111	0.087
				(3.1)	(0.15)	(0.011)	***
Pseudotsuga	Mainland	7	22	53.0	2.29	0.106	0.066
menziesii				(4.1)	(0.17)	(0.015)	***
	Island	6	22	52.0	2.33	0.116	0.061
				(4.6)	(0.12)	(0.017)	***
	Overall	—	—	61.0	2.43	0.142	0.093
				(1.5)	(0.09)	(0.006)	
Mean	Mainland	—	—	62.8	2.50	0.143	0.045
				(2.0)	(0.08)	(0.008)	
	Island	—	—	60.6	2.42	0.142	0.074
				(1.6)	(0.07)	(0.006)	

* P < 0.05.
*** P < 0.001.

those of *P. edulis*, a closely related species that occurs at the lower elevations of the western Rocky Mountains.

Variation among populations was analyzed separately for the mainland and island populations to determine whether partitioning of genetic variation differs between the two regions. Chi-square analyses were used to determine whether significant heterogeneity in allele frequencies exists among the populations within each region. Nei's (1973) G_{ST} statistic was used to partition genetic diversity within and among populations of each species. The mean G_{ST} values for mainland versus island populations and relict versus immigrant species were compared.

RESULTS

Levels of Genetic Diversity Within Populations

The nine Great Basin conifer species (including *P. edulis*) maintain relatively high levels of genetic diversity within their populations (Tables 8.2 and 8.3). When the populations are pooled, these nine Great Basin conifers had somewhat higher proportions of polymorphic loci (P = 63.6 percent vs. 53.4 percent), approximately the same number of alleles per polymorphic locus (A_p = 2.50 vs. 2.53), and higher proportions of expected heterozygosity per individual (H = 0.169 vs. 0.151) than the means for more than 100 conifer species reviewed by Hamrick et al. (1992). There were relatively large differences among the nine species for these genetic diversity parameters, however. Genetic diversity measures were highest for *P. longaeva* and *A. lasiocarpa* (Table 8.2) and lowest for *A. concolor* and *P. menziesii* (Table 8.3). The majority of the differences in genetic diversity (H) among these species appeared to be due to differences in the proportion of polymorphic loci. However, *A. concolor* and *P. menziesii* also had the lowest number of alleles per polymorphic locus.

Comparisons of the Pleistocene-relict and the Holocene-immigrant species (Tables 8.2 and 8.3) indicate that these two groups of species have similar proportions of polymorphic loci (P = 63.8 percent vs. 61.0 percent) and number of alleles per polymorphic locus (A_p = 2.45 vs. 2.43) but that the Pleistocene-relict species have a higher proportion of expected heterozygosity (H = 0.199 vs. 0.142). These results indicate that alleles at the polymorphic loci of the Pleistocene-relict species have more even allele frequencies within populations than those of the Holocene-immigrant species.

Species with limited and widespread distributions in the Great Basin (Table 8.1) had roughly equal proportions of polymorphic loci (P = 61.6 percent vs. 63.2 percent) and genetic diversity (H = 0.169 vs. 0.172). The widespread species had somewhat more alleles per polymorphic locus (A_p = 2.50) than the four species with more limited distributions in the Great Basin (A_p = 2.38).

Across the eight comparisons there were almost no differences between the levels of genetic diversity maintained in the Rocky Mountain mainland populations and in the Great Basin montane-island populations (P = 62.7 percent vs. 62.9 percent; A_p = 2.48 vs. 2.42; and H = 0.169 vs. 0.173). There were no real differences in these three genetic parameters between mainland and montane-island populations of the four Pleistocene-relict species (Table 8.2). The montane-island populations had somewhat higher levels of polymorphic loci (P) and genetic diversity (H) but had fewer alleles per polymorphic locus (A$_p$). For the four Holocene-immigrant species, the montane-island populations have marginally smaller P and A$_p$ values. Genetic diversity (H) within populations from these two areas is the same, however. Mainland and montane-island populations of individual Pleistocene-relict species have some rather large differences in genetic diversity (e.g., the H value for *P. flexilis* and the A$_p$ value for *P. engelmannii*), but there are no consistent trends (Table 8.2). Among the Holocene-immigrant species, mean A$_p$ values were lower for the island populations for three species (Table 8.3). For *P. menziesii*, the values were reversed.

To summarize, the major differences in the level of allozyme variation maintained within populations is between the mean genetic diversity (H) of the Pleistocene-relict and the Holocene-immigrant species. Also, although the differences are not statistically significant, there is some indication that the montane-island populations of the Holocene-immigrant species have somewhat lower mean values for the proportion of polymorphic loci and the number of alleles per polymorphic locus.

Distribution of Genetic Diversity Among Populations

Like most conifers, these nine Great Basin species have the majority of their genetic diversity within populations and relatively little among populations. Compared to mean values for the conifer species reviewed by Hamrick et al. (1992), the Great Basin species have more genetic diversity among populations. The G$_{ST}$ values for individual species based on all the populations analyzed are generally clustered close to the overall mean (Tables 8.2 and 8.3). Exceptions were the two pinyon pines, *P. edulis* and *P. monophylla*, which had particularly low G$_{ST}$ values (Table 8.3). At the other extreme was *P. longaeva* (Table 8.2), with an overall G$_{ST}$ value of nearly 0.15. The G$_{ST}$ values represent statistically significant differences in allele frequencies among populations in every instance due to the large number of populations and sample sizes used. Comparisons of allele frequencies among the four *P. edulis* populations were only weakly significant (P < 0.05), while all the rest were highly significant (P < 0.001).

Pleistocene-relict species, largely because of the presence of *P. longaeva*, had a mean G$_{ST}$ value approximately 24 percent higher than the value for the Holocene-immigrant species. Species with a widespread distribution in the Great Basin also have a higher mean G$_{ST}$ since *P. longaeva* is also a member of this group. The most significant differences among categories of populations occurred between the mean G$_{ST}$ values of the mainland and the montane-island populations (Tables 8.2 and 8.3). In seven of the eight comparisons, G$_{ST}$ values for the mainland populations were smaller than those for the montane-island populations. For some species (i.e., *P. flexilis*, *P. longaeva*, and *P. ponderosa*), the G$_{ST}$ values for the montane-island populations were more than two times the values for the mainland populations. Only P. menziesii had less variation among its island populations than among its mainland populations. The Pleistocene-relict species generally had larger differences between

G_{ST} values for mainland and montane-island populations (0.056 vs. 0.108, Table 8.2) than did the Holocene-immigrant species (0.045 vs. 0.074, Table 8.3).

The proportion of the total genetic diversity due to genetic heterogeneity among populations can be partitioned into two components. The first component is due to genetic heterogeneity between the two geographic regions represented in this study, the Rocky Mountain mainland and the Great Basin montane islands. The second component is due to genetic variation among populations within these two regions. For the Pleistocene-relict species, the mean G_{ST} value over all populations was 0.115, that between regions was 0.026, and that due to differences among populations within the two regions was 0.089. For the Holocene-immigrant species, the three values were 0.093, 0.018, and 0.075. Thus, it appears that genetic differences between the Rocky Mountain mainland populations and the Great Basin island populations are smaller for the Holocene-immigrant species. This conclusion is supported by the mean genetic distance (Nei 1972) values of the Holocene-immigrant species (D = 0.008) and the Pleistocene-relict species (D = 0.022) between the Rocky Mountain mainland and the Great Basin island populations.

DISCUSSION

With our understanding of the paleobiogeography of these conifer species, we made several predictions concerning the distribution of genetic diversity within and among their populations. Specifically, we predicted that the Holocene-immigrant species should have less variation within their Great Basin populations and more variation among these populations than among similar populations from the Rocky Mountain mainland. Pleistocene-relict species, in contrast, should show little or no difference between mainland and island populations in how their genetic variation is distributed. Furthermore, the Holocene-immigrant species should have relatively more genetic diversity among their montane-island populations and relatively less genetic diversity within populations than the Pleistocene-relict species with similar geographic distributions.

Our results do not support these predictions. Holocene-immigrant species have somewhat less genetic diversity within their montane-island populations than within their Rocky Mountain populations, but these differences are not statistically or biologically significant. Furthermore, Pleistocene-relict and Holocene-immigrant species have approximately the same proportion of polymorphic loci and the same number of alleles per locus within their populations. Nor do they differ in how genetic diversity is partitioned among populations. In fact, the Pleistocene-relict species have somewhat more genetic heterogeneity among both mainland and montane-island populations than the Holocene-immigrant species. The most striking result is that there is more genetic differentiation among the montane-island populations than among mainland populations for seven of the eight species. For most species, there is nearly twice as much variation among the montane-island populations.

Several historical factors affecting the founding of the Great Basin populations by the Holocene-immigrant species could alter our predictions. First, these populations could have been founded by relatively large numbers of individuals. This is a plausible explanation since the bird species involved can carry up to 95 pinyon seeds in specially adapted sublingual pouches (Van der Wall and Balda 1977). Also, these birds often fly in rather large flocks. If several birds were to cache seeds in a local area, several hundred seeds would be available to germinate. Thus, even if the probability of a seed or seed cache's surviving and the probability of a seedling's reaching maturity are low, several reproductive individuals could survive in a local area. In addition, several such colonizing events may have occurred within a mountain range, thereby increasing genetic diversity within the mountain range and within individual populations. Seeds may have also been constantly introduced into a population after the time of initial founding. Although the chance of a seed's becoming established may be lower in a pre-existing population, additional genetic diversity could have been introduced in this way. Once several populations become established on a mountain range, seed and pollen movement among these populations would further homogenize genetic diversity with the overall effect of increasing diversity in any one location and decreasing diversity among local populations on different mountain ranges.

It is also possible that populations of supposedly Holocene-immigrant species were present during the most recent glacial period in small, isolated refugia, readily missed by localized macrofossil samples. The present-day distribution of conifer species on many Great Basin ranges is often characterized by one or a few isolated sites. Often these populations contain several hundred reproductive individuals — more than enough to preserve the genetic diversity present when the species was more widely distributed. However, while small pleniglacial refugia could have existed for some of the immigrant species, we feel that the weight of paleoecological evidence (Wells 1983) precludes this explanation for every mountain range studied.

A final factor that would increase genetic diversity within and decrease genetic diversity among Great Basin populations would be the occurrence of relatively high levels of pollen flow between the Great Basin mountain ranges and the Rocky Mountain mainland. Recent genetic studies of pollen contamination in conifer seed orchards (El-Kassaby et al. 1988; Friedman and Adams 1985; Nagasaka and Szmidt 1985) indicate that the movement of conifer pollen can be quite extensive over several kilometers. In the Great Basin, however, significant levels of pollen movement among mountain ranges separated by 40 km or more or among the Great Basin ranges and the Rocky Mountain mainland are unlikely since the prevailing winds (westerly) are counter to the principal direction of immigration. Thus, pollen flow (eastward) would be unlikely to have reinforced seed dispersal (westward and northward).

Evidence against high rates of recent gene flow between the mainland and the Great Basin montane islands or among the Basin ranges is provided by the observation that genetic diversity among the Basin populations is almost twice that found among the western Rocky Mountain populations. The G_{ST} values of the mainland populations are similar to those found for conifer species with continuous or nearly continuous distributions (e.g., *Pinus contorta*, Yeh and Layton 1979; *P. ponderosa*, Hamrick et al. 1989; *Pseudotsuga menziesii*, Li and Adams 1989). Yet the higher G_{ST} values of the discontinuously distributed Great Basin populations are more similar to those of other discontinuously distributed conifer species (e.g., *Pinus brutia*, Conkle et al. 1988; *P. halepensis*, Schiller et al. 1985; *P. pungens*, Gibson and Hamrick 1991). An exception is the two pinyon pines, *P. edulis* from the Wasatch mainland and *P. monophylla* from the Great Basin. Both of these lowland woodland species have much smaller G_{ST} values than species from the more isolated montane and subalpine habitats. The more continuous current distributions of these two species coupled with the fact that the pinyons are the preferred food source for the jays and nutcrackers may lead to greater gene flow and less genetic differentiation among their populations. Additional gene movement among pinyon pine populations could have resulted from the action of humans. Betancourt et al. (1991) found relatively little reduction in genetic diversity in an isolated population of *P. edulis* in northern Colorado believed to have been unintentionally founded by humans within the past 750 years.

Two evolutionary forces could have acted to produce greater genetic diversity among the montane-island populations: genetic drift and disruptive selection. While we would not argue that the allozyme loci studied are not influenced by selection, it is unlikely that selection would increase genetic differentiation among populations for all of the species involved, Pleistocene-relict and Holocene-immigrant alike. Also, since both groups of species appear to show this pattern, their different biogeographical histories could not have had a major effect on their present population genetic structure. The larger differentiation of allele frequencies among the Great Basin populations could have been caused by population bottlenecks for the Pleistocene-relict species or a combination of founder events and bottlenecks for the Holocene-immigrant species. These bottlenecks and founder events have evidently not been so severe as to lead to the loss of significant amounts of genetic diversity (Nei et al. 1975), but they have led to shifts in allele frequencies. The long life span of conifers would buffer against the loss of genetic variation during periods of reduced population sizes. As the environmental stress that caused the bottleneck is removed, the presence of a few large individuals would enhance the ability of the population to recover and to maintain its genetic diversity (Nei et al. 1975). However, because of the isolation of the Great Basin populations, any changes in allele frequencies that occurred during the bottleneck would not be erased by subsequent gene flow. The near extinction of local populations may also occur on the mainland. However, the lack of geographic barriers to gene flow on the Wasatch mainland would tend to reduce any heterogeneity in allele frequencies that might arise.

In conclusion, our analyses of these Great Basin conifer species indicate that the establishment of populations by long-distance founding events has not played a major role in shaping the genetic structure of these populations. Our results show, however, that populations isolated by 40 km or more of unfavorable habitat have a tendency to diverge genetically. Gene flow over such long distances is evidently unable to counteract the genetic differences that have developed.

ACKNOWLEDGMENTS

We wish to acknowledge the field and laboratory assistance of Cathy Gorman, Jenna Hamrick, Karen Hamrick, Ron Lanner, Roger Laushman, and Linda Vescio. Without their good-natured assistance, a project of this magnitude could never have been possible. Financial support was provided by a National Science Foundation Grant, BSR-8320529, to J.L.H. and P.V.W.

LITERATURE CITED

Balda, R. P., and G. C. Bateman. 1971. Flocking and annual cycle of the pinon jay, *Gymnorhinus cyanocephalus*. Condor 73:287–302.

Betancourt, J. L., W. S. Schuster, J. B. Mitton, and R. S. Anderson. 1991. Fossil and genetic history of a pinyon pine (*Pinus edulis*) isolate. Ecology 72:1685–1697.

Conkle, M. T., G. Schiller, and C. Grunwald. 1988. Electrophoretic analysis of diversity and phylogeny of *Pinus brutia* and closely related taxa. Syst. Bot. 13:411–424.

El-Kassaby, Y. A., D. Rudin, and R. Yazdani. 1988. Levels of outcrossing and contamination in two *Pinus sylvestris* L. seed orchards in northern Sweden. Scan. J. For. Res. 4:41–49.

Friedman, S., and W. T. Adams. 1985. Estimation of gene flow into two seed orchards of loblolly pine (*Pinus taeda* L.). Theor. Appl. Genet. 69:609–615.

Gibson, J. P., and J. L. Hamrick. 1991. Genetic diversity and structure in *Pinus pungens* (Table Mountain pine) populations. Canad. J. For. Res. 21:635–642.

Hamrick, J. L., H. M. Blanton, and K. J. Hamrick. 1989. Genetic structure of geographically marginal populations of ponderosa pine. Amer. J. Bot. 76:1559–1568.

Hamrick, J. L., M.J.W. Godt, and S. L. Sherman-Broyles. 1992. Factors influencing levels of genetic diversity in woody plant species. New Forestry 6:95–124.

Hutchins, H. E., and R. M. Lanner. 1982. The central role of Clark's nutcracker in the dispersal and establishment of whitebark pine. Oecologia 55:192–201.

Lanner, R. M., and S. B. Van der Wall. 1980. Dispersal of limber pine seed by Clark's nutcracker. J. For. 78:637–639.

Li, P., and W. T. Adams. 1989. Range-wide pattern of allozyme variation in Douglas-fir (*Pseudotsuga menziesii*). Can. J. For. Res. 19:149–161.

Ligon, J. D. 1978. Reproductive interdependence of pinon jays and pinon pine. Ecol. Mono. 48:111–126.

Little, E. L. 1979. Checklist of United States Trees. U.S. Forest Service Agricultural Handbook 541.

Mitton, J. B., Y. B. Linhart, B. K. Sturgeon, and J. L. Hamrick. 1979. Allozyme polymorphisms detected in mature needle tissue of ponderosa pine, *Pinus ponderosa* Laws. J. Hered. 70:86–89.

Nagasaka, K., and A. E. Szmidt. 1985. Multilocus analysis of external pollen contamination of a Scots pine (*Pinus sylvestris* L.) seed orchard. In: Population Genetics in Forestry (ed. H.-R. Gregorius). Lecture Notes in Biomathematics 60:134–138.

Nei, M. 1972. Genetic distance between populations. Am. Nat. 106:283–292.

Nei, M. 1973. Analysis of gene diversity in subdivided populations. Proc. Natl. Acad. Sci. USA 70:3321–3323.

Nei, M., T. Maruyama, and R. Chakraborty. 1975. The bottleneck effect and genetic variability in populations. Evolution 29:1–10.

Schiller, G., M. T. Conkle, and C. Grunwald. 1985. Local differentiation among Mediterranean populations of Aleppo pine in their isozymes. Silv. Genet. 35:11–19.

Thompson, R. S., and J. I. Meade. 1982. Late quaternary environments and biogeography in the Great Basin. Quat. Res. 17:39–55.

Tomback, D. F. 1980. How nutcrackers find their seed stores. Condor 82:10–19.

Van der Wall, S. B., and R. P. Balda. 1977. Coadaptations of Clark's nutcracker and pinon pine for efficient seed harvest and dispersal. Ecol. Mono. 47:89–111.

Wells, P. V. 1976. Macrofossil analysis of woodrat (*Neotoma*) middens as a key to the Quaternary vegetational history of arid America. Quat. Res. 6:223–248.

Wells, P. V. 1979. An equable glaciopluvial in the West: pleniglacial evidence of increased precipitation on a gradient from the Great Basin to the Sonoran and Chihuahuan deserts. Quat. Res. 12:311–325.

Wells, P. V. 1983. Paleobiogeography of montane islands in the Great Basin since the last glaciopluvial. Ecol. Mono. 53:341–383.

Yeh, F. C., and C. Layton. 1979. The organization of genetic variability in central and marginal populations of lodgepole pine *Pinus contorta* spp. *latifolia*. Canad. J. Genet. Cytol. 21:487–503.

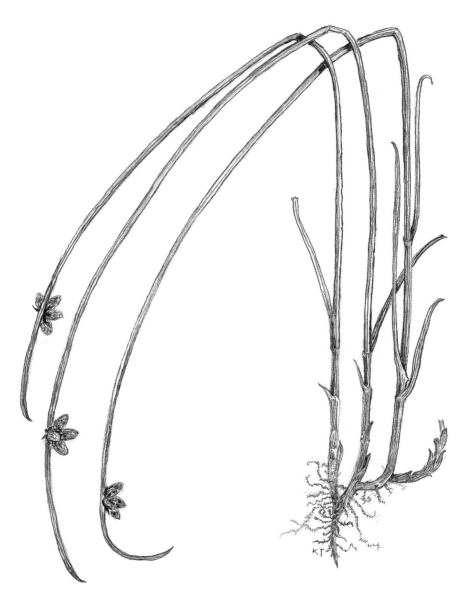

Scirpus americanus L. (alkali bulrush) was a common component of the periodically inundated and recolonized edges of saline marshes. This species produces large seeds that were avidly harvested by both waterfowl and native peoples.

CHAPTER 9

Fishes of the Great Basin and the Colorado Plateau: Past and Present Forms

John W. Sigler and William F. Sigler

OVERVIEW

This chapter includes a comprehensive list of the fish species reported to occur (currently and historically) in the Great Basin and the Colorado Plateau. The authors consider the impact of humans, both in terms of modification of natural habitats and the introduction of nonnative species to the area; they also review the status of native and introduced species. Currently, 44 percent of the native fishes of the region are at risk and are protected by either federal or state law, and the American Fisheries Society recommends protection for two additional species.

The geographical area this volume covers is hundreds of square miles and some of the most diverse desert habitat found in North America (see Figure 9.1). The Gila River Basin is excluded. The area's wide diversity has resulted in both fragile and unique ecosystems, often geographically separated from other similar ecosystems and each containing unique fishes.

New aquatic habitats have been formed by human activities. Reservoirs, ponds, and irrigation canals are neither unique nor fragile. Their original construction and transfer of water to them from natural systems harmed native fish directly and also provided habitat suitable for a host of introduced fish species. These nonnatives, directly and indirectly, further damaged the native fauna through competition for resources, predation, disease transfer, and other interactions.

We present brief information on the ecological concept of species survival. Why do some fish species survive and prosper whereas others fail when stocked outside of their native range? This is an often-discussed facet of fisheries management. Sometimes the reasons for failure are obvious. For example, Atlantic salmon stocked in Utah streams cannot complete the obligatory marine portion of their life cycle. In other instances reasons for success or failure are less clear. Common carp, generally considered to be an undesirable species by fisheries managers and fishing enthusiasts alike, have succeeded

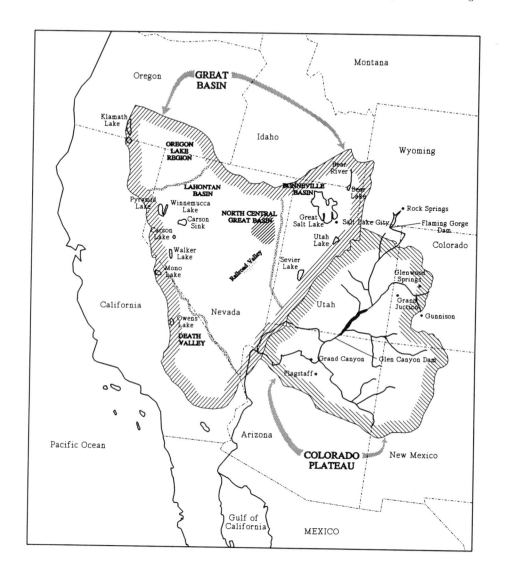

Figure 9.1   Map of the Great Basin and Colorado Plateau.

beyond reasonable belief. They have expanded their range in the United States and Canada at a phenomenal rate since their introduction in 1876 and now occupy habitats over a wide range of temperature, water quality, altitude, and interspecific interactions. The obvious conclusion is that carp seem physiologically adaptable to a wide range of environmental conditions.

The list of fishes that follows and the accompanying annotations include all species of fish ever known to be present naturally or stocked in waters in the Great Basin and

Colorado Plateau. The number of species and subspecies listed is 190. Of these, 109 (57 percent) are native and 81 (43 percent) are introduced. However, today 21 (26 percent) of the stocked fishes are no longer present, and nine (8 percent) of the native fishes are extinct.

Currently, there are 100 native and 60 exotic (160 total, 62 percent native) species and subspecies. Thirty-three (33 percent) of the native fishes have federal protection: nine (9 percent) are threatened, and 24 (24 percent) are endangered. An additional 11 (11 percent) are protected by the states in which they occur. The numbers of native fishes requiring special protection (federally listed as threatened or endangered, or protected by the states) is 44 (44 percent). In addition, the American Fisheries Society recommends protection for two additional species. Humans have not been kind to the native fishes of the area.

ENDEMISM, DIVERSITY, AND HABITAT

The tui chub, a small minnow of the Lahontan Basin, is perhaps better able to adapt to a wider range of habitats than any other fish we discuss in this chapter. Body form, number and size of gill rakers, and color respond readily to the available space and physical and chemical characteristics of their habitat. J. O. Snyder, an early American ichthyologist, described many new species, apparently based on their response to habitat. Most were later reduced to subspecies. The humpback chub is a highly specialized minnow that lives in the upper Colorado River. Over thousands of years, it adapted to the water's fast current and its extremes of temperature and volume. Spring floods scoured the bottom of its habitat so that there was a constant downstream movement of sediments. The humpback's torpedo-shaped body and large dorsal hump make it a survivor under the violent physical conditions in which it evolved. Early settlers saw this great river not as a unique fish habitat but as a wonderful source of water and electrical power. The resulting dams and diversions of water created a series of placid still water lakes and side streams that only remotely resembled the once roaring and uncontrolled river. The humpback chub has not been able to adjust to these altered conditions: it may not survive to the end of this century. Other native Colorado River fishes, including the bonytail, the large and predaceous squawfish, and perhaps the flannelmouth sucker, are suffering a somewhat similar fate.

The woundfin, another medium-size minnow, has an unusual adaptation for soft-rayed fishes. It is one of six species of New World minnows that is spiny-rayed. Some ponds in the Lahontan Basin are inhabited by a lone endemic, for example, the relict dace. The cui-ui, a native of prehistoric Lake Lahontan, has a mouth that is distinctly different from the mouth of most suckers. This genus, *Chasmistes*, has a near terminal mouth and feeds off the bottom. Utah Lake in the Bonneville Basin also has a lone species of this genus.

Pyramid Lake (and sections of the lower Truckee River), which has as its sole source of flowing water the stream flow from high-altitude Lake Tahoe, suffered a catastrophe possibly more violent than the havoc wreaked by the dams of the Colorado River system. In 1905 Derby Dam, located some 38.5 miles upstream from Pyramid Lake, effected a transbasin diversion from the Truckee River to the Carson

River Basin. In low-water years, this had the effect of diverting most, if not all, of the Truckee River flow away from Pyramid Lake. In the early 1930s the level of Pyramid Lake was so low that the native Lahontan cutthroat trout could not run upstream to spawn. Most of the population of these trout, the largest cutthroat in the world, were gone from the lake and from the river by 1938 (a few were reported in 1943).

Bear Lake, a nearly isolated, high mountain lake of the Bonneville Basin in Utah-Idaho, has four endemic fishes. Included in this high level of endemism are the Bear Lake sculpin, the Bear Lake whitefish, the Bonneville whitefish, and the Bonneville cisco, the most numerous fish in Bear Lake.

The Devils Hole pupfish is a lone endemic of Devil's Hole, Nevada. Its range of 23 square yards is the smallest of any vertebrate species. The subspecies of the Salt Creek pupfish inhabit a section of Salt Creek, Death Valley, California-Nevada, that ranges in altitude from 180 to 240 feet below sea level. Temperatures may reach 130°F. Numbers of these fish fluctuate in the extreme. The three-spine stickleback, circumpolar in both fresh- and saltwater, is native in Holcomb Creek, Mojave River, California.

ORIGINAL AND EXTENDED FISH RANGES: WHY SOME STOCKINGS FAIL

Most movement of fishes over land is accomplished by humans. There are rare instances of one stream's "capturing" another stream and thereby expanding the range of the fishes in both. Some fishes (e.g., walking catfish, American eel) are able to move short distances across land or around a dam if there is moisture on the ground or vegetation, but this is unusual. Birds may carry fertilized eggs from one body of water to another, and there are documented instances of hurricane-force winds transferring water and fishes from one body of water to another. Such means of dispersal are rare: all of these non-human-connected fish-transporting episodes are probably fewer than one in 1,000. The main culprit behind range changes is, as expected, humans. The whys are less easily defined.

Shortly after the Civil War, the U.S. Biological Survey and some states, including Iowa, rigged live-tanks on railroad cars, loaded them with fishes seined in Midwest floodwaters, and stocked them in streams or lakes at railroad crossings across the western states. This offers at least one explanation why the ubiquitous green sunfish exists in so many places where it is not now wanted.

Starting in 1831 and continuing until near the end of the century, common carp from Europe and Asia were stocked repeatedly in many of the 48 states. Their qualities as a food fish were described in glowing terms. Both the federal government and many state fish commissioners promoted the plantings. Most of the state commissioners were political appointees, and few, if any, had formal training in fisheries or even biology. In their defense it should be noted that we are still planting fish, sometimes without looking too far ahead.

Anglers stock fish. Sometimes it is in the careless dumping of a bait bucket of live minnows; more often it is a deliberate act to "improve fishing." This happens on a rather regular basis and rarely with desirable results. Thousands of pet aquarium fish are dumped in the wild each year because people are thoughtless or too softhearted to kill them. Often pet fishes are disposed of using the simple expedient of flushing them down the toilet. Species range from the small but destructive guppy to the large and pugnacious piranha. And with the official sanction of the state government, even trained fishery biologists plant exotic fishes as potential game fish or as forage (food) species for game species. Many of these stockings are not preceded by in-depth research regarding the potential impact of this planting on the ecosystem or its components (resident fishes in particular). Politics, in a subtle form, is often involved directly or indirectly. State fish and game directors and fishery biologists are asked to provide "more and better fishing" in the face of an increase in anglers and a decrease in quality habitats and funds. It is understandable why some decisions appear hasty. However, many plantings have substantially improved sport fishing.

A historical overview of the fishery in the Colorado River Basin offers perhaps the best example. The Colorado River heads high in the Rocky Mountains at over 14,000 feet elevation and winds its way 1,360 miles southwest to the Gulf of California. Originally a fast, highly variable, turbulent, and muddy river that fluctuated greatly over time, it has now become a series of dams and diversions that make it an almost totally alien habitat for native fishes. Originally, the native fauna that qualify under the current definition of game fish consisted of one trout (the cutthroat), the mountain whitefish, and the squawfish. All three of these fishes have suffered extensively from river modifications. Therefore, exotics, which were adapted to the changed environment, were the answer to better fishing. These include cold-, cool-, and warm-water species. The anglers saw this only as a vast improvement in fishing, and it was.

For every success story regarding fish stocking, there are a number of failures. The reasons are often obscure. Often there is no evidence on which to base judgment. There are, however, several reasons why failure is almost inevitable. Stocked fish may be unhealthy, either initially or as a result of being transported. The shock of moving and handling may be more than the fish can tolerate. The number stocked may be too low, that is, below the threshold of critical numbers wherein sufficient reproduction can occur to ensure continued existence of the species. In these cases the fish simply disappear. Additionally, predators may home in on the disoriented, tired stocked fish and seriously depredate them before they can acclimate and seek cover. The new arrivals in an area (or ecosystem) may be unable to utilize available food sources or compete for food and space with resident species. However, the number-one reason for failure of stocked fish is adverse (or unsuitable) habitat. There may be inadequate spawning ground or lack of cover or lack of acceptable food or unacceptable water quality (i.e., temperature, salinity, pH, oxygen, etc.). Or there may be diseases they cannot combat. The lack of survival at any one elemental life stage is fatal to the species.

Introduction to Fishes Past and Present

In Table 9.1 fishes past and present are listed phylogenetically; that is, they evolve from the least to the most specialized. Within this framework, the fishes are listed alphabetically by genus, then species, then subspecies. Orders may have many families, families many genera. The scientific name of each fish is followed by the author (the person who originally described the fish) and date of publication. If later taxonomists changed the scientific name of a species, the original author's name is placed in parentheses.

The Great Basin is made up of two major basins: the Lahontan Basin, which is largely in Nevada, and the Bonneville Basin, which is primarily in Utah but extends into Idaho on the north and Nevada on the west. The Lahontan Basin has five notable subdivisions, portions of which are in Nevada, California, Oregon, and Arizona (see Figure 9.1). The Colorado Plateau extends over approximately the eastern half of Utah, portions of Colorado, New Mexico, and Arizona and has tributary streams that arise in Wyoming. Abbreviations for each of these geographic units are used in the following table to designate locations of fish species. Additional abbreviations designate legal status of a species, states where species occur, and other information that appears in footnotes at the bottom of each page of the table.

Table 9.1   List of Species — Past and Present

Order Anguilliformes			
Family Anguillidae — freshwater eels			
American eel #BC	*Anguilla rostrata*[NP]	(Lesueur 1817)	
Order Clupeiformes			
Family Clupeidae — herrings			
American shad #BC	*Alosa sapidissima*[NP]	(Wilson 1811)	
gizzard shad #B	*Dorosoma cepedianum*	(Lesueur 1818)	UT
threadfin shad #C	*Dorosoma petenense*	(Günther 1867)	
Order Cypriniformes			
Family Cyprinidae — carps and minnows			
chiselmouth *O	*Acrocheilus alutaceus*	Agassiz and Pickering 1855	
longfin dace #C	*Agosia chrysogaster*	Girard 1856	
goldfish #BC	*Carassius auratus*	(Linnaeus 1758)	
grass carp #BC	*Ctenopharyngodon idella*[NP]	(Valenciennes 1844)	

Key: Fish species: * = native, # = introduced, NP = not present
Basins: O = Oregon Lakes, L = Lahontan Basin, N = North central Great Basin,
R = Railroad Valley, D = Death Valley, B = Bonneville Basin, C = Colorado Plateau
Names: Robins et al. 1991
U.S. Fish and Wildlife Service (Federal Endangered Species Act) legal status:
T = threatened, E = endangered
State legal status (not repeated when protected under federal law) reported under appropriate state, i.e.,
UT = Utah
American Fisheries Society designation (not reported when reported under state or
federal law): t = threatened, e = endangered

continues

Table 9.1   List of Species — Past and Present   (*continued*)

red shiner #C	*Cyprinella lutrensis*	(Baird and Girard 1853)
common carp #OLBC	*Cyprinus carpio*	Linnaeus 1758
desert dace *L	*Eremichthys acros*	Hubbs and Miller T 1948
Alvord chub *O	*Gila alvordensis*	Hubbs and Miller 1972
Utah chub *LB#C	*Gila atraria*	(Girard 1856)
tui chub *L	*Gila bicolor*	(Girard 1856)
Fish Creek Springs tui chub *L	*Gila bicolor euchila*	Hubbs and Miller t
Sheldon tui chub *OL	*Gila bicolor eurysoma*	Williams and Bond
Independence Valley tui chub *L	*Gila bicolor isolata* (extinct)	Hubbs and Miller
Mohave tui chub *D	*Gila bicolor mohavensis*	(Snyder) E
Newark Valley tui chub *L	*Gila bicolor newarkensis*	Hubbs and Miller
Lahontan Creek tui chub *OL	*Gila bicolor obesa*	(Girard)
Owens tui chub *D	*Gila bicolor snyderi*	Miller E
Cowhead Lake tui chub *O	*Gila bicolor vaccaceps*	Bills and Bond
Borax Lake chub *O	*Gila boraxobius*	Williams and E Bond 1980
leatherside chub *B#C	*Gila copei*	(Jordan and Gilbert 1881)
humpback chub *C	*Gila cypha*	Miller 1945 E
bonytail *C	*Gila elegans*	Baird and Girard E 1853
arroyo chub #L	*Gila orcutti*	(Eigenmann and Eigenmann 1890)
roundtail chub *C	*Gila robusta*	Baird and Girard UT 1853

Key: Fish species: * = native, # = introduced, NP = not present
Basins: O = Oregon Lakes, L = Lahontan Basin, N = North central Great Basin,
R = Railroad Valley, D = Death Valley, B = Bonneville Basin, C = Colorado Plateau
Names: Robins et al. 1991
U.S. Fish and Wildlife Service (Federal Endangered Species Act) legal status:
T = threatened, E = endangered
State legal status (not repeated when protected under federal law) reported under appropriate state, i.e.,
UT = Utah
American Fisheries Society designation (not reported when reported under state or
federal law): t = threatened, e = endangered

continues

Table 9.1   List of Species — Past and Present   *(continued)*

Colorado roundtail chub *C	*Gila robusta robusta*	Miller	AZ
Pahranagat roundtail chub *L	*Gila robusta jordani*	Tanner	E
Virgin roundtail chub *C	*Gila robusta seminuda*	Cope	E
California roach #L	*Hesperoleucus symmetricus*	(Baird and Girard 1854)	
brassy minnow #C	*Hybognathus hankinsoni*	Hubbs 1929	
plains minnow #C	*Hybognathus placitus*	Girard 1856	
least chub *B	*Iotichthys phlegethontis*	(Cope 1874)	UT
White River spinedace *C	*Lepidomeda albivallis*	Miller and Hubbs 1960	E
Pahranagat spinedace *L	*Lepidomeda altivelis* (extinct)	Miller and Hubbs 1960	
Virgin spinedace *LC	*Lepidomeda mollispinis*	Miller and Hubbs 1960	
Virgin River spinedace *C	*Lepidomeda mollispinis mollispinis*	Miller and Hubbs	NV, UT
Big Spring spinedace *L	*Lepidomeda mollispinis pratensis*	Miller and Hubbs	T
Little Colorado spinedace *C	*Lepidomeda vittata*	Cope 1874	T
common shiner #B	*Luxilus cornutus*[NP]	(Mitchill 1817)	
hornyhead chub #B	*Nocomis biguttatus*[NP]	(Kirtland 1840)	
golden shiner #LB	*Notemigonus crysoleucas*	(Mitchill 1814)	
emerald shiner #B	*Notropis atherinoides*	Rafinesque 1818	
spottail shiner #B	*Notropis hudsonius*	(Clinton 1824)	
sand shiner #C	*Notropis stramineus*	(Cope 1865)	
Sacramento blackfish #L	*Orthodon microlepidotus*	(Ayres 1854)	
bluntnose minnow #B	*Pimephales notatus*[NP]	(Rafinesque 1820)	
fathead minnow #BC	*Pimephales promelas*	Rafinesque 1820	
bullhead minnow #B	*Pimephales vigilax*[NP]	(Baird and Girard 1853)	

Key: Fish species: * = native, # = introduced, NP = not present
Basins: O = Oregon Lakes, L = Lahontan Basin, N = North central Great Basin,
R = Railroad Valley, D = Death Valley, B = Bonneville Basin, C = Colorado Plateau
Names: Robins et al. 1991
U.S. Fish and Wildlife Service (Federal Endangered Species Act) legal status:
T = threatened, E = endangered
State legal status (not repeated when protected under federal law) reported under appropriate state, i.e.,
UT = Utah
American Fisheries Society designation (not reported when reported under state or
federal law): t = threatened, e = endangered

continues

Table 9.1   List of Species — Past and Present   *(continued)*

woundfin *C	*Plagopterus argentissimus*	Cope 1874	E
Colorado squawfish *C	*Ptychocheilus lucius*	Girard 1856	E
northern squawfish *O	*Ptychocheilus oregonensis*	(Richardson 1836)	
relict dace *N	*Relictus solitarius*	Hubbs and Miller 1972	
blacknose dace #B	*Rhinichthys atratulus*[NP]	(Hermann 1804)	
longnose dace *B#C	*Rhinichthys cataractae*	(Valenciennes 1842)	
Las Vegas dace *C	*Rhinichthys deaconi* (extinct)	Miller 1984	
speckled dace *OLBC	*Rhinichthys osculus*	(Girard 1856)	
Sevier River speckled dace *B	*Rhinichthys osculus adobe*	(Jordan and Evermann)	
Bonneville speckled dace *B	*Rhinichthys osculus carringtoni*	(Cope)	
Big Smokey Valley speckled dace *L	*Rhinichthys osculus lariversi*	Lugaski	
Independence Valley speckled dace *L	*Rhinichthys osculus lethoporus*	Hubbs and Miller	E
Moapa speckled dace *D	*Rhinichthys osculus moapae*	Williams	
Ash Meadows speckled dace *D	*Rhinichthys osculus nevadensis*	(Gilbert)	E
Clover Valley speckled dace *L	*Rhinichthys osculus oligoporus*	Hubbs and Miller	E
Grass Valley speckled dace *L	*Rhinichthys osculus reliquus* (extinct)	Hubbs and Miller	
Lahontan speckled dace *L#N	*Rhinichthys osculus robustus*	(Rutter)	
Kendall Warm Springs dace *C	*Rhinichthys osculus thermalis*	Hubbs and Kuehne	E
White River speckled dace *C	*Rhinichthys osculus velifer*	Gilbert	
Colorado speckled dace *C	*Rhinichthys osculus yarrowi*	(Jordan and Evermann)	
redside shiner *LBC	*Richardsonius balteatus*	(Richardson 1836)	

Key: Fish species: * = native, # = introduced, NP = not present
Basins: O = Oregon Lakes, L = Lahontan Basin, N = North central Great Basin,
R = Railroad Valley, D = Death Valley, B = Bonneville Basin, C = Colorado Plateau
Names: Robins et al. 1991
U.S. Fish and Wildlife Service (Federal Endangered Species Act) legal status:
T = threatened, E = endangered
State legal status (not repeated when protected under federal law) reported under appropriate state, i.e.,
UT = Utah
American Fisheries Society designation (not reported when reported under state or
federal law): t = threatened, e = endangered

continues

Table 9.1   List of Species — Past and Present   *(continued)*

Columbia redside shiner balteatus #C	*Richardsonius balteatus*	(Richardson)	
Bonneville redside shiner *LB#C	*Richardsonius balteatus hydrophlox*	Cope	
Lahontan redside *L	*Richardsonius egregius*	(Girard 1858)	
creek chub #C	*Semotilus atromaculatus*	(Mitchill 1818)	
tench #L	*Tinca tinca*[NP]	(Linnaeus 1758)	

Family Catostomidae — suckers

Utah sucker *B#C	*Catostomus ardens*	Jordan and Gilbert 1881	
longnose sucker #C	*Catostomus catostomus*	(Forster 1773)	
desert sucker *C	*Catostomus clarki*	Baird and Girard 1854	
White River sucker *C	*Catostomus clarki intermedius*	(Tanner)	NV
bridgelip sucker *OL	*Catostomus columbianus*	(Eigenmann and Eigenmann 1893)	
white sucker #C	*Catostomus commersoni*	(Lacepède 1803)	
bluehead sucker *BC	*Catostomus discobolus*	Cope 1872	
Zuni bluehead sucker *C	*Catostomus discobolus yarrowi*	Cope	
Owens sucker *D#C	*Catostomus fumeiventris*	Miller 1973	
flannelmouth sucker *C	*Catostomus latipinnis*	Baird and Girard 1853	
largescale sucker *O	*Catostomus macrocheilus*	Girard 1856	
mountain sucker *OLBC	*Catostomus platyrhynchus*	(Cope 1874)	
Tahoe sucker *OL	*Catostomus tahoensis*	Gill and Jordan 1878	
Warner sucker *O	*Catostomus warnerensis*	Snyder 1908	T
cui-ui *L	*Chasmistes cujus*	Cope 1883	E
June sucker *B (historic)	*Chasmistes liorus liorus* (extinct)	Jordan 1878	

Key: Fish species: * = native, # = introduced, NP = not present
Basins: O = Oregon Lakes, L = Lahontan Basin, N = North central Great Basin,
R = Railroad Valley, D = Death Valley, B = Bonneville Basin, C = Colorado Plateau
Names: Robins et al. 1991
U.S. Fish and Wildlife Service (Federal Endangered Species Act) legal status:
T = threatened, E = endangered
State legal status (not repeated when protected under federal law) reported under appropriate state, i.e.,
UT = Utah
American Fisheries Society designation (not reported when reported under state or
federal law): t = threatened, e = endangered

continues

Table 9.1   List of Species — Past and Present   *(continued)*

June sucker *B (present)	*Chasmistes liorus mictus*	Miller and Smith E 1981
razorback sucker *C	*Xyrauchen texanus*	(Abbott 1861) AZ, CA, CO,UT, NV

Order Siluriformes

Family Ictaluridae — bullhead catfishes

white catfish #L	*Ictalurus catus*	(Linnaeus 1758)
black bullhead #LBC	*Ameiurus melas*	(Rafinesque 1820)
yellow bullhead #OC	*Ameiurus natalis*	(Lesueur 1819)
brown bullhead #L	*Ameiurus nebulosus*	(Lesueur 1819)
channel catfish #LBC	*Ictalurus punctatus*	(Rafinesque 1818)

Family Loricariidae — suckermouth catfishes

suckermouth catfish #L	*Hypostomus plecostomus*	(Linnaeus 1766)

Order Salmoniformes

Family Esocidae — pikes

northern pike #LBC	*Esox lucius*	Linnaeus 1758

Family Osmeridae — smelts

delta smelt #B	*Hypomesus transpacificus*[NP]	McAllister 1963

Family Salmonidae — trouts

lake whitefish #BC	*Coregonus clupeaformis*[NP]	(Mitchill 1818)
golden trout #LB	*Oncorhynchus aguabonita*	(Jordan 1893)
Apache trout *C	*Oncorhynchus apache*	(Miller 1972) T
cutthroat trout *OLBC	*Oncorhynchus clarki*	(Richardson 1836)
Yellowstone cutthroat trout #LB	*Oncorhynchus clarki bouvieri*	(Bendire)
Lahontan cutthroat trout *OL#B	*Oncorhynchus clarki henshawi*	(Gill and T Jordan)
Colorado cutthroat trout *C	*Oncorhynchus clarki pleuriticus*	(Cope)

Key: Fish species: * = native, # = introduced, NP = not present
Basins: O = Oregon Lakes, L = Lahontan Basin, N = North central Great Basin,
R = Railroad Valley, D = Death Valley, B = Bonneville Basin, C = Colorado Plateau
Names: Robins et al. 1991
U.S. Fish and Wildlife Service (Federal Endangered Species Act) legal status:
T = threatened, E = endangered
State legal status (not repeated when protected under federal law) reported under appropriate state, i.e.,
UT = Utah
American Fisheries Society designation (not reported when reported under state or
federal law): t = threatened, e = endangered

continues

Table 9.1   List of Species — Past and Present   *(continued)*

Paiute cutthroat trout *L	*Oncorhynchus clarki seleniris*	(Snyder)	T
greenback cutthroat trout *C	*Oncorhynchus clarki stomias*	(Cope)	T
Bonneville cutthroat trout *B	*Oncorhynchus clarki utah*	(Suckley)	UT
chum salmon #LC	*Oncorhynchus keta*[NP]	(Walbaum 1792)	
coho salmon #LC	*Oncorhynchus kisutch*[NP]	(Walbaum 1792)	
rainbow trout *L#ORBC	*Oncorhynchus mykiss*	(Walbaum 1792)	
steelhead trout #L	*Oncorhynchus mykiss*[NP] (not differentiated)		
Kamloops trout #B	*Oncorhynchus mykiss*[NP] (not differentiated)		
Eagle Lake rainbow trout *L	*Oncorhynchus mykiss aquilarum*	Snyder	
sockeye salmon (kokanee) #LBC	*Oncorhynchus nerka*	(Walbaum 1792)	
chinook salmon #LB	*Oncorhynchus tshawytscha*[NP]	(Walbaum 1792)	
Bear Lake whitefish *B	*Prosopium abyssicola*	(Snyder 1919)	
Bonneville cisco *B	*Prosopium gemmifer*	(Snyder 1919)	
Bonneville whitefish *B	*Prosopium spilonotus*	(Snyder 1919)	
mountain whitefish *LBC	*Prosopium williamsoni*	(Girard 1856)	
Atlantic salmon #LBC	*Salmo salar*[NP]	Linnaeus 1758	
brown trout #LBC	*Salmo trutta*	Linnaeus 1758	
brook trout #LBC	*Salvelinus fontinalis*	(Mitchill 1814)	
lake trout #LBC	*Salvelinus namaycush*	(Walbaum 1792)	
Arctic grayling #LBC	*Thymallus arcticus*	(Pallas 1776)	

Order Percopsiformes

Family Percopsidae — trout-perches

trout-perch #B	*Percopsis omiscomaycus*[NP]	(Walbaum 1792)	

Key: Fish species: * = native, # = introduced, NP = not present
Basins: O = Oregon Lakes, L = Lahontan Basin, N = North central Great Basin,
R = Railroad Valley, D = Death Valley, B = Bonneville Basin, C = Colorado Plateau
Names: Robins et al. 1991
U.S. Fish and Wildlife Service (Federal Endangered Species Act) legal status:
T = threatened, E = endangered
State legal status (not repeated when protected under federal law) reported under appropriate state, i.e.,
UT = Utah
American Fisheries Society designation (not reported when reported under state or
federal law): t = threatened, e = endangered

continues

Table 9.1   List of Species — Past and Present   (*continued*)

Order Atheriniformes

Family Cyprinodontidae — killifishes

White River springfish *RC	*Crenichthys baileyi*	(Gilbert 1893)	
Preston springfish *RC	*Crenichthys baileyi albivallis*	Williams and Wilde	NV
White River springfish *RC	Crenichthys baileyi baileyi	(Gilbert)	E
Hiko springfish *RC	*Crenichthys baileyi grandis*	Williams and Wilde	E
Moapa springfish *RC	*Crenichthys baileyi moapae*	Williams and Wilde	NV
Moorman springfish *RC	*Crenichthys baileyi thermophilus*	Williams and Wilde	NV
Railroad Valley springfish *RC	*Crenichthys nevadae*	Hubbs 1932	T
Devils Hole pupfish *D#C	*Cyprinodon diabolis*	Wales 1930	E
Amargosa pupfish *D	*Cyprinodon nevadensis*	Eigenmann and Eigenmann 1889	
Amargosa pupfish *D	*Cyprinodon nevadensis amargosae*	Miller	
Tecopa pupfish *D	*Cyprinodon nevadensis calidae* (extinct)	Miller	
Ash Meadows pupfish *D	*Cyprinodon nevadensis mionectes*	Miller	E
Saratoga Springs pupfish *D	*Cyprinodon nevadensis nevadensis*	Eigenmann and Eigenmann	
Warms Springs pupfish *D	*Cyprinodon nevadensis pectoralis*	Miller	E
Shoshone pupfish *D	*Cyprinodon nevadensis shoshone*	Miller	e
Owens pupfish *D	*Cyprinodon radiosus*	Miller 1948	E
Salt Creek pupfish *D	*Cyprinodon salinus*	Miller 1943	
Cottonball Marsh pupfish *D	*Cyprinodon salinus milleri*	LaBounty and Deacon	
Salt Creek pupfish *D	*Cyprinodon salinus salinus*	Miller	
Pahrump poolfish *D	*Empetrichthys latos*	Miller 1948	E

Key: Fish species: * = native, # = introduced, NP = not present
Basins: O = Oregon Lakes, L = Lahontan Basin, N = North central Great Basin,
R = Railroad Valley, D = Death Valley, B = Bonneville Basin, C = Colorado Plateau
Names: Robins et al. 1991
U.S. Fish and Wildlife Service (Federal Endangered Species Act) legal status:
T = threatened, E = endangered
State legal status (not repeated when protected under federal law) reported under appropriate state, i.e.,
UT = Utah
American Fisheries Society designation (not reported when reported under state or
federal law): t = threatened, e = endangered

continues

Table 9.1   List of Species — Past and Present   (*continued*)

Raycraft Ranch poolfish *D	*Empetrichthys latos concavus* (extinct)	Miller	
Manse Ranch poolfish *D#C	*Empetrichthys latos latos*	Miller	E
Pahrump poolfish *D	*Empetrichthys latos pahrump* (extinct)	Miller	
Ash Meadows killifish *D	*Empetrichthys merriami* (extinct)	Gilbert 1893	
plains topminnow #C	*Fundulus sciadicus*	Cope 1865	
plains killifish #BC	*Fundulus zebrinus*	Jordan and Gilbert 1883	
rainwater killifish #B	*Lucania parva*	(Baird and Girard 1855)	

Family Poeciliidae — livebearers

western mosquitofish #LBC	*Gambusia affinis*	(Baird and Girard 1853)
sailfin molly #L	*Poecilia latipinna*	(Lesueur 1821)
shortfin molly #LD	*Poecilia mexicana*	Steindachner 1863
guppy #L	*Poecilia reticulata*	Peters 1859
green swordtail #L	*Xiphophorus helleri*	Heckel 1848

Order Gasterosteiformes

Family Gasterosteidae — sticklebacks

brook stickleback #B	*Culaea inconstans*[NP]	(Kirtland 1841)
threespine stickleback *D	*Gasterosteus aculeatus*	Linnaeus 1758

Order Scorpaeniformes

Family Cottidae — sculpins

Utah Lake sculpin *B	*Cottus echinatus* (extinct)	Bailey and Bond 1963
mottled sculpin *BC	*Cottus bairdi*	Girard 1850
Paiute sculpin *LBC	*Cottus beldingi*	Eigenmann and Eigenmann 1891

Key: Fish species: * = native, # = introduced, NP = not present
Basins: O = Oregon Lakes, L = Lahontan Basin, N = North central Great Basin,
R = Railroad Valley, D = Death Valley, B = Bonneville Basin, C = Colorado Plateau
Names: Robins et al. 1991
U.S. Fish and Wildlife Service (Federal Endangered Species Act) legal status:
T = threatened, E = endangered
State legal status (not repeated when protected under federal law) reported under appropriate state, i.e.,
UT = Utah
American Fisheries Society designation (not reported when reported under state or
federal law): t = threatened, e = endangered

continues

Table 9.1   List of Species — Past and Present   *(continued)*

Bear Lake sculpin *B	*Cottus extensus*	Bailey and Bond 1963

Order Perciformes

Family Percichthyidae — temperate basses

white bass #LBC	*Morone chrysops*	(Rafinesque 1820)
striped bass #C	*Morone saxatilis*	(Walbaum 1792)

Family Centrarchidae — sunfishes

rock bass #BC	*Ambloplites rupestris*[NP]	(Rafinesque 1817)
Sacramento perch #LB	*Archoplites interruptus*	(Girard 1854)
green sunfish #LBC	*Lepomis cyanellus*	Rafinesque 1819
pumpkinseed #OL	*Lepomis gibbosus*	(Linnaeus 1758)
bluegill #OLBC	*Lepomis macrochirus*	Rafinesque 1819
redear sunfish #B	*Lepomis microlophus*[NP]	(Günther 1859)
smallmouth bass #OLC	*Micropterus dolomieu*	Lacepède 1802
spotted bass #L	*Micropterus punctulatus*	(Rafinesque 1819)
largemouth bass #OLNBC	*Micropterus salmoides*	(Lacepède 1802)
white crappie #LC	*Pomoxis annularis*	Rafinesque 1818
black crappie #LBC	*Pomoxis nigromaculatus*	(Lesueur 1829)

Family Percidae — perches

Iowa darter #C	*Etheostoma exile*	(Girard 1859)
johnny darter #C	*Etheostoma nigrum*	Rafinesque 1820
yellow perch #LBC	*Perca flavescens*	(Mitchill 1814)
logperch #B	*Percina caprodes*	(Rafinesque 1818)
walleye #LBC	*Stizostedion vitreum*	(Mitchill 1818)

Family Cichlidae — cichlids

jaguar cichlid #C	*Cichlasoma managuense*	(Günther 1867)
convict cichlid #L	*Cichlasoma nigrofasciatum*	(Günther 1867)
redbelly tilapia #D	*Tilapia zilli*	(Gervais 1848)

Key: Fish species: * = native, # = introduced, NP = not present
Basins: O = Oregon Lakes, L = Lahontan Basin, N = North central Great Basin,
R = Railroad Valley, D = Death Valley, B = Bonneville Basin, C = Colorado Plateau
Names: Robins et al. 1991
U.S. Fish and Wildlife Service (Federal Endangered Species Act) legal status:
T = threatened, E = endangered
State legal status (not repeated when protected under federal law) reported under appropriate state, i.e.,
UT = Utah
American Fisheries Society designation (not reported when reported under state or
federal law): t = threatened, e = endangered

Introduction to the Annotated List

In the following table we present a brief description of family characteristics for the listed fishes. The descriptive material for each fish varies with the level of known information and other factors. The range of natives, stocking records of exotics (including dates), unique or unusual characteristics such as adaptability, dangers native fishes face, and reasons for extinction or failure of stocking effort, where known, are given in the descriptive material for each species. Representative sub-species of some fishes are also listed. For example, both the tui chub and speckled dace have many (potential) subspecies, though authors or fish taxonomists are not always in agreement as to how many. Not all (potential) subspecies of the killifish family are listed. The importance of each fish is largely left undiscussed because of the complexity of that issue. Value for game fishes is not as difficult to determine as it is for native fish with no sport or commercial significance. The point we make here, however, is that no fish species be allowed to go extinct. Fishes are listed in the same order as in Table 9.1.

ANNOTATED LIST

ORDER ANGUILLIFORMES
ANGUILLIDAE — FRESHWATER EELS

These fishes, whose shape is commonly known, have well-developed jaws, a soft-rayed dorsal, and a long caudal fin. All members of this genus reproduce in the ocean.

American eel # B C — *Anguilla rostrata*[NP]

> This species migrates to an area known as the Sargasso Sea (northern Atlantic, east of the Bahamas, and southwest of Bermuda) to spawn and then presumably die. The young migrate (carried by currents) back to freshwater. Males remain in the brackiest water, and females move far inland. They (sex not specified) were stocked in Salt Lake City ponds in 1872. Since the Great Basin is landlocked, failure was inevitable. They were also stocked in the Colorado River in the 1800s and appeared in Lake Mead in the 1960s, presumably arriving there in the bilges of large boats brought in from the Atlantic Coast.

ORDER CLUPEIFORMES
CLUPEIDAE — HERRINGS

Herrings are small to medium-size, silvery, pelagic fishes. Most are laterally compressed. They have no adipose fin and no lateral line. Scales on the body only are cycloid and deciduous.

American shad # B C — *Alosa sapidissima*[NP]

> The shad is an anadromous (grows mainly at sea but returns to freshwater to spawn) fish with a native range from Sand Hill River, Labrador, to St. Johns

River, Florida. They were stocked in the Weber River, Utah, in 1871 but did not survive. They were also stocked in the Colorado River.

gizzard shad # B — *Dorosoma cepedianum*

The original range of the gizzard shad is much of the East Coast of the United States to as far west as eastern South Dakota and central Montana, south through eastern Colorado into New Mexico, and to the Gulf of California. They were stocked as forage for game fishes in 1990 and are reproducing in Willard Reservoir, Utah, where the main game fishes are black crappie, channel catfish, and walleye.

threadfin shad # C — *Dorosoma petenense*

The native range is from the Ohio River, Kentucky, and southern Indiana, west and south to Oklahoma, Texas, and Florida, along the coast of the Gulf of Mexico to northern Guatemala and Belize. They were first stocked in the Colorado River system (Lake Mead) in 1953. In 1968 they were stocked in upstream Lake Powell, Utah-Arizona, where they flourished for several years until predation by the introduced game fishes severely reduced their numbers.

ORDER CYPRINIFORMES
CYPRINIDAE — CARPS AND MINNOWS

Most people think of minnows as small fishes, and most are. Members of this family are usually less than 6 inches long. However, the introduced carp can reach 3.5 feet long, and the native Colorado squawfish 3.5 feet long. All species in this family do not have teeth on the jaws; rather, they have grinding teeth in the throat. Fin rays of most species are soft. They have cycloid scales, generally a lateral line, and no adipose fin. Some have one or two pairs of barbels. Breeding males may be quite colorful. This is one of the largest of all fish families, with over 1,500 species.

chiselmouth * O — *Acrocheilus alutaceus*

These 6- to 12-inch minnows are native to the Harney-Malheur system of southeastern Oregon and Nevada, as well as the Fraser and Columbia River systems. They appear to be prospering and are abundant.

longfin dace # C — *Agosia chrysogaster*

This species is native in Arizona south of the Colorado Plateau. They are a highly adaptable desert fish. Longfins are rare in the Colorado River near Moab, Utah, and the lower San Juan River. They have been introduced in the Virgin and Little Colorado Rivers.

goldfish # B C — *Carassius auratus*

This Asian fish has been stocked in a few Great Basin and Colorado River system locations in the wild. They are typically not abundant enough to be a nuisance but can prosper in situations too degraded for most other fishes. Additional stocking of them is discouraged.

grass carp # B C — *Ctenopharyngodon idella*[NP]

Agricultural irrigators have selectively stocked grass carp to control weeds. Some state natural resource departments forbid stocking unless the fish are sterile. Grass carp are a native of eastern Asia and were first stocked in the United States in 1968. They grow rapidly and adapt readily to a wide range of warm-water environments. Their palatability is on a par with or better than common carp.

red shiner # C — *Cyprinella lutrensis*

This highly adaptive exotic little minnow, rarely over 3 inches, is abundant over much of the upper Colorado River Basin. They tolerate high turbidities and moderately warm temperatures. They thrive in disrupted habitat where native minnows suffer. They also compete favorably with native fishes for food and space.

common carp # O L C B — *Cyprinus carpio*

Stocked in the United States in the 1800s from Europe and Asia, carp are common to abundant in the warm and cool waters of 47 of the 48 contiguous states (Florida excluded) and lower Canada. They are at best a mixed blessing. They degrade habitat of waterfowl and fish alike, and they often acquire a muddy taste in late spring and summer. However, some anglers enjoy catching and eating them. Carp are probably the most widely established of any exotic fish. The world-record carp from South Africa weighed 82.5 pounds. The U.S. record is 56 pounds.

desert dace * L — *Eremichthys acros*

These little fish occur only in warm springs in Humboldt County, Nevada. They are listed as threatened. They grow to about 2.5 inches in length and live 2 to 3 years. Habitat degradation and exotic fishes that prey on them, compete with them for food, and carry exotic diseases are reducing populations. Thousands of years in a solitary, specialized environment have not equipped them to cope with twentieth-century hazards.

Alvord chub * O — *Gila alvordensis*

This small native fish is restricted to limited warm waters in the Alvord Basin of southeastern Oregon and northwestern Nevada. There is concern for it because of habitat degradation and shrinkage.

Utah chub * L B # C — *Gila atraria*

This ubiquitous fish, native to the Great Basin and the Snake River, Idaho, above Shoshone Falls, appears to do as well or better outside its native range as within. They have been stocked widely outside of their range, mostly by well-meaning anglers. They fare well in deep, cold lakes and in warm irrigation ditches. They compete readily with other small fishes and may dominate a body of water where there are several species. Some populations may have 3- to 8-inch-long fish; others may have larger ones. Fishery biologists generally consider them a nuisance. Some desert spring populations have either become reduced in size or are extinct.

tui chub * L — *Gila bicolor*

These highly successful, small, native minnows, primarily of the basin of prehis-toric Lake Lahontan, are noted for their adaptability to a wide range of environ-mental conditions. At one time, J. O. Snyder, an early ichthyologist, was so impressed with different populations that he described many as new species. These were later reduced to subspecies. Their early and present range is presum-ably about the same.

Fish Creek Springs tui chub * L — *Gila bicolor euchila*

This small Nevada fish is listed as threatened by the American Fisheries Society.

Sheldon tui chub * O L — *Gila bicolor eurysoma*

This minnow is native to the Guano Basin of southeastern Oregon and north-western Nevada.

Independence Valley tui chub * L — *Gila bicolor isolata*

These fish were endemic to Warm Springs, Independence Valley, Nevada. Intro-duced largemouth bass may have caused their extinction. None was found in sur-veys by M. Rosenfeld in 1986, 1987, and 1988.

Mojave tui chub * D — *Gila bicolor mohavensis*

Mojave tui chub are present in Death Valley of the Mojave Desert, California, southwestern Lahontan Basin. They are endangered.

Newark Valley tui chub * L — *Gila bicolor newarkensis*

This chub is from Newark Valley, Nevada. This subspecies has habitat problems.

Lahontan Creek tui chub * O L — *Gila bicolor obesa*

These are present in California, Oregon, and Nevada.

Owens tui chub * D — *Gila bicolor snyderi*

Present only in a single location in California, this chub is endangered.

Cowhead Lake tui chub * O — *Gila bicolor vaccaceps*

These are native only to a small slough, the outlet of Cowhead Lake, California. Because of limited habitat, this subspecies is threatened with extinction. Cow-head Lake drained into the Warner Valley of Oregon during pluvial times.

Borax Lake chub * O — *Gila boraxobius*

These 2- to 4-inch fish live only in Borax Lake, Oregon, and its immediate out-fall. The water sources are thermal springs that may reach temperatures over 100°F. Most fish live only 1 year; a few (mostly females) may live 2 to 3 years. Their status is endangered.

leatherside chub * B # C — *Gila copei*

Leatherside chubs are so named because their skin has a leathery texture, even though they have very fine scales. They range primarily in the eastern part of pluvial Lake Bonneville. They have adapted, when stocked, in the Colorado

River Basin, especially Strawberry Reservoir (removed from there in 1990 by poisoning).

humpback chub * C — *Gila cypha*

This medium-size fish has adapted over several thousand years to the historically very turbulent and swift waters of the Colorado River and its tributaries. Their unusual dorsal hump, long torpedo-shaped body, and slender caudal peduncle enabled them to survive even in the Grand Canyon. The Colorado River, once swiftly turbulent and turbid, is now governed by a series of dams and diversions. Flows released through dams are dictated largely by downstream power demands. Behind the dams are deep, cold, stratified (three temperature layers: warm, cooling rapidly, and cold) lakes that in very few ways resemble the original river. Below the dams are clear, cold, silt-free waters that are much more uniform in temperature and flow than the original river. The now endangered humpback chub has not been able to adapt to this new set of habitat parameters. It may be doomed.

bonytail * C — *Gila elegans*

This medium-size, fast-water minnow once ranged throughout most of the Colorado River Basin. Today they are very rare in the Green River and Lake Mojave. Bonytails, like humpback chubs, have not been able to adapt to the vastly changed environment. See humpback chub.

arroyo chub # L — *Gila orcutti*

This California native was once adapted to the fluctuating streams of the Los Angeles Plain. They should be encouraged in their native range but probably not in the Lahontan Basin.

roundtail chub * C — *Gila robusta*

This species, which exists as a number of subspecies, is native to the Colorado River drainage from Wyoming to Mexico. They have not suffered from habitat alteration to the same extent that two other *Gila* spp. (*cypha* and *elegans*) have. However, the numbers are down substantially from early times. They are protected because laypeople may not be able to distinguish them from the two endangered species of *Gila*.

Colorado roundtail chub * C — *Gila robusta robusta*

Colorado roundtail chub are inhabitants of the mainstream Colorado and Green Rivers and most upper Basin tributaries. They may be hybridizing with two endangered *Gila* (*cypha* and *elegans*). Numbers are down substantially from earlier times.

Pahranagat roundtail chub * L — *Gila robusta jordani*

This subspecies has a very restricted range, the outflow of Ash Springs in eastern Nevada. Changes in the longtime stable habitat and exotic fish and invertebrate introductions may extirpate this now endangered fish.

Virgin roundtail chub * C — *Gila robusta seminuda*

This subspecies lives in the Virgin and Moapa Rivers, tributaries to the Colorado. Numbers are so greatly reduced from early times that they are endangered. Habitat varies in the extreme. Spring floods may be followed by high temperatures and dewatering caused by local irrigation practices. In order to survive, fishes in this type of habitat generally spawn early so that the fragile egg-larva stages are past when hot-weather-low-water conditions develop.

California roach # L — *Hesperoleucus symmetricus*

This nonnative fish occurs in intermittent streams and tolerates adverse environmental conditions that many native fishes in the Great Basin cannot. Their spread should not be encouraged.

brassy minnow # C — *Hybognathus hankinsoni*

Introduced from the central and eastern United States, brassy minnows have been reported as rare from the Yampa River, Colorado, and the Colorado River near Moab, Utah. Their future status is undetermined.

plains minnow # C — *Hybognathus placitus*

Plains minnows are natives of the upper Missouri River drainage as far south as southern Illinois. They are rare in the San Juan River, Utah. Future status is undetermined.

least chub * B — *Iotichthys phlegethontis*

These tiny fish are rarely over 2 inches long and most live only 2 or rarely 3 or 4 years. They were once present in the Bonneville Basin in the Great Salt Lake marshes, in several streams along the Wasatch Front, and Great Salt Desert Springs. They are present now only in Snake Valley, Millard County, western Utah, and Leland Harris Spring, Juab County. They are preyed on by exotic fishes, bullfrogs, and fish-eating birds. Exotic species introductions and habitat degradation or destruction are the primary causes of the reduced population. They are protected in Utah.

White River spinedace * C — *Lepidomeda albivallis*

This small dace occurs only in one area of the upper White River of southeastern Nevada. Both natural disasters such as flooding and drought and human practices such as agricultural development have led to their present status, endangered.

Pahranagat spinedace * L — *Lepidomeda altivelis*

This subspecies is extinct.

Virgin spinedace * L C — *Lepidomeda mollispinis*

The future of this subspecies is not encouraging.

Virgin River spinedace * C — *Lepidomeda mollispinis mollispinis*

The native range of this dace is the Virgin River drainage of Utah, Arizona, and Nevada (Colorado River Basin). The present range is much reduced because of water demands for agriculture. In low-water years some stretches of the river may be dry in mid- to late summer. Although the Virgin River spinedaces' existence is threatened, they survive apparently by their ability to adapt to extremely harsh conditions. They are also stressed from the competition for food and space by exotic fishes, especially the red shiner. They are protected in Utah and Nevada.

Big Spring spinedace * L — *Lepidomeda mollispinis pratensis*

The Big Spring spinedace is presumably extinct from its original range, Big Spring, in the spring-fed marsh northeast of Panaca, Nevada. The spinedaces have a precarious existence in Meadow Valley Wash, Carpenter River, Nevada. Having evolved over thousands of years in a stable environment, they are ill prepared for water development projects and exotic fishes. They are threatened.

Little Colorado spinedace * C — *Lepidomeda vittata*

Distribution of this species is limited to the upper part of the Little Colorado River system. They are not abundant but adaptable to a wide range of habitat conditions. They are threatened.

common shiner # B — *Luxilus cornutus*[NP]

This is another Mississippi River system fish stocked as forage in Willard Reservoir, Utah. They did not survive.

hornyhead chub # B — *Nocomis biguttatus*[NP]

This native of the Great Lakes area and west to Wyoming prospers in Midwest glaciated areas. They were stocked in Willard Reservoir, Utah, in 1982 but did not reproduce.

golden shiner # L B — *Notemigonus crysoleucas*

This 8- to 10-inch golden minnow is native to the central and eastern United States. They have been stocked widely in western states as forage. Golden shiners are reared for bait more than any other minnow. They are prospering but not abundant in the Great Basin.

emerald shiner # B — *Notropis atherinoides*

These natives of the Mississippi River system and the Great Lakes were stocked as forage in 10,000-acre, 12-foot-deep Willard Reservoir and Utah Lake, Utah, in 1983. They are reproducing.

spottail shiner # B — *Notropis hudsonius*

The native range of the spottail shiner is the eastern United States, west to the Mississippi River and north to lower Canada. They were stocked in Willard Bay Reservoir, Utah, as forage in 1982. Unlike some other fishes stocked there, the spottail are reproducing.

sand shiner # C — *Notropis stramineus*

Introduced sand shiners are abundant from Cataract Canyon to the Colorado-Utah state line in the Colorado River. They are also abundant in the Yampa

River and rare in the Green River, Utah. They thrive in this exotic environment but not to the extent the red shiner does.

Sacramento blackfish # L — *Orthodon microlepidotus*

These medium-size minnows, averaging less than 3 pounds, were introduced into Lahontan Reservoir in 1939 on the Carson River, Nevada, where they are prospering. They hybridize with native tui chub. Hybrids have been found at the mouth of the Humboldt River. They were also introduced near Reno, Nevada, but did not survive. They are a popular food fish in some San Francisco markets but are not popular in Nevada.

bluntnose minnow # B — *Pimephales notatus*[NP]

The bluntnose were introduced in Willard Reservoir, Utah, as forage in 1982. They did not survive. The relatively low numbers stocked may have contributed to their failure to reproduce. They are native to the Mississippi and Great Lakes Basins, south to the Gulf of California slope.

fathead minnow # B C — *Pimephales promelas*

Fatheads were stocked in Utah Lake, Utah, in 1969. They also invaded or were stocked in the upper Colorado River system, where they are abundant. It is difficult to pinpoint a reason why one member of their genus (*Pimephales*) prospers, but two more (bluntnose and bullhead) do not. A reason that is at least logical is that the fathead invaded one or more tributary streams, built up large populations, and then moved on to establish a new range.

bullhead minnow # B — *Pimephales vigilax*[NP]

The bullhead minnow was introduced in Utah Lake, Utah, in 1969. Small populations were reported around Currant Creek and the Spanish Fork River. None has been seen recently.

woundfin * C — *Plagopterus argentissimus*

Original range of this species is throughout the Virgin and Gila River Basins. Today they are present only in the Virgin River below LaVerkin, Utah, and LaVerkin Creek. They are one of six species of New World minnows that are spiny-rayed. Woundfin are endangered.

Colorado squawfish * C — *Ptychocheilus lucius*

The Colorado squawfish, once very abundant in the Colorado River Basin, is now endangered. This largest of North American minnows, reportedly reaching a length of 3.5 feet, has not been able to adapt to the drastically changed environment (see humpback chub). They are rare in the upper Colorado River Basin and are listed as endangered. They once provided abundant food for Native Americans and later for pioneers. They are an atypical minnow in that they have a pikelike body and at an early age turn to feeding on fishes. They can be caught readily on artificial lures such as red and white spoons.

northern squawfish * O — *Ptychocheilus oregonensis*

These squawfish, native to the Pacific slope of North America, are doing so well that the Oregon Fish and Wildlife Department has put a bounty on them. It seems that these squawfish have developed a taste for downstream migrating salmon and steelhead smolts on the Columbia River. The Oregon department believes this predator is seriously depleting these young game fishes. It is interesting to note that water developments on the Colorado River system have created serious problems for the Colorado squawfish, but dams on the Columbia River provide habitat favorable to the northern squawfish. Perhaps part of the reason is that the Columbia is the only route to the sea for millions of young salmon and steelhead trout, which are highly vulnerable to predation.

relict dace * N — *Relictus solitarius*

This small, native dace lives in a few thermal springs and marsh areas in the north central Great Basin valleys of Nevada between the Lahontan and Bonneville Basins. Both range and numbers have been reduced by agricultural developments and the introduction of exotic fishes along with diseases to which the dace are vulnerable. No other fishes occur naturally within this range.

blacknose dace # B — *Rhinichthys atratulus*[NP]

This native to northeastern America and as far west as the lower Missouri River drainage was introduced in Utah Lake and Willard Reservoir, Utah, in 1983. They did not survive, probably in part because the total numbers stocked were low.

longnose dace * B # C — *Rhinichthys cataractae*

The native range of this dace is from the East Coast west to Washington State. They occur naturally in the upper reaches of the Bonneville system in the Great Basin and in the Columbia River Basin. Because of their body form, they adapt easily to fast streams, generally living near the bottom. They also prosper in lakes, mostly inshore in cool weather (70°F or less) and in deeper water in hot months. They are prospering throughout most of their range. They are rare in the upper Colorado River Basin.

Las Vegas dace * C — *Rhinichthys deaconi*

Endemic to springs in Las Vegas, Nevada, the Las Vegas dace is believed to be extinct.

speckled dace * O L B C — *Rhinichthys osculus*

This species ranges from the Colorado River Basin west to the Pacific but is rare in coastal streams. At one time the species was listed as 12 different species. The number of subspecies is large today. This taxonomic problem can be stated simply. They adapt to a wide range of habitats, ranging from cold mountain streams to warm, spring-fed ponds, and the body form and color change accordingly. The solution to the taxonomic problem is complex. The speckled dace's adaptability indicates it is a survivor, but many of its isolated population numbers are becoming rare.

Sevier River speckled dace * B — *Rhinichthys osculus adobe*

These dace are native to the Sevier River drainage, Utah, part of the region covered by pluvial Lake Bonneville. There have been several local extinctions.

Bonneville speckled dace * B — *Rhinichthys osculus carringtoni*

Bonneville speckled dace are native to the northern Bonneville Basin, part of the region covered by pluvial Lake Bonneville, and the contiguous upper Snake River, into which Lake Bonneville discharged. Several local extinctions have occurred.

Big Smoky Valley speckled dace * L — *Rhinichthys osculus lariversi*

These are native to Charnock Springs, central Big Smoky Valley, Nevada.

Independence Valley speckled dace * L — *Rhinichthys osculus lethoporus*

This Nevada subspecies described by Hubbs and Miller is currently endangered.

Moapa speckled dace * D — *Rhinichthys osculus moapae*

This species occurs in the disrupted White River.

Ash Meadows speckled dace * D — *Rhinichthys osculus nevadensis*

This Death Valley speckled dace is endangered.

Clover Valley speckled dace * L — *Rhinichthys osculus oligoporus*

This Lahontan Basin subspecies of speckled dace is endangered.

Grass Valley speckled dace * L — *Rhinichthys osculus reliquus*

This species, endemic to Grass Valley in central Nevada, is believed to have become extinct before 1969.

Lahontan speckled dace * L # N — *Rhinichthys osculus robustus*

These dace are native to the Humboldt River system, Nevada, including semi-isolated Diamond Valley. Introduced into Ruby Valley, they were extirpated or depleted in several locations.

Kendall Warm Springs dace * C — *Rhinichthys osculus thermalis*

This subspecies of speckled dace is present only in Kendall Warm Springs, Green River, Wyoming. It is listed as endangered.

White River speckled dace * C — *Rhinichthys osculus velifer*

Native to the White River and Meadow Valley Wash, Nevada, this subspecies has suffered because of habitat alterations.

Colorado speckled dace * C — *Rhinichthys osculus yarrowi*

These are native to the Colorado River system upstream from the Grand Canyon and to the Virgin River.

redside shiner * L B C — *Richardsonius balteatus*

Redside shiners are native in western North America from Washington and Oregon to as far east as the Bonneville Basin.

Columbia redside shiner * L B — *Richardsonius balteatus balteatus*

This subspecies is originally from the Columbia River drainage. Subspecies are often difficult to distinguish in the field.

Bonneville redside shiner * L B # C — *Richardsonius balteatus hydrophlox*

This subspecies is native to the Virgin River and parts of the Great Basin. They are also present in the Yampa, Duschesne, and Little Colorado Rivers.

Lahontan redside * L — *Richardsonius egregius*

This relative of the redside shiner is native to the Lahontan Basin of Nevada and California. They have been stocked outside their native range in Nevada, but the status is unknown. They appear ecologically similar to redside shiners, but their ranges do not overlap. They are prospering throughout most or all of their range.

creek chub # C — *Semotilus atromaculatus*

Creek chub are native to the Atlantic slope and as far west as Montana. They have been introduced in the upper Colorado River Basin, where they are rare to common near the junction of the Green and Yampa Rivers. As the name indicates, they are most at home in creeks, usually cool to warm ones. They may spread further in the Colorado River system.

tench # L — *Tinca tinca*[NP]

This small minnow of western Europe was reportedly introduced in as many as 36 states by the U.S. Fish Commission in 1886–1889. They were also stocked privately in California. They were presumably brought in to provide food for game fishes. They were stocked near Virginia City, Nevada, in 1885 or 1886 but did not survive.

CATOSTOMIDAE — SUCKERS

The family name is derived from the ventral (underneath) mouth that enables them to feed effectively on or near the bottom. They range in size from small to large. There are no jaw teeth, but, as in the minnows, there are pharyngeal (throat) teeth that grind food. There is no adipose fin, and no barbel is present. The tail is forked, the scales are cycloid, and the swim bladder is large, with two or three chambers. This large family of freshwater fishes is mainly North American.

Utah sucker * B # C — *Catostomus ardens*

The native range of the Utah sucker is the Bonneville Basin and the upper Snake River above Shoshone Falls. They have been introduced, source unknown, in the Colorado River Basin in the Duschesne and Dirty Devil Rivers, where they are rare. Since they are highly adaptable to a wide range of habitats, they probably will continue to flourish in the Colorado River system.

longnose sucker # C — *Catostomus catostomus*

The longnose sucker has the most northern and widespread range of any sucker. They are present in the arctic drainage of eastern Siberia and as far south as Great Lakes states and Wyoming and northern Colorado. They have been stocked in the upper Gunnison River, Colorado River Basin, where they are locally common. They appear to be in no trouble throughout most or all of their range.

desert sucker * C — *Catostomus clarki*

The native range of this small (16 inches or less) sucker is the lower Colorado River Basin from the Grand Canyon southward. They are also present in the White River. There is no record of transplants. The species does not appear to be threatened.

White River sucker * C — *Catostomus clarki intermedius*

The population in the pluvial White River, eastern Nevada, is protected by the state.

bridgelip sucker * O L — *Catostomus columbianus*

The range of this sucker is northwest America, including the Harney Basin in Oregon. The range is not extensive, and there is no record of native range extension. They frequent cold, fast streams with gravelly bottoms. They appear to be in no danger.

white sucker # C — *Catostomus commersoni*

The widespread and abundant white sucker ranges from the Arctic Circle (Mackenzie River drainage) south to New Mexico and Georgia. Their range has not been extended, and they appear to be in no trouble. They are common to abundant in parts of the upper Colorado River Basin.

bluehead sucker * B C — *Catostomus discobolus*

This small cool- to cold-water sucker's native range is the upper Colorado River Basin, where they are common, as far south as the Grand Canyon. Below this they are supplanted by the desert sucker. They are also in the Bear and Weber River drainages and in the Snake River, Idaho, above Twin Falls. They appear to be prospering over most of their range.

Zuni bluehead sucker * C — *Catostomus discobolus yarrowi*

There is a limited population of this sucker in the lower Colorado Plateau, New Mexico.

Owens sucker * D # C — *Catostomus fumeiventris*

Native range of the Owens sucker is the Owens River and tributaries in Death Valley, California. They have been introduced in the Santa Clara River system by escape from the Los Angeles aqueduct, and they are in a native fish sanctuary in Owens Valley, California. The fate of those at this last site is unknown. In spite of hazards faced, they seem to be existing, if not prospering.

flannelmouth sucker * C — *Catostomus latipinnis*

The native range of flannelmouth includes both the upper and lower Colorado River Basins. They are common to abundant in the upper Basin but are extinct below the Virgin River. Unlike the razorback sucker, which has the same native range, flannelmouths have not suffered as extensively from water development projects in the upper Colorado River Basin. See humpback chub.

largescale sucker * O — *Catostomus macrocheilus*

The native range of the largescale sucker is western North America, primarily west of the Rocky Mountains. They are also in the Harney Basin, Oregon. The native range has not been extended.

mountain sucker * O L B C — *Catostomus platyrhynchus*

These 5- to 6-inch cold-water suckers' native range is mountainous western North America, the Pacific, Gulf (upper Missouri River), and arctic drainages. They are common throughout the Great Basin and much of the Colorado Plateau. Their widespread range and abundance assures the species' continuance. One population of dwarfed individuals is restricted to a desert spring in the Bonneville Basin, a relict of pluvial Lake Bonneville.

Tahoe sucker * O L — *Catostomus tahoensis*

The native range of the Tahoe sucker is mainly the Lahontan Basin, where it is common to abundant. They are faring well in most of their range, excluding Walker Lake, where total dissolved solids are very high.

Warner sucker * O — *Catostomus warnerensis*

Confined to the Warner Lake Basin of southeastern Oregon, the Warner sucker has suffered from agricultural practices and the introduction of exotic fishes. It is listed as threatened.

cui-ui * L — *Chasmistes cujus*

Cui-ui are present only in Pyramid Lake and the lower Truckee River that feeds the lake. The adults are in the river only at spawning time; the young remain there 4 weeks or more. Cui-ui, unlike most other suckers, have a large, near terminal mouth. They feed partly in the water column just off the bottom. In 1905 Derby Dam on the Truckee River was completed. This affected a transbasin diversion of some, and sometimes almost all, of the Truckee River water to the Carson River Basin. This caused the Pyramid Lake level to drop so low that a large delta was formed at the mouth of the river. The cui-ui could not navigate this delta in drought years, such as the 1930s, and therefore could not spawn. In the 1970s a fish ladder was built at the mouth of the Truckee River; after several modifications it functioned minimally. The cui-ui is endangered.

June sucker * B (historic) — *Chasmistes liorus liorus*

This June sucker was native only in Utah Lake until the 1930s, when drought and agricultural practices led to its extinction.

June sucker * B (present) — *Chasmistes liorus mictus*

The present June sucker is the result of a cross between the Utah sucker and the original June sucker. They are present only in Utah Lake and are endangered.

razorback sucker * C — *Xyrauchen texanus*

The native range of the razorback is the Colorado River and tributaries. Today they are rare in the upper Colorado River Basin and down to the Grand Canyon. They are present in Lakes Mead, Mojave, and Havasu, and some side ditches and small impoundments. This rather large sucker, once abundant enough to be a staple in the diet of Native Americans and pioneers, is almost gone. They have not been able to adjust to ecological changes. Predation on young may be preventing recruitment. They are protected in Arizona, California, Colorado, Nevada, and Utah. See humpback chub.

ORDER SILURIFORMES
ICTALURIDAE — BULLHEAD CATFISHES

This family has members that range in size from small to quite large. They are native to North and Central America. The head is large and flattened, the body is naked (without scales), the teeth on the jaws and palatines (raised bones in the roof of the mouth) are small and comblike, and there are several pairs of whiskerlike barbels. They have an adipose fin and fin spines. For all species, populations in the United States west of the Continental Divide are introduced.

white catfish # L — *Ameiurus catus*

The native range of the white catfish is the Atlantic Coast states, Florida to New York. They are abundant in Lahontan Reservoir on the Carson River, Indian Lakes and Stillwater Marsh (until recently), and the Humboldt and Truckee Rivers (in 1887). All of these areas were stocked. They are larger than bullheads and popular with catfish anglers.

black bullhead # L B C — *Ameiurus melas*

Native range of black bullheads is from southern Ontario south to northern Mexico, west to Montana and eastern Colorado, east to the mideastern states. The range has been extended to improve sport fishing in the Great Basin, where they are common, and the Colorado Plateau, where they are less abundant. This .75- to 2-pound catfish is the favorite of youngsters and casual anglers. They are most often present in sloughs; gravel pits; shallow, turbid lakes; ponds; and small creeks.

yellow bullhead # O C — *Ameiurus natalis*

This species is native to the eastern and central United States. They have been stocked in Warner Valley, Oregon, and Lake Powell. Yellow bullheads are stream fish. Fishing for them is much the same as for the black bullhead.

brown bullhead # L — *Ameiurus nebulosus*

The native range of the brown bullhead is the eastern United States and southern Canada. They have been stocked in the Truckee, Carson, and Humboldt Rivers in Nevada. Brown bullheads are big, clearwater, vegetated lakes fish. They are fished much like the other two bullheads; patience is required.

channel catfish # L B C — *Ictalurus punctatus*

The native range of this important sport and commercial catfish is the central drainages of the United States and southern Canada and possibly parts of the Atlantic Coast. Their range has been extended substantially. They were first stocked in Utah Lake, Utah, in 1888 and the Colorado River in 1892. They are the number-one cultured warm-water fish in the United States, and their sport value is high. They are much larger than the previously discussed catfishes and are sought by more anglers. They strike a wide range of lures and baits, and they range from small, warm ponds to large lakes to fast, cool rivers.

LORICARIIDAE — SUCKERMOUTH CATFISHES

These armored (coated with bony plates) catfishes are elongate and flattened with a thick coating of fine prickles. They have a mouth that forms a sucking disc under the head.

suckermouth catfish # L — *Hypostomus plecostomus*

The native range of this catfish is much of South America and Trinidad. Once pets, they were released in Indian Springs, southeastern Nevada. They have the unusual ability to travel short distances over land. They are considered a nuisance in the wild.

ORDER SALMONIFORMES
ESOCIDAE — PIKES

This is a family of medium-size to large fishes, with an elongate body, forked tail, and large prominent teeth on the jaws. Their distinctive features are their large heads and the elongate, flat snouts that look a bit like a duck's bill. Some become piscivorous at an early age.

northern pike # L B C — *Esox lucius*

The northern pike is circumpolar in distribution in the Northern Hemisphere. In North America the native range is from the north central and northeastern United States north through much of Canada to Alaska. Introductions that enlarged the range have not been extensive. The northern pike is a long-lived, large fish. In northern climates they may live 20 or more years and weigh 30 pounds.

OSMERIDAE — SMELTS

This family of small, slender, silvery fishes may be anadromous or marine or live in freshwater. They have large mouths, cycloid scales, an adipose fin, and a lateral line. They are circumpolar in the Northern Hemisphere only.

delta smelt # B — *Hypomesus transpacificus*[NP]

This small smelt's native range is confined to the Sacramento–San Joaquin Delta region. They are listed as threatened. They were stocked in Willard Reservoir, Utah, in 1982 but did not survive.

SALMONIDAE — TROUTS

This family includes the trouts, salmon, chars, whitefishes, and grayling. It has both freshwater and anadromous cool-water and cold-water species of medium to large size. The body is terete, the scales are cycloid, and there is a lateral line. Most members of this family are important as game fish: some are taken commercially. Species of western trout were, until recently, members of the genus *Salmo*. Cutthroat trout were *Salmo clarki*, and rainbow trout were *Salmo gairdneri*.

lake whitefish # B C — *Coregonus clupeaformis*[NP]

The native range of this species is from Atlantic Coast watersheds, west across Canada and the northern United States, to British Columbia, the Yukon, and Alaska. They were stocked in streams around Salt Lake City, Utah, in 1873, in Lake Tahoe, Nevada-California, in 1877, and in the Colorado River drainage before 1881. None survived.

golden trout # L B — *Oncorhynchus aguabonita*

This species is native to the upper Kern River Basin, California. They have been stocked in the Humboldt River Basin, Nevada, the Uinta Mountains, Utah, and some lakes in Colorado. They have survived, but not flourished, in most of these areas. These small (12- to 14-inch), beautiful trout are not able to compete well with other trouts. They prosper in a monoculture in high, cold wilderness areas.

Apache trout * C — *Oncorhynchus apache*

Historically there was a substantial population in the Salt River, Arizona. Now there is only a small population of Apache trout on the lower Colorado Plateau in Arizona that is threatened.

cutthroat trout * O L B C — *Oncorhynchus clarki*

The cutthroat has the largest native range of any western trout. Coastal forms that range from California to Alaska are anadromous. Inland forms range from Alberta, south through California, and as far east as Colorado and Montana. Numbers have dwindled and the range has shrunk in many areas. Practices of industry and agriculture have degraded much of the original range, and in this disrupted habitat the cutthroat has fared poorly in competition with exotic trouts. In places where changes have been minimal, it prospers. The cutthroat is one of the trouts most prized by anglers.

Yellowstone cutthroat trout # L B — *Oncorhynchus clarki bouvieri*

These natives of Yellowstone Lake, Yellowstone National Park, Wyoming, were stocked extensively in the Great Basin around the midcentury mark.

Lahontan cutthroat trout * O L # B — *Oncorhynchus clarki henshawi*

The native range of the Lahontan cutthroat is the western part of the Lahontan Basin, including Pyramid, Walker, and Tahoe Lakes. The largest of all cutthroat trout, they are listed as threatened. Stocks are maintained, largely by plantings. They have been stocked in Utah.

Colorado cutthroat trout * C — *Oncorhynchus clarki pleuriticus*

These cutthroat trout have limited range and numbers in the upper Colorado River Basin.

Paiute cutthroat trout * L — *Oncorhynchus clarki seleniris*

This threatened subspecies of cutthroat occurs in the western area of the Lahontan Basin in California.

greenback cutthroat trout * C — *Oncorhynchus clarki stomias*

The greenback population of cutthroat, high in the Rockies, is threatened.

Bonneville cutthroat trout * B — *Oncorhynchus clarki utah*

This subspecies ranged at one time throughout much of the Bonneville Basin and was commercially harvested in tonnage amounts from Utah Lake in the mid- to late 1800s. They are confined today to a remnant population in Snake Valley, western Utah; in isolated streams near Salt Lake City; and in eastern Nevada. Another subpopulation is in Smith's Fork on the Bear River in Wyoming, and there are a few other scattered remnants. They are protected in Utah.

chum salmon # L C — *Oncorhynchus keta*[NP]

This anadromous species is native to the west coast of North America from California to Alaska and elsewhere. They were stocked in Strawberry Reservoir and Fish Lake, Utah, and Lahontan Reservoir, Nevada in 1939. Reports indicate some individuals reached a fairly large size in Strawberry Reservoir. None reproduced.

coho salmon # L C — *Oncorhynchus kisutch*[NP]

This anadromous species inhabits the Pacific. In North America they range from Monterey Bay, California, north to Point Hope, Alaska. They were stocked in Strawberry Reservoir and Fish Lake, Utah, in 1925, and in the Truckee River, Nevada, in 1913. None reproduced.

rainbow trout * L # O R B C — *Oncorhynchus mykiss*

Original range of this species was the West Coast of North America from southern California to Alaska. Rainbow have been stocked more extensively in North America than any other trout. They thrive in a wide range of environments from cool farm ponds to high, cold rivers and lakes. This is the trout that is raised commercially, one reason being that they are easier to raise in hatcheries than most other trouts, and probably more rainbow trout are caught by anglers than any other trout. Part of the reason for this is that more are stocked.

steelhead trout # L — *Oncorhynchus mykiss*[NP] (not differentiated)

This sea-run (anadromous) form of rainbow trout was stocked in Nevada in 1904. They did not survive.

Kamloops trout # B — *Oncorhynchus mykiss*[NP] (not differentiated)

This lake form of rainbow trout grows to a large size in lakes having an abundance of food. They were stocked in Bear Lake, Utah-Idaho, in the 1950s but did not reproduce.

Eagle Lake rainbow trout * L — *Oncorhynchus mykiss aquilarum*

Present only in Eagle Lake, California, this is the only rainbow trout native to the Great Basin.

sockeye salmon (kokanee) # L B C — *Oncorhynchus nerka*

Native to the west coast of North America, the anadromous form of sockeye salmon has many landlocked populations. Landlocked populations are generally small (12 to 16 inches) but often abundant, and many populations reproduce. The range has been extended by stocking.

chinook salmon # L B — *Oncorhynchus tshawytscha*[NP]

The original range of this anadromous Pacific salmon in North America is Ventura River, California, to Point Hope, Alaska, the southern end of the range extirpated because of habitat degradation. This largest (about 125 pounds) of the Pacific salmon is the least abundant. They were stocked in the Jordan River, Utah, in 1873, and in the Lahontan Basin, Nevada, in 1879. None survived. In general, this is a difficult species to establish in a new range. Two exceptions are the Great Lakes and New Zealand.

Bear Lake whitefish * B — *Prosopium abyssicola*

Endemic to Bear Lake, Utah-Idaho, this species has not been stocked elsewhere. It is one of four species endemic to Bear Lake. The others are Bonneville cisco, Bonneville whitefish, and Bear Lake sculpin. This small (10 to 12 inches), deepwater whitefish is moderately abundant and prospering.

Bonneville cisco * B — *Prosopium gemmifer*

This small (7.5 to 8 inches) fish is endemic to Bear Lake, Utah-Idaho. They have been stocked in several other habitats, but there is no record of survival. They are the most numerous fish in Bear Lake. Each year in mid-January, thousands of these little fish move inshore to spawn. Some are dipnetted by anglers.

Bonneville whitefish * B — *Prosopium spilonotus*

Endemic to Bear Lake, Utah-Idaho, this species has not been stocked elsewhere. The Bonneville whitefish is somewhat larger than the Bear Lake whitefish and probably more abundant.

mountain whitefish * L B C — *Prosopium williamsoni*

The native range of the mountain whitefish is western North America, from northern Utah and Nevada north to the Yukon Territory–British Columbia border. They are not considered a particularly good game fish and therefore have not been stocked much, if any, outside their original range.

Atlantic salmon # L B C — *Salmo salar*[NP]

Native range of Atlantic salmon is the North Atlantic Ocean from Portugal to the Arctic Circle and from northern Quebec south to the Connecticut River in the west. There are also landlocked forms. They have been stocked widely with minimal success. They were reportedly stocked in Utah in 1873 and in Lake Tahoe, Nevada-California, in 1881 and in the Colorado River. None survived.

brown trout # L B C — *Salmo trutta*

The brown trout, a native of Europe and western Asia, has been stocked widely in North America. They are a popular sport fish because they reproduce readily in the wild and are a challenge to anglers. Some of the largest brown trout in North America are in Flaming Gorge Lake on the Green River, in the upper Colorado River Basin.

brook trout # L B C — *Salvelinus fontinalis*

The brook trout is native to eastern North America. They have been stocked extensively in the western states and western Canada. Brook trout are high mountain, cold-water fish that have a tendency to stunt when they are crowded. Small ones are relatively easy to catch. Brook trout produce a significant fishery.

lake trout # L B C — *Salvelinus namaycush*

This species is a native of the northeastern lake states and much of Canada. They have been stocked, but not as extensively as most other trouts, in several western states. The lake trout live in deep, cold, infertile lakes and occasionally rivers. They grow to trophy size in Flaming Gorge Lake and elsewhere.

Arctic grayling # L B C — *Thymallus arcticus*

This fish is native to the headwaters of the Missouri River, Montana, and north through Canada to Alaska, once in rivers flowing into Lake Michigan. The range in the United States has been reduced through habitat disruption. Stocking has produced limited populations in eastern California and the Uinta Mountains, Utah. They are medium-size fish (12 to 18 inches) that thrive in the coldest lakes and streams.

ORDER PERCOPSIFORMES
PERCOPSIDAE — TROUT-PERCHES

These small fishes look superficially like both trout (with an adipose fin) and perch (in body shape).

trout-perch # B — *Percopsis omiscomaycus*[NP]

The native range of trout-perch is central and northern North America. They live in both lakes (inshore) and streams. They were introduced (inadvertently) in Utah Lake and Willard Reservoir, Utah, in 1983. They did not survive. Numbers stocked are not known but were probably quite low.

ORDER ATHERINIFORMES
CYPRINODONTIDAE — KILLIFISHES

Small, stout-bodied fishes with a small terminal (jaws equal) mouth, most killifishes are 2 to 3 inches long and may live no more than 1 or 2 years. They have cycloid scales; the body is laterally compressed, usually with no lateral line. These are warm-water to tropical fishes.

White River springfish * R C — *Crenichthys baileyi*

The native range is the warm springs along the now disrupted pluvial White River in eastern Nevada.

Preston springfish * R C — *Crenichthys baileyi albivallis*

This species is endemic to the White River Basin in eastern Nevada. They are protected.

White River springfish * R C — *Crenichthys baileyi baileyi*

The native range is the same as that of *C. baileyi*. Their range has been abbreviated by various human activities. They are endangered.

Hiko springfish * R C — *Crenichthys baileyi grandis*

The Hiko springfish is endemic to warm springs along the disrupted White River, eastern Nevada. They are endangered.

Moapa springfish * R C — *Crenichthys baileyi moapae*

This species is endemic to the headwater warm springs of the Moapa River along the disrupted pluvial White River in eastern Nevada. They are protected.

Moorman springfish * R C — *Crenichthys baileyi thermophilus*

Moorman springfish are endemic to the warm springs along the disrupted White River in eastern Nevada. They are protected.

Railroad Valley springfish * R C — *Crenichthys nevadae*

Native to Railroad Valley, Nye County, Nevada, their range has been extended to warm springs in Mineral County, Nevada. They are threatened.

Devils Hole pupfish * D # C — *Cyprinodon diabolis*

Native range of this small fish is Devil's Hole, Death Valley National Monument, Nevada. The surface area of Devil's Hole is 23 square yards, making it the smallest known range for a vertebrate. They have been transplanted to two other areas as insurance against extirpation, but these transplants have not fared well. They are listed as endangered.

Amargosa pupfish * D — *Cyprinodon nevadensis*

They are native to the Amargosa River Basin, Nevada-California. Some subspecies are listed below.

Amargosa pupfish * D — *Cyprinodon nevadensis amargosa*

This subspecies of pupfish's native range is from Tecopa Bore (an artesian well) downstream to the Amargosa River.

Tecopa pupfish * D — *Cyprinodon nevadensis calidae* (extinct)

These fish were extirpated when their spring habitat was modified.

Ash Meadow pupfish * D — *Cyprinodon nevadensis mionectes*

This subspecies is native from springs and water holes of Ash Meadows, Nye County, Nevada. The subspecies is endangered.

Saratoga Springs pupfish * D — *Cyprinodon nevadensis nevadensis*

These pupfish are native to Saratoga Springs, Amargosa River, Nevada-California.

Warm Springs pupfish * D — *Cyprinodon nevadensis pectoralis*

Warm Springs pupfish are native to Scruggs Springs 1 and 2, and School Spring, near Devil's Hole, Nevada. They are endangered.

Shoshone pupfish * D — *Cyprinodon nevadensis shoshone*

Shoshone pupfish are native to Shoshone Springs, Amargosa River Basin. They are listed as endangered by the American Fisheries Society.

Owens pupfish * D — *Cyprinodon radiosus*

This endemic to Owens Valley, in the vicinity of Lone Pine, Inyo County, California, was once abundant along the Owens River. They have survived in three areas near Bishop, California, but are endangered.

Salt Creek pupfish * D — *Cyprinodon salinus*

Salt Creek pupfish are restricted to Death Valley.

Cottonball Marsh pupfish * D — *Cyprinodon salinus milleri*

These are restricted to Cottonball Marsh and the floor of Death Valley.

Salt Creek pupfish * D — *Cyprinodon salinus salinus*

This subspecies was originally confined to a 1.5-mile section of Salt Creek in northern Death Valley, 180–249 feet below sea level. Transplanted populations are established in Soda Lake, San Bernardino County, and River Springs, Mono County, California.

Pahrump poolfish * D — *Empetrichthys latos*

This species was originally confined to three springs in Pahrump Valley, Nye County, Nevada. One subspecies population still exists in refugia outside its native range.

Raycraft Ranch poolfish * D — *Empetrichthys latos concavus* (extinct)

This subspecies became extinct when the spring that made up its habitat dried up as a result of pumping in Pahrump Valley.

Manse Ranch poolfish * D # C — *Empetrichthys latos latos*

This subspecies was transplanted to a spring outside its native range just before its habitat was destroyed by efforts to control mosquitoes. It now persists as the only living representative of its genus, in nonnative habitat. It is endangered.

Pahrump poolfish * D — *Empetrichthys latos pahrump* (extinct)

See information on Raycraft Ranch poolfish above.

Ash Meadows poolfish * D — *Empetrichthys merriami* (extinct)

The native range of this fish was Ash Meadows, Amargosa Desert, California-Nevada border. There was a thermal isolate known from five separate springs that is thought to have been extirpated through interactions with introduced fishes.

plains topminnow # C — *Fundulus sciadicus*

This species has two native centers, one primarily in Nebraska and one in south central Missouri. They were introduced in the upper White River, Colorado River Basin, where they remain rare.

plains killifish # B C — *Fundulus zebrinus*

The native range of the plains killifish is southeastern Montana, east to Missouri, and south to Texas. They were introduced in the Bonneville Basin, Juab County, Utah.

rainwater killifish # B — *Lucania parva*

The native range of these little killifish is the Atlantic slope of North America, from Massachusetts to Tampico, Mexico. They are in Timpie Springs and Blue Lake, Utah. They were introduced to Blue Lake along with a shipment of largemouth bass. Dispersants from the Timpie Springs have established breeding populations along the southern shore of Great Salt Lake.

POECILIIDAE — LIVEBEARERS

Members of this family bring forth their young alive. They resemble the killifishes in size and general appearance. Livebearers have the dorsal fin placed far back, and the male has a gonopodium that is used to fertilize the female. Gravid females have distended abdomens.

mosquitofish # L B C — *Gambusia affinis*

The native range of the mosquitofish is the central United States from southern Illinois and Indiana south to the mouth of the Rio Grande, Texas. They have been introduced widely in the southwestern United States, where they often compete with or prey upon native fishes.

sailfin molly # L — *Poecilia latipinna*

The native range of the sailfin is from South Carolina to Florida and west into Mexico. They were introduced in Indian Springs, Pahranagat Valley, Nevada.

shortfin molly # L D — *Poecilia mexicana*

The native range of the shortfin molly is from northern Mexico to South America. They have been stocked in several places in Nevada, including Ash Springs.

guppy # L — *Poecilia reticulata*

The native range of the guppy is Venezuela, Barbados, Trinidad, northern Brazil, and Guyana. They have been stocked in the Sheldon National Wildlife Refuge, Nevada, and in certain other waters.

green swordtail # L — *Xiphophorus helleri*

The native range of this pet fish is the Atlantic slope from Rio Nautla, Veracruz, Mexico, to northern Honduras. They have been introduced in Indian Springs, Nevada.

ORDER GASTEROSTEIFORMES
GASTEROSTEIDAE — STICKLEBACKS

The sticklebacks have well-developed, distinctive spines ahead of the dorsal fin. They are small, laterally compressed fishes, with tiny, well-developed teeth. The pelvic fins are thoracic (on the chest), usually posterior to the pectoral fin base, with a single strong, well-developed spine.

brook stickleback # B — *Culaea inconstans*[NP]

Native range of this fish is Nova Scotia west to Iowa, Nebraska, and Montana. They were inadvertently stocked in Willard Reservoir, Utah, in 1983.

threespine stickleback * D — *Gasterosteus aculeatus*

Threespine stickleback are nearly circumpolar in their native range in both freshwater and marine habitats. They are native to Holcomb Creek, Mojave River, California.

ORDER SCORPAENIFORMES
COTTIDAE — SCULPINS

In this largely marine family, the genus *Cottus* has invaded freshwater. They are small (3- to 7-inch) fishes with large flattened heads and fanlike pectoral fins, and are devoid of true scales. The ctenii, or hooks on the body, are remnants of ctenoid scales. They have two dorsal fins; the first has feeble spines, and the anal fin lacks spines. The skull is broad and low, the eyes are high on the head, and the jaws are strong, with well-developed teeth.

mottled sculpin * B C — *Cottus bairdi*

The mottled sculpin ranges in the cool to cold waters in much of North America. They are found from the Tennessee River system of Georgia and Alabama to Labrador on the north to west of the Great Lakes Basin. They are in the Missouri and Columbia River systems, the Bonneville Basin in Utah, and the Colorado River Basin. This small fish, said to be an indicator of trout waters, prospers or suffers along with the trout. They appear to be prospering over much of their range.

Paiute sculpin * L B C — *Cottus beldingi*

The Paiute sculpin is the only sculpin occurring naturally in the Lahontan Basin. They are also native to parts of the Columbia River drainage, the Bear River, and the upper Colorado River. They are short-lived and slow growing; 4 years and 5 inches is typical. They are prospering reasonably well.

Utah Lake sculpin * B — *Cottus echinatus* (extinct)

Indigenous to Utah Lake, this sculpin was extirpated around 1930, when drought and agricultural practices reduced the lake level to an all-time low.

Bear Lake sculpin * B — *Cottus extensus*

This sculpin is endemic to Bear Lake, Utah-Idaho. They live mostly in the deep, cold waters of Bear Lake, moving inshore in late winter to spawn. In high-water years inshore rocks provide cover; in low-water years many of the rocky areas are exposed.

ORDER PERCIFORMES
PERCICHTHYIDAE — TEMPERATE BASSES

These are perchlike fishes that are deep bodied and laterally compressed. The jaws are well developed, with numerous small, strong teeth. The pelvic fins are thoracic; the fish have one spine, five soft rays, and no axillary or scaly process. There are seven branchiostegal rays.

white bass # L B C — *Morone chrysops*

The native range of the white bass is the eastern United States, throughout the river systems of the Mississippi and Ohio Valleys and the Great Lakes. At one time Lake Erie had one of the largest populations. The largest transplanted population in the Great Basin is in Utah Lake. Here the numbers are so large that the species' main competition is itself. The result is many small (8 to 10 inches) white bass and few large ones. They were also stocked in Nevada and the Colorado Plateau. They are considered an important sport fish. Unlike many native species that suffer from river water development, the white bass thrives in impoundments.

striped bass # C — *Morone saxatilis*

Original range of the striped bass is from the St. Lawrence River south to St. Johns River, Florida. There were disjunct populations in the Gulf of Mexico. One of the great success stories in fish stocking is that a relatively few individuals transplanted in the West Coast waters produced a major fishery. Originally this species lived along the coast and moved into freshwater to spawn; there are now many landlocked populations. In Lake Powell they are reproducing in large enough numbers to produce a fishery. They are large, fast-growing, important sport fish.

CENTRARCHIDAE — SUNFISHES

The sunfishes are highly colorful, fresh- and warm-water fishes of North America. Their range has been greatly expanded by stockings starting in the 1800s, when discrimination was usually lacking. The size range is from small to medium; the mouth may be small or large; there are ctenoid scales; the lateral line is complete; the dorsal fin consists of a spinous portion (six to 13 spines) and a soft-rayed section, the two joined in varying degrees. This is one of the most, if not the most, important warm-water sport fish families in the United States. The pan-size sunfishes are sought by youngsters and other anglers, the black basses by both amateurs and professionals. Except for the Sacramento perch, all species are native to regions east of the Continental Divide.

rock bass # B C — *Ambloplites rupestris*[NP]

Its original range the eastern United States and as far west as eastern North and South Dakota, rock bass were introduced in Utah Lake in 1983 and in the Colorado River Basin but apparently did not survive.

Sacramento perch # L B — *Archoplites interruptus*

This medium-size sunfish is endemic to the Sacramento–San Joaquin drainage, California. They are the only sunfish native this far west. They were introduced in Pyramid Lake, Nevada, where they once were relatively abundant. They were stocked in other areas of Nevada and in Gunnison and Cutler Reservoirs, Utah. They are not abundant where they have to compete with other sunfishes. They are not often important game fish outside their native range.

green sunfish # L B C — *Lepomis cyanellus*

The native range of this small, pugnacious sunfish is east central North America. They have been stocked widely and indiscriminately in the western states, where they are rarely considered a sport fish but often a nuisance.

pumpkinseed # O L — *Lepomis gibbosus*

The original distribution of this small to medium-size panfish is much of the Atlantic slope, the Great Lakes, and the upper Mississippi. There has been limited stocking in southeastern Oregon and northwest Nevada. Their contribution to sport fishing is minimal.

bluegill # O L B C — *Lepomis macrochirus*

The original range of the bluegill is central and eastern North America. They have been stocked perhaps more extensively in the United States than any other fish. They are popular with anglers of all ages. In the southern states bluegills are often stocked in ponds with largemouth bass. They are also stocked in large impoundments such as Lake Powell and other downstream lakes.

redear sunfish # B — *Lepomis microlophus*[NP]

The redear is native to the Florida Peninsula, the lower Atlantic and Gulf slopes drainage west to Texas, and north to southern Indiana. They were stocked in

Holmes Creek Reservoir, Utah, in 1959. Scott Strong of Kaysville confirmed they were present in 1981.

smallmouth bass # O L C — *Micropterus dolomieu*

The native range of the smallmouth is from Minnesota and southern Quebec, south to the Tennessee River system in Alabama, and west to eastern Oklahoma. Stocking in western states has been extensive but not intensive. They provide only moderate fishing because the range is restricted and numbers are limited in the Great Basin and Colorado Plateau. There is probably more popular literature on the smallmouth bass than any other warm-water fish.

spotted bass # L — *Micropterus punctulatus*

The original range of this medium-size bass is the central and lower Mississippi Basin and along the Gulf Coast from western Texas through northwestern Florida. They were stocked in western Nevada.

largemouth bass # O L N B C — *Micropterus salmoides*

The native range of the largemouth is from northeastern Mexico to Florida, much of the Mississippi River Basin, north to southern Quebec and Ontario, and on the Atlantic slope north to central South Carolina. They have been stocked abundantly in the Great Basin and the Colorado Plateau. This is by far the largest (more than 22 pounds) member of the sunfish family. They are also the most popular: bass clubs and tournaments abound just to enjoy and pursue this rather amazing fish. Prized not only for their size, they leap repeatedly when hooked and are not easy to hook. Their culinary qualities are also tops. In many bodies of warm water, the difference between largemouth and no largemouth is the difference between good and fair to poor fishing. They thrive in small, warm ponds and large, warm to cool lakes. They appear to do exceptionally well in reservoirs. They have been introduced into many desert springs from which native fishes have subsequently disappeared or been drastically decreased in numbers. Most desert spring populations of largemouth bass are stunted.

white crappie # L C — *Pomoxis annularis*

The native range of the white crappie (pronounced "croppie") is central and eastern North America. There are a few populations in the Great Basin and the Colorado Plateau.

black crappie # L B C — *Pomoxis nigromaculatus*

The native range of the black crappie is eastern and central North America. They have been stocked extensively in the western states. The black crappie fares better than the white in warm, clear lakes and reservoirs. Crappies are larger than most sunfishes but much smaller than the black basses. There are often amazing surges in population numbers. They tend to stay very near cover.

PERCIDAE — PERCHES

These are long, streamlined, somewhat laterally compressed fishes. Mouth size varies; there are teeth on the jaws, palatines, and vomer. There are two dorsal fins

— one spiny, one soft — that are well separated. Darters, the small, colorful members of this family, are most numerous (over 100). The family inhabits warm to cold arctic water and is circumpolar in distribution. Most species are restricted to North America.

Iowa darter # C — *Etheostoma exile*

The native range of this little fish is much of the interior of southern Canada and the northern United States. They were introduced in the Colorado River Basin, where they are rare.

johnny darter # C — *Etheostoma nigrum*

The johnny darter's native range is from Hudson and James Bay drainages, south to Arkansas, west to Colorado, and east to North Carolina. They were introduced and are rare in the upper Colorado River Basin.

yellow perch # L B C — *Perca flavescens*

The native range of the yellow perch is from Nova Scotia to South Carolina, west of the Appalachians from Pennsylvania to upper Missouri, from eastern Kansas to western Montana, north to Great Slave Lake, then southeast to James Bay. This fish also occurs naturally in northern Europe and Asia. They have been stocked in Nevada and Utah, where they are common in some waters, and the Colorado Plateau, where they are rare to occasionally common. These usually 12- to 14-inch fish furnish good sport where they are common. They may be stunted (7 to 8 inches) and of little interest to anglers.

logperch # B — *Percina caprodes*

The range of this largest of the darters is much of the east central United States and far north in eastern Canada. They were inadvertently stocked in Willard Reservoir, Utah, in 1983, where they are prospering moderately.

walleye # L B C — *Stizostedion vitreum*

The native range of the walleye is much of the United States as far west as eastern Colorado, Wyoming, and Montana. The range in Canada is north to the Mackenzie River and Great Slave Lake. They have been stocked extensively in Nevada, Utah, Arizona, and Colorado. They are a large, fast-growing, long-lived fish that is much sought after by anglers. They are soft biters and not easy to catch, which adds to the sport. Although they reach sizes comparable to largemouth bass, they are not as popular. This is probably because they are both hard to find at times and harder to catch than largemouth.

CICHLIDAE — CICHLIDS

This family is native to Africa, South America, Central America, and the southwestern United States. They are sold throughout the United States as pet fishes. This has led to their introduction in the wild far outside their original range.

jaguar cichlid # C — *Cichlasoma managuense*

This large cichlid's native range is Atlantic drainages of Central America, from southern Costa Rica north to Rio Patuco, Honduras. They are present in a spring pool in the Virgin River Basin. This species could be a substantial threat to native fishes were they to escape into the Virgin River.

convict cichlid # L — *Cichlasoma nigrofasciatum*

The native range includes Guatemala and other areas of Central America. They were released, probably by pet owners or dealers, in Ash and Crystal Springs in Pahranagat Valley, Nevada. They are hazardous to small native fishes.

redbelly tilapia # D — *Tilapia zilli*

This species is native to north and central Africa. They were introduced in Cottonwood Park, Pahrump Valley, Nevada.

SUMMARY

The Great Basin is a closed drainage; that is, no water that accumulates from surface flow or runoff flows naturally to the sea. The largest accumulations of water in the Great Basin are the Great Salt Lake in Utah and Pyramid Lake in Nevada. In prehistoric times much of the Great Basin was covered by Lake Lahontan and Lake Bonneville.

The Colorado Plateau consists roughly of the upper Colorado River watershed and extends over portions of several states. Species diversity among fishes is much less than that in the great rivers of the Midwest, where high nutrient loads and a wider range of nonadverse conditions contribute to higher species diversity. The mark of humans is cut deeply on the Colorado River and its tributaries: it has been dammed and diverted for water use and power generation more than any river in North America with the possible exception of the Columbia in the Pacific Northwest. It is very much changed in character and condition from the unaltered state under which the fish fauna evolved. There is no comparison between the original lower reaches of the river and what now reaches the Gulf of California.

For some very small bodies of water, some less than an acre, the changes in water chemistry, sediment levels, and other characteristics have been drastic. Some of the severely impacted species, particularly in the Lahontan Basin, have become extinct.

While fish species diversity in the Basin is not as high as in many areas of the country, a total of 190 stocked and native species and subspecies are present. Today 26 percent of the fish stocked historically are no longer present, and 8 percent of the native fishes are extinct. Federal protection (primarily by the Endangered Species Act) has been given to 33 percent of the native fishes, and 11 percent have state protection. With few exceptions, movement of fish outside their original range is accomplished by humans. These stockings are done for a variety of reasons, many with little logic or biological basis. Anglers stock fish because they believe their efforts will improve fishing success at the favorite angling location, or they thoughtlessly dump exotic bait minnows from their holding pails when they finish fishing for the day. People flush exotic fishes down the drain rather than kill them.

Most will die, but a few hardy individuals may survive, with potential adverse impacts that include spread of exotic diseases, predation on native species, and competition for food and other resources. Biologists stock exotic species to improve sport fishing, to improve the structure of the food web, or to add another sport fish to the fishery. Some of these introductions are carefully thought out and accomplished by biologists who have studied both the water and the fish species in detail; those by well-meaning or uninformed individuals rarely have positive results. Many western waters were stocked indiscriminately with exotics in the late nineteenth and early twentieth centuries. Common carp are perhaps the best-known example. These fish were praised as a fine food fish and stocked extensively by the federal and state governments and private individuals. Today common carp are a detriment to the majority of the waters in which they exist. Overall, indiscriminate stocking, in addition to being illegal in some situations, is strongly discouraged by resource agencies with management responsibility and by ichthyologists attempting to study, catalog, and document species status.

Within the fish fauna of the Great Basin and Colorado Plateau area, there are several examples of highly specialized fishes that developed in extreme conditions. One of these species, humpback chub, does not adapt well to extreme change, and populations in the modified Colorado River have not fared well. The tui chub, in contrast, responds readily to habitat alterations and is apparently affected little by many of the dramatic changes in habitat structure. The Salt Creek pupfish in Death Valley, which lives in waters as hot as 130°F and as much as 249 feet below sea level, is unique.

The transbasin diversion of much of the flow of the Truckee River into the Carson River in 1905 is an example of extreme habitat alteration. The lower Truckee River (below the Derby Dam) and Pyramid Lake (which depends upon river flows) were drastically altered when the dam was completed. The original Lahontan cutthroat trout in Pyramid Lake were doomed by the drop in lake elevation, which severely reduced then terminated river spawning access and success.

Perhaps the most useful summation with respect to fish fauna of the vast area of the western United States inside the Great Basin and the Colorado Plateau is a reflection on the great diversity of habitat types in the aquatic environment and the responses this diversity elicited from the fauna over centuries of evolution. Humans have altered both these habitats and the faunal structure: it is significant that many of the species, both native and exotic, have survived in spite of these modifications.

ACKNOWLEDGMENTS

We acknowledge the helpful input and reviews of the following individuals or organizations: W. L. Minckley, professor of zoology, Arizona State University, Tempe; Mark Rosenfeld, curator, Museum of Natural History, University of Utah, Salt Lake City; R. M. Bailey, Museum of Zoology, University of Michigan, Ann Arbor; Gerald R. Smith, curator of fishes, Museum of Zoology, University of Michigan, Ann Arbor; Spectrum Sciences and Software, Logan, Utah, and Fort Walton Beach, Florida. Margaret Sigler and Sydney Peterson, Logan, Utah, provided editorial and review assistance.

REFERENCES AND FURTHER READING

Bailey, R. M., and T. Uyeno. 1964. Nomenclature of the blue chub and the tui chub, cyprinid fishes from western United States. Copeia: 238–239.

Baxter, G. T., and J. R. Simon. 1970. Wyoming fishes. Cheyenne: Wyoming Game and Fish Department, Bull. 4. 168 pp.

Behnke, R. J. 1992. Native trout of western North America. American Fisheries Society Monograph 6. 275 pp.

Bills, F. T., and C. E. Bond. 1980. A new subspecies of tui chub (Pices: Cyprinidae) from Cowhead Lake, California. Copeia.

Bisson, P. A. and C. E. Bond. 1971. Origin and distribution of the fishes of Harney Basin, Oregon. Copeia: 268–281.

Bond, C. E. 1979. Biology of fishes. New York: Holt, Rinehart and Winston, CBS College Publishing. 514 pp.

Dill, W. A., and L. Shapovolov. 1939. An unappreciated California game fish, the Rocky Mountain Whitefish, *Prosopium williamsoni* (Girard). California Fish and Game 25(3): 226–227.

Everhart, W. H., and W. R. Seaman. 1971. Fishes of Colorado. Denver: Colorado Game, Fish, and Parks Division. 75 pp.

Hubbs, C. L., and R. R. Miller. 1948. The zoological evidence. The Great Basin, with emphasis on glacial and post-glacial times. Bull. Univ. Utah. Biol. Ser. 11: 18–166.

Hubbs, C. L., R. R. Miller, and L. C. Hubbs. 1974. Hydrographic history and relict fishes of the north-central Great Basin. Mem. Calif. Acad. Sci. 7: 1–259.

Johnson, J. E. 1987. Protected fishes of the United States and Canada. Bethesda, MD: American Fisheries Society. 45 pp.

LaRivers, I. 1962. Fishes and fisheries of Nevada. Reno: Nevada State Fish and Game Commission. 782 pp.

Lee, D. S., C. R. Gilbert, C. H. Horcutt, R. E. Jenkins, D. E. McAllister, and J. R. Stauffer, Jr. 1980. Atlas of North American freshwater fishes. Raleigh: North Carolina State Museum of Natural History. 854 pp.

Lugaski, T. 1972. A new species of speckled dace from Big Smoky Valley, Nevada. Biol. Soc. Nev. Occ. Pap. 30: 1–8.

Marsh, P. C., T. A. Burke, B. D. DeMarais, and M. E. Douglas. 1989. First North American record of *Cichlasoma managuense* (Pices: Cichlidae). Great Basin Naturalist 49(3): 387–389.

Miller, R. R., and G. R. Smith. 1981. Distribution and evolution of *Chasmistes* (Pices: Catostomidae) in western North America. Occ. Pap. of the Museum of Zoology, University of Michigan, No. 696. 46 pp.

Minckley, W. L. 1973. Fishes of Arizona. Phoenix: Arizona Game and Fish Department. 293 pp.

Minckley, W. L., D. A. Hendrickson, and C. E. Bond. 1986. Geography of western North American freshwater fishes. Description and relationships to intracontinental tectonism. Pp. 519–613 in H. C. Hocutt and E. O. Wiley (eds.), Zoogeography of North American freshwater fishes. New York: Wiley Interscience.

Moyle, P. B. 1976. Inland fishes of California. Berkeley: University of California Press. 405 pp.

Robins, C. R., R. M. Bailey, C. E. Bond, J. R. Brooker, E. A. Lachner, R. N. Lea, and W. B. Scott. 1991. Common and scientific names of fishes from the United States and Canada. 5th ed. Bethesda, MD: American Fisheries Society Special Publication 20. 183 pp.

Scott, W. B., and E. J. Crossman. 1973. Freshwater fishes of Canada. Fisheries Research Board of Canada Bull. 184. 966 pp.

Sigler, W. F., and R. R. Miller. 1963. Fishes of Utah. Salt Lake City: Utah Department of Fish and Game. 203 pp.

Sigler, W. F., and J. W. Sigler. 1987. Fishes of the Great Basin: A Natural History. Reno: University of Nevada Press. 425 pp.

————. 1993. Fishes of Utah: A Natural History Review. Manuscript.

Simpson, J. C., and R. C. Wallace. 1978. Fishes of Idaho. Moscow: University of Idaho Press. 237 pp.

Smith, G. R. 1978. Biogeography of intermountain fishes. Great Basin Naturalist Mem. 2: 17–42.

Tomelleri, J. R., and M. E. Eberle. 1990. Fishes of the Central United States. Lawrence: University Press of Kansas. 226 pp.

Tyus, H. M., B. D. Burdock, R. A. Valdez, C. M. Haynes, T. A. Lytle, and C. R. Berry. 1982. Fishes of the upper Colorado River Basin: distribution, abundance, and status. Pp. 12–70 in W. H. Miller, H. M. Tyus, and C. A. Carlson (eds.), Fishes of the upper Colorado River system: Present and Future. Washington, D.C.: Western Division, American Fisheries Society.

Williams, J. D. 1981. Threatened desert fishes and the Endangered Species Act. Pp. 447–475 in R. J. Naiman and D. L. Soltz (eds.), Fishes in North American deserts. New York: John Wiley and Sons.

Williams, J. E. 1978. Taxonomic status of *Rhinichthys osculus* (Cyprinidae) in the Moapa River, Nevada. SW Nat. 23: 511–518.

Williams, J. E., and C. E. Bond. 1980. *Gila boraxobius*, a new species of cyprinid fish from southeastern Oregon with a comparison to G. *alvordensis* Hubbs and Miller. Proceedings of the Biological Society of Washington 93(2): 291–298.

Williams, J. E., J. E. Johnson, D. A. Hendrickson, S. Contreras-Balderas, J. D. Williams, M. Navarro-Mendoza, D. E. McAllister, and J. E. Deacon. 1989. Fishes of North America: Endangered, threatened or of special concern. Fisheries 14(6): 2–20.

Wiltzius, W. J. 1985. Fish culture and stocking in Colorado, 1872–1978. Denver: Colorado Division of Wildlife 12.

Chrysothamnus nauseosus (Pall.) Britt. (rubber rabbitbrush) is a common invader of road edges both on the Colorado Plateau and in the Great Basin. When this shrub flowers in September, it produces a waist-high mound of spectacular yellow flowers. The long, tubular flowers produce abundant nectar that attracts a rich diversity of bees and butterflies.

CHAPTER 10

Insects of the Great Basin and Colorado Plateau

C. Riley Nelson

OVERVIEW

This chapter is a review of selected groups of insects reported to occur in the Great Basin and Colorado Plateau. The author discusses general distribution patterns, species diversity, ecological roles, and human-related impacts for each group. He also examines available data concerning the insect fossil record for the region, phylogenetic affinities, endemicity, and dispersal barriers and corridors.

Insects are more diverse than all the rest of the animal kingdom combined (Eisner and Wilson 1977). The number of species of insects on earth has been estimated by several methods and ranges from the approximately 800,000 species formally described by scientists to appraisals of 30 million based on rain forest canopy fogging studies (Erwin 1983). This amazing diversity makes mere identification, much less an assessment of the biological significance, of the species that inhabit a large area such as the Great Basin and Colorado Plateau a Herculean task.

The Great Basin and Colorado Plateau are inhabited by thousands of species of insects (Nelson 1983), each the result of individual phylogenetic histories and each playing one or more of a multitude of ecological roles. The regional geography of insects — and any other group of organisms, for that matter — can be studied from two major frames of reference that indeed are not completely exclusive: historical and ecological. In simplistic form the historical component consists of the genetic histories and identities of species interacting with the geologic histories of the areas they inhabit. Interesting questions in historical biogeography of the region would include: What range patterns are seen in Great Basin and Colorado Plateau insect species? What are the genealogical or phylogenetic relationships among the species of an area? Did these groups evolve in the Great Basin? If not, from where did they come? What roles have geographical barriers or corridors played in the isolation or dispersal of these organisms?

The questions of interest in ecological biogeography are somewhat different, being more related to proximal factors that restrict a species to a limited area called its geographical range (Brown and Gibson 1983). These factors can be either abiotic or biotic. Abiotic factors, which are most relevant in the context of biogeography of insects of the Great Basin and Colorado Plateau, are rainfall patterns, temperature regimes, soil types and salinities, and, for aquatic insects, stream or lake size. The biotic factors are diverse and defined in terms of niche, habitat usage, and community-level interactions such as predator-prey relations, competition, and mutualisms. The relative importance of historical versus ecological factors in biogeography has spurred considerable discussion between workers in the two fields (Humphries and Parenti 1986; Rosen 1990). For the purposes of this chapter, I focus more on the historical component while agreeing that the ecological component has indeed played a very important role in shaping the insect fauna of the Great Basin and Colorado Plateau.

Information concerning the insect fauna of the region is dispersed throughout the scientific literature. Haws et al. (1988) reported more than 6,000 species of insects in an extensive but not exhaustive search of literature relating to insects associated with western wildland shrubs, most of which occur in the Great Basin and Colorado Plateau region. This insect/plant literature component is but a small subset of the information available in systematic revisionary studies and zoogeographic syntheses of the majority of insect groups. In this chapter I provide examples of studies on a number of insect groups to emphasize similarity of distributions in many cases as well as indications of unique patterns in others.

DIVERSITY

How many species of insects inhabit the Great Basin and Colorado Plateau? A simple enough question but unanswered to date for a variety of reasons. Foremost of these reasons is the amazing diversity of the organisms to consider. Approximations of the size of some components of the insect fauna of the region are given in Table 10.1. I estimate a total of 14,000 to 26,000 described species for the region. This figure was calculated by using the estimated North American insect fauna (88,090 species) times the proportion of the fauna of the less inclusive taxa, which ranged from 0.16 (16 percent) for robber flies and 0.30 (30 percent) for ants. This proportion was calculated by dividing the number of species in the region by the number of North American species. The groups represented in Table 10.1 were chosen somewhat arbitrarily according to readily available information but are generally some of the more completely collected of insects in the region. In general the stonefly families and genera found in the study area are of boreal affinities (Zwick 1973), and the robber flies have a large component of more southern distribution (Nelson 1985). Ants most certainly increase in diversity as one nears the tropics (Hölldobler and Wilson 1990). The number of species in the region was estimated using publications with coverage based on political boundaries, not the composite "natural" boundaries of the Great Basin and Colorado Plateau. As such the approximations given are not directly comparable but are thought to be reasonable estimates of the numbers in the composite area. In any event since the numbers in column two of Table 10.1 are taken from subsets of the Great Basin and Colorado Plateau area, they represent a more conservative approximation of the number of species present. Are the Great Basin and Colorado Plateau species rich or species poor? The answer to this question must be tempered with the caveat, in relation to what? If disparate areas are compared, of course the tropical rain forests are richer; for example, recent collecting in the state of Rondonia in the Amazon Basin of Brazil has produced 1,300 butterfly species compared to the 155 of the Great Basin (C. J. Durden, personal communication; Austin and Murphy 1987). Perhaps a better comparison would be with a neighboring area such as the mountains of California to the west. On a single trip to this area, Nelson and Stark (1988) recorded 81 stonefly species collected during a seven-day period. Comparing this to the 40 captured during extensive collecting of stoneflies in the Great Basin (Sheldon 1979), we must judge the Great Basin depauperate. A second type of assessment of species richness could include diversity through time. One aspect of this would consist of the fossil record for insects of the Great Basin and Colorado Plateau. A third comparison of richness could be comparison of species in a single genus in two areas. In the case of *Athysanella* leafhoppers (Cicadellidae) examined by Hicks and colleagues (1988), the Great Basin was found to be particularly rich in endemics.

Table 10.1   Number of Insects in Great Basin and Colorado Plateau (GB/CP) and Percentage of North American Insect Fauna Represented Therein

Taxon	GB/CP	North America	Percentage
Stoneflies	90[a]	537[a]	17
Butterflies	155[b]	763[c]	20
Robber flies	160[d]	1,012[e]	16
Ants	77[f]	580[g]	30
Insects	14,000–26,000[h]	88,090[i]	16–30

(a) Stark, Szczytko, and Baumann 1986, for Utah and Nevada; (b) Austin and Murphy 1987, for Great Basin; (c) Miller and Brown 1981; (d) Nelson 1987, for Utah; (e) Fisher and Wilcox 1987, Catalog of Nearctic Asilidae (unpublished list); (f) Wheeler and Wheeler 1986, for Nevada; (g) Smith 1979; (h) my calculations gave 14,094–26,427; (i) Borror, Triplehorn, and Johnson 1989

So the question, Is the region species rich? can be answered on at least four scales: broad geographic, neighboring geographic, temporal occurrence, and lower-level phylogenetic. Examples from the last three scales are most applicable to this chapter and are discussed under the individual groups that follow.

Fossil Insects

Fossil insects are known from very few localities in the Great Basin and Colorado Plateau. The few sites known, however, are of great importance in the history of the group as a whole. Indications of insects from the Paleozoic, Mesozoic, and Cenozoic Eras have all been found. In fact, the oldest formation bearing fossil insect remains in western North America (Paleozoic: Pennsylvanian) is in the Great

Basin in the Manning Canyon Shale Formation found near Utah Lake in central Utah (Durden 1984).

The Manning Canyon Shale is well known for its extensive plant fossils (Tidwell 1967; Tidwell et al. 1974). With 43 genera and 103 species of plants found therein, the Manning Canyon Shale represents the most diversified flora of Carboniferous age presently known in western North America (Nelson and Tidwell 1987). The plant assemblage indicates that the area was a swampy, moist lowland with perpetual summerlike conditions (Tidwell 1975).

A number of arthropods have been found in the Manning Canyon Shale, including an arachnid (probably the extinct family Trigonotarbidae), a crustacean, a millipede, an orthopteroid resembling a cockroach, a disassociated insect wing, and a nearly complete specimen of *Brodioptera stricklani* Nelson and Tidwell in the extinct order Megasecoptera. Megasecoptera contains some of the oldest of winged insects (Wooton 1981). *Brodioptera stricklani* is remarkable in the reduction of the veins of the wing compared to other insects of similar age (Nelson and Tidwell 1987). This reduced venation is phylogenetically significant because current models of insect wing evolution imply that many veins, particularly pairs of anterior and posterior members of several series, are the ancestral or plesiomorphic condition (Kukalová-Peck 1983). That the veins are reduced in this insect of similar age to that proposed for the hypothetical first winged insect may partially refute the multiple-vein generalization. A reappraisal of these generalizations and consideration of additional hypotheses is required as well as a re-evaluation of the stratigraphy involved. It is also interesting to note that the only other specimen of *Brodioptera*, a hind wing, is known from Nova Scotia in eastern Canada. Presence of two closely related species currently separated by such long distances indicates a zoogeographic affinity between the two areas at that early date.

Indications of Mesozoic insects in the Great Basin and Colorado Plateau are limited to apparent larval borings in the trunklike structures of *Tempskya* tree ferns from the Lower Cretaceous Dakota Sandstone in the central Colorado Plateau (W. D. Tidwell, personal communication). Fortunately, insect fossils and traces are more common from the Cenozoic strata. Cenozoic insects are readily placed in recent families with genera and sometimes species virtually the same as extant forms. The Green River Formation of Eocene age, probably most famous for beautifully preserved fish fossils, contains extensive insect remains. Two sites on the Colorado Plateau, near Bonanza, Utah, and Douglas Pass, Colorado, have yielded particularly extensive and relatively well preserved insect material. Oligocene insects are not well represented in the Great Basin and Colorado Plateau but are extraordinarily rich in the Florissant Shales to the east of the Colorado Plateau in central Colorado (Scudder 1890). Miocene insects are represented in the Great Basin at two sites in western Nevada. Angiosperm woods contain borings of insects, probably beetles, at a site in Virgin Valley in the extreme northwestern corner of Nevada north of Pyramid Lake (W. D. Tidwell, personal communication). A fine-grained substrate of Miocene age in Stewart Valley near Hawthorne, Nevada, has yielded numerous specimens of lightly built insects like nematocerous flies and aphids. Future excavations at these sites will undoubtedly reveal many more specimens (H. I. Scudder, personal communication). Pleistocene insects have been noted in studies of packrat middens in the Great Basin and in the caves along the Colorado River in the Grand Canyon.

SELECTED INSECT GROUPS

Orthoptera

The grasshoppers, crickets, and their relatives are a conspicuous component of the fauna of the Great Basin and Colorado Plateau. Historically members of the order Orthoptera have played an important role in the history of the region. When Mormon settlers arrived in the Great Basin in 1847, they found that members of the Ute tribe in the vicinity of the Great Salt Lake often gathered large numbers of the wingless "crickets," *Anabrus simplex* Haldeman, for food. By the year after the white settlers' arrival, these tettigoniids formed large hordes that threatened to decimate the first meager crops. After numerous attempts at controlling these "Mormon crickets" with water-filled trenches and beating devices, the pioneers asked for divine intervention as a solution to their problem. Flocks of sea gulls made a timely appearance and began feeding on the insects in earnest. Reports of the time include mentions of the gulls' flying to the Great Salt Lake and emptying their engorged crops of the insects, then returning to the fields for another load. As a result of this incident, the state bird of Utah is the sea gull, and the Mormons have erected a monument to the sea gulls and placed it on Temple Square in central Salt Lake City.

Mormon crickets continue to be a problem to ranchers and farmers in the Great Basin and on the Colorado Plateau. In the summer of 1990, reports of outbreaks near Winnemucca, Nevada, were given national news coverage on several network stations. Several other areas of perennially high Mormon cricket populations include the valleys near Oak City in Millard County, Utah, and the foothills of the Uinta Mountains north of Vernal, Utah, and nearby northwest Colorado. Several government agencies monitor these populations and treat the pests in these areas with a variety of control measures (Capinera and Sechrist 1982).

Grasshoppers are of perennial concern to inhabitants of this region. High populations of grasshoppers attract the attention of the ranching and farming industries as well as suburban homeowners. Several species of acridid grasshoppers continue to attain outbreak population levels in the region (Capinera and Sechrist 1982) and are continuously monitored by agencies such as the U.S. Department of Agriculture's Animal and Plant Health Inspection Service (APHIS) and state agencies. A summary of the cultural, chemical, and biological control measures frequently used in the region is given by Capinera and Sechrist (1982).

The Orthoptera of North America have also attracted the attention of biologists for reasons other than the economic situation alone (Helfer 1987; Rehn 1958), with special attention given several of the acridid subfamilies (Otte 1981, 1984). Taxonomic identification guides and reviews of selected Orthoptera of the region include those for Orthoptera (in the broad sense) of Utah (Barnum 1954) and grasshoppers of Colorado (Capinera and Sechrist 1982).

Capinera and Sechrist (1982) provide distribution maps summarizing then current distributions of acridids in Colorado. As determined from these maps, the portion of the Colorado Plateau in the state of Colorado harbors 61 of the 131 species of grasshoppers found in Colorado.

Gilbert (1988) listed 99 species of acridids in Utah and examined the distributional relationship of these species to various floristic (e.g., Cronquist et al. 1972), faunal (e.g., Durrant 1952), and community mapping systems, including those of Clements and Shelford (1939), Dice (1943), and Holdridge (1947). She also compared these distributions to maps of abiotic factors such as precipitation (broken down into several seasonal categories), temperature (maxima and minima, again placed in several seasonal categories), annual potential evapotranspiration, and soil type. She concluded that the most useful of community classifications for grasshopper distributions should be framed in repeatable, flexible, nonhierarchical units based on abiotic factors. In her study the Holdridge life zone system provided better correlations with the grasshopper distribution than any of the other community-type mapping systems. The zones of this system, based on abiotic factors, produced repeating combinations of species whenever given combinations of conditions repeated. She stated that the major problem with the life zone model was that it was specifically designed to predict the distribution of plant architecture, which is only one of several environmental factors to which the grasshoppers could respond, and that the relationship between the grasshoppers and the life zones was not simple. She further noted that the scale of resolution important to plants may be smaller than that important to grasshoppers and that their communities reflected individually distributed species that usually formed indistinctly bound overlapping assemblages. Thus, she concluded, problems in overlap are only regarded as such if mapping is the ultimate goal of community classification. She suggested that such mapping is not the ultimate goal and that better correlations between animal distributions and community classification might be found in systems designed from on-site descriptions of abiotic conditions and plant physiognomy (Gilbert 1988).

Plecoptera

Stoneflies (Plecoptera) are excellent model animals for studies of comparative and cladistic biogeography. They serve particularly well in boreal areas because they have low dispersal tendencies, are speciose (over 550 species in North America), have a high proportion of endemic species, and are readily collected from predictable habitats. Systematic reviews of the stoneflies of the Great Basin and Colorado Plateau are found in more general works such as Baumann et al. (1977) and Jewett (1960).

Prior to the efforts of Sheldon (1979), the isolated ranges within the Great Basin had attracted little attention from aquatic biologists, and the running-water fauna of the region was very poorly known. Sheldon's (1979) collecting efforts yielded 40 species of stoneflies from 15 of the mountain ranges in the Great Basin of Nevada and Utah (Table 10.2). He caught no more than 15 species of stoneflies from any one range. The number of stonefly species he collected in any one of these ranges is much smaller than from even single streams in two potential source areas, the Sierra Nevada and the Wasatch Mountains. On the western margin of the Great Basin, Sheldon and Jewett (1967) reported 31 species of stoneflies from Sagehen Creek in the central Sierra Nevada, while Baumann (1967) reported 32 species in

Big Cottonwood Creek in the Wasatch Mountains on the Great Basin's eastern border. Since both Sagehen and Big Cottonwood Creeks drain into the Great Basin and are of approximately the same size as many of the streams in the Basin ranges, these streams are fair representatives of the biotic potential of some of the streams in the Great Basin. Still, these streams have only half as many species as those of the neighboring major mountain masses. The Great Basin streams are depauperate, therefore, compared to nearby ranges of larger area.

Table 10.2 Mountain Ranges and Number of Plecoptera Species

Deep Creek Mountains	9	Schell Creek Range	15
Humboldt Range	7	Snake Range	9
Jackson Mountains	12	Sonoma Range	8
Jarbidge Mountains	12	Spring Mountains	2
Pine Forest Range	11	Toiyabe Range	14
Quinn Canyon–Grant Range	5	White Mountains	9
Ruby Mountains	10	White Pine Range	7
Santa Rosa Range	15		

Source: Sheldon 1979.

The distributional affinities of the 40 species of stoneflies reported by Sheldon (1979) are summarized in Table 10.3. Of these 40 species, 26 are known from both the Sierra Nevada to the west and the central or southern Rocky Mountains. Six species in the Great Basin clearly have affinities to those in the Sierra Nevada, and five of these six are known only from the White Mountains, which are nearly contiguous with the Sierra Nevada south of Mono Lake. One of these five, *Capnia hornigi* Baumann and Sheldon, is limited in distribution to the White Mountains and further is a member of the Barberi group, which otherwise is limited to the Sierra Nevada (Nelson and Baumann 1989). The sixth species, *Moselia infuscata* Claassen, is widespread in the Sierra Nevada and Cascade Ranges to the west of the Great Basin but is known only from the Pine Forest Range in Nevada near the northwest limits of the Great Basin. Five species collected in the Great Basin are uniquely shared with the central and southern Rocky Mountains. It is notable, then, that the Great Basin uniquely shares about the same number of species with either the Rocky Mountains or the Sierra Nevada despite the richer stonefly fauna of the Sierra Nevada (C. R. Nelson, unpublished data). In fact, the species shared only with the Sierra Nevada are limited to the extreme western border of the Great Basin, while the species of Rocky Mountain affinity occur as far west as the eastern foothills of the Sierra Nevada (*Capnura wanica* Frison: Nelson and Baumann 1987) as well as the various ranges in the central Great Basin.

A single species, *Malenka* sp. A of Sheldon (1979), from the Spring Mountains in the Mojave Desert of southern Nevada is most closely related to *Malenka biloba* (Claassen) from the ranges of southern California near Los Angeles north to Kern

County (R. W. Baumann, personal communication). Two species reported by Sheldon (1979) were identified to only the generic level, and both genera are represented by several species in the purported source areas, therefore eliminating the possibility of making assignment of affinity to zoogeographic area.

Table 10.3   Stoneflies Reported From the Great Basin, Sorted
                 by Geographic Affinities

Shared With Both Sierra Nevada and Rocky Mountains

1. *Alloperla severa* (Hagen)
2. *Capnia gracilaria* Claassen
3. *Capnia utahensis* Gaufin and Jewett
4. *Diura knowltoni* (Frison)
5. *Doddsia occidentalis* (Banks)
6. *Eucapnopsis brevicauda* Claassen
7. *Hesperoperla pacifica* (Banks)
8. *Isoperla quinquepunctata* (= *patricia*) (Banks)
9. *Isoperla sobria* (= *ebria*) (Hagen)
10. *Malenka californica* (Claassen)
11. *Paraleuctra occidentalis* (Banks)
12. *Paraleuctra vershina* Gaufin and Ricker
13. *Plumaperla* (= *Triznaka) diversa* (Frison)
14. *Podmosta delicatula* (Claassen)
15. *Prostoia besametsa* (Ricker)
16. *Pteronarcys princeps* Banks
17. *Skwala americana* (= parallela) Klapálek
18. *Suwallia pallidula* (Banks)
19. *Sweltsa borealis* (Banks)
20. *Sweltsa coloradensis* (Banks)
21. *Taenionema nigripenne* (Banks)
22. *Triznaka pintada* (Ricker)
23. *Zapada cinctipes* (Banks)
24. *Zapada frigida* (Claassen)
25. *Zapada haysi* (Ricker)
26. *Zapada oregonensis* (Claassen)

Shared with Sierra Nevada

27. *Capnia hornigi* (= sp. A) Baumann and Sheldon
28. *Frisonia picticeps* (Hanson)
29. *Kogotus nonus* (= sp.)
30. *Moselia infuscata* (Claassen)
31. *Sweltsa townesi* (Ricker)
32. *Yoraperla brevis* (Banks)

continues

Table 10.3   Stoneflies Reported From the Great Basin, Sorted
               by Geographic Affinities   *(continued)*

Shared with Rocky Mountains

33. *Capnia uintahi* Gaufin
34. *Capnura (= Capnia) wanica* (Frison)
35. *Megarcys signata* (Hagen)
36. *Pteronarcella badia* (Hagen)
37. *Utacapnia lemoniana* (Nebeker and Gaufin)

Southern Mountains Endemic

38. *Malenka* sp. A

Not Enough Information

39. *Cultus* sp.
40. *Doroneuria* sp. (= *baumanni*)

Note: Names in current usage followed in parentheses by
names used by Sheldon 1979. Current usage as in Stark,
Szczytko, and Baumann 1986.
Sources: For data, Sheldon 1979.

Studies of the phylogenetic relationships among members of stonefly groups found in the Great Basin are sparse. A reconstructed phylogeny for a few members of the winter stonefly family Capniidae, however, is available (Nelson and Baumann 1987). The genus *Capnura* occurs from coast to coast in North America, with one species in eastern North America and the remaining six found in the West. In the western United States, the genus can be split into two groups based on morphological characters. These two groups also differ in their distributional patterns, with one group found north and west of the Front Range of the Rocky Mountains and the other more to the south and west. No *Capnura* have been collected from the main cordillera of the Rocky Mountains or Sierra Nevada; rather, they are limited to streams at generally low elevations and are somewhat unique among stoneflies for their ability to live in ephemeral streams. One species, *Capnura wanica*, has been collected from the eastern foothills of the Rockies in streams entering the Great Plains in Wyoming, Colorado, and New Mexico. *Capnura wanica* has also been collected from tributaries of the Colorado River in Colorado National Monument and in the Virgin River of southern Utah. In the Great Basin this species has been collected from the Humboldt River system and from Long Valley Creek near Hallelujah Junction north of Reno. This Long Valley Creek is less than 5 miles from the divide separating the Great Basin drainage basin from that of the Central Valley in California. No other *Capnura* have been collected in California. This underlines the overall zoogeographic trend noted above for more species found in the Great Basin having affinities to those of the Rocky Mountains than to those of the Sierra Nevada. Vascular plants in general follow this trend of Rocky Mountain affinities (Harper et al. 1978). This same trend was noted in particular by Wells (1983) for conifers in the Great Basin and is noted in a variety of groups that follow. The sister species of *Capnura wanica* is *C. intermontana* Nelson and Baumann (1987, fig. 46), known from several streams draining into the Snake River scattered from the Raft River of northwestern Utah in the east to the Malheur River drainage in eastern Oregon on the west. Morphological similarities in this species pair indicate a relatively recent vicariance event between the Columbia–Snake River Basin and the Great Basin. Current records show the two species separated by less than 100 miles, with the Jarbidge Mountains intervening between the two species' ranges at this area of closest contact. Since the next sister out to these two species, *C. fibula* Claassen, is found only as far north as the Mogollon Rim of Arizona (and extending south into Chihuahua, Mexico), the hypothesized route of dispersal for the pair is from the south.

The specific route of *C. wanica* through the Great Basin, however, is unclear. Two competing hypotheses are a northeastern penetration route, coursing through the foothills of the nearly contiguous, high-elevational land mass of east central Nevada to the headwaters of the Humboldt River system, or a southern skirting hypothesis, where the westward trending route would follow the foothills of this same high-elevational area until extending northward into the sinks of the Humboldt River and thence eastward in the Humboldt River to its headwaters. Support for the penetration route could come from additional collecting in such localities with appropriate habitat in the Meadow Valley Wash near Panaca, Nevada, from streams draining the southern flank of the Ruby Mountains, or from the White River and its tributaries near Lund, Nevada. Support for the skirting hypothesis could be gained from collecting in southern drainages of the Pancake, Monitor, and Toquima ranges, if appropriate stream habitats exist there.

This *Capnura* example, then, illustrates an invasion of the Great Basin from the south by a relatively warm-tolerant stonefly genus. In contrast, members of the large winter stonefly genus *Capnia* are much less tolerant of warm waters, most being found only in streams of high gradient and high water quality. Many of these species are therefore limited to high mountain regions and as such might be expected to have come to the Great Basin from the northern mass of the Rocky Mountains. One monophyletic group in *Capnia* is the Excavata Group (Nelson and Baumann 1989). This group is composed of three species: *C. excavata* Claassen exists from the Sierra Nevada, Coast, and Cascade Ranges but no further inland than the Hood River in western Oregon; *C. cheama* Ricker occurs in several river systems near the juncture of Idaho, Montana, and Alberta; *C. uintahi* has been collected inland from eastern Nevada to western Colorado, far removed from the current ranges of the other two members of the species group. Morphological characters support a grouping of *C. cheama* and *C. uintahi* as sister species (Figure 10.1). Among the hypotheses for this sort of distribution, two are most attractive. One is the standard allopatric model where the former range of the ancestor is fragmented into the two ranges of the descendant species. The Snake River Plain coupled with the lowland pass of the Continental Divide between the Snake River headwaters and the Missouri River headwaters form a substantial barrier splitting the ancestral range in this case. A second plausible hypothesis is that the ancestral species was displaced southward during the Wisconsinan glaciation and left a relict

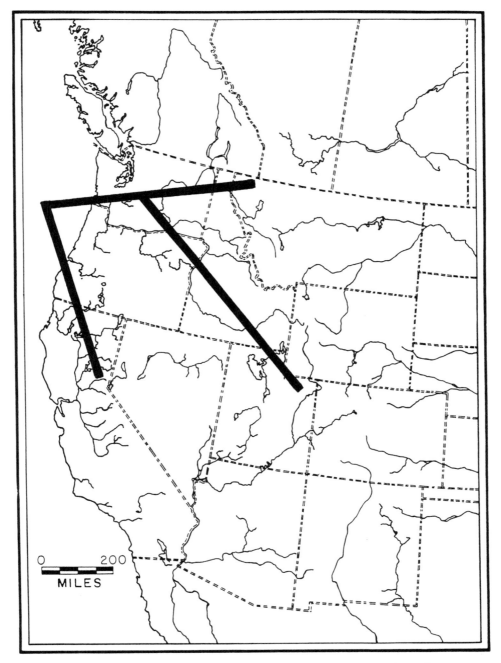

Figure 10.1 Cladogram of relationships of *Capnia excavata* group. Terminal taxa (top to bottom) are *C. cheama*, *C. uintahi*, and *C. excavata*.

population in the south as the continental glaciers retreated northward. This second hypothesis also accounts for the limited northward expansion of C. *cheama* into Canada since the full retreat of the ice sheet. Indeed reality may well be a combination of these two hypotheses such that the glaciation first pushed the ancestor south then the barrier divided its gene pool.

In summary, the zoogeographic affinities of stoneflies of the Great Basin are in large part with the Rocky Mountains and to a lesser degree with the Sierra Nevada, and the region has served as an arena for speciation in some genera. Further detailed coverages of distribution including more finely tuned hypotheses will undoubtedly be testable as the phylogenies of more and more groups of stoneflies are recovered.

Hemiptera

The order Hemiptera consists of two groups: Heteroptera, commonly called true bugs, and Homoptera, composed of cicadas, hoppers, psyllids, whiteflies, aphids, and scale insects. All these groups have sucking mouthparts with which they feed on a variety of liquid foods of both animal and plant origin (Borror et al. 1989).

HETEROPTERA   True bugs are an important component of the insect fauna of the Great Basin and Colorado Plateau. Seed bugs (family Lygaeidae) of the genus *Nysius* can be extremely abundant in the region, particularly on sites dominated by peppergrass (*Lepidium* spp.) and cheatgrass (*Bromus tectorum* Linnaeus). The plant bugs (Miridae) are the most commonly encountered family of Heteroptera in the region. The family Miridae is the largest heteropteran family in North America (Slater and Baranowski 1978). Most of the 1,750 species (Borror et al. 1989) are plant feeders. Knight (1968) reviewed the Miridae of western North America and provided taxonomic coverage for 622 species, which he placed in 122 genera. It is also important to note that in this work he described a total of 245 new species and hinted that many more are in need of description. Knight (1968) emphasized southwestern Nevada, especially the vicinity of the Nevada test site near Mercury in Nye and Lincoln Counties. Of significant consideration in the context of Great Basin biogeography is the geographic position of the test site in relation to the Great Basin and Mojave Desert. Knight (1968) reported that this area reflected a complex of plant and animal types previously recorded as being either Great Basin or Mojave Desert. In other words, this area is a region of intermixing of the two faunas or floras. It is interesting to note that the three plants with the richest mirid fauna at the test site were gymnosperms: *Pinus monophylla* Torrey and Fremont, *Juniperus osteosperma* (Torrey) Little, and *Ephedra nevadensis* Watson. Singleleaf pinyon (*P. monophylla*) is widespread throughout the Great Basin, often in association with Utah juniper (*J. osteosperma*), and the ranges of both these species extend into most areal concepts of the Mojave Desert. At the test site, this pinyon harbored 12 species of mirids, more than any other plant species sampled. Knight (1968) described nine of these species as new, an indication perhaps of the limited information regarding this speciose family of insects. Other plant hosts sampled that produced several species of mirids were *Artemisia*, *Atriplex*, and *Chrysothamnus*. It is also interesting to note that blackbrush (*Coleogyne ramosissima* Torrey), a dominant rosaceous shrub forming extensive, almost pure stands, yielded no mirid associates despite extensive collecting.

After widespread reports of shrub die-off in the region (Nelson et al. 1989), several studies intending to associate a proximal cause for this event were undertaken. Haws et al. (1990) surveyed the Great Basin and Colorado Plateau for insects associated with several of the shrub species that were dying in vast stands. Several plant-feeding insects, mirids among others (Haws et al. 1990; C. R. Nelson, unpublished data), were collected in association with dying members of the genus *Atriplex*. Four-wing saltbush (*Atriplex canescens* [Pursh] Nuttall) and shadscale (*A. confertifolia* [Torrey and Fremont] Watson) harbored substantial populations of *Melanotrichus*, *Europiella*, and several species tentatively placed in *Europiella* but thought to represent new genera (determinations by R. T. Schuh and M. D. Schwartz).

HOMOPTERA   The Homoptera is a large insect group closely related to Heteroptera and includes leafhoppers, aphids, and scale insects. All are typically plant feeders with juice-sucking mouthparts. Despite the morphological uniformity of their mouthparts, they exhibit diversity of feeding behavior on their host plants by specializing on various plant parts such as leaves for some and stems or roots for others (Nelson et al. 1990). This feeding specialization is further subdivided to finer scales of plant morphology with certain homopteran specialists draining individual cells or feeding entirely in either xylem or phloem tissue.

The plants of the Great Basin and Colorado Plateau are attacked by a wide array of homopterans. In Utah big sagebrush (*Artemesia tridentata* Nuttall) alone serves as host to 46 aphid species (Knowlton 1983). Leafhoppers (Cicadellidae) were particularly targeted as part of a larger survey of insects inhabiting shrubs of the Great Basin and Colorado Plateau (Haws et al. 1990). These leafhopper collections revealed 112 species in 55 genera taken predominantly on *Artemesia* and *Atriplex* spp. Twelve of the 55 genera contain species that are implicated vectors of plant diseases.

The phylogenetic study of cicadellids in the Great Basin and Colorado Plateau certainly has much potential for delineating biogeographic affinities. An excellent example of this sort of treatment is Whitcomb and Hicks (1988), in which the grass-feeding leafhopper genus *Flexamia* was revised and a phylogeny given based on morphological characters proposed for the 44 species contained therein. This phylogeny was compared with that of the grass hosts and the hypothesis of specialization on warm-season grasses supported. Specialization was determined in their study by use of an "oligophagy coefficient" calculated by taking the number of specimens of a given leafhopper species collected on a given taxon (e.g., plant family, genus, or species) divided by the total number of specimens of that species collected, with 1.0 representing total specialization on that plant taxon and lower values indicating use of a variety of other hosts. They also produced a series of hypothesized colonization events, host transfers, and phenological shifts that were proposed in a context of explaining speciation of phytophagous insects in general.

Whitcomb and Hicks (1988) proposed that the ancestor of *Flexamia* resembled the extant genus *Spartopyge* and thus used this genus as their outgroup for character polarization. They proposed that the diversification of the *Spartopyge* lineage in Mexican grasslands led to several genera, including *Flexamia*. *Flexamia* later diversified into the 13 species groups recognized by Whitcomb and Hicks. They also reported many more species in mesic grasslands east of the Great Basin and Colorado Plateau.

The initial divergence of the *Flexamia* line resulted from specialization of a generalist ancestor on side oats grama (*Bouteloua curtipendula* [Michaux] Torrey). Side oats grama is extremely widespread in North America, with a northern range extending from the Maritime Provinces of Canada west to Alberta and a southern range extending from central Texas and Mexico west to the Mojave Desert in California. Side oats grama is absent from the Pacific Northwest but is irregularly encountered in the Great Basin and Colorado Plateau. In the context of this treatment of the biogeography of the Great Basin and Colorado Plateau, it is interesting to note that none of the species of *Spartopyge* deemed closely related to *Flexamia* occur there despite the presence of side oats grama. Although interesting, it is not surprising, because the range of these host-specialized herbivores is of necessity limited to regions of dominance (or at least critical "mass" of population size) by the grass host, owing to extreme patchiness of the host near the periphery of its range and reinforced by unfavorable climatic factors (Whitcomb and Hicks 1988). Two species with origins in this initial *Flexamia* diversification (*F. abbreviata* Osborn and Ball and *F. canyonensis* Young and Beirne) did indeed reach the Colorado Plateau presumably by shifting to novel hosts. *Flexamia abbreviata* switched to blue grama (*Bouteloua gracilis* [Humboldt, Bonpland, and Kunth] Lagasca ex Steudel), which is a dominant grass in the region. But even this species of leafhopper becomes spotty in distribution near the periphery of blue grama's range. Still, all near relatives of *F. abbreviata* are from the southwestern United States or Mexico, indicating a colonization route from points south. The second product in this initial clade was from a lineage specializing on *Muhlenbergia*. This lineage is represented by *F. canyonensis* from the extreme southern Colorado Plateau near Kingman, Arizona. Its host there and southward is bush muhly (*M. porteri* Schribner ex Beal), which also occurs further north into southern Utah but has not been sampled there (R. F. Whitcomb, personal communication).

The second diversification event in *Flexamia* germane to the biogeography of the Great Basin and Colorado Plateau involves seven species: *F. serrata* Beamer and Tuthill, *F. decora* Beamer and Tuthill, *F. youngi* Whitcomb and Hicks, *F. arenicola* Lowry and Blocker, *F. stylata* (Ball), *F. inflata* Osborn and Ball, and *F. flexulosa* (Ball). One of these species, *F. serrata*, specializes on mat muhly (*M. richardsonis* [Trinius] Rydberg), which is a typical warm-season grass host for *Flexamia* but is also typically a host island surrounded by a sea of cool-season grasses unacceptable for *Flexamia* (Whitcomb and Hicks 1988). These conditions of host islands were ideal for the evolution of a specialist lineage of *Flexamia*. Vicariance with host fidelity, presumably during glacial episodes, yielded two more species, *F. decora* in the Rocky Mountains and *F. youngi* in the Great Basin. *Flexamia youngi* thus represents the only Great Basin endemic in the genus.

Host transfer to *M. pungens* Thurber in Gray by the mat-muhly-using ancestor yielded *F. arenicola*, with one form endemic to the Colorado Plateau (and points south) but virtually indistinguishable from a form endemic to the Nebraska Sand

Hills (Whitcomb 1989). The mat-muhly-feeding ancestor transferred to the more common spike muhly (M. *wrightii* Vasey ex Coulter) to yield *F. stylata*, which has been collected on the Great Plains skirting the eastern flanks of the Rocky Mountains and rounding westward into northern New Mexico and Arizona. Note that this distribution is similar to the eastern clade of the winter stonefly *Capnura* reported in the Plecoptera section of this chapter. These two species, *arenicola* and *stylata*, thus represent colonization of the Colorado Plateau from the north in contrast with the southern routes exhibited by the other species mentioned above.

The remaining two species of this second diversification event apparently used different strategies to become two of the most widespread and common species of *Flexamia* in the West. *Flexamia flexulosa* is a specialist on blue grama who emerged from a clade of muhly specialists. This transfer was undoubtedly facilitated by the approximation of the vast stands of blue grama to the ancestor on the relatively patchy mat muhly. This approximation allowed phenological expansion onto the dominant followed by loss of use of the patchy ancestral host. The apparent option taken by *F. inflata*, however, was not a transformation from specialist A to specialist B as in *F. flexulosa* but the conversion of a specialist to a generalist. Whitcomb and Hicks (1988) list the oligophagy coefficient of *F. flexulosa* as 1.0 on grasses as a whole and 0.889 on blue grama (n = 380), while that of *F. inflata* is much lower, at 0.725 on grasses (of which 0.562 is accounted to specimens taken on M. *asperifolia* [Nees and Meyen] Parodi) and 0.275 on Juncaceae. Thus, these two widespread species have become the most commonly collected *Flexamia* in the Great Basin and Colorado Plateau.

In brief, the Great Basin and Colorado Plateau harbor nine *Flexamia* species. Two species have immediate ancestors from the grasslands of central western Mexico or the southwestern United States. One species has a range encompassing northern mountain islands of warm-season grass surrounded by cool-season grasses. Two more species, a vicariant pair, have descended from an ancestor currently found to the north, with the isolating barrier between the pair corresponding to that separating the Great Basin from the Rocky Mountain highlands (including the Colorado Plateau). Another species in the Colorado Plateau has specialized on grass of sandy sites with conspecifics in the Nebraska Sand Hills. The connection of these disjunct populations is through the Great Plains corridor of the Uinta Basin (Nelson 1985). A species currently found on the Colorado Plateau has descended from a northern mountains ancestor. This Colorado Plateau inhabitant has a distribution skirting the east flank of the Rocky Mountains and swinging west through the grasslands of northern New Mexico to reach the Colorado Plateau via a south central route. The two remaining species are of widespread distribution, one of northern origins being a specialist on the widespread dominant blue grama and the other a generalist able to use a variety of monocots as host.

In contrast to the genus *Flexamia*, which prefers mesic grasslands and spills over into the Great Basin from the east, the genus *Athysanella* (Blocker and Johnson 1988, 1990a, 1990b; Blocker et al. 1990; Hicks and Whitcomb in press) is adapted to semi-arid regions. This adaptation has no doubt allowed this genus to colonize and perhaps speciate in the Great Basin and Colorado Plateau. Most species of

Athysanella are short-winged (flightless) forms of low vagility that have ranges con-siderably smaller than the areas composing the Great Basin or Colorado Plateau. Of the 133 known species in *Athysanella*, 11 occur in the Great Basin but not the Col-orado Plateau, five occur in the Colorado Plateau but not the Great Basin, and six occur in both regions (R. F. Whitcomb, personal communication).

Species occurring solely in the Great Basin include those of the subgenus *Amphipyga*, which, unlike other *Athysanella* subgenera, abounds in the far western and northern or montane grasslands and whose hosts are often cool-season grasses. This contrasts as well with *Flexamia*, which generally prefers the warm-season grasses usually found more to the south. Other species of the genus *Athysanella* that occur in the Great Basin include those of the subgenus *Athysanella*, which shows extensive evolution with host plants of saline areas. Thus, some of the Great Basin endemics are associated with saline bottoms and others with suites of cool-season grasses.

Species of *Athysanella* occurring solely in the Colorado Plateau tend to be in the subgenus *Gladionura*, which is predominantly Mexican, usually Chihuahuan (Whitcomb et al. 1990; Blocker et al. 1990; Hicks et al. 1990), and thus more tuned to track warm-season grasses. Only one of these species, A. (G.) *casa*, occupies most of the Colorado Plateau. Another species, A. (G.) *itawana*, appears to be an endemic of the San Juan Basin. Several additional species occupy the southeastern part of the Colorado Plateau, which is adjacent to the high plains of New Mexico, a region that is rich in grassland cicadellid species and no doubt a source area for many of the Plateau species. Occupancy of the Plateau by these species is readily explained by the presence of their hosts.

Species shared by the two regions include a few widely distributed species that are more oligophagous than most *Athysanella* species and a few species generally confined to one of the two regions but whose distributions overlap the border between the regions. Although the presence of host-specific *Athysanella* species can be explained by host presence, it cannot be predicted on the basis of host occur-rence. This paradox stems from the complex pattern of partitioning of host range by leafhopper specialists (Whitcomb et al. 1987) and is most pronounced in the semi-arid grasslands of the southwestern United States (Hicks et al. 1988, 1990). The native dominant grasses of the Southwest have many specialist cicadellids, none of which occupies a major portion of the range of its host. There are two bases for this confinement. One basis is insularity of host patches (e.g., saltgrass, *Distichlis spicata* [L.] Greene, which occurs in alkaline bottomlands and saline riparian areas). The other basis appears to be climatic, with blue grama in New Mexico partitioned by seven to eight species of *Athysanella*, each with unique climatic adaptations (Hicks et al. 1988). Both mechanisms appear to be involved in the development of ende-mism in the Great Basin and Colorado Plateau. Two endemics of the San Juan Basin, for example, colonize alkali sacaton (*Sporobolus airoides* [Torrey] Torrey) and galleta (*Hilaria jamesii* [Torrey] Bentham), respectively, and seem to be climatically constrained, since their hosts (particularly galleta) are common throughout the Southwest. In the regions discussed herein, the partitioning of galleta, which is superbly adapted to the two regions, is especially spectacular. The several species that colonize this host all have small ranges (Hicks et al. 1990; R. F. Whitcomb, personal communication). The most obvious reason for such partitioning is climate, as discussed above. *Distichlis,* in contrast, is partitioned by even more species than is galleta or blue grama (Hicks et al., 1990; R. F. Whitcomb, personal communication). The basis for this is almost certainly the insularity of saltgrass habitats in saline bottomlands or riparian areas. This islandlike pattern of saltgrass habitat is the stage on which individual genetic differentiation of populations is set on each isolated valley floor, a scenario similar to that proposed for shadscale ploidy races by Stutz and Sanderson (1983).

Thus, the availability of the Great Basin and Colorado Plateau to leafhoppers over a long period of Quaternary time has permitted the development of endemic species with ranges much smaller than the area of either region taken singly. Nonetheless, the integrity of these regions over time has been the staging ground for these speciations, and the relative stability through glaciations has reduced the extinction rates, relative to more northern grassland as well as the potential for post-Pleistocene differentiations in isolated patches.

Diptera

The two-winged flies (Diptera) are a diverse order of insects with a wide variety of feeding strategies. As adults they vary from the nonfeeding crane flies and plant-feeding gall midges to the bloodsucking mosquitoes, predatory robber flies, and carrion-feeding blow flies. For general identification, flies fall into two categories: Nematocera and Brachycera. Nematocera are easily recognized by the whip of their antennae, which have six or more segments. Examples of Nematocera are mosquitoes, midges, and crane flies. Additionally, the Nematocera are usually frail-bodied flies with long, delicate legs. In contrast, the Brachycera nearly always have the antennal whip with six or fewer segments and are generally stout-bodied, with shorter, more bristly legs. Examples of Brachycera include horseflies, deerflies, robber flies, and houseflies.

It is of historical interest that tularemia, a bacterial disease transmitted by deerflies, was first recognized as a disease of humans in the Great Basin of central Utah (Francis 1919; Francis and Mayne 1921), where it was referred to as Pahvant Valley plague. This had earlier been reported among rodents in Tulare County, California, and from thence is the common name of the disease. In the western United States, rabbits constitute an important reservoir for the bacteria, which can be transmitted to humans by deerflies, ticks, or even the skinning of infected rabbits (Harwood and James 1979).

The family Tipulidae, crane flies, is the single largest family of Diptera, with approximately 14,000 species worldwide and about 1,600 in North America. Many people will recognize crane flies as the spindly-legged "giant mosquitoes" or "mosquito eaters" that sometimes enter houses in the warmer months. Neither of these common names is appropriate, however, because they are not mosquitoes nor do they eat them. In fact, the adults of most species don't feed at all. The majority of the larvae of crane flies live in aquatic or semi-aquatic habitats (Byers 1984), but many feed underground, presumably on leaf litter, in rangelands and deserts, including those of the Great Basin and Colorado Plateau (Gelhaus 1989). Desert crane flies, especially the subgenus *Eremotipula* of the genus *Tipula,* were the basis of biogeographic analysis of Gelhaus (1989). Gelhaus (1989) found that most species are endemic to the Mojave or Great Basin Deserts and that, surprisingly, none is endemic to the Chihuahuan or Sonoran Deserts. His phylogenetic analysis revealed that most species of basal lineages occur at lower elevations and in highly xeric areas, whereas the more recently derived lines inhabit comparatively mesic habitats at higher elevations. Gelhaus postulated that *Eremotipula* possibly first evolved during the Miocene from a *Tipula (Lunatipula)*-like ancestor when xeric shrubby habitats first became available in western North America (Axelrod 1979). Of most interest in the context of this chapter is the high number of Great Basin and Colorado Plateau endemics reported by Gelhaus (1989). This endemism in parts of the Great Basin is somewhat puzzling, as several species probably did not inhabit much or any of their present ranges during the last glacial maximum. Wells (1983) reported that major latitudinal displacement of vegetation in the northern Great Basin probably left the area without the appropriate pinyon-juniper woodland that is the current habitat for most of these *Eremotipula* endemics. Additionally, much of the range of these endemics was inundated by Lake Bonneville and several other pleniglacial lakes. Still, these endemics may have retreated much to the south, tracking the appropriate habitat harboring *Artemisia* and *Atriplex* as far as southern Nevada, where these plants were apparently common 12,000 years ago. But current records show no specimens of these endemics in southern Nevada. In contrast, the Colorado Plateau, with its substantial areas of diverse shrubs in the understory and as steppe, continuously offered appropriate habitat to the flies during the Tertiary, particularly in northern and central Arizona, where several endemic species are found today. These southern Colorado Plateau endemics regularly show sister species relationships in the phylogenetic analysis to widely distributed vicars in the north, while pairs basal to these Plateau pairs show east-west vicariance in the hotter deserts further south.

The family Asilidae, robber flies, is another large group of Diptera, with over 1,000 species in North America. These predatory flies are commonly encountered in the Great Basin and Colorado Plateau, where they range in size from 3 mm to more than 50 mm in length. They have large, well-separated eyes used in locating prey, usually flying insects, which are taken on the wing then subdued with a fast-acting toxin injected with formidable stabbing mouthparts. Robber flies inhabit all the life zones of the region from the desolate saline flats on up to the alpine mountaintops. They are most apparent, however, in the shrub/scrub-dominated communities, where several genera are usually sitting on rocks or low shrubs waiting for potential prey to pass. Many species of robber flies are able to tolerate direct sun during the hottest parts of summer days, but in these conditions they often move into the shade and sally out on short foraging flights. Nelson (1987) reported 158 species for Utah, and I estimate that as many as 200 species will be found to inhabit the Great Basin and Colorado Plateau when records for the entire region are compiled. In discussing the biogeography of the 158 species in Utah, I proposed a system for classifying the distributions of the Utah species (Table 10.4). By far the most prevalent category for distribution of Utah robber flies was "widespread," with 68 species included. A species was classified as widespread if it occurred in three or more of the other areas and/or was known to occur in several other states. The next most speciose grouping was the Mojave Desert, which consisted of the drainage basin of the Virgin River below Zion National Park. This area harbored 23 species found nowhere else in Utah, and thus this area warrants unique biogeographic recognition. Many of these species are restricted to the north-south–trending riparian zones along the Virgin River and other Colorado River tributaries.

Table 10.4 Numbers of Asilidae Species by Area in Utah

Distribution	Number of Species
Widespread[a]	68
Mojave Desert (Virgin River Basin)	23
Colorado River drainage (minus Virgin River Basin)	17
Great Basin	13
Wasatch Mountains	13
Utah Mountains (Wasatch, Uinta, La Sal, and Abajo Mountains)	10
Information too limited	14
Total	158

[a]A composite area inhabited by species present in several of the other areas as well.

Seven robber flies are currently known from specimens taken only from the Great Basin or Colorado Plateau: *Efferia utahensis* (Bromley), *Laphystia annulata* Hull, *L. rubra* Hull, *L. tolandi* Wilcox, *L. utahensis* Wilcox, *Megaphorus pallidus* Johnson, and *Stichopogon salinus* (Melander). *Efferia utahensis* was named from material collected in Price, Utah, and has since been collected from several localities on the Colorado Plateau in Utah (Nelson 1987). The genus *Efferia* is the most speciose genus of Asilidae in North America, with well over 100 species. Most species in *Efferia* are of generally rather wide distribution, although several endemics are reported (Wilcox 1966).

The genus *Laphystia* is particularly interesting in studies of the region because they are found on sandy beaches and on saline or alkaline flats (Wilcox 1960), which abound in the Great Basin and Colorado Plateau. The four species that occur in Utah are all endemic to the area, with *L. annulata* and *L. rubra* limited to the Colorado Plateau, *L. tolandi* known only from the Great Basin (with specimens having been collected in both the Bonneville and Lahontan Basins), and *L. utahensis* from the Mojave Desert near St. George, Utah, where it is known only from the type series and a tentatively identified specimen from Yuma, Arizona (Wilcox 1960).

Most species in the genus *Megaphorus* are densely yellow haired; M. *pallidus*, however, is a white-haired species known from several localities on the saline flats of the eastern Great Basin in Utah. This species is most closely related to M. *frustra* (Pritchard), a bright yellow-haired species that has been collected in close proximity to M. *pallidus*. Color variations of this sort are not normally accorded specific rank in Asilidae, but in this case the obvious color difference may indeed be indica-tive of specific isolation, with M. *pallidus* being an ecological segregate limited to the white habitats available on salt flats. Further discussion of pale forms in the Great Basin is given in the Lepidoptera section of this chapter.

The last known endemic is *Stichopogon salinus*, which occurs only in the Bon-neville Basin of the eastern Great Basin. A brief phylogenetic analysis of *Sticho-pogon* in North America (10 species) reveals this species to be the sister species of the widespread (coast-to-coast) species *Stichopogon trifasciatus* (Say); both of these species inhabit sandy areas, usually near watercourses.

Lepidoptera

Butterflies are attractive models for biogeographic studies because general interest in the group has produced large collections upon which distributional studies can be based. Butterflies are also attractive study animals because of the wealth of infor-mation available concerning host-plant preference, genetic differentiation, con-trasts of adult and larval behaviors, and vagility estimates.

Austin and Murphy (1987) outlined distributional patterns emerging from the ranges of the 155 butterfly species occurring in the Great Basin. They noted some 240 subspecies and well-differentiated segregates among these 155 species yet con-sidered this to be depauperate compared to neighboring areas. More than half of the species were geographically polytypic in the Great Basin, Rocky Mountains, or the Sierra Nevada. None of these species was endemic to the Great Basin alone, but about 50 subspecies or other distinct infraspecific groups or populations were. While nearly 90 percent of the Great Basin butterfly species were also found in the Rocky Mountains, only about two-thirds were shared with the Sierra Nevada. When the species occurring only on the margins of the Great Basin were removed from the analysis, the species shared with the Rocky Mountains outnumbered those shared with the Sierra Nevada by about three to one.

Austin and Murphy (1987) recognized four distinct groups of Great Basin butter-flies: (1) widespread species whose Great Basin forms represented the most pallid phenotype, (2) widespread species with little or no differentiation, (3) some south-ern desert taxa reaching their northern limits in the Great Basin, and (4) a few but-terflies of mainly northern affinity ranging south into the northern Great Basin. They also recognized two "centers of differentiation" for the Great Basin forms. These centers consisted of eastern and western components that were further divided. The most clearly defined center in the eastern component was the Jarbidge Subregion, in which three subspecies were found to be narrowly restricted to the Jarbidge and Independence Mountains. The western component's most well defined center was the Inyo Subregion, comprising the Inyo Mountains, White Mountains, and Owens Valley.

Perhaps the most striking element of Great Basin biogeography of butterflies was the predominance of the Rocky Mountain fauna in relative proximity to the east slope of the Sierra Nevada. A latitudinal transect of three Great Basin ranges exemplifies this concept. The Snake Range, near the center of the Great Basin, had 54 percent of its 86 species represented by subspecies or segregates shared with the Rocky Mountains. Only 3 percent of the species, in contrast, were of Sierra Nevadan affinity. Further west, the Toiyabe Range had 50 percent of its 92 species represented by Rocky Mountain forms and only 4 percent by those of the Sierra Nevada. Finally, the White Mountains, in sight of the Sierra Nevada and only a few tens of kilometers to their east, shared forms of 34 percent of its species with the Rocky Mountains but only 17 percent with the Sierra Nevada! Thus, the east slope of the Sierra Nevada can be expected to be an area of vigorous interaction of the two faunas and a fertile ground for studies of general biological interest, including speciation, hybridization, competition, phenotypic plasticity, host-plant preference evolution, as well as comparisons of vicariance versus dispersal biogeography.

Twenty species exhibit their most pallid phenotype in the Great Basin. These pale forms are often restricted to certain regions, but the phenomenon is widespread in the region taken as a whole. Light or white alkaline soils have been suggested as a proximal cause for the differentiation, with the key mechanism being predator-mediated selection for paler butterfly forms (Emmel and Emmel 1969). This general principle is further supported by the presence of very dark forms of some Great Basin species in dark-background marshy areas. Paleness in the Great Basin forms, however, is also consistent with findings associating lighter basal wing color with warmer thermal regimes (Watt 1968).

In summary, there is a general impoverishment of butterfly species richness inward from the periphery of the Great Basin. Montane or boreal species appear to be relicts isolated after fragmentation of extensive boreal habitats in the Pleistocene. Affinities of Great Basin butterfly species are predominantly with the Rocky Mountains to the east (or northeast) and a narrow zone of affinity on the western edge with the Sierra Nevada. Differentiation of forms is most striking along the western and northeastern edges but is not restricted to those areas. Distinct areas of interaction and speciation are clearly indicated by the butterfly data (Austin and Murphy 1987) within the whole of the Great Basin.

Hymenoptera

Ants are probably the most obvious of the insects inhabiting the Great Basin and Colorado Plateau. The foothills and flats are dotted with the gravelly nest mounds of the seed-feeding harvester ant (*Pogonomyrmex* spp.), while the forested areas present the extensive thatched mounds of generalist-feeding *Formica* spp. Other regularly seen ants include the large carpenter ants (*Camponotus* spp.), which commonly create nests in downed timber, and the honey ants (*Myrmecocystus* spp.), in which certain members of the colony become storage containers for plant secretions and other liquids, including the honeydew secretions of Homoptera such as aphids. Additionally, the more rarely encountered army ants and ponerines in the area are almost exclusively carnivorous. But these large, obvious, or specialized species by no means make up the entire ant fauna of the region. Certainly a total of more than 150 species occur in the Great Basin and Colorado Plateau. Several researchers have published extensively on the ants of the region. Creighton (1950) provided an overview to the ants of all of North America, and each of the states of Colorado (Gregg 1963), Nevada (Wheeler and Wheeler 1986), and Utah (Allred

1982) have lists, taxonomic keys, and species treatments summarizing their respective ant faunas.

Gregg (1963) produced an extensive treatment of the ants of Colorado in which he recognized 164 species and 29 genera and presented summaries of the known ecological and geographical distributions. Gregg also gave a general review of the geology, geography, and ecology of the entire state. After the primary division of the ant fauna into northern and southern components, the most striking feature was the crossroads position of Colorado with regard to the Nearctic realm: different species of ants apparently reached Colorado from all directions, and the Rocky Mountains have been an important secondary center for evolution and dispersal. Wheeler and Wheeler (1986) recognized 177 ant species in Nevada, which makes this work especially useful in identifying ants from the Great Basin. Their chapter on bionomics should prove useful to persons interested in the ecology of the group. Their collection data were particularly well presented in their succinct table 10.2, which summarized the ant faunal constituents of each of the biomes in Nevada. Wheeler and Wheeler (1986) also supported the "all points of the compass" origin of Nevada ants, as did Gregg (1963) for the ants of Colorado. They did, however, recognize the Sierra Nevada as harboring a distinctive fauna of six species found nowhere else in the state, while seven montane species from elsewhere in Nevada were not found in the Sierra Nevada. These observations support the east-to-west direction of colonization of the Great Basin by many species noted in several groups throughout this chapter. The 177 species of ants in 30 genera found in Nevada represent 31 percent of the 578 native Nearctic species of ants. By subtracting the 115 species collected only in states bordering the Gulf of Mexico and other states along the southern border of the United States and the 80 species known only from type material or in only one place, Wheeler and Wheeler found 383 species that one might expect to collect in the temperate part of the Nearctic realm. Of this number, the Nevada fauna makes up 46 percent, which they would consider a rich fauna. This is amply supported from the data presented in Wheeler and Wheeler's table, where ants seem to be overrepresented in the study region compared with other groups.

The ants of Utah were listed in Allred (1982). The size of the ant fauna of Utah therein reported, 169 species in 29 genera, was comparable to that of Colorado and Nevada. Ants, then, are taxonomically rich in the Great Basin and Colorado Plateau as well as being obvious to the casual observer. This species richness, apparency, and their diverse ecological habits make ants important targets for future study in the Great Basin and Colorado Plateau.

CONCLUSIONS

At the beginning of this chapter, I posed several questions. These I have answered.

1. What are the range patterns for insects of the Great Basin and Colorado Plateau? The most common pattern is a widespread distribution, with the same species represented in regions to the east and west. The second most common pattern is to range in the Great Basin, Colorado Plateau, and Rocky Mountains.

2. What biogeographic patterns emerge from studies of phylogenetic relations of Great Basin and Colorado Plateau species with close relatives from other areas?

The most common discernible pattern of phylogenetic affinities for Great Basin and Colorado Plateau species is with the Rocky Mountains. Other distinctive patterns include examples from each of the points of the compass as well as a roundabout pattern of expansion to the north by way of a southern route in a clade of northern affinity (e.g., stoneflies: *Capnura wanica*; leafhoppers: *Flexamia stylata*; and flies, as in some recently derived lineages of *Eremotipula*).

3. Did Great Basin and Colorado Plateau species evolve in place? Many endemics for the region exist, for example, *Capnura intermontana* in Plecoptera, many Miridae in the Heteroptera, a large number of *Athysanella* in the Homoptera, many species of *Eremotipula* crane flies, a variety of robber flies, and several subspecies and genetic segregates of butterflies. One interesting consequence of endemicity in the Great Basin is the pale general appearance of many of the butterfly and robber fly endemics, purportedly to match soil color and avoid predation.

4. What are probable barriers to dispersal in Great Basin and Colorado Plateau insects? The lowlands just east of the Sierra Nevada and White Mountains isolate the montane faunas of the west from those of the Basin and Range as well as the Rocky Mountains. For lowland forms of the Colorado Plateau, the southern Rocky Mountains prevent expansion to the north and east. The Snake River Plain, or the mountain masses to its north or south, marks the northern extent of the ranges in a number of groups. The hot deserts to the south of the Great Basin and Colorado Plateau served as a filtering barrier for species found more generally in the south.

5. What are probable corridors for range extension? For montane species, the numerous mountain ranges have served as refugia and corridors of geographic expansion for species currently found more commonly in the north. Foothill and lowland species have in some cases expanded into the Great Basin and Colorado Plateau by skirting to the south of the unsuitable (to them) high montane habitats of the southern Rocky Mountains. The low-elevation plains between the eastern flank of the Uinta Mountains and the western slope of the Colorado Rockies have allowed migration of some northern Great Plains forms into the Colorado Plateau. Mesic-adapted southern forms have penetrated the Great Basin and Colorado Plateau along north-south–trending riparian zones of several rivers.

6. How many species of insects are in the Great Basin and Colorado Plateau? Some 14,000 to 26,000, estimated using proportions of the number of species in relatively well studied groups compared to the number of species known for the same groups for North America as a whole. In this analysis ants were represented by a higher percentage in the Great Basin and Colorado Plateau than the other groups.

7. Is the Great Basin and Colorado Plateau a species-rich region? A qualified yes, depending on the group studied and the temporal or spatial scale examined. A balanced spectrum of narrow endemic, widespread Nearctic, and cosmopolitan species all manage to maintain populations in the Great Basin and Colorado Plateau.

ACKNOWLEDGMENTS

I thank R. W. Baumann, J. K. Gelhaus, Andrew Sheldon, and R. F. Whitcomb for sharing unpublished data. I am most grateful to J. Gillaspy, E. Vargo, and R. Patrock for providing useful suggestions after reading the manuscript. I also thank the Department of Zoology and Brackenridge Field Laboratory at the University of Texas, Austin, for logistic support.

LITERATURE CITED

Allred, D. M. 1982. Ants of Utah. Great Basin Natur. 42: 415–511.

Austin, G. T., and D. D. Murphy. 1987. Zoogeography of Great Basin butterflies: patterns of distribution and differentiation. Great Basin Natur. 47: 186–201.

Axelrod, D. I. 1979. Desert vegetation, its age and origin. In Goodin, U. R., and D. K. Northington, eds., Arid land plant resources. Texas Tech. Univ., Lubbock.

Barnum, A. H. 1954. A taxonomy of Utah Orthoptera. Great Basin Natur. 14: 39–60.

Baumann, R. W. 1967. A study of the stoneflies (Plecoptera) of the Wasatch Front, Utah. M.S. thesis, Univ. of Utah. 114 pp.

Baumann, R. W., A. R. Gaufin, and R. F. Surdick. 1977. The stoneflies (Plecoptera) of the Rocky Mountains. Mem. Amer. Entomol. Soc. 31: 1–208.

Blocker, H. D., A. L. Hicks, and R. F. Whitcomb. 1990. Host and biogeography as factors in speciation in the genus Athysanella. Proc. Seventh Auchenorrhyncha Meeting, Wooster, Ohio, 1990.

Blocker, H. D., and J. W. Johnson. 1988. Subgenera of the genus Athysanella Baker (Homoptera: Cicadellidae: Deltocephalinae) and a proposed phylogeny. Proc. Sixth Auchenorrhyncha Meeting, Turin, Italy, 1987, pp. 39–46.

Blocker, H. D., and J. W. Johnson. 1990a. Classification of Athysanella (Amphipyga) (Homoptera: Cicadellidae: Deltocephalinae). J. Kansas Entomol. Soc. 63: 101–132.

Blocker, H. D., and J. W. Johnson. 1990b. Classification of five subgenera of Athysanella (Homoptera: Cicadellidae: Deltocephalinae). J. Kansas Entomol. Soc. 63: 304–315.

Borror, D. J., C. A. Triplehorn, and N. F. Johnson. 1989. An introduction to the study of insects, 6th edition. Saunders College Publishing, San Francisco. 875 pp.

Brown, J. H., and A. C. Gibson. 1983. Biogeography. C. V. Mosby, St. Louis, Missouri. 643 pp.

Byers, G. W. 1984. Tipulidae. Pp. 491–514 in Merritt, R. W., and K. W. Cummins, eds., An introduction to the aquatic insects of North America. Kendall Hunt, Dubuque, Iowa. 722 pp.

Capinera, J. L., and T. S. Sechrist. 1982. Grasshoppers (Acrididae) of Colorado: identification, biology, and management. Colorado State University Experiment Station Fort Collins Bull. 584S. 161 pp.

Clements, F. E., and V. E. Shelford. 1939. Bio-ecology. John Wiley and Sons, New York.

Creighton, W. S. 1950. The ants of North America. Bull. Museum of Comparative Zoology, Harvard 104: 1–585.

Cronquist, A., A. H. Holmgren, and J. L. Reveal. 1972. Intermountain flora: vascular plants of the Intermountain West, U.S.A., Vol. 1: Geographical and botanical history of the region, its plant geography and a glossary. The vascular cryptogams and the gymnosperms. Hafner, New York. 270 pp.

Dice, L. R. 1943. The biotic provinces of North America. Univ. Michigan Press, Ann Arbor.

Durden, C. J. 1984. Carboniferous and Permian entomology of western North America. Pp. 81–89 *in* Sutherland, P. K., and W. L. Manger, Vol. 2 of Proceedings of International Congress on Carboniferous Stratigraphy and Geology held in Washington, D.C., and Champaign, IL, May 17–26, 1979. Southern Illinois University, Carbondale.

Durrant, S. D. 1952. Mammals of Utah, taxonomy, and distribution. Univ. Kansas Publ. Natur. Hist. 6: 1–549.

Eisner, T., and E. O. Wilson. 1977. The insects. W. H. Freeman, San Francisco. 334 pp.

Emmel, T. C., and J. F. Emmel. 1969. A new subspecies of the *Cercyonis meadi* group (Satyridae). J. Lepid. Soc. 23: 161–164.

Erwin, T. L. 1983. Tropical forest canopies: the last biotic frontier. Bull. Entomol. Soc. Amer. 29: 14–19.

Francis, E. 1919. Deer fly fever or Pahvant Valley plague. Public Health Rep. 34: 2061–2062.

Francis, E., and B. Mayne. 1921. Experimental transmission of tularemia by flies of the species *Chrysops discalis*. Public Health Rep. 36: 1738–1746.

Gelhaus, J. K. 1989. Systematics and biogeography of the desert crane fly subgenus *Tipula* (*Eremotipula*). Ph.D. dissertation, Department of Entomology, Univ. of Kansas. 467 pp.

Gilbert, C.A.B. 1988. The distribution of Utah grasshopper species (Order: Orthoptera) in relation to the distributions of community types and abiotic factors. M.S. thesis, Department of Biology, Utah State University. 120 pp.

Gregg, R. E. 1963. The ants of Colorado. Univ. of Colorado Press, Boulder. 792 pp.

Harper, K. T., D. C. Freeman, W. K. Ostler, and L. G. Klikoff. 1978. The flora of Great Basin mountain ranges: diversity, sources, and dispersal ecology. *In* Intermountain biogeography: a symposium. Great Basin Natur. Mem. 2: 81–103.

Harwood, R. F., and M. T. James. 1979. Entomology in human and animal health. Macmillan, New York. 548 pp.

Haws, B. A., G. E. Bohart, C. R. Nelson, and D. L. Nelson. 1990. Insects and shrub die-off in western states: 1986–1989 survey. Pp. 127–151 *in* McArthur, E. D, E. M. Romney, S. D. Smith, and P. T. Tueller, comps., Proceedings — Symposium on cheatgrass invasion, shrub die-off, and other aspects of shrub biology and management, 1989, April 5–7, Las Vegas. Gen. Tech. Rep. INT-276. USDA, Forest Service, Intermountain Forest Research Station, Ogden, Utah. 351 pp.

Haws, B. A., A. H. Roe, and D. L. Nelson. 1988. Index to information on insects associated with western wildland shrubs. Gen. Tech. Rep. INT-248. USDA, Forest Service, Intermountain Forest Research Station, Ogden, Utah. 296 pp.

Helfer, J. R. 1987. How to know the grasshoppers, crickets, cockroaches, and their allies. Dover, New York. 363 pp.

Hicks, A. L., and R. F. Whitcomb. In press. Notes on the cicadellid gyp fauna of southeastern New Mexico, with description of a new species of *Athysanella*. Proc. Entomol. Soc. Washington.

Hicks, A. L., R. F. Whitcomb, and H. D. Blocker. 1990. Species richness and host partitioning in southwestern grasslands: evidence from the genus *Athysanella*. Proc. Seventh Auchenorrhyncha Meeting, Wooster, Ohio, 1990.

Hicks, A. L., R. F. Whitcomb, H. D. Blocker, and K. A. Allred. 1988. Why are there so many species of *Athysanella*? Proc. Sixth Auchenorrhyncha Meeting, Turin, Italy, 1987, pp. 397–403.

Holdridge, L. R. 1947. Determination of world plant formations from simple climatic data. Science 105: 367–370.

Hölldobler, B., and E. O. Wilson. 1990. The ants. Harvard Univ. Press, Cambridge. 732 pp.

Humphries, C. J., and L. R. Parenti. 1986. Cladistic biogeography. Clarendon Press, Oxford. 98 pp.

Jewett, S. G., Jr. 1960. The stoneflies (Plecoptera) of California. Bull. California Insect Survey 6: 125–177.

Knight, H. H. 1968. Taxonomic review: Miridae of the Nevada Test Site and the western United States. Brigham Young Univ. Science Bull. Biol. Ser. 9: 1–282.

Knowlton, G. F. 1983. Aphids of Utah. Utah Agric. Exper. Sta. Res. Bull. 509. 155 pp.

Kukalová-Peck, J. 1983. Origin of the insect wing and wing articulation from the arthropodan leg. Canad. J. Zool. 61: 1618–1669.

Miller, L. D., and F. M. Brown. 1981. A catalogue/checklist of the butterflies of America, north of Mexico. The Lepidopterists' Soc. Memoir 2.

Nelson, C. R. 1983. Invertebrates. In Workman, G.W., ed., Aquatic and riparian ecological relationships of the North Fork of the Virgin River and its Deep Creek–Crystal Creek tributary, Zion National Park, Utah. Report to National Park Service, NPS CX-1200-0-B041 and USU 246 2760 1009 16501. 272 pp.

Nelson, C. R. 1985. Distribution of robber flies in Utah (Diptera: Asilidae). Encyclia 62: 25–33.

Nelson, C. R. 1987. Robber flies of Utah (Diptera: Asilidae). Great Basin Natur. 47: 38–90.

Nelson, C. R., and R. W. Baumann. 1987. The winter stonefly genus Capnura (Plecoptera: Capniidae) in North America: systematics, phylogeny, and zoogeography. Trans. Amer. Entomol. Soc. 113: 1–28.

Nelson, C. R., and R. W. Baumann. 1989. Systematics and distribution of the winter stonefly genus Capnia (Plecoptera: Capniidae) in North America. Great Basin Natur. 49: 289–363.

Nelson, C. R., B. A. Haws, and D. L. Nelson. 1990. Mealybugs and related Homoptera of Shadscale: possible agents in the die-off problem in the Intermountain West of North America. Pp. 152–165 in McArthur, E. D., E. M. Romney, S. D. Smith, and P. T. Tueller, comps., Proceedings—Symposium on cheatgrass invasion, shrub die-off, and other aspects of shrub biology and management, 1989, April 5–7, Las Vegas. Gen. Tech. Rep. INT-276. USDA, Forest Service, Intermountain Forest Research Station, Ogden, Utah. 351 pp.

Nelson, C. R., and B. P. Stark. 1988. The Salmoperla safari: hit and run stonefly collecting in Nevada and California. Perla 8 (1986–1987): 7–11.

Nelson, C. R., and W. D. Tidwell. 1987. Brodioptera stricklani n. sp. (Megasecoptera: Brodiopteridae), a new fossil insect from the upper Manning Canyon Shale Formation, Utah (Lowermost Namurian B). Psyche 94: 309–316.

Nelson, D. L., B. A. Haws, K. T. Harper, K. C. Boyer, D. J. Weber, and J. R. Marble. 1989. Wildland shrub dieoffs in Utah: an approach to understanding the cause. Pp. 5–22 in Wallace, A. E., D. McArthur, and M. R. Haferkamp, comps., Proceedings — Symposium on shrub ecophysiology and biotechnology, 1987, June 30–July 2, Logan, Utah. Gen. Tech. Rep. INT-256. USDA, Forest Service, Intermountain Forest Research Station, Ogden, Utah. 183 pp.

Otte, D. 1981. The North American grasshoppers, Vol. 1: Acrididae Gomphocerinae and Acridinae. Harvard Univ. Press, Cambridge. 275 pp.

Otte, D. 1984. The North American grasshoppers, Vol. 2: Acrididae Oedipodinae. Harvard Univ. Press, Cambridge. 366 pp.

Rehn, J. A. 1958. The origin and affinities of the Dermaptera and Orthoptera of western North America. Pp. 253–298 in Hubbs, C. L., ed. Zoogeography. Amer. Assoc. Advance. Sci., Washington, D.C.

Rosen, B. R. 1990. Biogeographic patterns: a perceptual overview. Pp. 23–55 in Myers, A. A., and P. S. Giller, eds., Analytical biogeography: an integrated approach to the study of animal and plant distributions. Chapman and Hall, New York. 578 pp.

Scudder, S. H. 1890. The Tertiary insects of North America. Rep. U.S. Geol. Survey Terr., Dep. Interior 13. 734 pp.

Sheldon, A. L. 1979. Stonefly (Plecoptera) records from the basin ranges of Nevada and Utah. Great Basin Natur. 39: 289–292.

Sheldon, A. L., and S. G. Jewett, Jr. 1967. Stonefly emergence in a Sierra Nevada stream. Pan-Pac. Entomol. 43: 1–8.

Slater, J. A., and R. M. Baranowski. 1978. How to know the true bugs. Wm. Brown, Dubuque, Iowa. 256 pp.

Smith, D. R. 1979. Superfamily Formicoidea. Pp. 1323–1467 *in* Krombein, K. V., P. D. Hurd, D. R. Smith, and B. D. Burks, eds., Catalog of Hymenoptera in America north of Mexico, Vol. 2. Smithsonian Institution Press, Washington, D.C.

Stark, B. P., S. W. Szczytko, and R. W. Baumann. 1986. North American stoneflies (Plecoptera): systematics, distribution, and taxonomic references. Great Basin Natur. 46: 383–397.

Stutz, H. C., and S. C. Sanderson. 1983. Evolutionary studies of *Atriplex*: chromosome races of *A. confertifolia* (shadscale). Amer. J. Botany 70: 1536–1547.

Tidwell, W. D. 1967. Flora of Manning Canyon Shale, Part 1: a lowermost Pennsylvanian flora from the Manning Canyon Shale, Utah, and its stratigraphic significance. Brigham Young Univ. Geol. Studies 14: 1–66.

Tidwell, W. D. 1975. Common fossil plants of western North America. Brigham Young Univ. Press, Provo, Utah, 197 pp.

Tidwell, W. D., D. A. Medlyn, and A. D. Simper. 1974. Flora of the Manning Canyon Shale, Part 2: Lepidodendrales. Brigham Young Univ. Geol. Studies 21: 119–146.

Watt, W. B. 1968. Adaptive significance of pigment polymorphisms in *Colias* butterflies, Part 1: Variation of melanin pigment in relation to thermoregulation. Evolution 22: 437–458.

Wells, P. V. 1983. Paleobiogeography of montane islands in the Great Basin since the last glaciopluvial. Ecol. Monog. 53: 341–382.

Wheeler, G. C., and J. N. Wheeler. 1986. The ants of Nevada. Natural History Museum of Los Angeles County, Los Angeles. 138 pp.

Whitcomb, R. F. 1989. Nebraska Sand Hills: the last prairie. Proc. 11th North Amer. Prairie Conf.: 57–69.

Whitcomb, R. F., H. D. Blocker, D. E. Lynn, and A. L. Hicks. 1990. Evolution of life history traits in grassland cicadellids: analysis of a five taxon natural experiment. Proc. Seventh Auchenorrhyncha Meeting, Wooster, Ohio, 1990.

Whitcomb, R. F., and A. L. Hicks. 1988. Genus *Flexamia*: new species, phylogeny, and ecology. Great Basin Natur. Memoirs 12: 224–323.

Whitcomb, R. F., A. L. Hicks, D. E. Lynn, K. A. Allred, and H. D. Blocker. 1987. Geographic variation in host relationships of leafhoppers (Homoptera: Cicadellidae) in North American grasslands. Pp. 293–325. *in* Wilson, M. R., and L. R. Nault, eds., Proc. 2nd inter. workshop on leafhoppers and planthoppers of economic importance, Commonwealth Institute of Entomol., London.

Wilcox, J. 1960. *Laphystia* Loew in North America (Diptera: Asilidae). Ann. Entomol. Soc. Amer. 53: 328–346.

Wilcox, J. 1966. *Efferia* Coquillett in America north of Mexico (Diptera: Asilidae). Proc. California Acad. Sci. 34: 85–234.

Wooton, R. J. 1981. Palaeozoic insects. Ann. Rev. Entomol. 26: 319–344.

Zwick, P. 1973. Insecta: Plecoptera, Phylogenetisches System und Katalog. Das Tierreich. Berlin, 94. 465 pp.

Penstemon humilis Nutt. ex Gray (low penstemon) is one of over 100 penstemons native to the region considered in this volume. All penstemons have showy flowers, some genuinely elegant. This species extends from desert edges to treeline on rocky, open ridges.

CHAPTER 11

Elevational Patterns of Insects in the Great Basin and Colorado Plateau

Steven D. Warren and
Kimball T. Harper

OVERVIEW

In this chapter the authors consider the influence of elevation on the distribution patterns of insects in the Great Basin and Colorado Plateau. Generally, species richness and relative abundance of insect orders decline at higher elevations and in hot, lower-elevation desert sites. As shown here, insects are able to survive climatic extremes because of various adaptations (morphological, behavioral, and physiological).

A variety of climatic factors important to the survival and distribution of insects is known to vary along elevational gradients. These include temperature, humidity, amount and kind of precipitation, moisture in the substrate, solar radiation, magnitude of diel temperature fluctuations, and wind. Within the Great Basin region, elevation ranges from a low of 86 m below sea level in Death Valley, California, to a high of 3,970 m above sea level at Wheeler Peak, Nevada. The maximum temperature recorded in the Great Basin was 56°C (134°F) in 1913 at Death Valley; the minimum temperature was –56°C (–69°F) at an elevation of approximately 2,735 m near Logan, Utah (National Weather Service, personal communication). Average annual precipitation for the period 1951–1980 ranged from 51.6 mm at Death Valley to 1,072 mm at an elevation of 2,663 m near Brighton, Utah (National Oceanic and Atmospheric Administration 1982). Most precipitation at the higher elevations falls as snow.

The ability of insects to survive at elevational extremes is limited by their ability to cope with the environmental conditions at those locations. Indeed, it has been suggested that climatic severity and unpredictability may be more important in determining the relative success of insects than the abundance of food resources (Downes 1964; Heithaus 1974; Moldenke 1975). In view of the apparently harsh conditions existing at elevational extremes in the Great Basin and Colorado Plateau regions, it seems logical to expect fewer insect species and smaller numbers of individuals in those locations than at intermediate sites. In addition, one might expect to encounter a variety of unique behavioral, morphological, and physiological adaptations among the various insect groups found at these elevational extremes. In this chapter we examine the elevational patterns of insects in the Great Basin and Colorado Plateau and make comparisons with insect populations along similar elevational gradients worldwide. Unfortunately, the bulk of published information regarding insect numbers along elevational gradients is limited to comparisons at high-elevation extremes. This is probably true since low elevation in other regions does not necessarily correspond to climatically harsh conditions, as is the case in the Great Basin and Colorado Plateau. We present a discussion of insect adaptations to harsh climatic conditions at both high and low elevational extremes.

ELEVATIONAL PATTERNS IN TOTAL INSECT NUMBERS

A general decline in the total number of insects and in the number of insect species has been documented along a gradient of increasing elevation for most major high-elevation regions of the world (Mani 1968), including the Great Basin and Colorado Plateau of North America (Fernandes and Price 1988; Gaufin 1959). The generalized trend is true for all insect orders that have been investigated along elevational gradients (Table 11.1). All major behavioral groups of insects — for

Table 11.1 Taxonomic Orders of Insects with Evidence of Declining Numbers of Species and Individuals at High Elevations

Insect Order	Representative Forms	Sources of Documentation
Ephemeroptera	Mayflies	Ward and Berner 1980
Odonata	Dragonflies and damselflies	Evans 1988
Plecoptera	Stoneflies	Knight and Gaufin 1966; Ward 1982; Sanchez-Ortega and Alba-Tercedor 1989
Orthoptera	Grasshoppers and crickets	Alexander and Hilliard 1969; Bey-Bienko and Peshev 1960; Pascual 1978
Hemiptera	True bugs	Janzen 1973
Coleoptera	Beetles	Elias 1987; Janzen 1973; Mani 1968
Hymenoptera	Bees, wasps, and ants	Arroyo et al. 1983; Janzen 1973; Raw 1985
Trichoptera	Caddisflies	Herrmann et al. 1986
Lepidoptera	Butterflies and moths	Arroyo et al. 1983; Janzen 1973
Diptera	Flies, mosquitoes, and midges	Arroyo et al. 1983; Rajput and Singh 1988

example, pollinators (Arroyo et al. 1983; Moldenke 1976; Müller 1881), herbivores (Alexander and Hilliard 1969; Pascual 1978), predators (Evans 1988), gall-forming insects (Fernandes and Price 1988), aquatic insects (Gaufin 1959; Knight and Gaufin 1966; Ward 1982; Ward and Berner 1980), and litter dwellers (Walter 1985) — seem to be similarly affected by elevation.

ELEVATIONAL PATTERNS IN SPECIES COMPOSITION

Although all groups of insects apparently decline in numbers in harsh environments, some groups decline at a faster rate than others. The net result is a shift in relative species richness and relative abundance of the various insect orders along an elevational gradient.

Perhaps the most studied functional group of insects is the pollinators. Pollinating insects are predominantly from the taxonomic orders Hymenoptera, Lepidoptera, Diptera, and Coleoptera (see Table 11.1 for representative forms). Studies of these groups in the Great Basin and Colorado Plateau reveal trends of diminishing relative species richness among hymenopterans and coleopterans and an increasing contribution by dipterans with increasing elevation (Table 11.2). The relative contribution of lepidopteran pollinators is apparently variable, increasing with elevation on the Colorado Plateau but declining in the Great Basin. The poor representation of lepidopterans at high elevations in the Great Basin may be related to biogeographical insularity of the Great Basin mountain systems in general (Wilcox et al. 1986) rather than the effects of elevation per se.

Table 11.2   Relative Species Richness (Percentage of All Species Encountered) and Number of Pollinating Species (in Parentheses) of Four Insect Orders

| | | Elevational Zone (m) | | | |
| | | 0–999 | 1,000–1,999 | 2,000–2,999 | 3,000–3,999 | >4,000 |
Location	Insect Order					
Great Basin (Warren et al. 1988)	Hymenoptera		53 (31)		27 (27)	
	Diptera		25 (15)		62 (62)	
	Lepidoptera		10 (6)		5 (5)	
	Coleoptera		12 (7)		6 (6)	
Colorado Plateau (Moldenke and Lincoln 1979)	Hymenoptera				53 (58)	36 (37)
	Diptera				30 (33)	41 (43)
	Lepidoptera				9 (10)	20 (21)
	Coleoptera				7 (8)	3 (3)
Chilean Andes (Arroyo et al. 1982)	Hymenoptera			40 (37)	13 (5)	
	Diptera			48 (45)	63 (24)	
	Lepidoptera			12 (11)	24 (9)	
	Coleoptera			NA*	NA*	

continues

Table 11.2 Relative Species Richness (Percentage of All Species Encountered) and Number of Pollinating Species (in Parentheses) of Four Insect Orders   *(continued)*

Location	Insect Order	Elevational Zone (m)				
		0–999	1,000–1,999	2,000–2,999	3,000–3,999	>4,000
European Alps (Müller 1881)	Hymenoptera		33 (276)	18 (88)		
	Diptera		36 (301)	44 (210)		
	Lepidoptera		18 (150)	31 (148)		
	Coleoptera		13 (106)	7 (33)		
California (Moldenke 1976)	Hymenoptera	55 (145)	59 (176)		39 (74)	55 (42)
	Diptera	18 (49)	19 (56)		35 (67)	17 (13)
	Lepidoptera	8 (21)	7 (21)		16 (31)	25 (19)
	Coleoptera	19 (49)	15 (45)		9 (18)	3 (2)
Costa Rica (Heithaus 1974)	Hymenoptera	51 (153)			22 (14)	
	Diptera	8 (24)			57 (37)	
	Lepidoptera	24 (73)			9 (6)	
	Coleoptera	17 (52)			12 (8)	

Note: For any given study location, if more than one site was sampled within an elevational zone, an average of the sites has been determined.
* Information not available.

Various other studies from around the world provide data suitable for similar quantitative comparisons of the relative importance of these groups as pollinators at various elevations. Analyses of these data sets indicate that the trends seen in the Great Basin and Colorado Plateau are similar to those worldwide (Table 11.2). Numerous, less quantitative studies also support those trends. Dipterans are reported to be the most abundant flower-visiting insects at high altitudes in the Himalaya Mountains (Mani and Giddings 1980) and in New Zealand (Primack 1983). In a study conducted in the Rocky Mountains of the Colorado Plateau, the percentage of pollinator visits attributable to dipterans increased from 1 percent at 2,590 m to 36 percent at 3,660 m, even though observations were made only on plant species that the author considered to be pollinated primarily by bees (Pleasants 1980). Increased importance of lepidopterans as flower visitors has been alluded to in literature treating the subalpine areas of British Columbia (Pojar 1974). The replacement of bees as pollinators at higher elevations is also common on tropical mountain systems (Raw 1985), although the function of pollination has been relinquished to birds rather than other insects for at least some species of plants in tropical Mexico (Burquez and Sarukhan 1980; Cruden 1972) and Hawaii (Carpenter 1976).

Faegri and van der Pijl (1979) suggested that dipterans increase in importance as pollinators in most areas of frigid climatic conditions. This appears to be true in most alpine regions of the world. In addition, where the temperate alpine zone merges into tundra in the high arctic near Lake Hazen in the Northern Territories of Canada, dipterans were reported to make up 66 percent of the pollinator fauna and participate in 74 percent of all flower-insect associations (Hocking 1968; Kevan 1972). More than 85 percent of the dipteran specimens captured at Lake Hazen were identified as pollen vectors (McAlpine 1965). Even among nonpollinating insects, dipterans are considered the most abundant group of insects in both the arctic and sub-antarctic (Gressitt and Yoshimoto 1974; Weber 1954).

Considering the relative abundance of the various insect groups in general, without regard to trophic habits, elevational shifts are evident that parallel those observed for pollinators. Of the insect orders that include pollinators, hymenopterans are the first group to disappear from the general insect fauna at high elevations in the Himalayas, followed successively by coleopterans, lepidopterans, and finally dipterans (Mani 1968). Along an elevational gradient in Costa Rica, hymenopteran, lepidopteran, and coleopteran foliage insects declined in relative species richness and relative numbers of individuals along a gradient of increasing elevation, while dipterans reached a proportional peak at the highest elevational zone (Janzen 1973). Among other insect orders, the relative contribution of hemipterans declined at higher elevations in the Costa Rica study, while the relative number of homopteran species (cicadas, leafhoppers, aphids, etc.) increased. Similar elevational trends in relative abundance of these six insect orders were reported for the Great Smoky Mountains of Tennessee and North Carolina (Whittaker 1952).

Within the Great Basin and Colorado Plateau, the number of plecopteran species and individuals tends to reach a peak at higher elevations than most other insects, thus lending them increased importance in the high-elevation insect fauna (Knight and Gaufin 1966). The same general phenomenon is true for ephemeropterans, although peak species richness occurs at a somewhat lower elevational range than for plecopterans (Ward and Berner 1980). Numbers of orthopteran species decline progressively above about 1,500 m (Alexander and Hilliard 1969). However, the number of individuals remains relatively high, and grasshoppers constitute a significant numeric component of the total insect fauna of the alpine zone (Alexander 1951). At the opposite end of the environmental spectrum, orthopterans as well as coleopterans and hymenopterans (primarily ants) are among the most prominent insects in lowland desert ecosystems (Crawford 1981).

INSECT ADAPTATIONS FOR HARSH ENVIRONMENTS

Temperature appears to be the single most important factor affecting the ability of insects to survive at elevational extremes. The effects of temperature may be intensified by other climatic factors, including humidity, precipitation, and wind. Length of the plant growing season, which is abbreviated in both very hot and very cold climates, is also an important factor controlling the distribution of insects (Alexander and Hilliard 1969). Insect adaptations in harsh environments at elevational extremes are varied, but they can be categorized into three basic types: morphological, behavioral, and physiological.

Morphological Adaptations

Dark pigmentation, or melanism, is perhaps the most ubiquitous adaptive characteristic of high-altitude insects (Mani 1968). Black, dark brown, and reddish brown are among the most common colors. When red, yellow, and orange insects occur, they are often of darker, more subdued tones than their lower-elevation counterparts. Among insect species that occur across a wide elevational range, individuals inhabiting higher elevations are often darker than their lower elevation relatives. In addition, dark spots, bands, or other markings common on lower-elevation individuals become larger and may fuse on higher-elevation individuals. Melanism is also common among arctic insects (Downes 1964, 1965). At the opposite end of the temperature spectrum, insects inhabiting very hot environments at low elevations in the temperate zone are often light colored and have relatively few dark markings (Hamilton 1975).

The functional significance of dark versus light coloration is generally attributed to efficiency of absorption of solar energy. Light coloration tends to reflect rather than absorb solar radiation and is therefore favored in hot environments where heat avoidance is necessary for survival. This has been illustrated in the Namib Desert of southwest Africa, where tenebrionid beetles with white elytra have been shown to have significantly lower body temperatures than those having black elytra (Hadley 1970), thus allowing them to remain active during the hotter parts of the day (Hamilton 1973).

Dark coloration enhances absorption of sunlight, facilitating rapid warming in cold environments. Perhaps the best-documented example of the adaptive significance of melanism in insects from cold environments is that of the butterfly genus *Colias*, a group that is well represented in the Great Basin and Colorado Plateau regions. Populations of *Colias* butterflies at high elevations and latitudes have more heavily melanized wings than populations from warmer climates. The darker individuals heat more rapidly in sunlight and maintain a steady temperature approximately 15 percent higher than lighter individuals under the same conditions (Watt 1968).

Reduction in the size and utility of wings is also common among high-altitude insect species. Nearly 60 percent of the insect species above 4,000 m in the northwest Himalaya Mountains are wingless (apterous); many of the remaining species have reduced wings (are brachypterous) or seldom fly (Mani 1962). Flightless, apterous, and brachypterous conditions are also common at high elevations in the United States (Alexander 1951; Mani 1968) and in the arctic in general (Downes 1964). As a possible selective force for winglessness, Darlington (1943) suggested that cold temperatures may hinder normal flight muscle activity, thus retarding the need for the development of wings. Strong winds common at high altitudes also restrict flight activity and may be a selective force for reduction or loss of wings (Digby 1958). Winged pollinators may resort to crawling from flower to flower in very cold, windy conditions (Downes 1962) or may relinquish their role to ants or other wingless insects (Peterson 1977; Primack 1978).

In addition to increased melanism and reduction or loss of wings, small body size is characteristic of many high-elevation insects (Mani 1968). Within any given taxonomic order of insects, it is not uncommon to encounter smaller forms at higher altitudes than in lowlands. Small insects with a greater ratio of surface to volume reach an equilibrium body temperature more rapidly than large insects under similar conditions (Casey 1981; Digby 1955). Small body size, therefore, allows insects to respond more rapidly to brief periods of sunshine at high elevations. The relationship of body size to temperature may help explain why small-sized insect orders such as Diptera and Collembola are proportionally more successful than other insect orders at high elevations.

In cold habitats at high elevations and at high latitudes, there is an increase in the number of insect species with dense coverings of bristles, pubescence, scales, and waxy coatings (Downes 1965; Mani 1968). It has been postulated that the coverings may help absorb warmth from sunshine and insulate the body from heat loss (Church 1960; Kingsolver and Moffat 1982; Lindner 1956), although work by Digby (1955) seems to indicate that pubescence may have little effect on heat absorption. In low-elevation desert regions and other warm environments, selective pressures may discourage thick body coverings that could result in overheating.

Behavioral Adaptations

The level of activity of an insect is dependent, at least in part, on its body temperature. Activity is limited by very high or very low temperatures. Through the selection of habitat, insects can partially avoid climatic extremes of temperature and humidity. They can also ameliorate the effects of large diel fluctuations in temperature. Both soil and water tend to moderate daily and seasonal fluctuations in ambient temperature. Soil-dwelling and aquatic insect species are particularly well represented in climatically stressful environments (Downes 1964; Mani 1968). Even insects that are terrestrial as adults may spend their immature stages in the soil or in water.

Not all insects spend their lives in protected environments. However, this does not preclude their use of such refugia. In both cold, high-elevation environments and low-elevation deserts, there is a tendency for insects to seek refuge under rocks and in the soil during the most stressful portions of the day (Arroyo et al. 1982; Cloudsley-Thompson 1963; Gamboa 1976). During hot daylight hours at low elevations, many insects seek the shelter of shade, tracking it as the sun moves (Chappell 1983). On cold days or in cold environments, many insects typically seek open, sunny locations where they can bask in sunlight (Downes 1964; Heinrich and Pantle 1975; Watt 1968). Some insects seek brightly colored surfaces that reflect sunlight, as in mosquitoes that use cup-shaped flowers as parabolic reflectors (Hocking and Sharplin 1965; Kevan 1975). Other insects bask or crouch on substrates that have already been warmed by the sun, presumably to warm themselves through conduction (Arroyo et al. 1982; Chappell 1983; Tinker 1952). Figure 11.1a illustrates the crouching behavior of *Melanoplus sanguinipes*, a grasshopper common in cold alpine areas of the Great Basin and Colorado Plateau.

Warmth collected through basking behavior can be enhanced by posture and orientation to the sun. By orienting the long axis of their bodies perpendicular to the sun, insects maximize the surface area exposed to solar radiation, thus maximizing radiative heat gain (Casey 1981). This behavior has been encountered in dragonflies

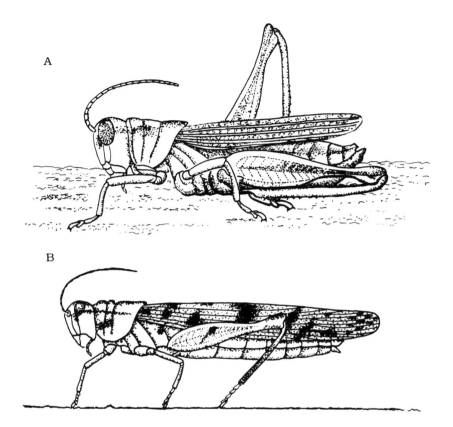

Figure 11.1 Postural adaptations of two grasshoppers in response to environmental conditions. (a) Under cold conditions, the crouching behavior of *Melanoplus sanguinipes* facilitates conductive warming from a warm substrate. (b) In hot environments, the stilting behavior of *Trimerotropis pallidipennis* elevates the body above a hot substrate and enhances convective cooling.

(Heinrich and Casey 1978; May 1976), grasshoppers (Chappell 1983; Gillis and Smeigh 1987; Uvarov 1977), cicadas (Heath 1967; Heath and Wilkin 1970; Heath et al. 1972), beetles (Hamilton 1971; Henwood 1975), butterflies (Clench 1966; Kevan and Shorthouse 1970), and caterpillars (Casey 1976a; Sherman and Watt 1973). High-elevation *Colias* butterflies common to the Great Basin and Colorado Plateau combine basking behavior with increased melanism of the hindwing undersides to enhance the efficiency of radiative warming. Butterflies of this genus typically present themselves perpendicular to the sun and hold their wings closed over their backs (Figure 11.2a). This exposes the darker surfaces of the hindwing undersides to the sun, thus maximizing absorption of solar energy (Watt 1968). Figure 11.2b illustrates an alternative posture used by *Papilio bairdii*, a butterfly common to the Colorado Plateau, in which the wings are held open, presenting their dark backsides to the sun. In this manner maximum surface area is exposed to the sun (Casey 1981).

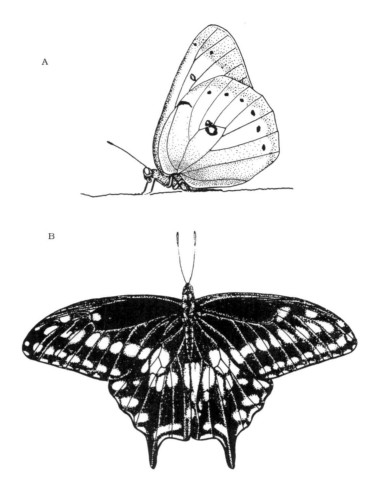

Figure 11.2 Sun-basking postures of *Colias eurytheme* (a) and *Papilio bairdii* (b) that maximize exposure of heavily melanized portions of the wings to the sun.

Under conditions where heat avoidance is essential to survival, insect posture and orientation are often altered to minimize exposure to direct sunlight. This is accomplished by orienting the long axis of the body parallel to the sun (Clench 1966; May 1976; Uvarov 1977). In addition, many desert insects have evolved long legs that are useful in raising the body above a hot soil surface, a behavior that minimizes heat conduction from the ground to the body, moves the body into a cooler temperature regime above the thin surface boundary layer, and enhances convective cooling by exposing more body surface area to higher wind velocities (Casey 1981; May 1979). Figure 11.1b illustrates this behavior in *Trimerotropis pallidipennis*, a grasshopper found in hot desert habitats of the Great Basin. Insects that are overheated may also orient themselves perpendicular to the prevailing wind to increase convective cooling (Casey 1976a; Waloff 1963).

By selecting the most favorable time of day, insects can minimize exposure to harsh climatic conditions. In hot deserts many insects are crepuscular, becoming most active during the early morning and evening hours, thereby avoiding the hottest daytime hours (Crawford 1981). Many lowland moths and some other insects are nocturnal, but at high elevations where low temperatures become a limiting factor, nocturnal and crepuscular species are generally absent (Alexander 1951; Cruden et al. 1976), and most insects achieve maximum activity during the warmest part of the day. Some species that are crepuscular in low-elevation environments become strictly diurnal at higher elevations (Douglas 1978).

In order to initiate flight, particularly at high elevations, winged insects must often achieve a minimum thoracic temperature that is greater than ambient temperatures (Heinrich 1972, 1975; Heinrich and Pantle 1975). While some insects rely on ectothermic forms of temperature regulation such as basking, others generate their own heat through endothermic mechanisms. Flight is often preceded by wing-whirring or shivering of the thoracic muscles. Although the muscle movement is not always visible, the net result is an increase in thoracic temperature to a level required for flight (Kammer 1981; May 1979). This behavior is particularly evident in high-elevation bees (Arroyo et al. 1982) but has also been observed in some butterflies and moths (Dotterweich 1928; Kammer 1968; Krogh and Zeuthen 1941), dragonflies (Pond 1973), beetles (Bartholomew and Casey 1977; Leston et al. 1965), and flies (Heinrich and Pantle 1975). Dependence on endothermic thermoregulation is energetically costly. The high cost of endothermy may be reflected in the replacement of bees as pollinators at high elevations and latitudes by flies and butterflies. Bees warm up by shivering and are continuously active during the day so long as conditions permit. Flies and butterflies, however, are known to supplement their daily energy budgets with regular and rather prolonged periods of basking. Bees also expend considerable energy provisioning their nest and warming their brood (Arroyo et al. 1982; Heinrich 1974), a behavior unknown among flies and butterflies.

Insects in flight generate a significant quantity of heat. Indeed, as much as 80–90 percent of the energy produced through muscle movement during flight may appear as heat in the thorax (Kammer and Heinrich 1978). For insects in cold environments, the heat can be beneficial. However, for insects inhabiting hot desert environments, the additional heat can be troublesome. Most desert insects avoid flight during the hot hours of the day. When forced to fly, they minimize flight distances (Chappell 1983). Honeybees (Apis mellifera) have developed an efficient behavioral mechanism that permits sustained flight even at temperatures as high as 46°C (115°F) (Heinrich 1979, 1980). At high temperatures honeybees in flight will regurgitate small droplets of fluid. Evaporation of the fluid may reduce the body temperature of the bee by 2° to 8°C (4° to 14°F).

Physiological Adaptations

Physiological means of regulating heat loss may also be used by insects in flight. Some moths (Heinrich 1971; Casey 1976b), dragonflies (Heinrich and Casey 1978), beetles (Bartholomew and Heinrich 1978), and bumblebees (Heinrich 1975) are able to regulate body temperature during flight by controlling the flow of hemolymph from the thorax to the abdomen. At low ambient temperatures the flow is restricted, thereby conserving warmth in the thorax; at high ambient temperatures the rate of circulation is increased, causing the abdomen to function as a heat radiator (Kammer 1981).

Both winged and nonwinged insects have demonstrated adaptive changes in physiological tolerance to temperature extremes under the stimulus of severe environments. While some species of insects become inactive or die at temperatures near the freezing point, other species are well within their preferred temperature range. Cold-adapted species have been known to survive temperatures as low as –50° to –80°C (–58° to –112°F) (Mani 1968). Some high-elevation collembolans are so well adapted to cold that they die if exposed briefly to the warmth of a human hand (Mani 1962). The exact mechanisms of cold tolerance are not fully understood, although it has been suggested that enzyme systems are unusually efficient at low temperature; in other cases a high glycerol content in the body tissues may play a significant role in preventing formation of damaging ice crystals in cells (Salt 1961a, 1961b).

Alterations in life cycles may occur in insects inhabiting harsh environments. Whereas insects of temperate areas typically complete one or more life cycles in a single year, individuals of the same species may require two or more years to complete a life cycle at high elevations and latitudes because of the brevity and irregularity of favorable conditions (Downes 1965; Mani 1968). Insects that manage to complete their life cycles in a single year in harsh environments may spend extended periods in a state of diapause and then become active and complete their life cycles at an accelerated pace when conditions become favorable (Alexander and Hilliard 1969; Dingle et al. 1990; Downes 1964; Mani 1968).

CONCLUSIONS

Virtually all groups of insects decline in total numbers at very high elevations and in hot, low-elevation deserts where climatic conditions are severe. However, the decline is not uniform among orders. Some groups are less capable of surviving climatic extremes and are less well represented in those environments. The result is a shift in relative species richness and relative abundance of the various insect orders along an elevational gradient. Insects have evolved a variety of mechanisms that enhance survival in hot or cold habitats where the primary limiting factor is temperature. Morphological, behavioral, and physiological adaptations provide the insects with some degree of control of body temperatures. Some physiological adaptations may also enhance tolerance to temperature extremes.

LITERATURE CITED

Alexander, G. 1951. The occurrence of Orthoptera at high altitudes with special reference to Colorado Acrididae. Ecology 32: 104–112.

Alexander, G., and J. R. Hilliard, Jr. 1969. Altitudinal and seasonal distribution of Orthoptera in the Rocky Mountains of northern Colorado. Ecol. Monogr. 39: 385–431.

Arroyo, M.T.K., J. Armesto, and R. Primack. 1983. Tendencias altitudinales y latitudinales en mecanismos de polinización en la zona andina de los Andes templados de Sudamérica. Rev. Chil. Hist. Nat. 56: 159–180.

Arroyo, M.T.K., R. Primack, and J. Armesto. 1982. Community studies in pollination ecology in the high temperate Andes of central Chile. I. Pollination mechanisms and altitudinal variation. Am. J. Bot. 69: 82–97.

Bartholomew, G. A., and T. M. Casey. 1977. Endothermy during terrestrial activity in large beetles. Science 195: 882–883.

Bartholomew, G. A., and B. Heinrich. 1978. Endothermy in African dung beetles during flight, ball making, and ball rolling. J. Exp. Biol. 73: 65–83.

Bey-Bienko, G. Y., and G. P. Peshev. 1960. A study of the fauna of Orthopterans (Orthoptera) in Bulgaria. Bull. Inst. Zool. Acad. Sci. Bulg. 9: 3–51.

Burquez, A., and Y. J. Sarukhan K. 1980. Biología de poblaciones silvestres y cultivadas de Phaseolus coccineus L. I. Relaciones planta-polinizador. Bol. Soc. Bot. Méx. 39: 5–24.

Carpenter, F. L. 1976. Plant-pollinator interactions in Hawaii: Pollination energetics of Metrosideros collina (Myrtaceae). Ecology 57: 1125–1144.

Casey, T. M. 1976a. Activity patterns, body temperature, and thermal ecology in two desert caterpillars (Lepidoptera: Sphingidae). Ecology 57: 485–497.

Casey, T. M. 1976b. Flight energetics of sphinx moths: Heat production and heat loss in Hyles lineata during free flight. J. Exp. Biol. 64: 545–560.

Casey, T. M. 1981. Behavioral mechanisms of thermoregulation, pp. 79–114. In: B. Heinrich (ed.), Insect thermoregulation. John Wiley & Sons, New York.

Chappell, M. A. 1983. Metabolism and thermoregulation in desert and montane grasshoppers. Oecologia 56: 126–131.

Church, N. S. 1960. Heat loss and the body temperature of flying insects. II. Heat conduction within the body and its loss by radiation and convection. J. Exp. Biol. 37: 186–213.

Clench, H. K. 1966. Behavioral thermoregulation in butterflies. Ecology 47: 1021–1034.

Cloudsley-Thompson, J. L. 1963. Light responses and diurnal rhythms in desert Tenebrionidae. Entomol. Exp. Appl. 6: 75–78.

Crawford, C. S. 1981. Biology of desert invertebrates. Springer-Verlag, Berlin. 314p.

Cruden, R. W. 1972. Pollinators in high-elevation ecosystems: Relative effectiveness of birds and bees. Science 176: 1439–1440.

Cruden, R. W., S. Kinsman, R. E. Stockhouse II, and Y. B. Linhart. 1976. Pollination, fecundity, and the distribution of moth-flowered plants. Biotropica 8: 204–210.

Darlington, P. J., Jr. 1943. Carabidae of mountains and islands: Data on the evolution of isolated fauna and on atrophy of wings. Ecol. Monogr. 13: 37–61.

Digby, P.S.B. 1955. Factors affecting the temperature excess of insects in sunshine. J. Exp. Biol. 32: 279–298.

Digby, P.S.B. 1958. Flight activity in the blowfly Calliphora erythrocephala in relation to wind speed, with special reference to adaptation. J. Exp. Biol. 35: 775–795.

Dingle, H., T. A. Mousseau, and S. M. Scott. 1990. Altitudinal variation in life cycle syndromes of California populations of the grasshopper, Melanoplus sanguinipes (F.). Oecologia 84: 199–206.

Dotterweich, H. 1928. Beiträge zur Nervenphysiologie der Insekten. I. Das Schwirren der Schmetterlinge vor dem Fluge. Zool. Jahrb. Abt. Allg. Zool. Physiol. Tiere. 44: 399–425.

Douglas, M. M. 1978. Thermal niche partitioning in the Sphingidae. Am. Zool. 18: 573.

Downes, J. A. 1962. What is an arctic insect? Can. Entomol. 94: 143–162.

Downes, J. A. 1964. Arctic insects and their environment. Can. Entomol. 96: 279–307.

Downes, J. A. 1965. Adaptations of insects in the arctic. Annu. Rev. Entomol. 10: 257–274.

Elias, S. A. 1987. Colorado ground beetles (Coleoptera: Carabidae) from the Rotger collection, University of Colorado Museum. Great Basin Nat. 47: 631–637.

Evans, M. A. 1988. Checklist of Odonata of Colorado. Great Basin Nat. 48: 96–101.

Faegri, K., and L. van der Pijl. 1979. The principles of pollination ecology. Pergamon Press, Oxford. 244p.

Fernandes, G. W., and P. W. Price. 1988. Biogeographical gradients in galling species richness. Oecologia 76: 161–167.

Gamboa, G. J. 1976. Effects of temperature on the surface activity of the desert leaf-cutter ant, *Acromyrmex versicolor versicolor* (Pergande). Am. Midl. Nat. 95: 485–491.

Gaufin, A. R. 1959. Production of bottom fauna in the Provo River, Utah. Iowa State Coll. J. Sci. 33: 395–419.

Gillis, J. E., and P. A. Smeigh. 1987. Altitudinal variation in thermal behavior of the grasshopper *Circotettix rabula* (Rehn & Hebard) from central Colorado. Southwest. Nat. 32: 203–211.

Gressitt, J. L., and C. M. Yoshimoto. 1974. Insect dispersal studies in northern Alaska. Pac. Insects 16: 11–30.

Hadley, N. F. 1970. Micrometeorology and energy exchange in two desert arthropods. Ecology 51: 434–444.

Hamilton, W. J. 1971. Competition and thermoregulatory behavior of the Namib Desert tenebrionid beetle genus *Cardiosis*. Ecology 52: 810–822.

Hamilton, W. J. 1973. Life's color code. McGraw-Hill, New York. 238p.

Hamilton, W. J. 1975. Coloration and its thermal consequences for diurnal desert insects, pp. 67–89. *In*: N. F. Hadley (ed.), Environmental physiology of desert organisms. Dowden, Hutchinson & Ross, Stroudsburg, Pennsylvania.

Heath, J. E. 1967. Temperature responses of the periodical "17-year" cicada, *Magicicada cassinii* (Homoptera, Cicadidae). Am. Midl. Nat. 77: 64–76.

Heath, J. E., and P. J. Wilkin. 1970. Temperature responses of the desert cicada, *Diceroprocta apache* (Homoptera, Cicadidae). Physiol. Zool. 43: 145–154.

Heath, J. E., P. J. Wilkin, and M. S. Heath. 1972. Temperature responses of the cactus dodger, *Cacama valvata* (Homoptera, Cicadidae). Physiol. Zool. 45: 238–246.

Heinrich, B. 1971. Temperature regulation of the sphinx moth, *Manduca sexta*. II. Regulation of heat loss by control of blood circulation. J. Exp. Biol. 54: 153–166.

Heinrich, B. 1972. Thoracic temperatures of butterflies in the field near the equator. Comp. Biochem. Physiol. 43A: 459–467.

Heinrich, B. 1974. Thermoregulation in bumblebees. I. Brood incubation by *Bombus vosnesenskii* queens. J. Comp. Physiol. 88: 129–140.

Heinrich, B. 1975. Thermoregulation in bumblebees. II. Energetics of warm up and free flight. J. Comp. Physiol. 96: 155–166.

Heinrich, B. 1979. Keeping a cool head by honeybees, *Apis mellifera*. Science 205: 1269–1271.

Heinrich, B. 1980. Mechanisms of body-temperature regulation in honeybees *Apis mellifera*. I. Regulation of head temperature. J. Exp. Biol. 85: 61–87.

Heinrich, B., and T. M. Casey. 1978. Heat transfer in dragonflies: "Fliers" and "perchers." J. Exp. Biol. 74: 17–36.

Heinrich, B., and C. Pantle. 1975. Thermoregulation in small flies (*Syrphus* sp.) basking and shivering. J. Exp. Biol. 62: 599–610.

Heithaus, E. R. 1974. The role of plant-pollinator interactions in determining community structure. Ann. Missouri Bot. Gard. 61: 675–691.

Henwood, K. 1975. A field-tested thermoregulation model for two diurnal Namib Desert tenebrionid beetles. Ecology 56: 1329–1342.

Herrmann, S. J., D. E. Ruiter, and J. D. Unzicker. 1986. Distribution and records of Colorado USA Trichoptera. Southwest Nat. 31: 421–458.

Hocking, B. 1968. Insect-flower associations in the high Arctic with special reference to nectar. Oikos 19: 359–388.

Hocking, B., and C. D. Sharplin. 1965. Flower basking by arctic insects. Nature 206: 215.

Janzen, D. H. 1973. Sweep samples of tropical foliage insects: Effects of seasons, vegetation types, elevation, time of day, and insularity. Ecology 54: 687–708.

Kammer, A. E. 1968. Motor patterns during flight and warm-up in Lepidoptera. J. Exp. Biol. 48: 89–109.

Kammer, A. E. 1981. Physiological mechanisms of thermoregulation, pp. 115–158. In: B. Heinrich (ed.), Insect thermoregulation. John Wiley & Sons, New York.

Kammer, A. E., and B. Heinrich. 1978. Insect flight metabolism. Adv. Insect Physiol. 13: 133–228.

Kevan, P. G. 1972. Insect pollination of high arctic flowers. J. Ecol. 60: 831–847.

Kevan, P. G. 1975. Sun-tracking solar furnaces in high arctic flowers: Significance for pollination and insects. Science 189: 723–726.

Kevan, P. G., and J. D. Shorthouse. 1970. Behavioral thermoregulation by high arctic butterflies. Arctic 23: 268–279.

Kingsolver, J. G., and R. J. Moffat. 1982. Thermoregulation and the determinants of heat transfer in *Colias* butterflies. Oecologia 53: 27–33.

Knight, A. W., and A. R. Gaufin. 1966. Altitudinal distribution of stoneflies (Plecoptera) in a Rocky Mountain drainage system. J. Kansas Entomol. Soc. 39: 668–675.

Krogh, A., and E. Zeuthen. 1941. The mechanism of flight preparation in some insects. J. Exp. Biol. 18: 1–9.

Leston, D., J.W.S. Pringle, and D.C.S. White. 1965. Muscle activity during preparation for flight in a beetle. J. Exp. Biol. 42: 409–414.

Lindner, E. 1956. Zur Verbreitung der Diptera (Zweiflügler) in den Hochregionen der Alpen. Jahrb. Ver. Schutz. Alpenpflanz. Tiere. 1956: 121–128.

Mani, M. S. 1962. Introduction to high altitude entomology. Methuen, London. 304p.

Mani, M. S. 1968. Ecology and biogeography of high altitude insects. Dr. W. Junk, The Hague. 455p.

Mani, M. S., and L. E. Giddings. 1980. Ecology of highlands. Dr. W. Junk, The Hague. 530p.

May, M. L. 1976. Thermoregulation and adaptation to temperature in dragonflies. Ecol. Monogr. 46: 1–32.

May, M. L. 1979. Insect thermoregulation. Annu. Rev. Entomol. 24: 313–349.

McAlpine, J. F. 1965. Observations on anthophilous diptera at Lake Hazen, Ellesmere Island. Can. Field Nat. 79: 247–252.

Moldenke, A. R. 1975. Niche specialization and species diversity along a California transect. Oecologia 21: 219–242.

Moldenke, A. R. 1976. California pollination ecology and vegetation types. Phytologia 34: 305–361.

Moldenke, A. R., and P. G. Lincoln. 1979. Pollination ecology in montane Colorado: A community analysis. Phytologia 42: 349–379.

Müller, H. 1881. Alpenblumen, ihre Befruchtung durch Insekten und ihre Anpassungen an dieselben. Verlag von Wilhelm Engelmann, Leipzig. 612p.

National Oceanic and Atmospheric Administration. 1982. Monthly normals of temperature, precipitation, and heating and cooling degree days 1951–1980. National Climatic Center, Asheville, North Carolina.

Pascual, F. 1978. Estudio preliminar de Ortópteros de Sierra Nevada. IV. Distribución altitudinal. Bol. Asoc. Esp. Entomol. 2: 49–63.

Peterson, B. 1977. Pollination by ants in the alpine tundra of Colorado. Trans. Illinois State Acad. Sci. 70: 349–355.

Pleasants, J. M. 1980. Competition for bumblebee pollinators in Rocky Mountain plant communities. Ecology 61: 1446–1459.

Pojar, J. 1974. Reproductive dynamics of four plant communities of southwestern British Columbia. Can. J. Bot. 52: 1819–1834.

Pond, C. M. 1973. Initiation of flight and preflight behavior of anisopterous dragonflies *Aeshna* spp. J. Insect Physiol. 19: 2225–2229.

Primack, R. B. 1978. Variability in New Zealand montane and alpine pollinator assemblages. N.Z.J. Ecol. 1: 66–73.

Primack, R. B. 1983. Insect pollination in the New Zealand mountain flora. N.Z.J. Bot. 21: 317–333.

Rajput, K. B., and T. K. Singh. 1988. Vertical distribution of mosquitoes in Manipur, India. Entomon. 13: 295–302.

Raw, A. 1985. The ecology of Jamaican bees (Hymenoptera). Rev. Bras. Entomol. 29: 1–16.

Salt, R. W. 1961a. Principles of insect cold-hardiness. Annu. Rev. Entomol. 6: 55–73.

Salt, R. W. 1961b. Resistance of poikilothermic animals to cold. Br. Med. Bull. 17: 5–8.

Sánchez-Ortega, A., and J. Alba-Tercedor. 1989. Características de fenología y distribución de las especies de Plecóptera de Sierra Nevada (Insecta: Plecoptera). Bol. Asoc. Esp. Entomol. 13: 213–230.

Sherman, P. W., and W. B. Watt. 1973. The thermal ecology of some *Colias* butterfly larvae. J. Comp. Physiol. 83: 25–40.

Tinker, M. E. 1952. The seasonal behavior and ecology of the box-elder bug *Leptocoris trivittatus* in Minnesota. Ecology 33: 407–414.

Uvarov, B. 1977. Grasshoppers and locusts, a handbook of general acridology, volume 2. Centre for Overseas Pest Research, London. 588p.

Waloff, Z. 1963. Field studies on solitary and *transiens* desert locusts in the Red Sea area. Anti Locust Bull. 40: 1–93.

Walter, D. E. 1985. The effects of litter type and elevation on colonization of mixed coniferous litterbags by oribatid mites. Pedobiologia 28: 383–387.

Ward, J. V. 1982. Altitudinal zonation of Plecoptera in a Rocky Mountain stream. Aquat. Insects 4: 105–110.

Ward, J. V., and L. Berner. 1980. Abundance and altitudinal distribution of Ephemeroptera in a Rocky Mountain stream, pp. 169–177. *In:* J. F. Flannagan and K. E. Marshall (eds.), Advances in Ephemeroptera biology. Plenum Press, New York.

Warren, S. D., K. T. Harper, and G. M. Booth. 1988. Elevational distribution of insect pollinators. Am. Midl. Nat. 120: 325–330.

Watt, W. B. 1968. Adaptive significance of pigment polymorphisms in *Colias* butterflies. I. Variation of melanin pigment in relation to thermoregulation. Evolution 22: 437–458.

Weber, N. A. 1954. Arctic Alaskan Diptera. Proc. Entomol. Soc. Washington. 56: 86–91.

Whittaker, R. H. 1952. A study of summer foliage insect communities in the Great Smoky Mountains. Ecol. Monogr. 22: 1–44.

Wilcox, B. A., D. D. Murphy, P. R. Ehrlich, and G. T. Austin. 1986. Insular biogeography of the montane butterfly faunas in the Great Basin: Comparison with birds and mammals. Oecologia 69: 188–194.

Ceratoides ianata (Pursh) J. T. Howell (winterfat) is a beautiful shrub and a nutritious forage plant. Two forms of the plant occur in the area: a large, stiffly branched shrub that grows as a component of floristically diverse shrub-grass communities on the Colorado Plateau, and a small subshrub that forms widespread, essentially monotypic stands in the Great Basin.

CHAPTER 12

Late Pleistocene and Holocene Herpetofaunas of the Great Basin and Colorado Plateau

Jim I. Mead and Christopher J. Bell

OVERVIEW

The authors of this chapter describe the herpetofauna of the late Pleistocene and Holocene of the Great Basin and Colorado Plateau. Relative to the amount of information available concerning the mammals, little is known about the herpetofaunas of the late Pleistocene and Holocene in the Intermountain Area. The authors compare the modern herpetofauna to the late Pleistocene–Holocene fossil herpetofauna. In spite of the limited number of study sites, 61 percent of the modern herpetofauna are represented in the fossil record of the late Pleistocene and Holocene. Species missing in the fossil record, especially salamanders and anurans, are likely absent because fossil sites in critical habitat types have not been excavated.

This is a review of the late Pleistocene and Holocene (late Quaternary) herpetofaunas recovered from various deposits in the greater Intermountain Region, which here includes the Great Basin and the adjacent Colorado Plateau as shown in Figure 12.1. The area encompassed in this study is partly biased — we avoid most of the warm desert biomes to the south and west and the Snake River Plains region to the north. We are not discussing the Mojavian Biogeographic Province, except for the thin strip that follows up the Colorado River into the western part of the Grand Canyon, Colorado Plateau. This means that we do not include some important herpetofaunas in southern Nevada.

The Great Basin encompasses some 390,000 km^2 and, although centered in Nevada, also extends into several adjoining states. This arid region is generally characterized by linear, north-south trending fault-block mountain ranges (igneous, metamorphic, and limestone), separated by closed-drainage valleys. Elevations range from below sea level (Death Valley, California) to valley bottoms well above 1,525 m and mountain masses up to 3,970 m in the central Great Basin (eastern Nevada) and the eastern-western boundaries.

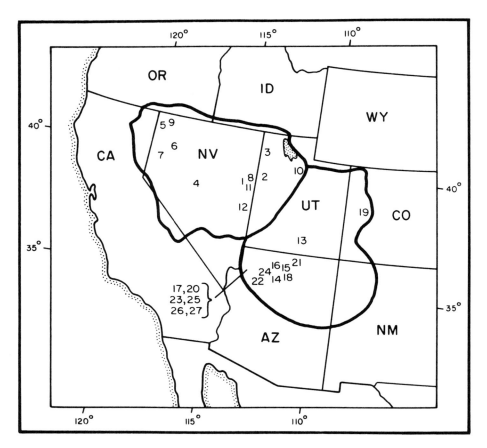

Figure 12.1 Map of western North America locating the greater Intermountain Region, including the interior Great Basin and the Colorado Plateau. Numbers refer to site location names in Table 12.1.

Although the Colorado Plateau adjoins the Great Basin on its eastern boundary, the Plateau is a region in complete contrast. Encompassing some 336,000 km², the Colorado Plateau is composed of predominantly flat-lying sedimentary rock units. Elevations typically are below 1,525 m along the Colorado River corridor, with upland plateaus usually approximately 1,830 m to 2,130 m; surrounding and interior igneous and some sedimentary masses range from between 3,350 m to 3,840 m above sea level. Present plant communities for both areas have been reviewed by Reveal (1979).

Grayson and Brown have illustrated in detail that the Great Basin has a remarkably dynamic record of mammalian extirpation, extinction, and colonization (Grayson 1982, 1987, Chapter 4 of this volume; Brown 1978). Although the small mammals have been studied in fair detail, the large extinct mammals of the late Pleistocene are only beginning to be understood for the Great Basin (Grayson, Chapter 4).

The study of the early Holocene and late Pleistocene zoogeography of the Colorado Plateau is still in its infancy, other than for Mammuthus (mammoth; Agenbroad and Mead 1989). Outside of the Grand Canyon, the Colorado Plateau is essentially unknown for late Pleistocene and early Holocene faunal remains. Although faunas have been studied, these are usually either the rare skeletal remains recovered from packrat middens or the copious amounts of dried megaherbivore dung (Mead and Agenbroad 1992). Most of these deposits are from localities along the Colorado River corridor region (Mead 1981). Almost nothing is known from the higher elevations outside of this river conduit; however, there are notable exceptions from high elevations (Miller 1987). If the late Pleistocene and early Holocene mammals are known in "fair detail" for the Great Basin and somewhat on the Colorado Plateau, then the herpetofaunas are certainly "inadequately" known for the same region. Late Pleistocene and Holocene localities known to contain a herpetofauna are presented in Table 12.1. An overview of late Pleistocene and Holocene herpetofaunas has not been attempted prior to this.

Table 12.1   Late Pleistocene and Holocene Herpetofaunas and
Their Radiocarbon Ages

Locality	Radiocarbon Age (yr B.P.)	Major Reference
Great Basin		
1. Council Hall Cave 1b midden	4220 + 60	Thompson 1979; Mead, Thompson, and Van Devender 1982
2. Crystal Ball Cave	< 23,000	Heaton 1985; Mead, Heaton, and Mead 1989
3. Danger Cave Stratum V	1930–4900	Jennings 1957; Grayson 1988; Mead 1988
4. Gatecliff Rock Shelter Strata 1–56	0–7100	Thomas 1983; Mead, Grayson, and Casteel 1983
5. Hanging Rock Shelter Strata 2, 4, 5	Holocene	Grayson 1988; Mead 1988
6. Hidden Cave All strata	< 8000	Thomas 1983; Mead 1988
7. Kramer Cave	3620 + 80– 3900 + 100	Hattori 1982
8. Ladder Cave Modern midden 3 midden 2a midden	modern 13,230 + 110 27,280 + 970	Thompson 1979; Mead, Thompson, and Van Devender 1982
9. Last Supper Cave Strata 3, 4	6000–9000	Grayson 1988; Mead 1988
10. Silver Creek Local Fauna	> 40,000	Miller 1976

continues

Table 12.1   Late Pleistocene and Holocene Herpetofaunas and
              Their Radiocarbon Ages   *(continued)*

Locality	Radiocarbon Age (yr B.P.)	Major Reference
11. Smith Creek Cave		Brattstrom 1976; Thompson
Sediment	12,600–28,650	1979; Mead, Thompson,
1 midden	11,660 + 245	and Van Devender 1982
No provenience	late Quaternary	
12. Snake Creek Burial Cave		Mead, Heaton, and Mead
2 layers	7860 + 160–15,100 + 700	1989; Mead and Mead 1989
Colorado Plateau		
13. Bechan Cave		Mead, Agenbroad, Davis, and
Dung unit	11,670 + 300–13,050 + 580	Martin 1986; Mead, Stuart, and Agenbroad ms; Mead and Agenbroad 1992
14. Bida Cave		Cole and Mead 1981; Cole
6b	6800 + 220	1990; Mead 1983
1c midden	13,340 + 150	
Layers 5, 8	> 16,150 + 600	
15. Chuar Valley		Cole and Mead 1981; Cole
4 midden	12,015 + 365	1990
16. Clear Creek		Cole and Mead 1981; Cole
1 midden	9400 + 270	1990
17. Desert Almond Canyon*		Van Devender, Phillips,
7a and b midden	8560 + 260–9650 + 360	and Mead 1977
1 midden	10,100 + 200	
5 midden	10,310 + 500	
6 midden	10,910 + 450	
3 midden	11,190 + 150	
18. Hance Canyon		Cole and Mead 1981; Cole
1 midden	10,150 + 120	1990
8 midden	12,030 + 220	
19. Haystack Cave		Emslie 1986
Levels 1–8	12,154 + 1,700 –14,935 + 610	
20. Muav Gate		Van Devender, Phillips,
1 midden	12,430 + 550	and Mead 1977
21. Nankoweep Canyon		Cole and Mead 1981; Cole
7a midden	12,170 + 210	1990
22. Peach Springs Wash		Van Devender, Phillips,
1 midden	12,040 + 400	and Mead 1977

continues

Table 12.1   Late Pleistocene and Holocene Herpetofaunas and
Their Radiocarbon Ages   (*continued*)

Locality	Radiocarbon Age (yr B.P.)	Major Reference
23. Rampart Cave		Van Devender, Phillips,
Stake 50	9770 + 160	and Mead 1977; Mead and
Stake 35	12,230 + 350	Agenbroad 1992
Pit B floor	12,600 + 260	
Roof crack	13,510 + 910	
Rat layer	14,810 + 230–	
	18,890 + 500	
Pit B front	16,330 + 270	
24. Shinumo Creek		Van Devender, Phillips,
1 midden	13,660 + 160	and Mead 1977
25. Vulture Canyon		Van Devender, Phillips,
12 midden	8540 + 180	and Mead 1977
2 midden	10,250 + 290	
14 midden	11,870 + 190	
1 midden	12,770 + 440	
26. Vulture Cave		Mead and Phillips 1981
18–3 midden	1160 + 110	
25–1 midden	11,830 + 140	
20 midden	12,000 + 260	
8 midden	13,820 + 220	
18–1 midden	14,390 + 300	
15 midden	15,260 + 270	
17 midden	17,100 + 680	
26 midden	17,290 + 240	
6 midden	17,610 + 290	
10 midden	19,050 + 390	
7 midden	22,720 + 610	
9 midden	29,810 + 1,980–	
	33,600 + 1,000	
WTMTd layer	13,430 + 460	
WTMTb layer	17,030 + 760	
Ringtail deposit	1930 + 150	
27. Window Rock		Van Devender, Phillips,
1 midden	11,310 + 380	and Mead 1977

Note: Number of locality refers to location in Figure 12.1. Details about radiocarbon dates can be found in the references.
*Name changed from Emery Falls Canyon to Desert Almond Canyon (Phillips 1984).

ZOOGEOGRAPHY

Amphibia

Amphibians living in the Intermountain Region include the salamanders (order Caudata) and the frogs, spadefoots, and toads (order Anura).

CAUDATA   Salamanders are diverse along the Pacific Northwest coastal region today, but to the east of the Sierra Nevada and Cascade Mountains and south of the Snake River Plains, the arid environment eliminates all but one species of salamander, *Ambystoma tigrinum* (tiger salamander; Stebbins 1962; Table 12.2). This salamander is not living within the interior Great Basin, although it occurs widely in permanently wet/moist canyons on the Colorado Plateau (Stebbins 1962; Tanner 1978).

Table 12.2 Living Species of Amphibians and Reptiles in the Interior Great Basin and Colorado Plateau

Order	Family	Genus	Species	Common Name
		Amphibia		
Caudata	Ambystoma-tidae	*Ambystoma*	*tigrinum*	tiger salamander
Anura	Pelobatidae	*Scaphiopus*	*bombifrons*	plains spadefoot
		Scaphiopus	*multiplicatus*	southern spadefoot
		Scaphiopus	*intermontanus*	Great Basin spadefoot
	Ranidae	*Rana*	*catesbeiana*	bullfrog
		Rana	*onca*	relict leopard frog
		Rana	*pipiens*	northern leopard frog
		Rana	*pretiosa*	spotted frog
	Bufonidae	*Bufo*	*boreas*	western toad
		Bufo	*woodhousei*	Woodhouse's toad
	Hylidae	*Pseudacris*	*triseriata*	chorus frog
		Reptilia		
Testudines	Emydidae	*Clemmys*	*marmorata*	western pond turtle
	Testudinidae	*Gopherus**	*agassizii*	desert tortoise
Squamata (Sauria)	Gekkonidae	*Coleonyx**	*variegatus*	banded gecko
	Iguanidae	*Callisaurus*	*draconoides*	zebra-tailed lizard
		Crotaphytus	*collaris*	collared lizard
		Crotaphytus	*insularis*	desert collared lizard
		Gambelia	*wislizenii*	leopard lizard
		Holbrookia	*maculata*	lesser earless lizard

continues

Table 12.2   Living Species of Amphibians and Reptiles in the Interior Great Basin and Colorado Plateau   (*continued*)

Order	Family	Genus	Species	Common Name
		Phrynosoma	*douglassi*	short-horned lizard
		Phrynosoma	*platyrhinos*	desert horned lizard
		Sauromalus*	*obesus*	chuckwalla
		Sceloporus	*graciosus*	sagebrush lizard
		Sceloporus	*magister*	desert spiny lizard
		Sceloporus	*occidentalis*	western fence lizard
		Sceloporus	*undulatus*	eastern fence lizard
		Urosaurus	*ornatus*	common tree lizard
		Uta	*stansburiana*	side-blotched lizard
	Helodermatidae	*Heloderma**	*suspectum*	gila monster
	Xantusiidae	*Xantusia*	*vigilis*	desert night lizard
	Teiidae	*Cnemidophorus*	*inornatus*	little striped whiptail
		Cnemidophorus	*tigris*	western whiptail
		Cnemidophorus	*velox*	plateau striped whiptail
	Scincidae	*Eumeces*	*multivirgatus*	many-lined skink
		Eumeces	*skiltonianus*	western skink
(Serpentes)	Boidae	*Charina*	*bottae*	rubber boa
	Colubridae	*Arizona*	*elegans*	glossy snake
		Chionactis	*occipitalis*	western shovel-nosed snake
		Coluber	*constrictor*	racer
		Diadophis	*punctatus*	ringneck snake
		Elaphe	*gutata*	corn snake
		Hypsiglena	*torquata*	night snake
		Lampropeltis	*getulus*	common kingsnake
		Lampropeltis	*pyromelana*	Sonora mountain kingsnake
		Lampropeltis	*triangulum*	milk snake
		Masticophis	*flagellum*	coachwhip
		Masticophis	*taeniatus*	striped whipsnake
		Opheodrys	*vernalis*	smooth green snake
		Pituophis	*melanoleucus*	gopher snake
		Rhinocheilus	*lecontei*	long-nosed snake
		Salvadora	*hexalepis*	western patch-nosed snake
		Sonora	*semiannulata*	ground snake

continues

Table 12.2 Living Species of Amphibians and Reptiles in the Interior Great Basin and
Colorado Plateau (continued)

Order	Family	Genus	Species	Common Name
		Tantilla	*planiceps*	western black-headed snake
		Thamnophis	*couchi*	western aquatic garter snake
		Thamnophis	*cyrtopsis*	black-necked garter snake
		Thamnophis	*elegans*	western terrestrial garter snake
		Trimorphodon	*biscutatus*	lyre snake
	Viperidae	*Crotalus*	*cerastes*	sidewinder
		Crotalus	*mitchelli*	speckled rattlesnake
		Crotalus	*scutulatus*	mojave rattlesnake
		Crotalus	*viridis*	western rattlesnake

* These species barely range into the region covered by this review, mainly along the low, hot desert Colorado River region within the western Grand Canyon. They usually live in the hot, arid Mojavian Biogeographic Province, reaching their northern limits in southwestern Utah in the Virgin River drainage, immediately outside our review area.

There are no published reports of salamanders occurring in the interior Great Basin or on the Colorado Plateau during the late Pleistocene or into the Holocene until historic records (Table 12.3). If the tiger salamander ever lived along the late Pleistocene lakes of the interior Great Basin, it has yet to be recovered. Its absence from fossil deposits might be due in part to a bias of taphonomic destruction and the researchers' collecting techniques. Had the species been living along the western shores of Pleistocene Lake Bonneville, it should have been found in the raptor deposits in Smith Creek Cave, along with all the other aquatic taxa.

The tiger salamander is not known from late Pleistocene deposits on the Colorado Plateau, although it is rare to occasional there today. Detailed excavations have not been made in areas where *Ambystoma* is likely to be preserved. Reconstructions of the local biotic community outside of Bechan Cave at approximately 12,000 B.P. indicate the presences of grasses, sedges, woody shrubs, and a riparian boreal forest (Mead et al. 1986). A fauna from such an environment should have included *Ambystoma tigrinum*, but Bechan Cave is approximately 100 m from and well above the area where the riparian forest would have been situated — too far for the species to happen into the locality on its own. The depositional environment of the fossils in the cave does not include raptor remains (Mead, Stuart, and Agenbroad ms), probably the only other means of introducing the salamander into the deposit. It is our opinion that researchers have not looked in the correct environmental setting to recover salamanders, if indeed they were present during the late Pleistocene or early Holocene on the Colorado Plateau.

ANURA   Ten species of frogs and toads presently live in both the Great Basin and on the Colorado Plateau (Table 12.2). Most species are found in areas of at least

Table 12.3   Late Pleistocene and Holocene Amphibians from the Great Basin and Colorado Plateau

	Bufo sp.	B. boreas	B. woodhousei	B. boreas/woodhousei	Pseudacris triseriata	Rana sp.	R. piipiens	Scaphiopus sp.	S. hammondi	S. intermontanus
Great Basin										
Gatecliff	—	—	—	—	—	—	—	—	—	X
Hanging	—	—	—	—	X	—	—	—	—	—
Haystack	—	—	—	X	—	—	—	—	—	—
Hidden	X	X	—	—	—	X	—	X	—	X
Last Supper	X	—	—	—	—	—	—	—	—	—
Silver Creek	—	—	—	—	—	—	—	X	—	—
Smith Creek	X	—	—	—	—	X	—	—	X	—
Sed.	X	X	X	—	—	X	—	—	—	X
1	—	—	—	—	—	—	—	—	—	X
Colorado Plateau										
Bechan	—	—	—	—	—	—	—	—	—	X

Note: Locality names as in Table 12.1.

local, perennial moisture. *Scaphiopus* (*Spea*; Kluge 1966) (spadefoot) are known to live in arid areas in both regions, as long as there is a summer moisture period. We have observed *Bufo boreas* (western toad) on small patches of wet grass surrounded by major snowfields at 2,990 m elevation in the Ruby Mountains.

Six species of spadefoots, toads, and frogs have been identified from the late Pleistocene and Holocene deposits in the Great Basin (Table 12.3). Most of the anurans recovered from the various deposits in the Great Basin are expected, based upon modern species distributions. The recovery of one tibiofibula of *Pseudacris triseriata* (chorus frog) from the early to middle Holocene deposits in Hanging Rock Shelter (Mead 1988) was unexpected, since the chorus frog lives no closer to the shelter than the Snake River Valley, approximately 360 km to the northeast (Figure 12.2). The species is terrestrial, frequenting damp marshes, swamps, and lake- and pond sides (Stebbins 1962).

Anurans are demonstratively absent from the late Pleistocene and Holocene deposits on the Colorado Plateau, except for the remains of *Scaphiopus intermontanus* (Great Basin spadefoot) from Bechan Cave (Table 12.3; Figure 12.2). If we are to understand adequately anurans of the late Pleistocene on the Colorado Plateau outside of the Grand Canyon, it will be necessary to excavate lacustrine and raptor deposits; this is at present completely inadequate in the published record.

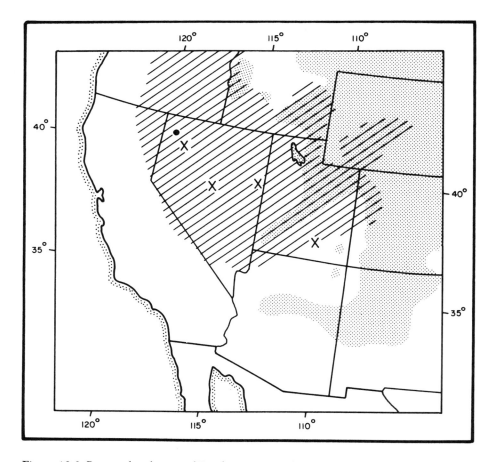

Figure 12.2 Present distribution of *Pseudacris triseriata* (stippled, with fossil as dot) and *Scaphiopus intermontanus* (hachured, with fossil as x), based on Stebbins 1985.

Reptilia

Reptiles living in the Great Basin and on the Colorado Plateau include the turtles (order Testudines), the lizards (order Squamata; suborder Sauria), and the snakes (order Squamata; suborder Serpentes).

TESTUDINES   Turtle species are rare in the Intermountain Region today and in the late Pleistocene, with only *Clemmys* and *Gopherus* being found (Tables 12.1 and 12.4). *Clemmys marmorata* (western pond turtle) was recovered from Kramer Cave on Falcon Hill, adjacent to Winnemucca Lake, part of the Pleistocene Lake Lahontan system (Hattori 1982). Although a rare find, it is reasonable given the present distribution and habitat requirements of the species. It is the most aquatic species of *Clemmys* and inhabits ponds, marshes, and slow-moving streams with rocky or muddy bottoms and abundant aquatic vegetation. It is also found in clear, swift streams up to an elevation of 1,830 m (Ernst and Barbour 1972).

Table 12.4 Late Pleistocene and Holocene Turtles and Lizards from the Great Basin and Colorado Plateau

	Gopherus agassizii	*Clemmys marmorata*	*Cnemidophorus sp.*	*C. tigris*	*Coleonyx variegatus*	*Crotaphytus sp.*	*C. collaris*	*Gambelia wislizenii*	*Heloderma suspectum*	*Phrynosoma sp.*	*P. douglassi*	*P. platyrhinos*	*Sauromalus obesus*	*Sceloporus sp.*	*S. graciosus*	*S. magister*	*S. occidentalis*	*S. undulatus*	*S. undulatus/occidentalis*	*Uta stansburiana*
Great Basin																				
Crystal	—	—	—	X	—	X	X	X	—	—	X	X	—	X	X	—	—	—	X	X
Gatecliff	—	—	—	—	—	—	X	X	—	X	—	X	—	X	X	X	X	—	X	X
Hanging	—	—	—	—	—	—	—	—	—	—	—	—	—	X	X	X	X	—	—	—
Hidden	—	—	—	X	—	X	X	—	—	—	—	—	X	—	X	—	X	—	—	X
Kramer	—	X	—	—	—	—	—	—	—	—	—	—	—	—	—	—	—	—	—	—
Ladder Mod.	—	—	—	—	—	—	—	—	—	—	—	—	—	—	—	—	—	—	—	X
2a	—	—	—	—	—	—	—	—	—	—	—	—	X	—	—	—	—	—	X	—
3	—	—	—	—	—	—	—	—	—	—	—	—	X	—	—	—	—	—	—	—
Last Supper	—	—	—	—	—	—	—	—	—	—	—	—	—	X	—	—	X	—	—	—
Snake Creek	—	—	—	—	—	—	—	—	—	—	—	—	X	—	—	—	—	—	X	X
Smith Creek	—	—	—	—	—	X	—	—	—	—	—	X	—	—	X	X	—	—	—	—
Sed.	—	—	—	X	—	X	X	X	—	—	X	X	—	X	X	X	—	—	X	—
Colorado Plateau																				
Bida 1c	—	—	—	—	—	—	—	—	—	—	—	—	—	X	—	—	—	—	—	—
6c	—	—	—	X	—	—	—	—	—	—	—	—	—	—	—	—	—	—	—	—
Layers 5, 8	—	—	—	X	—	—	—	—	—	—	—	—	X	—	—	—	—	—	—	X
Chuar 4	—	—	—	—	—	X	—	—	—	—	—	—	—	—	—	—	—	—	—	—
Clear 1	—	—	—	—	—	—	—	—	—	—	—	—	—	—	—	—	X	—	—	—
Desert 1	—	—	—	—	—	—	—	—	—	—	—	—	—	—	—	X	—	—	—	—
3	—	—	—	—	—	—	—	—	—	—	—	—	X	—	—	—	—	—	—	—
5	—	—	—	—	X	—	X	—	—	—	—	—	—	X	—	X	—	X	—	X
6	—	—	X	—	X	—	X	—	—	—	—	—	—	—	—	X	—	X	—	X
7b	—	—	—	X	—	—	—	—	—	—	—	—	—	—	X	—	—	—	—	—
Hance 1	—	—	—	—	—	—	—	—	—	—	—	—	—	—	—	—	X	—	—	—
8	—	—	X	—	—	—	—	—	—	—	—	—	X	—	—	—	—	—	—	—
Haystack	—	—	—	—	—	—	—	—	—	—	—	—	—	—	—	—	X	—	—	—
Muav 1	X	—	—	—	—	—	—	—	—	—	—	—	—	—	—	—	—	—	—	—
Nankoweap 7a	—	—	—	—	—	—	—	—	—	—	—	—	X	—	—	—	—	—	—	—
Peach	—	—	—	—	—	—	—	—	—	—	—	—	X	—	X	—	—	—	—	—
Rampart Stake 50	—	—	—	—	—	—	—	—	—	—	—	—	—	—	X	—	—	—	—	—
Stake 35	X	—	—	—	—	—	—	—	—	—	—	—	—	—	—	—	X	—	—	—

continues

Table 12.4 Late Pleistocene and Holocene Turtles and Lizards from the Great Basin and Colorado Plateau   (*continued*)

	Gopherus agassizii	*Clemmys marmorata*	*Cnemidophorus sp.*	*C. tigris*	*Coleonyx variegatus*	*Crotaphytus sp.*	*C. collaris*	*Gambelia wislizenii*	*Heloderma suspectum*	*Phrynosoma sp.*	*P. douglassi*	*P. platyrhinos*	*Sauromalus obesus*	*Sceloporus sp.*	*S. graciosus*	*S. magister*	*S. occidentalis*	*S. undulatus*	*S. undulatus/occidentalis*	*Uta stansburiana*
Pit B Fl.	X	—	—	—	—	—	—	—	—	—	—	—	—	—	—	—	—	—	—	—
Rat	X	—	—	—	—	—	—	—	—	—	—	—	X	—	—	X	—	—	—	—
Pit B Fr.	X	—	—	—	—	—	—	—	—	—	—	—	—	—	—	X	—	—	—	—
Shinumo	—	—	—	—	—	—	—	—	—	—	—	—	—	—	—	—	—	—	X	—	—
Vulture Can. 12	—	—	—	—	—	—	—	—	—	—	—	—	X	—	—	—	—	—	—	—
2	X	—	—	—	—	—	—	—	—	—	—	—	X	—	—	—	—	—	—	—
14	—	—	—	—	—	—	—	—	—	—	—	—	—	—	—	—	—	—	—	—
1	—	—	—	—	—	—	—	—	—	—	—	—	—	—	—	—	—	—	X	—	—
Vulture Cave 18–3	—	—	X	—	—	—	—	—	—	—	—	—	X	—	—	X	—	—	—	—
25–1	—	—	—	—	—	—	—	—	—	—	—	—	—	X	—	—	—	—	—	—
20	—	—	—	—	—	—	—	—	—	—	—	—	—	X	—	X	—	—	—	—
8	X	—	—	—	—	—	—	—	—	—	—	—	X	X	—	X	—	X	—	—
18–1	—	—	—	—	—	—	—	—	—	—	—	—	—	X	—	—	—	—	—	—
15	—	—	—	—	—	—	—	—	—	—	—	—	—	X	—	—	—	—	—	—
26	—	—	—	—	—	—	—	—	—	—	—	—	—	X	—	—	—	—	—	—
10	—	—	—	—	—	—	—	—	—	—	—	—	—	X	—	—	—	—	—	—
7	—	—	—	—	—	X	—	—	—	—	—	—	—	—	—	—	—	—	—	—
9	X	—	—	—	—	—	—	—	—	—	—	—	—	X	—	—	—	—	—	—
WTMTd	—	—	—	X	—	—	X	—	X	—	—	—	X	—	—	X	—	—	—	—
Ringtail	—	—	—	X	X	—	X	—	—	—	—	—	X	—	—	X	—	X	—	—
Window 1	—	—	—	—	—	—	—	—	—	—	—	—	X	—	—	X	—	X	—	—

Note: Locality names as in Table 12.1.

Gopherus agassizii (desert tortoise; sometimes placed in *Xerobates*) is known from the Colorado River corridor area of the Colorado Plateau and even then only a short distance upriver from the western terminus at the Grand Wash Cliffs (Van Devender, Phillips, and Mead 1977; Mead and Phillips 1981).

Remains of *Chelydra serpentina* (snapping turtle) are in the lacustrine late Pleistocene vertebrate fauna near Glendale, Clark County, Nevada, immediately west of the Colorado Plateau and south of our terminus of the Great Basin region (Figure 12.1; Van Devender and Tessman 1975). To better the understanding of turtles in the study region, analysis of more xeric cave deposits (for *Gopherus*) and lacustrine deposits (for the various aquatic turtles, including *Clemmys*) will have to be undertaken.

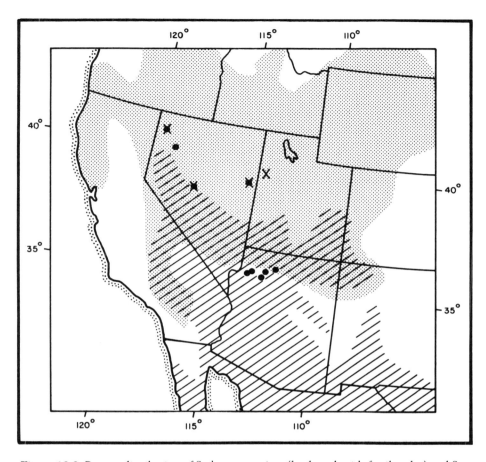

Figure 12.3 Present distribution of *Sceloporus magister* (hachured, with fossil as dot) and *S. graciosus* (stippled, with fossil as x) based on Parker 1982 and Censky 1986, respectively.

SAURIA   Lizards are numerous in late Pleistocene and Holocene deposits in the Great Basin and Colorado Plateau. There are presently 22 species living in these regions (including the Colorado River corridor; Table 12.1); 14 species are identified from the late Pleistocene and Holocene deposits (Table 12.4). The most common taxa recovered in the late Pleistocene and Holocene deposits are the various species of *Sceloporus*. *Sceloporus graciosus* (sagebrush lizard) appears not to have changed its distribution since the late Pleistocene (Figure 12.3). During the late Pleistocene *Sceloporus magister* (desert spiny lizard) occurred farther north in the Great Basin than it does presently (Figure 12.3; Brattstrom 1976; Mead, Thompson, and Van Devender 1982; Mead 1985, 1988). The hot desert species in the study region, including *Heloderma suspectum* (gila monster) and *Coleonyx variegatus* (banded gecko), occur today and occurred in the late Pleistocene only along the low elevations adjacent to the Colorado River, westernmost portion of the Colorado Plateau.

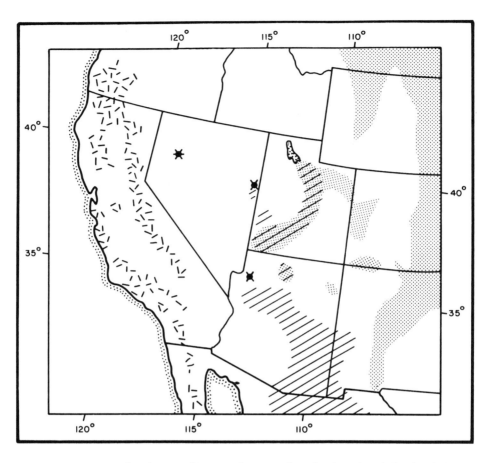

Figure 12.4 Present distribution of *Lampropeltis pyromelana* (hachured, with fossil as dot), *L. zonata* (mixed, with fossil as *), and *L. triangulum* (stippled, with fossil as x), based on Tanner 1983, Zweifel 1974, and Stebbins 1985, respectively.

SERPENTES   Snake genera are the most numerous of reptiles presently living in the interior Great Basin and on the Colorado Plateau (26 species; Table 12.2). Most species of the 15 recovered in the late Pleistocene and Holocene deposits (Table 12.5) are expected based on the present distributions. Exceptions are the unusual occurrences of *Lampropeltis* (kingsnake) species. *Lampropeltis zonata* (California kingsnake) was tentatively identified from Hidden Cave. Today it does not live east and away from the effects of the Sierra Nevada environment, and therefore it does not enter the interior of the Great Basin (Figure 12.4; Mead 1988). *L. pyromelana* (Sonora mountain kingsnake) and *L. triangulum* (milk snake) were both identified from Smith Creek Cave, with the former species also recovered from Hidden Cave (Figure 12.4; Mead 1988; Mead, Thompson, and Van Devender 1982). *L. pyromelana* has a disjunct population presently living in the Snake

Range; other than this isolate, it is extirpated from the interior Great Basin. *L. triangulum* does not presently live in the interior Great Basin. The locations where fossil remains of the species have been recovered indicate that both species had much more northern and western extensions into the Great Basin during the late Pleistocene. After more specimens and localities of *Lampropeltis* are recovered, all kingsnake specimens should be re-examined. The hot desert snake, *Trimorphodon biscutatus*, is known to occur in the study region only along the Colorado River corridor of the Colorado Plateau.

DISCUSSION AND CONCLUSIONS

The living herpetofauna of the Great Basin and the Colorado Plateau is listed in Table 12.2; of these, no species of the salamander (of one living species), six anuran (of 10), two turtle (of two), 14 lizard (of 22), and 15 snake (of 26) have been recovered from late Pleistocene and Holocene deposits in the Great Basin and the Colorado Plateau. This is actually a reasonable fossil representation of the living species, although there is obviously a bias in the distribution of investigated fossil localities. Sites have not been investigated based on their potential of recovering a certain herpetofauna. In the Great Basin, most of the examined sites are selected for investigation based on the surface potential of stratified archaeological remains. On the Colorado Plateau the reported fossil localities are heavily biased toward packrat midden studies (rocky habitat areas located in the Grand Canyon corridor) or dry dung deposits. The excavation of a rare, small carnivore bone accumulation has produced an abundance of reptile remains from the late Holocene of the Grand Canyon (Mead and Van Devender 1981).

The lizard and snake taxa are fairly well represented in the various localities in both the Great Basin and on the Colorado Plateau. This is to be expected because the localities investigated are arid sites, environments where these species have both an abundance and richness today. Lizard and snake remains are common in sites incorporating raptor-vulturid pellet, commensal living, and packrat midden taphonomies (for example, Gatecliff Shelter and Vulture Cave). Natural trap localities (for example, Snake Creek Burial Cave) do include both snake and lizard species. However, fewer species of lizards are incorporated into such deposits because of their better climbing abilities.

The amphibians seem inordinately absent in the fossil localities, especially the salamanders. Localities that incorporate anuran remains usually contain raptor deposits and are adjacent to an aquatic system (for example, Hidden Cave), although the spadefoots can be found in other taphonomic, xeric situations. Detailed excavations have not occurred in riparian, paludal, or lacustrine deposits where salamanders and various other aquatic species are likely to be recovered.

Herpetofaunas are useful for paleoenvironmental reconstructions, especially when incorporated with the mammalian data. Certain localities indicate that there were disharmonious faunas in the Great Basin during the late Pleistocene and/or the early Holocene. The same stratum of Hanging Rock Shelter that provided the *Pseudacris* specimen contained *Sceloporus magister* and *Ochotona princeps* (pika; Rodentia), also presently extralimital species. Assuming that this unit is not bioturbated

Table 12.5 Late Pleistocene and Holocene Snakes from the Great Basin and Colorado Plateau

	Charina bottae	*Crotalus* sp.	*C. viridis*	*C. viridis/mitchelli*	*Coluber constrictor*	*Masticophis* sp.	*Masticophis/Coluber*	*M. flagellum*	*Hypsiglena torquata*	*Lampropeltis* sp.	*L. getulus*	*L. pyromelana*	*L. triangulum*	*L. zonata*	*Pituophis melanoleucus*	*Rhinocheilus lecontei*	*Salvadora hexalepis*	*Sonora semiannulata*	*Thamnophis* sp.	*Trimorphodon biscutatus*
Great Basin																				
Council Hall 1b	—	—	—	—	—	—	—	X	—	—	—	—	—	—	—	—	—	—	—	—
Crystal	—	—	—	—	—	—	—	—	—	X	—	—	—	—	—	—	—	—	X	—
Danger	—	—	—	—	—	—	—	—	—	—	—	—	—	—	X	—	—	—	—	—
Gatecliff	—	X	X	—	X	X	—	—	—	—	X	—	—	—	X	—	X	—	X	—
Hanging	X	—	X	—	—	X	—	—	—	—	—	—	—	—	X	—	—	—	X	—
Hidden	—	—	X	—	X	X	X	—	—	X	X	X	—	X	X	X	X	X	X	—
Ladder Mod.	—	—	—	—	—	—	—	—	—	—	—	—	—	—	—	X	—	—	—	—
Last Supper	—	—	X	—	—	X	—	—	X	X	X	—	—	—	X	—	—	—	X	—
Snake Creek	—	—	X	—	—	—	—	—	—	X	—	—	—	—	X	—	—	—	—	—
Smith Creek	—	—	X	—	X	—	—	X	X	—	X	—	—	—	X	—	—	—	—	—
Sed.	—	—	X	—	—	—	—	—	—	X	—	—	X	X	—	X	X	—	X	—
Colorado Plateau																				
Bechan	—	X	—	—	—	—	—	—	—	—	—	—	—	—	X	—	—	—	—	—
Desert 5	—	—	—	—	—	—	—	—	—	—	—	—	—	—	X	—	—	X	—	—
6	—	—	—	X	—	—	—	—	X	—	—	—	—	—	—	—	—	—	—	—
Rampart Pit B. Fl.	—	—	—	—	—	—	—	—	—	—	—	—	—	—	X	—	—	—	—	—
Pit B Fr.	—	—	—	—	—	—	—	—	—	—	—	—	—	—	—	—	X	—	—	—
Vulture Can. 14	—	—	—	—	—	—	—	—	X	—	—	—	—	—	—	—	—	—	—	—
1	—	X	—	—	—	—	—	—	—	—	—	—	—	—	—	—	—	—	—	—
18-3	—	—	—	X	—	—	—	—	—	—	—	—	—	—	—	—	X	X	—	—
15	—	—	—	X	—	—	—	—	—	—	—	—	—	—	—	—	—	—	—	—
6	—	—	—	—	—	—	—	—	—	—	—	—	—	—	—	—	—	—	—	—
WTMTd	—	—	X	—	—	—	—	—	X	—	X	X	—	—	—	—	—	—	—	—
WTMTb	—	—	—	—	—	—	—	—	—	—	—	—	—	—	—	—	—	X	—	—
Ringtail	—	—	X	—	—	X	—	—	—	—	X	X	—	—	—	—	—	X	—	X

Note: Locality names as in Table 12.1.

and that these species actually coexisted, *Pseudacris* and *Ochotona* suggest a late Pleistocene/early Holocene climatic regime, certainly with summer temperatures cooler than in the area today and possibly with more available local moisture. The presence of *S. magister* (a disharmonious entity in this case) suggests winters that were at least no colder than those of today at its northern extent around Pyramid Lake, northwestern Nevada. If the associations are valid, the Hanging Rock Shelter fauna may suggest that the late Pleistocene/early Holocene was a period of more equable climate than it is today. The middle Holocene may have been a time of greater aridity, colder winters, and increased seasonality, thus causing the breakup of late Pleistocene/early Holocene (then harmonious) vertebrate communities.

The change from a "typical" glacial biotic community in the Grand Canyon to a "typical" postglacial community apparently took place over a number of thousands of years. The packrat midden record for plant remains both in the Great Basin and on the Colorado Plateau indicates a gradual or a series of small changes from a late glacial to a more modern community (see various authors in Betancourt, Van Devender, and Martin 1990). Each species of plant and animal reacted individually to the climatic changes of the Wisconsin late glacial; there was not a zonal or community-wide change.

The best record of such a change in the herpetofauna is with the various remains recovered from the packrat midden sequences from the Grand Canyon, especially from Vulture Cave (Van Devender, Phillips, and Mead 1977; Mead and Phillips 1981). Here there is a fairly detailed record of the herpetofauna in direct association with the changing local plant community. We see that certain species of plants either "move in" or "move out" of the lower, western end of the Grand Canyon over a period of 5,000 to 7,000 years. Xeric desert dwellers like *Coleonyx variegatus* first show up in the cave and packrat midden record at about 16,000 B.P. (Bida Cave; Mead 1983). *Gopherus*, although in the Grand Canyon prior to the Wisconsin full glacial, reappears in the record again by about 16,000 B.P. (Rampart Cave Pit B Front; Van Devender, Phillips, and Mead 1977). *Crotaphytus collaris* (collared lizard), although present at the beginning of the full glacial, reappears in the record by 14,000 to 13,000 B.P. The snakes *Rhinocheilus* (long-nosed) and *Hypsiglena* (night snake) first appear in the packrat midden record in the western end of the Grand Canyon at approximately 16,500 to 17,500 B.P., respectively (Mead 1981).

The herpetofauna record of the Great Basin and the Colorado Plateau dating to the late Pleistocene and early Holocene is not as well known as those faunas to the immediate south in the warm deserts. Packrat midden studies have been largely responsible for this detailed account of late Pleistocene herpetofaunas from the present Sonoran and Chihuahuan Deserts (for example, Van Devender and Mead 1978; Van Devender, Mead, and Rea 1991; Van Devender and Bradley in press). Limestone cave deposits containing raptor and small carnivore bone accumulations have also provided a herpetofaunal record in this region.

In whatever detail the herpetofaunal record for the Great Basin, the Colorado Plateau, and the southwestern warm deserts is known only for the Wisconsin glacial and the Holocene interglacial. Records of the herpetofaunas for the preceding interglacial (Sangamonian) are not known from the Great Basin or the Colorado Plateau, as they are in rare instances in southern Arizona and northern Sonora, Mexico (Skinner 1942; Van Devender, Rea, and Smith 1985; Czaplewski, Mead, Ku, and Agenbroad 1989). This is probably only a bias produced by the researchers and is not a taphonomic problem.

It is apparent that there is a herpetofauna record for both the Great Basin and the Colorado Plateau for the late Pleistocene and the Holocene; however, it is plagued with large temporal gaps, taphonomic biases, and physiographic biases. These are to be expected with any faunal record for such a large region and for one that has been consistently studied in detail only since the late 1970s. What is needed is: (1) for more packrat midden series to be studied, both from numerous isolated settings and from single sites with long temporal chronologies; (2) detailed studies of raptor deposits with long temporal records; and (3) detailed studies of lacustrine, paludal, and riparian settings. Analyses of combinations of these settings will provide the best-case scenario for reconstructing the local herpetofaunas of any given region through time.

ACKNOWLEDGMENTS

We extend our sincere thanks to our colleagues Tom Van Devender (Arizona-Sonora Desert Museum, Tucson), Don Grayson (Burke Museum, University of Washington, Seattle), Larry Agenbroad (Quaternary Studies, Northern Arizona University, Flagstaff), and Emilee Mead (University of Arizona, Tucson) for their work on the various faunas of the Great Basin and the Colorado Plateau. We appreciate the help and suggestions of Kiisa Nishikawa (Northern Arizona University) and Wade E. Miller (Brigham Young University). Emilee Mead drafted the figures.

REFERENCES

Agenbroad, L. D., and Mead, J. I. 1989. Quaternary Geochronology and Distribution of *Mammuthus* on the Colorado Plateau. *Geology* 17: 861–864.

Betancourt, J. L., Van Devender, T. R., and Martin, P. S. 1990. *Packrat Middens. The Last 40,000 Years of Biotic Change*. University of Arizona Press, Tucson.

Brattstrom, B. H. 1976. A Pleistocene Herpetofauna from Smith Creek Cave, Nevada. *Southern California Academy of Science Bulletin* 75: 283–284.

Brown, J. H. 1978. The Theory of Insular Biogeography and the Distribution of Boreal Mammals and Birds. In K. T. Harper and J. L. Reveal (eds.), *Intermountain Biogeography: A Symposium*. Great Basin Naturalist Memoirs 2: 209–228.

Censky, E. J. 1986. *Sceloporus graciosus*. *Catalogue of American Amphibians and Reptiles* No. 386.

Cole, K. L. 1990. Late Quaternary Vegetation Gradients Through the Grand Canyon. In J. L. Betancourt, T. R. Van Devender, and P. S. Martin (eds.), *Packrat Middens. The Last 40,000 Years of Biotic Change*, University of Arizona Press, Tucson, pp. 240–258.

Cole, K. L., and Mead, J. I. 1981. Late Quaternary Animal Remains from Packrat Middens in the Eastern Grand Canyon, Arizona. *Journal of the Arizona-Nevada Academy of Science* 16: 24–25.

Czaplewski, N. J., Mead, J. I., Ku, T.-L. , and Agenbroad, L. D. 1989. Radiometric Age Assignment for Papago Springs Cave Deposits, Southeastern Arizona. Southwestern Naturalist 34: 278–281.

Emslie, S. D. 1986. Late Pleistocene Vertebrates from Gunnison County, Colorado. *Journal of Paleontology* 60: 170–176.

Ernst, C. H., and Barbour, R. W. 1972. *Turtles of the United States*. University of Kentucky Press, Lexington.

Grayson, D. K. 1982. Toward a History of Great Basin Mammals During the Past 15,000 Years. In D. B. Madsen and J. F. O'Connell (eds.), *Man and Environment in the Great Basin*. Society for American Archaeology Papers 2: 82–101.

Grayson, D. K. 1987. The Biogeographic History of Small Mammals in the Great Basin: Observations on the Last 20,000 Years. *Journal of Mammalogy* 68: 359–375.

Grayson, D. K. 1988. *Danger Cave, Last Supper Cave, and Hanging Rock Shelter: The Faunas*. American Museum of Natural History Anthropological Papers 66 (1).

Hattori, E. M. 1982. *The Archaeology of Falcon Hill, Winnemucca Lake, Washoe County, Nevada*. Nevada State Museum Anthropological Papers 18.

Heaton, T. H. 1985. Quaternary Paleontology and Paleoecology of Crystal Ball Cave, Millard County, Utah: With Emphasis on Mammals and Description of a New Species of Fossil Skunk. *Great Basin Naturalist* 45: 337–390.

Jennings, J. D. 1957. *Danger Cave*. University of Utah Anthropological Paper 27.

Kluge, A. G. 1966. A New Pelobatine Frog from the Lower Miocene of South Dakota with a Discussion of the Evolution of the *Scaphiopus-Spea* Complex. Los Angeles County Museum, *Contributions in Science* 113: 1–26.

Mead, E. M., and Mead, J. I. 1989. Snake Creek Burial Cave and a Review of the Quaternary Mustelids of the Great Basin. *Great Basin Naturalist* 49: 143–154.

Mead, J. I. 1981. The Last 30,000 Years of Faunal History Within the Grand Canyon, Arizona. *Quaternary Research* 15: 311–326.

Mead, J. I. 1983. Harrington's Extinct Mountain Goat (*Oreamnos harringtoni*) and Its Environment in the Grand Canyon, Arizona. Ph.D. dissertation, University of Arizona, Tucson.

Mead, J. I. 1985. Paleontology of Hidden Cave: Amphibians and Reptiles. In D. H. Thomas, ed., *The Archaeology of Hidden Cave, Nevada*. American Museum of Natural History Anthropological Papers 61 (1): 162–170.

Mead, J. I. 1988. Herpetofauna from Danger Cave, Last Supper Cave, and Hanging Rock Shelter. In D. K. Grayson, ed., *Danger Cave, Last Supper Cave, and Hanging Rock Shelter: The Faunas*. American Museum of Natural History Anthropological Papers 66 (1): 116–120.

Mead, J. I. and Agenbroad, L. D. 1989. Pleistocene Dung and the Extinct Herbivores of the Colorado Plateau, Southwestern USA. *Cranium* 6: 29–44.

Mead, J. I., and Agenbroad, L. D. 1992. Isotope Dating of Pleistocene Dung Deposits from the Colorado Plateau, Arizona and Utah. *Radiocarbon* 34: 1–19.

Mead, J. I., Agenbroad, L. D., Davis, O. K., and Martin, P. S. 1986. Dung of Mammuthus in the Arid Southwest, North America. *Quaternary Research* 25: 121–127.

Mead, J. I., Grayson, D. K., and Casteel, R. W. 1983. Fish, Amphibians, Reptiles and Birds. In D. H. Thomas, ed., *The Archaeology of Monitor Valley*. 2. *Gatecliff Shelter*. American Museum of Natural History Anthropological Papers 59 (1).

Mead, J. I., Heaton, T. H., and Mead, E. M. 1989. Late Quaternary Reptiles from Two Caves in the East-Central Great Basin. *Journal of Herpetology* 23: 186–189.

Mead, J. I., and Phillips, A. M. 1981. The Late Pleistocene and Holocene Fauna and Flora of Vulture Cave, Grand Canyon, Arizona. *Southwestern Naturalist* 26: 257–288.

Mead, J. I., Stuart, A. J., and Agenbroad, L. D. Ms. Late Pleistocene Vertebrates from Bechan Cave, Utah. Department of Geology, Arizona State University, Flagstaff.

Mead, J. I., Thompson, R. S., and Van Devender, T. R. 1982. Late Wisconsinan and Holocene Fauna from Smith Creek Canyon, Snake Range, Nevada. *Transactions of the San Diego Society of Natural History* 20: 1–26.

Mead, J. I., and Van Devender, T. R. 1981. Late Holocene Diet of *Bassariscus astutus* in the Grand Canyon. *Journal of Mammalogy* 62: 439–442.

Miller, W. E. 1976. Late Pleistocene Vertebrates of the Silver Creek Local Fauna from North Central Utah. *Great Basin Naturalist* 36: 387–424.

Miller, W. E. 1987. *Mammut americanum*, Utah's First Record of the American Mastodon. *Journal of Paleontology* 61: 168–183.

Parker, W. S. 1982. *Sceloporus magister. Catalogue of American Amphibians and Reptiles* No. 290 (also Tanner 1983 and Zweifel 1974).

Phillips, A. M. 1984. Shasta Ground Sloth Extinction. Fossil Packrat Midden Evidence From the Western Grand Canyon. In P. S. Martin and R. G. Klein (eds.), *Quaternary Extinctions: A Prehistoric Revolution*. University of Arizona Press, Tucson, pp. 148–158.

Reveal, J. L. 1979. Biogeography of the Intermountain Region. A Speculative Appraisal. *Mentzelia* 4: 1–92.

Skinner, M. F. 1942. The Fauna of Papago Springs Cave, Arizona, and a Study of *Stockoceros*; with Three New Antilocaprines from Nebraska and Arizona. Bulletin of the American Museum of Natural History 80: 143–220.

Stebbins, R. C. 1962. *Amphibians of Western North America*. University of California Press, Berkeley.

Stebbins, R. C. 1985. *A Field Guide to Western Reptiles and Amphibians*. Petersen Field Guide Series. Houghton Mifflin, Boston.

Tanner, W. W. 1978. Zoogeography of Reptiles and Amphibians in the Intermountain Region. In K. T. Harper and J. L. Reveal (eds.), *Intermountain Biogeography: A Symposium*. Great Basin Naturalist Memoirs 2: 43–53.

Tanner, W. W. 1983. *Lampropeltis pyromelana. Catalogue of American Amphibians and Reptiles* No. 342.

Thomas, D. H. 1983. *The Archaeology of Monitor Valley. 2. Gatecliff Shelter*. American Museum of Natural History Anthropological Papers 59 (1).

Thompson, R. S. 1979. Late Pleistocene and Holocene Packrat Middens from Smith Creek Canyon, White Pine County, Nevada. In D. R. Tuohy and D. L. Rendall (eds.), *The Archaeology of Smith Creek Canyon, Eastern Nevada*. Nevada State Museum Anthropological Papers 17: 361–380.

Van Devender, T. R., and Bradley, G. L. In press. The Paleoecology and Historical Biogeography of the Herpetofauna of Maravillas Canyon, Texas. *Copeia*.

Van Devender, T. R., and Mead, J. I. 1978. Early Holocene and Late Pleistocene Amphibians and Reptiles in Sonoran Desert Packrat Middens. *Copeia* 1978: 464–475.

Van Devender, T. R., Mead, J. I., and Rea, A. M. 1991. Late Quaternary Plants and Vertebrates from Picacho Peak, Arizona. *Southwestern Naturalist* 36: 302–314.

Van Devender, T. R., Phillips, A. M., and Mead, J. I. 1977. Late Pleistocene Reptiles and Small Mammals from Lower Grand Canyon Arizona. *Southwestern Naturalist* 22: 49–66.

Van Devender, T. R., Rea, A. M., and Smith, M. L. 1985. The Sangamon Interglacial Vertebrate Fauna from Rancho La Brisca, Sonora, Mexico. *Transactions of the San Diego Society of Natural History* 21: 23–55.

Van Devender, T. R., and Tessman, N. T. 1975. Late Pleistocene Snapping Turtles (*Chelydra serpentina*) from Southern Nevada. *Copeia* 1975: 249–253.

Zweifel, R. G. 1974. *Lampropeltis zonata. Catalogue of American Amphibians and Reptiles* No. 174.

Atriplex canescens (Pursh) Nutt. (four wing saltbush) is one of the most valuable forage
shrubs of western America. Since it is widespread, genetically diverse, and able to hybridize
freely with a variety of cogeners, it is the focus of much modern research.

CHAPTER 13

Recommendations for Future Research

*Larry L. St. Clair, Kimball T. Harper, Kaye
H. Thorne, and W. M. Hess*

Intermountain North America has a diversity of habitats, ranging from hot deserts in the south to alpine tundra in the Rocky Mountains. As we prepared this volume, it became apparent that significant research on the biology of the Great Basin has been done but comparatively little is known about the biological diversity, evolutionary relationships, and ecological structure of the Colorado Plateau. The Plateau is rich in habitats that support diverse and complicated plant and animal communities. Climatic patterns that result in substantial summer rain have had a definite impact on the distribution of plants and animals on the Plateau. Richness in geologic substrates and topography on the Plateau have also played important roles in shaping the composition, structure, and dynamics of biological communities there.

THE NEED FOR DESCRIPTIVE WORK

Little is known about the various biological components of the Colorado Plateau. Unlike the Great Basin, where plant and animal communities are more uniform and have been more extensively studied, biodiversity on the Colorado Plateau is poorly understood. Generally, the Plateau is more biologically diverse than the Great Basin. In large measure the differences seem to be a function of the incredible diversity of geological substrates and complicated topography found on the Plateau. Even to the inexperienced eye, the living communities effectively mirror the inherent habitat diversity of this province. Unfortunately, the magnitude of habitat diversity, compounded by the relative inaccessibility of many areas of the Plateau, has presented a formidable barrier to most local biologists.

Much work will be required to accurately and completely characterize the vascular plants, algae, bryophytes, lichenized and nonlichenized fungi, mammals, birds, reptiles, fish, amphibians, and insects of this important region. As such information becomes available, it will stimulate productive questions concerning species distribution, evolution, and ecology on the Plateau.

EVOLUTIONARY QUESTIONS

It comes as no surprise that our lack of information about the biodiversity of the Colorado Plateau obscures our understanding of biogeographical, evolutionary, and ecological patterns in the area. Many questions need to be answered, and as we answer some questions a multitude of others will invariably arise.

Specifically, we suggest several basic questions that merit attention:

1.   How do the flora and fauna of the Great Basin and the Colorado Plateau compare in terms of diversity and similarity of species in the large genera, and what is the relative importance of historic and environmental factors in the origin of these differences?

2.   Is the occurrence of ancestral forms (diploids vs. polyploids as well as surviving relictual taxa) equal on the Colorado Plateau and in the Great Basin? Why or why not?

3.   Several deciduous forest species occur as disjunct populations in the deep, narrow canyons of the Colorado Plateau and the Virgin River drainage, including *Brickellia grandiflorum*, *Cercis occidentalis*, *Eupatorium herbaceum*, *Forestiera pubescens*, *Ostrya knowltonii*, *Parthenocissus vitacea*, *Parietaria pensylvanica*, *Ptelea trifoliata*, and *Vitis arizonica*. Do such widely disjunct populations represent examples of recent long-range dispersal (or recurrent long-range dispersal), or are they relictual fragments of the Arctotertiary forest that was once circumpolar and is now fragmented into many disjunct, lower-latitude fragments?

ECOLOGICAL QUESTIONS

Many basic questions about the structure and dynamics of the communities and ecosystems of the Colorado Plateau should be answered. Biologists who have worked on the Colorado Plateau have often expressed concern about the fragile nature of this province. Arid and semi-arid lands tend to be particularly vulnerable to human perturbation and following impact frequently require significant time for recovery. Since human-related resource development and extraction of energy resources are having a dramatic impact on the global environment, it seems particularly appropriate that we address some of these issues as they relate specifically to the Colorado Plateau. We should also carefully consider the general vulnerability of the Colorado Plateau to such human-related impacts. Several specific questions deserve attention:

1.   How has the greater importance of summer rain in deep southeastern Utah influenced biotic distributions and evolution there?

2.   What is the integrated influence of cryptogamic soil crusts on vascular plant communities? What specific physical, biological, and nutritional factors need to be considered if we are fully to evaluate the effects of such crusts on associated vascular plant communities? What are the dimensions and dynamics of nutrient flow between the soil microbiota, vascular plants, and herbivores?

3. What are the most successful exotic invaders of the different ecosystems of the Colorado Plateau, and what has been their impact on the indigenous biotic systems?

4. Is biotic diversity greater on the Colorado Plateau because of the increased topographic and geologic diversity of the region?

5. What is the effect of highly predictable annual precipitation versus unpredictable variation from year to year when average annual precipitation is comparable among regions of concern?

SUMMARY

Much work remains to be done in both the Great Basin and the Colorado Plateau. We hope that this volume clearly defines what we do know about the biology of these regions so that in the future we can more effectively address critical areas of uncertainty or concern.

Index

Note: Species are indexed by common name when the common name is given in the text. Otherwise, species are listed by their Latin name.